Pluralism by Default

Pluralism by Default

Weak Autocrats and the Rise of Competitive Politics

LUCAN WAY

Johns Hopkins University Press

BALTIMORE

© 2015 Johns Hopkins University Press
All rights reserved. Published 2015
Printed in the United States of America on acid-free paper
9 8 7 6 5 4 3 2

Johns Hopkins University Press
2715 North Charles Street
Baltimore, Maryland 21218-4363
www.press.jhu.edu

Library of Congress Cataloging-in-Publication Data

Way, Lucan, 1968–
  Pluralism by default : weak autocrats and the rise of competitive
politics / Lucan Way.
    pages cm
  Includes bibliographical references and index.
  ISBN 978-1-4214-1812-4 (paperback : acid-free paper) —
ISBN 1-4214-1812-6 (paperback : acid-free paper) — ISBN
978-1-4214-1813-1 (electronic) — 1-4214-1813-4 (electronic)
  1. Political participation—Belarus. 2. Political participation—
Moldova. 3. Political participation—Ukraine. 4. Democratization—
Belarus. 5. Democratization—Moldova. 6. Democratization—
Ukraine. 7. Belarus—Politics and government—1991–
8. Moldova—Politics and government—1991– 9. Ukraine—Politics
and government—1991– I. Title.
  JN6649.A15W38 2015
  323'.040947—dc23   2015010633

A catalog record for this book is available from the British Library.

*Special discounts are available for bulk purchases of this book. For
more information, please contact Special Sales at 410-516-6936 or
specialsales@press.jhu.edu.*

Johns Hopkins University Press uses environmentally friendly book
materials, including recycled text paper that is composed of at least
30 percent post-consumer waste, whenever possible.

For Idris and Kamran:
Like this book, you demonstrate the upside of chaos.

Contents

Acknowledgments   *ix*

Acronyms   *xiii*

1 Introduction   1

2 Perestroika and the Origins of Post-Soviet Pluralism
by Default   32

3 Pluralism by Default in Ukraine   43

4 Pluralism by Default in Moldova   92

5 Authoritarian Consolidation in Belarus   115

6 Consolidated and Unconsolidated Authoritarianism
in the Former Soviet Union   143

7 Conclusion   166

Appendix A: Coding Rules for Main Variables   *181*

*Appendix B: National Identity, Organizational Capacity,
and Regime Outcomes among Post-Soviet Incumbents*   *190*

Notes   *195*

Bibliography   *231*

Index   *251*

Acknowledgments

This book began as an off-handed comment in graduate school about the sources of pluralism under Yeltsin and became a book project when I was an Academy scholar at Harvard. The Harvard Academy provided me the original freedom and stimulation to conceive of this project. During my time there, I benefitted in particular from the encouragement and inspiration of Samuel Huntington, who then headed the Academy. His *Political Order in Changing Societies* had already pushed me to move beyond narrow institutionalism in graduate school and inspired the core ideas of this book.

The Department of Political Science at Temple University, where I had my first job, also gave early financial support and warm encouragement for this project. I benefitted in particular from interactions with Richard Deeg and Joe Schwartz. More recently, the Department of Political Science and the Centre for European, Russian, and Eurasian Studies at the University of Toronto have offered an unmatched intellectual community for the study of comparative and postcommunist politics. I owe particular gratitude to Susan Solomon for her friendship, comments on early drafts, and discussions about the concept of pluralism. The Connaught Fund at the University provided key assistance for this project. I also thank Olga Kesarchuk and Elena Maltseva for their assistance and Adam Casey, the hardest working RA in show business, for his extraordinary help on penultimate drafts.

Larry Diamond, Kathryn Stoner and the Center on Democracy, Development, and the Rule of Law at Stanford provided a sublime setting for a sabbatical and an opportunity to write substantial portions of this manuscript. I am thankful to Larry as well as to Marc Plattner at the *Journal of Democracy* for providing an early platform for my ideas.

Others have offered invaluable feedback at various stages of the project. Jerry

Easter, Steve Fish, Anna Grzymala-Busse, Axel Hadenius, Pauline Jones Luong, and Mike McFaul provided early advice and encouragement. Mark Beissinger was gracious enough to read the entire manuscript closely and offered many invaluable insights. Igor Botanu, Sergiu Buscaneanu, Charles King, and Vladimir Solonari gave invaluable assistance during my first trip to Moldova. Vitali Silitski assisted me in Belarus and inspired me with his wisdom and courage. I have also benefitted from innumerable conversations with Paul D'Anieri, Serhyi Kudelia, Taras Kuzio, and Oxana Shevel, about Ukraine. Dominique Arel was brave enough to host a seminar on my Ukraine chapter when it was 150 pages long. Antoinette Handley, Adrienne Lebas, and Will Prichard allowed me to benefit from their deep knowledge of African politics. I also thank Ben Smith for responding to my repeated missives about the resource curse. I am grateful for feedback by participants in seminars at Lund University, New York University, Princeton, University of Michigan, Uppsala University, and Yale.

Henry Hale organized a fantastic book incubator conference at George Washington University's Institute for European, Russian, and Eurasian Studies. I thank Henry, Margarita Balmaceda, Rebecca Chamberlain-Creanga, Evgeny Finkel, Gene Fishel, William Hill, Mike Miller, Maria Popova, and Andrew Wilson for their perspectives at this event. I am also much obliged to Marc Howard for his friendship and for pushing me to break up the conclusion into two separate chapters. I also owe thanks to Suzanne Flinchbaugh, Catherine Goldstead, and Greg Britton at Johns Hopkins University Press, and two anonymous reviewers for their support and comments on this manuscript. The late Henry Tom, who edited many of the classics on political regimes for the Press, provided early encouragement for this project.

Portions of the book draw on material previously published as "Pluralism by Default in Moldova" *Journal of Democracy* 13: 4 (October 2002), 127–41; "Deer in Headlights: Incompetence and Weak Authoritarianism after the Cold War." *Slavic Review,* 71, No. 3 (2012): 619–646; and "The Sources of Authoritarian Control after the Cold War: East Africa and the former Soviet Union." *Post-Soviet Affairs*, 28, No. 4 (2012): 424–48.

This project has also benefitted from the support of my close friends. Chrystia Freeland and I shared an early passion for Soviet politics as classmates. It was she who first introduced me to Ukraine when it was on the cusp of independence. Ed Schatz has provided consistent good cheer and sanity since we first met as postdocs in 2001. Keith Darden has inspired me and injected just the right amount of insanity into my life since we first met at Berkeley. And above all, Steve Levitsky, my intellectual comrade-in-arms, my frog and toad, Lennon and McCartney, has been there through thick and thin. Steve, I could not imagine academia without you and hope that we will be co-authoring until the end.

Fate has also given me an unimaginably supportive family. My mother and stepfather—Brenda Way and Henry Erlich—have both been editing my work since I learned the alphabet and gave wonderful feedback on several chapters. Thanks to my father, Peter Way, whose intense curiosity has always inspired me. My glorious wife, Zareen Ahmad, is an accomplished physician, an acute critic, and splendid wordsmith. She has provided unending feedback and emotional support during this project's ups and downs. Finally, my twin boys, Idris and Kamran, were not even a twinkle in my eye when this book began. But now I cannot imagine life without them. Pussycats, you cannot read yet, but this book is for you.

Acronyms

ADP: Agrarian Democratic Party (Moldova)
ADR: Alliance for Democracy and Reform (Moldova)
AEI: Alliance for European Integration (Moldova)
ANM: Armenian National Movement
BDPM: Bloc for a Democratic and Prosperous Moldova
BKGB: Belarusian Committee for State Security
BPF: Belarusian Popular Front
BYuT: Yulia Tymoshenko Bloc (Ukraine)
CIS: Commonwealth of Independent States
CPD: Congress of People's Deputies (USSR)
CPSU: Communist Party of the Soviet Union
IMF: International Monetary Fund
KGB: Committee for State Security
KGK: Committee for Government Control (Belarus)
KIIS: Kyiv International Institute of Sociology
LDPM: Liberal Democratic Party of Moldova
NDP: National Democratic Party (Ukraine)
PCRM: Communist Party of Moldova
PPCD: Christian-Democratic People's Party (Moldova)
SBU: Security Service of Ukraine
UDP: Presidential Business Administration (Belarus)
UES: United Energy System (Ukraine)

Pluralism by Default

1

Introduction

Ukraine's first president, Leonid Kravchuk, had had enough. Months before, he had agreed with the legislature to hold early presidential elections. But now, in early 1994, he argued that the decision to hold "unlawful" elections had only created "new problems." Such an election would create "unpredictable consequences for the country" and make it impossible for him to solve the economic crisis facing Ukraine. Thus he decided to disband parliament and delay presidential elections. He prepared to make a public announcement of this decision on central TV on January 11, 1994.[1]

Up to this point, the story reads like so many other tales of transition to authoritarianism. Like autocrats before him, Kravchuk saw his continued tenure as essential to the country's stability and prosperity. And like so many before him, he claimed that the suppression of elections was necessary to prevent chaos. At the same time, Ukraine's weak civil society, lack of democratic history, and relative international isolation meant that Kravchuk confronted few apparent obstacles in his efforts to reassert authoritarian rule.

But what happened next was more unusual and under-theorized in comparative politics. Heads of the police and security forces met with Kravchuk to tell him that they would not back his decision to suspend elections. As holdovers from the Soviet period, these officials were hardly committed democrats. Nor had they ever shown a particular respect for the rule of law. Instead, they resisted because they had little stake in Kravchuk's survival, while their subordinates, who had not been paid in months, could not be counted on to follow orders. As a consequence, Kravchuk was forced to back down from efforts to impose authoritarian rule. Elections went ahead as scheduled, and Kravchuk lost to the former prime minister, Leonid Kuchma, resulting in a nonviolent and democratic transfer of power.

Electoral turnover is widely seen as evidence of democratic institutional strength or elite acceptance of democratic norms—and thus an important step toward democratic consolidation.[2] However, Ukraine's first electoral turnover was caused less by strong institutions or democratically minded leaders and much more by the fact that the police and security services were weak and unwilling to follow orders. Ukraine's weak state, rather than undermining democracy as is so often assumed, was key to the survival of robust political competition in the 1990s. Indeed, Ukraine has witnessed four electoral turnovers since 1991 but is still barely democratic and far from consolidated.

The story of Ukraine's first electoral turnover provides an important clue to the central puzzle of this book: namely, why did pluralism emerge in so many countries under inhospitable conditions characterized by weak civil societies, underdevelopment, or lack of democratic history? Since the collapse of the USSR in 1991, a large number of poor and underdeveloped countries—including Albania and Macedonia in Eastern Europe; Kyrgyzstan and Moldova in the former Soviet Union; Benin, Mali, and Senegal in Africa—witnessed the rise and persistence of competitive authoritarian and democratic institutions familiar to Western observers: regular and competitive elections, powerful legislatures, and free media. Indeed, the share of democracies among low- and lower-middle-income countries nearly doubled from the mid-1980s to the 2000s.[3]

Despite real similarities of such regimes to established democracies, newly democratic or semi-democratic political competition has often been grounded less in robust institutions, emerging civil society, or the victory of a "democratic spirit"[4] and much more in the failure of authoritarianism. In many cases, democratic contestation has persisted because autocrats have been too weak to steal elections, repress opposition, or keep allies in line—resulting in *pluralism by default*.[5] Pluralism by default describes a range of democratic, competitive authoritarian, and soft authoritarian regimes in which political competition survives, not because leaders are especially democratic or because institutions or societal actors are particularly strong, but because the government is too fragmented and the state too weak to monopolize political control. In such cases, leaders lack the resources, authority, or coordination to prevent today's allies from becoming tomorrow's challengers, to control the legislature, impose censorship, manipulate elections, or use force against political opponents.

To understand the underpinnings of democratic competition in many post–Cold War regimes, we thus, paradoxically, need to pay greater attention to the sources of authoritarianism.

An investigation into the dynamics of pluralism by default reveals an important but largely unrecognized contradiction in the transition process in many countries—namely, that the same factors that facilitate democratic political competition may *also* thwart the development of stable, well-functioning democratic institutions.[6] Thus, the literature on democratization has focused on the ways in which weak parties, weak states, and divisions over national identity undermine democracy. Party weakness is thought to harm democratic accountability and create a "crisis of governability."[7] Weak states are said to facilitate civil conflict and thwart the protection of individual rights;[8] and divisions over national identity are typically considered "one of the major threats to any democracy."[9]

Each of these arguments finds support in the literature as well as in the case studies in this book. Yet after the Cold War, when multiparty elections became the minimal requirement for international legitimacy, weak ruling parties, weak states, and divided national identities also hindered efforts by authoritarian leaders to concentrate power and maintain political control—often resulting in relatively open elections, powerful legislatures, and serious opposition challenges. This paradox played out before the world in Ukraine in early 2014, when a combination of weak authoritarian institutions and national divisions resulted in the stunning overthrow of a brutal autocrat but also set the stage for violent conflict.

This book explores the sources of pluralism in countries "without prerequisites"[10] for democracy through an exploration of post–Soviet[11] regime trajectories since 1991. I offer one of the first book-length attempts to explain divergent regime trajectories across the region.[12] In particular, I compare three neighboring countries on the western border of the former Soviet Union: Belarus, Moldova, and Ukraine. Without democratic leadership, strong civil societies, or democratic histories, all three countries initially experienced highly competitive political regimes with open media, powerful legislatures, and democratic transfers of power. Twenty years later, however, their trajectories diverged considerably: Moldova and Ukraine were the most democratic countries in the former Soviet Union; while Belarus had one of the most closed autocracies outside of Central Asia.[13] I seek to explain both differences across these cases and changes in political competition in each case over time.

I find two sets of factors that help account for pluralism in these cases and in the rest of the post-Soviet region. First, a weak authoritarian state and the lack of a well-established ruling party facilitated pluralism by encouraging high-level defections and depriving incumbents of the means to repress opposition. Second, divisions in the titular national identity between two relatively equal groups exposed incumbents to greater external pressures and made it easier for otherwise weak opposition to mobilize support. These two sets of factors resulted in political competition that arose from an inability to create *any* kind of political order, whether democratic or authoritarian.

Authoritarianism and the Study of "New Democracies"

After the Cold War, studies of transitional and semi-competitive regimes were overwhelmingly driven by "the compelling power of democratic norms."[14] Scholars tended to view democratization from the point of view of those trying to build and consolidate democracy. Studies often focused on the presence or absence of factors considered key to long-term democratic development—for example, well-designed constitutions, economic development, strong parties, and strong states[15]—and paid less attention to features such as repressive capacity that are primarily important to authoritarian survival.

The problem with such a focus on democracy has not just been that scholars see democracy where it doesn't exist.[16] As we see in this book, the pluralism that emerged was frequently quite real. More importantly, the normative bent toward democracy has blinded scholars to the range of potential causes of pluralism. The pitfalls of this bias are most evident in studies of institutional or state capacity, which has been overwhelmingly viewed in terms of goals shared by analysts—and the author of this book—such as the capacity to deliver public goods, including the rule of law, public order, and economic development.[17] Even Brian Taylor's impressive study of policing and coercion under Putin centers on "state quality" and "good governance."[18] As this book shows, problems of capacity also affect leaders' ability to engage in "bad" behavior such as repressing opposition, stealing elections, or shutting down democratic institutions.

In the 2000s, the field of regime studies moved beyond democratization and saw an explosion of articles and books on authoritarianism as scholars focused on the conceptualization of new forms of authoritarian rule,[19] the dynamics of dictatorship, and the sources of authoritarian durability.[20] And long ago, the transitions literature drew attention to the importance of splits within authoritarian regimes.[21] However, the study of authoritarianism is critical, not just for understanding dictatorships, authoritarian durability, or the transition from authoritarianism, but also for the persistence of democratic or hybrid rule.

This book examines the origins of competitive and sometimes democratic politics by focusing on the development of institutions and mechanisms to limit opposition and control dissent. My approach is to study regime evolution from the perspective of an "autocrat," which I define broadly as any leader willing to use both legal and extra-legal means to stay in power and concentrate political control. This perspective focuses on the organizational and institutional strategies that leaders use to preserve unity, reward supporters, and punish enemies. Rather than concentrating on the evolution of state institutions that provide public goods (e.g., rule of law, public welfare), this viewpoint draws attention to mechanisms of state coercion to suppress and intimidate political opponents and sideline independent actors. Instead of centering on the factors that promote elite consensus around democratic rules of the game,[22] this perspective examines the forces that facilitate elite cohesion around a specific autocrat or ruling group.

I am not arguing that all leaders seek absolute power. Nor do I deny that key differences exist in leaders' tolerance of dissent or readiness to use violence. My point is rather that such differences in democratic support are rarely sufficient for understanding regime outcomes. Authoritarian state building has been central to the politics of many post-authoritarian regimes. Indeed, even "democratic" leaders in the post-Soviet context engaged in concerted—if often unsuccessful—efforts to abuse power and monopolize political control. For example, Yeltsin's government in Russia preserved the core of the Soviet-era KGB, bombed a recalcitrant parliament in 1993, and carried out electoral manipulation and media harassment in 1993 and 1996.[23] Similarly, Kyrgyzstan's Askar Akaev, widely considered "a strong advocate of political pluralism," pushed through an election law that allowed him to run as the only candidate in presidential elections in 1991, banned several opposition newspapers in 1994, and revoked the registration of three out of six presidential candidates in 1995.[24] These and other leaders such as Mikheil Saakashvili in Georgia, Mircea Snegur in Moldova, and Kravchuk in Ukraine were widely regarded as democratic because they acquiesced to elections and put up with media criticism. Yet they also made serious and repeated efforts to intimidate journalists, manipulate elections, harass opposition, and crack down on parliamentary opposition. Many leaders sought to build formal and informal institutions—new police and investigative units—to monitor and suppress opposition challenges. Such efforts should be taken seriously in their own right.

Paradoxically, putting ourselves in the shoes of an autocrat can give us significant insight into the sources of democratic or semi-democratic political competition. Autocrats often fail. Frequently hidden from public view, such failures—to prevent allies from defecting, to convince police to suppress opposition, or to preserve national unity—have been important causes of dynamic political contestation in countries with few constraints on authoritarian rule. While studies of democracies "without prerequisites"[25] have often looked first for democratically minded leaders or an "emerging" civil society, it is worthwhile considering the possibility that pluralism arises instead because leaders lack the capacity to abuse power or face down even modest opposition.

Obstacles and Opportunities for Authoritarianism after the Cold War

To comprehend the emergence of pluralism by default, we first need to understand the constraints on authoritarian rule that arose after the Cold War. The fall of Communism and the end of the Cold War generated new limits on autocratic behavior. After 1989, dictators in Africa, Central America, and Eastern Europe lost key sources of external support. Simultaneously, the combined explosion of new communications technologies[26] and the growth of international human rights organizations and other INGOs (international nongovernmental organizations such as Human Rights Watch and Amnesty International)[27] made it extraordinarily difficult for autocrats to hide abuses. Extensive election observation became much more widespread—complicating efforts at large-scale election fraud.[28] Further, a prodemocratic *zeitgeist* was created by the dominance of rich Western liberal democracies in the early 1990s.[29] Simultaneously, this period witnessed the growth of bilateral and multilateral democratic conditionality. Most strikingly, European Union conditionality was critical in promoting democratization in Romania, Slovakia, and other Eastern European countries in the 1990s and early 2000s.[30]

Thus, the end of the Cold War significantly raised the costs of full-scale authoritarian rule. Outright military intervention into politics declined significantly, and most coups that did take place resulted in elections.[31] Facing the threats of international isolation, all but a few leaders in the world adopted formal democratic institutions, including regular multiparty elections, in the aftermath of the Soviet collapse. Among 26 postcommunist states, Turkmenistan was the only one *not* to adopt a formal multiparty system.

At the same time, countries faced different external constraints on authoritarian behavior.[32] In contrast to their Eastern European counterparts, autocrats in the former Soviet Union confronted softer and more sporadic demands for democratic change.[33] Not a single autocrat in the non-Baltic former Soviet Union was pressured to meet EU membership conditionality or experienced direct Western military intervention of the scale applied in the Balkans in the 1990s. Aid was only weakly tied to democracy, and where pressure was employed, it was often ineffective.[34]

Domestically as well, post-Soviet incumbents confronted few apparent limits on autocratic behavior. First, societal mobilization was hampered by the Communist legacy. Marc Howard shows that postcommunist civil society was "distinctively weak" as compared to other post-authoritarian societies.[35] Most postcommunist countries lacked the powerful institutionalized networks of trade unions, churches, or political parties that would be in a position to challenge incumbent abuse. Moreover, the rule of law presented few constraints on autocrats. Law was selectively applied and used to bludgeon opposition through libel suits aimed at independent journalists and through prosecution of tax violations targeted at businesses that fund opposition.[36] Furthermore, post-Soviet leaders inherited a centralized economy that bolstered authoritarian control. State control over economic resources allowed incumbents to pay off supporters and starve opposition.[37] Finally, post-Soviet leaders regularly engaged in anti-democratic behavior.

To understand how robustly competitive and sometimes democratic regimes emerged from such barren soil, we need to look more closely into the dynamics of pluralism by default.

Pluralism by Default

Scholarship on democratization can roughly be divided between theories concentrating on factors that promote *competition and the dispersion of power* and those that highlight *political order and consensus on the rules of the game*. First, factors such as economic development are thought to promote democracy by facilitating mass mobilization[38] and deconcentrating control over economic resources,[39] thereby making it more difficult for any single group to monopolize political control. At the same time, other theories have drawn attention to factors promoting political order. Numerous scholars have focused on the important role played by a strong state in creating political order and enforcing individual rights necessary for a democracy to function.[40] Still others have concentrated on the importance of national unity in preventing polarized conflict and inter-communal violence.[41]

Obviously, both contestation and consensus are central to long-term democratic development. But the dilemma for many countries in the world with weak democratic prerequisites is that the most available sources of contestation are often the same factors that threaten disorder and undermine long-term democratic consolidation. This dilemma is central to *pluralism by default*, which describes a range of democratic, competitive authoritarian, and soft authoritarian regimes where political competition is rooted more in authoritarian weakness than in the strength of prodemocratic forces. In cases of pluralism by default, political competition endures not because leaders are especially tolerant or because civil society is particularly robust but because the government is too divided and the state too weak to impose authoritarian rule in a democratic international context. Such weakness promotes competition but undermines the development of stable democracy by leaving opportunities for authoritarian abuse and by thwarting efforts to establish stable rules of the game. In fact, pluralism by default rarely translates into full democracy—and when it does, such democracy is likely to be highly unstable. Thus, the vast majority of such cases became competitive authoritarian regimes characterized by a combination of genuine democratic competition and serious authoritarian abuse.[42] While often referred to as "emerging" or "new" democracies, such cases may be more usefully understood as unconsolidated authoritarian regimes.[43]

Despite the prevalence of competitive authoritarianism among cases of pluralism by default, this book focuses less on this or any other specific regime type but rather treats political competition-closure as a continuous variable.[44] As we shall see, cases of pluralism by default are often characterized by significant instability in regime type—slipping back and forth between more open democratic and more authoritarian rule. Thus, it makes sense to examine countries across a range of regimes.

My analysis focuses on the ways in which pluralism by default may emerge from state and party weakness and divided national identities. These factors have often undermined governance and long-term democratic consolidation. Yet they have also limited the ability of leaders to hold onto allies, curb public criticism, suppress opposition mobilization, and rig elections (see figure on p. 9). Their role in promoting political competition is examined below.

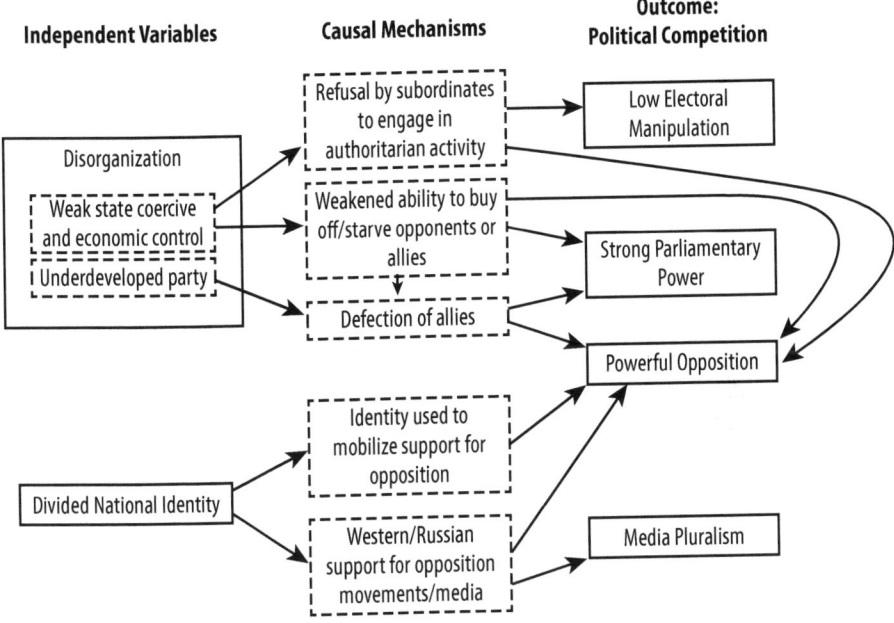

Causal mechanisms of pluralism by default

Disorganization and Failed Authoritarianism

Inspired by the work of Samuel Huntington, this book takes an *organizational* approach to regime evolution—focusing on the existence or absence of stable, incumbent-dominated structures through which allies cooperate to conduct affairs.[45] *Organizational capacity* describes incumbents' access to organizational tools to suppress popular dissent and promote elite cohesion. The analysis centers on two types of organizations—states and ruling parties—that are key sources of authoritarian durability. Incumbent state and party weakness has promoted competition in four key dimensions: elections, the media, the legislature, and opposition challenges (see figure above). The absence of a single well-established ruling party may strengthen opposition by facilitating high-level defections and undermining control over the legislature—thereby providing the opposition with a key base of operations. Simultaneously, an underfunded coercive apparatus and weak economic control may reduce the ability of autocrats to repress opposition and use economic resources to starve opposition and reward supporters. In the post-Soviet context, such weak organization has often—in the short run at least—strengthened key democratic institutions such as elections and the legislature that otherwise have little historical grounding or autonomous sources of power. In turn, party and state building, in the absence of other constraints on authoritarian rule, have often closed off key sources of contestation and facilitated more effective repression of opposition forces.

Parties and Authoritarian Power

First, the degree of pluralism has been shaped by the strength of the ruling party, or the extent to which the ruling coalition is organized around a single, extensive, well-organized, and cohesive political party.[46] Students of postcommunist democratization have generally viewed political parties as central to democratic development. In fact, many have argued that Yeltsin's resistance to party building at the start of the 1990s weakened democratic forces and undermined democratic development Russia.[47] Yet, if Russia and other countries in the 1990s are viewed as unconsolidated authoritarian regimes rather than as emerging democracies, a very different view of parties emerges. A well-organized ruling party may do more to help executives monopolize political control than to promote accountability. Thus, a significant literature focusing on authoritarian regimes contends that single-party regimes have historically been more durable than military or other types of nondemocratic regimes.[48] By contrast, the absence of ruling parties has encouraged instability.

Indeed, while seventy years of Soviet rule decimated civil society and atomized the population,[49] the collapse of the Soviet Union also left the ruling elite fluid and divided. In the 1990s, ruling parties in most post-Soviet countries were weaker than in just about any other region at the time. Following the sudden dissolution of the Soviet Communist Party, leaders were faced with the daunting task of creating new political structures on the fly—a task that necessarily requires time.[50] In the meantime, early leaders such as Yeltsin in Russia, Kravchuk in Ukraine, and Mircea Snegur in Moldova were forced to rely on popular support and loose coalitions of high-level supporters. They lacked not only parties but even "party substitutes" such as established regional patronage networks.[51]

Underdeveloped party structures facilitated pluralism by strengthening opposition challenges and weakening executive control over the legislature. Above all, weak parties have bolstered opposition by making elite defection more likely. Patronage, a critical source of cohesion in almost all authoritarian coalitions, needs to be organized. In the absence of organization, regime elites cannot be sure that loyalty will be repaid in the future and are thus prone to defect the minute they do not get what they want.[52] By providing institutional mechanisms to regulate access to the spoils of public office and by lengthening actors' time horizons through the provision of future opportunities for career advancement, ruling parties "create incentives for long-term loyalty."[53]

Absent a single dominant ruling party, regime elites may see fewer opportunities for career advancement from within and are thus more likely to seek power from outside the regime. Loosely organized non-party ruling coalitions give executives the flexibility to dump allies, but they also make it less costly for allies to defect with their organizational resources intact. Especially where civil society is weak and opposition is under-resourced, such defection has been a central source of opposition strength. Given the paucity of resources and media access outside the state, former prime ministers, cabinet members, and other regime insiders are often best positioned to seriously challenge incumbent power. Indeed, some of the main threats to incumbents in the former Soviet Union have come from appointees and former allies.[54]

High-level defections also offer important "political opportunities" for opposition mobilization.[55] Elite divisions first encourage leaders to mobilize support from outside the regime in order to strengthen their political influence relative to other elites within the ruling coalition.[56] Thus, in Georgia in 2003 and Ukraine in 2004, former regime elites were the primary leaders and organizers of protest efforts.[57] Defection of powerful insiders often gives protesters key financial and media resources as well as protection from government repression that can mean the difference between opposition success and failure.[58]

Disorganization also helps explain the quite surprising strength of parliament throughout much of the former Soviet Union in the 1990s—including Kazakhstan, Kyrgyzstan, Moldova, Russia, and Ukraine. While much has been written about confrontations between the executive and parliament that emerged in Russia and other republics after the Soviet collapse,[59] few observers have addressed the question of why legislatures were so strong despite the fact that they had no tradition of parliamentary power to draw on, little effective means to assert their power, and confronted executives with access to significant material and bureaucratic resources. While on paper legislatures sometimes had significant power, the rules themselves were often changed as frequently as they were ignored.[60] Given the extraordinarily weak rule of law and the fact that legislative power had been purely fictitious just a few years earlier in the Soviet period, it is not obvious why executives sitting atop large state bureaucracies could not simply ignore parliament.

The relative strength of the legislature can best be explained by the disorganization of executive power. Despite the executive's often disproportionate access to material resources, the absence of well-established parties to distribute spoils in a regularized manner meant that presidents often got little bang for their patronage buck as deputies defected the minute they did not get what they want. Thus, while Yeltsin in 1993 was backed by enormous power resources—virtually the entire security forces, economic ministries, all major TV stations, and a vast array of patronage appointments—he lacked the organization to manage elite rivalries and exert legislative control.[61] Consequently, Yeltsin's parliamentary support rapidly fell apart in early 1992, just months after the president's chosen successor, Ruslan Khasbulatov, had been put in charge of the legislature. On the other hand, the emergence of more institutionalized ruling parties—as in Russia under Putin, Ukraine under Yanukovych, and Moldova under the Communists—rapidly weakened legislative power. The combination of executive control over patronage and a relatively cohesive pro-governmental organization reduced elite defection and deprived the opposition of a key source of support.

In sum, well-established ruling parties have limited political competition in important ways. Party organization is obviously not inherently autocratic. However, such organization may greatly enhance regime closure by reducing conflict within the ruling coalition—conflict that is often a central source of democratic contestation in countries that lack other constraints on authoritarianism.

The Authoritarian State and Political Competition

State power is also key to authoritarian durability and regime closure.[62] While the postcommunist state received extensive attention after the fall of the USSR, studies were rooted almost entirely in a benign conception of state power consistent with the "quest for democratic governance,"[63] rule of law, and the ability to "recognize social problems, fashion cogent responses to them and effectively deliver corrective action."[64]

While partly justified by constitutional and regulatory reforms undertaken throughout the former Soviet Union in the 1990s, this focus on the *liberal* state has encompassed only part of the state building process. As we see in the chapters that follow, leaders simultaneously sought to promote and build state institutions for distinctly *illiberal* ends—including new, reinvigorated, or repurposed repressive agencies and institutions to investigate and harass opposition. Examples include Yeltsin's efforts to turn the presidential security service into a "mini KGB"; Kuchma's transformation of the state tax administration into an "organ of repression;" Lukashenka's building up of the State Control Commission (KGK) to reassert control over economic actors; and the creation of new investigatory units to collect compromising material on opposition (*kompromat*) under Kebich in Belarus and Lucinschi in Moldova.[65] Post-Soviet leaders also built formal and informal hierarchies that allowed them to use subnational state officials—from governors to police, teachers, and doctors—to harass opposition and manipulate elections.[66] While such dimensions of state building have nothing to do with the rule of law or the protection of rights, they have been core to the *actual* state building projects carried out by leaders in many "new democracies."

To understand the relationship between state power and authoritarian rule, I therefore move away from recent approaches that focus on the state's role in providing public goods and draw instead on discussions of early modern state building that center on the maintenance of internal order, the elimination or pacification of rival power centers, and the centralization of control over territory.[67] The focus of this book is on *authoritarian state power*, which refers to the willingness and capacity of state agencies to repress and distribute resources in support of incumbent power.[68] Two dimensions of state power are important for autocratic control: coercion and economic control. An extensive and cohesive coercive apparatus is important to monitor, intimidate, and suppress potential sources of opposition and to manipulate elections. Simultaneously, discretionary state control over the economy provides incumbents with increased capacity to buy off supporters, starve opposition, and undermine independent media.

Coercive State Power

First, coercion is central to autocracy. Police, local prefects, tax officials, and other agents of the state provide key support for autocratic rule by harassing, monitoring, and infiltrating opposition; facilitating vote fraud; and mobilizing regime support. Coercive capacity refers to the effective reach and cohesion of the state's coercive apparatus (see appendix A for coding rules).

While recent discussions of the state have emphasized the significant obstacles to liberal state building, the end of the Cold War also generated enormous problems for coercive state power—challenges that are key to understanding pluralism by default. The recent spread of global communications technologies and increased Western commitment to democratic norms means that large-scale abuse opens perpetrators to international condemnation—and in some cases punitive action. Such conditions make it more likely that major regime actors will defect when faced with demands to engage in risky behavior. Indeed, the collapse of Yanukovych's authoritarian regime in Ukraine in early 2014 was directly caused by the rapid defection of security officials who feared taking blame for large-scale, regime-backed violence.[69]

Simultaneously, in the post–Cold War context, many countries adopted laws that criminalized authoritarian activity such as voter fraud. With such laws on the books, lower-level officials carrying out abuse must be able to trust that their superiors will not hang them out to dry should things go wrong. At the same time, contemporary autocrats often resist giving signed or written orders to shoot at demonstrators, censor media, or steal elections.[70] Reliance on oral commands makes sense for leaders seeking to avoid accountability for risky actions. Yet such behavior may discourage subordinates from following orders because they do not want to take the fall for decisions made by their bosses. The lack of written orders can also be disastrous for administrative coordination. As anyone who has played "Telephone" knows, oral commands passed from person to person are prone to distortion. As we will see in chapter 3, these dynamics greatly undermined vote fraud in Ukraine in 2004.

Coercive power has had an important impact on regime competitiveness. In another era, weak central control often led to a military coup. However, in the post–Cold War era, external pressures have generally dissuaded those in the military from such overtly nondemocratic solutions. Instead, the default option has often been rough adherence to democratic procedure. As Marinov and Goemans demonstrate, the number of successful military coups declined dramatically after 1991; and among successful post–1991 coups, most resulted in elections.[71]

Coercive weakness has strengthened pluralism by thwarting incumbent attempts to suppress opposition, manipulate elections, and control parliament. First, it has undermined efforts to repress opposition. In cases of extremely weak repressive capacity (characterized by wage arrears and underfunding as in Ukraine in the early 1990s or in Kyrgyzstan), leaders have faced difficulties carrying out *any* large-scale coordinated authoritarian action and have therefore been vulnerable to even weak opposition challenges. Indeed, weak coercive capacity has provided key political opportunities for opposition mobilization and often underlies "people power."[72] As Sidney Tarrow notes, "[r]ational people do not often attack well-fortified opponents."[73] In Georgia in November 2003, police passivity caused by significant wage arrears allowed relatively modest numbers of protesters to storm and take over the legislature in the face of no resistance. Similarly, in Kyrgyzstan in 2005 and again in 2010, underfunded police forces largely stood aside as relatively small numbers of protesters throughout the country seized regional governments and ultimately national power. While successful revolts in Georgia and Kyrgyzstan have often been referred to as examples of "people power," they were not especially large and are thus arguably better understood as products of state failure.

In other cases where coercive capacity is greater and police are better financed, autocrats may still face significant obstacles to extremely visible, large-scale, "high intensity" repression.[74] Absent tight bonds of trust, or non-material ties among top regime elites and security forces,[75] regime allies tend to be risk averse and avoid taking responsibility for large-scale violent actions that invite international sanctions, prosecution, travel bans, and frozen bank accounts. In such cases, autocrats are often unable to motivate police to engage in consistent, large-scale repression over a long period of time. A spectacular example of this dynamic occurred in Ukraine in 2014 when the relatively well-funded Ukrainian security services remained loyal and cohesive for nearly three months of large-scale protest but dissolved as the government began to fire on crowds in the center of the capital (see chapter 3).

Next, coercive weakness undermines efforts to manipulate electoral outcomes. Thus in Russia in 1996, Yeltsin decided to back down from a decision to postpone the presidential elections after the head of the police, Anatolii Kulikov, strongly resisted this action.[76] In other cases, incumbent control has been so weak that leaders face opposition even among their own local subordinates at election time. For example, in Ukraine in 1994, Kravchuk appointees in eastern Ukraine actively campaigned on behalf of Kravchuk's main opponent.

Finally, weak coercive capacity strengthens otherwise weak legislatures by creating openings for competing forces to use informal measures to influence state policy. Even in the absence of a strong rule of law, tradition of parliamentary power, or robust legislative apparatus, parliamentary forces can affect policy by making deals with state ministers and those responsible for implementation.[77]

In turn, state building has often reduced the space for pluralism. Strengthening central control over coercive agencies and local agents of the state is not necessarily undemocratic. However, in the absence of other checks on central power—civil society or a robust judicial system—such state building may eliminate key sources of contestation. There is often little to prevent leaders from using their new-found central authority for strictly partisan ends. In Russia, for example, increased central control in the 2000s made it easier for Putin to carry out far more systematic and widespread electoral fraud than had existed in the 1990s under Yeltsin.[78] Similarly, strengthening key state institutions such as the tax authorities in Ukraine in the late 1990s resulted in much more systematic fraud in the 1999 election than in 1994 (see chapter 3).

State Control over Wealth

Discretionary state economic control has also been key to authoritarian consolidation.[79] State economic control is considered high where the state maintains control over key means of production and finance, as in command economies,[80] or where a large percentage of national income takes the form of rents effectively controlled by the state, as in many mineral-based rentier states. As Barrington Moore noted long ago, "The concentration of economic authority in a single body inevitably carries with it the concentration of political authority."[81] Above all, discretionary economic control has affected the ability of leaders to suppress opposition—both by preventing key defections that might otherwise strengthen opponents and by starving existing opposition of the resources necessary to survive.[82]

In the Soviet Union, Mikhail Gorbachev dismantled institutional mechanisms of state economic control in the late 1980s (see chapter 2). In the 1990s, leaders in Belarus, Uzbekistan, and Turkmenistan rebuilt mechanisms of state economic control and never engaged in large-scale privatization. Such autocrats had an easier time concentrating political power than did leaders in countries like Georgia, Kyrgyzstan, and Ukraine, who privatized and failed to reestablish such control.[83] In the latter context, even flawed privatization undermined efforts to concentrate political control.[84] As we see in subsequent chapters, business "oligarchs" who benefitted from insider privatization were often sufficiently autonomous to act as a potential resource for opposition during periods of regime crisis. Such oligarchs have played an important role in helping to organize anti-incumbent activity and funding opposition media.[85] While oligarchs are unlikely to provide a stable social base for democracy and are hardly committed democrats, they may facilitate the fragmentation of authoritarian power.[86] Because they have relatively independent resources and seek to end up on the winning side, oligarchs often amplify regime vulnerabilities. Thus, if a regime is perceived to be weak or if a viable challenger emerges, oligarchs—lacking any strong loyalty to the regime—are likely to spread their resources in order to ensure that they have ties to whoever comes out on top.

Organizational capacity is admittedly a somewhat messy, multifaceted variable encompassing diverse forms of party, economic, and coercive organizational power. Yet there are important theoretical reasons for combining these different factors into a single variable—namely, that strength in one area may compensate for weakness in another. Above all, a high degree of discretionary economic control reduces the importance of party strength in maintaining incumbent power. Where incumbents monopolize control of the economy, defectors will have a much harder time garnering the resources necessary to build a serious opposition movement. As I argue in chapter 5, highly centralized state economic control in Belarus under Lukashenka reduced the need for him to build a strong party. Rather than giving allies a long-term interest in his incumbency in a ruling party, Lukashenka increased the costs of opposition by depriving opponents and allies of any resources outside his direct control. By contrast, where incumbents lack such control, defectors can more easily build and sustain finances and create a viable opposition movement. The greater dispersion of resources increases opportunities for elite defection. Partly as a result, ruling parties were more important for maintaining elite cohesion in countries with fragmented economic control such as Moldova, Russia, and Ukraine. The fact that strength in one dimension compensates for weakness in another makes it useful to conceptualize organizational capacity as a single variable rather than as separate party and state variables.

Finally, it is worth emphasizing that organizational capacity is here defined in a way that can be clearly distinguished from regime competitiveness. Each of my measures can either be assessed before a leader is in power[87] or can easily be differentiated from the level of pluralism.[88] (See appendix A for full coding rules.)

In sum, authoritarian weakness offers an important explanation for the emergence of dynamic and often democratic competition in otherwise inhospitable conditions. Underdeveloped parties and states constrain autocratic behavior and often account for the failure of autocrats to suppress opposition, control the legislature, restrict media freedom, and manipulate elections.

National Divisions and Regime Contestation

Divisions over national identity[89] have provided another constraint on efforts to monopolize political control. As defined in this book, divided national identities exist where there are relatively equal and politically salient divisions in titular national identities along regional, cultural, ethnic or other lines. By "relatively equal," I mean that each of the main competing identity groups has sufficient support either to gain national power by itself or as an equal member in a coalition with other groups. I focus on divisions in the *titular* identity because such groups are most likely to fight for national power rather than demand separation. This definition excludes national divisions involving separatist minorities that do not seek national power (e.g., Abkhaz in Georgia, Chechens in Russia). It also excludes minorities (e.g., Coptic Christians in Egypt) that are far too small to gain national power.

Discussions of national identity and democracy have focused almost entirely on the dangers posed by splits along ethnic, religious, cultural or regional lines. Such divisions are typically considered "one of the major threats to any democracy" that threaten "instability and breakdown," undermine opposition unity, "place a dangerous strain" on democracy, and "contribute to state weakness and . . . violence."[90]

I do not deny that deep divisions may create serious problems for democracy, nor do I question that homogeneity can facilitate peaceful democratic development. Yet an exclusive focus on democratization provides only a limited understanding of the influence of divisions on regime trajectories. The fact that deep divides often undermine democracy does not mean that they facilitate authoritarian consolidation. Indeed, under certain circumstances, the very factors that make divisions so dangerous for democratic development may also make it more difficult for autocrats to monopolize political control. By contrast, in countries where opposition is otherwise weak and under-resourced, the absence of salient national divisions may deprive opposition of critical resources to challenge incumbent rule.

This book suggests three mechanisms by which splits in national identity may facilitate political pluralism. First, such divisions have provided opposition forces with potent *mobilizational appeals* to attract broad and passionate support even where opposition and civil society are weak. Second, polarized divisions have undermined efforts at *elite collusion* that might otherwise reduce political competition. Third, divisions increase the *external constraints* confronting incumbent power. Divisions between Russian and non-Russian groups in the post-Soviet context have enhanced the degree of incumbent exposure to international pressure—both from Russia and from the West.

Identity and Mobilization

Appeals to national identity are often effective sources of mobilization. Nationalism holds "unusual force and attraction"[91] and serves as a powerful "vehicle of political emotion."[92] Heightened emotion in turn motivates individual activism by shaping "both the assessment of potential gains and the costs involved in any line of action" and helps explain "activists' determination in the face of high risk and their willingness to endure suffering and self-sacrifice, including torture and death."[93]

All of this makes nationalism a particularly effective tool for oppositions possessing few resources and confronting significant repression. By framing regime opposition in terms of national identity, opposition has been able to draw on a committed activist base and stimulate sustained personal sacrifice that may be necessary in order to confront a repressive regime and generate regime crisis.

Such identities have been key to mobilizing support at the ballot box and on the streets. First, divisions in identity often create stable cleavage structures that make it easier for opposition to mobilize electoral support in the face of even a hostile media environment and in the absence of significant organizational and material resources.[94] Such appeals have also facilitated street protest. Thus, Mark Beissinger, in his study of protest behavior during the collapse of the Soviet Union, shows that nationalism played a significant role in providing opposition with a social base.[95] In the post-Soviet era, nationalism continued to give the opposition a powerful mobilizational tool. Regime opponents successfully mobilized support by framing opposition not simply as a push for democracy but as a fight for a national way of life.

The strength of opposition mobilization is heavily determined by the relative size of support for different identities. The larger the share of the population in which national identity can be mobilized against incumbent rule, the more powerful the potential opposition. Thus, we would expect opposition to be most powerful where incumbents confront opposition identities shared by the large majority of the population—as in many anticolonial struggles.

In the absence of other constraints on authoritarian rule (such as EU-style democracy promotion), identity conflicts would seem most likely to undermine authoritarian stability where there is a division between two relatively equal and politically salient ethnic, regional, cultural or other groups. Where support for competing identities is large enough that each side can plausibly take national power, both sides will be able to utilize significant symbolic power when they are out of power. Such splits give opposition a durable mobilizational tool and base of operations that can be used to limit incumbent control and mount serious challenges for national control. Thus, in Bangladesh, which witnessed three turnovers between 1991 and 2010, a relatively equal national division between a pro-Pakistani, non-ethnic "Bangladeshi" identity and a pro-Indian, ethnic "Bengali" identity provided the basis for a dynamic (but highly dysfunctional) two-party system.[96] Here, splits in identity have contributed to stalemate and conflict but made it harder for either side to monopolize political control. In general, such divisions make it harder for autocrats to use nationalism in the classic dictatorial fashion to unify the country, justify repressive actions, and bludgeon the opposition.

By contrast, in countries where the domestic and external push for democracy is otherwise weak, the dominance of a single national identity can deprive opposition of a powerful mobilizing resource. Unable to tap into any salient cleavages, the opposition may have a harder time motivating large numbers of supporters to take the necessary risks to challenge incumbent rule in the absence of a serious economic crisis. For example, the absence of salient national divisions and the relative success of nation-building efforts in Tanzania under Julius Nyerere may partly explain why the ruling party was able to garner 80 to 90 percent of the legislature in the 1990s and 2000s with little overt fraud.[97] Absent strong civil society or salient cleavages, Tanzanian opposition had "no clear message or ideological mission and has been unable to crack the suspicion that it is running simply to get into power."[98]

Polarization and Elite Collusion

Next, polarized national identities can create barriers to collusion. Indeed, one of the central threats to pluralism by default is agreement among otherwise competing parties and political leaders. If the main political actors can successfully agree ahead of time on how to divide the political pie, they are in a position to exclude outsiders, limit media freedom, and encourage electoral violations. By fostering polarization, national divisions often complicate such collusion. Thus, Adrienne LeBas argues that intense polarization sharpens "us-them" distinctions between opposition and incumbents that can bolster opposition unity and can make it more costly for opposition leaders to cooperate with incumbent power.[99] Such polarization may complicate efforts by incumbents to coopt opposition.

Identity Divisions and External Vulnerability

Finally, the types of passionate divisions over identity and culture discussed here rarely remain confined within domestic borders. They are thus likely to have a critical impact on countries' exposure to *external pressure*. By tapping into broader geopolitical divisions, polarized splits between Russophile and non-Russophile groups in the post-Soviet context have opened incumbents to pressure from both Russia and the West (see figure on p. 9). The existence of a relatively strong anti-Russian nationalism has led to the emergence of anti-Russian leaders who have faced Russian pressure and complicated efforts by autocrats to obtain "black knight" Russian support that might otherwise bolster authoritarian stability.[100] Russian hostility has in turn made countries more dependent on Western diplomatic and material assistance—thereby making these countries more vulnerable to Western democratizing pressure.

In Moldova and Ukraine, strong anti-Russian movements in the late 1980s encouraged the emergence of anti-Russian leaders who confronted significant tensions with Russia in the early 1990s. In each of these countries, disruptions in Russian energy deliveries seriously exacerbated economic crises.[101] Identity politics also encouraged the Russian government to finance opposition candidates and to use Russian dominance of post-Soviet media to disseminate negative information about anti-Russian candidates—making it impossible for leaders to monopolize domestic media. For example, Moldova, sandwiched between competing powers, became host to "two separate autonomous media subsystems"—one dominated by Romanianist and the other by Russophile forces that were difficult for any government to control.[102]

Hostility from Russia also enhanced dependence on Western support—thereby strengthening the impact of Western democracy promotion. This was a particularly important source of pluralism in Moldova in the 1990s and 2000s and, arguably, in Ukraine after the fall of Yanukovych in 2014. In stark contrast, relative unity around a Russophile identity in Belarus strengthened Russian support for Lukashenka and insulated the country from Western democratizing pressure.

In sum, splits in national identity have constrained autocrats by making it easier for opposition to tap into a passionate, committed base of support, undermining elite collusion, and heightening external constraints on authoritarian behavior. Thus, in each of the four turnovers in Ukraine, opposition succeeded in part by mobilizing either Russophile (1994 and 2010) or Ukrainophile (2004 and 2014) sentiment. Similarly in Moldova, opposition overturned incumbent power three times—in 1996, 2001, and 2009—by mobilizing either pro-European/Romanianist or Russophile sentiment.

At the same time, several caveats are in order. First, national identity is obviously not the only source of opposition mobilization and authoritarian failure. A range of factors—robust civil society, powerful labor organizations, economic crisis, strong external democratizing pressure—both facilitate mobilization and constrain autocratic behavior.[103] My point is that in the many countries where opposition *lacks* such resources or constraints, identity divisions are often virtually the only means for mobilizing political opposition.

Moreover, splits in national identity are not primordial. This book highlights the ways in which the various patterns of identity were constructed over the course of the last century. Nevertheless, national identity cannot easily "be cut from whole cloth" but must derive from "the repertoire of available emotive cultural symbols and practices."[104] This is all the more so for oppositions lacking access to state educational institutions and media that might be used to shape identity.

Interaction between National Identity and Organizational Strength

While conceptually and empirically separate, national identity and state and party strength may interact in important ways. Thus, strong state and party power in the Soviet context (as well as in cases such as Syria) have suppressed powerful opposition identities or channeled them in ways that support regime survival for many years. Identity divisions are thus not insurmountable barriers to authoritarian rule. Indeed, in the late 1980s, identity mobilization was precipitated *first* by institutional breakdown caused by Gorbachev's reforms (see chapter 2). In turn, where anti-Soviet national identity was strong (as in the Baltics and western Ukraine), nationalism encouraged the further destruction of authoritarian state institutions—a process that was much less evident in republics where anti-Russian/Soviet national identity was originally weaker.

Democracy and Chaos

The argument laid out above resonates with a widespread public perception in the former Soviet Union that "democracy means chaos"—a view bolstered by the fact that democracy was accompanied by economic crisis and state collapse in the early 1990s.[105] This association has been adroitly exploited by autocrats across the region.

The evidence presented here does not suggest that democratic institutions or participation per se create dysfunction as some have argued.[106] Instead, we see how dysfunction and political competition may sometimes have the same roots. Polarized stalemate and high fragmentation that characterize many cases of pluralism by default undermined both authoritarian consolidation and economic and other reforms.

Relatedly, this analysis highlights the fact that the forces that promote political pluralism may be different from those that facilitate the development of stable democratic institutions. Party weakness and fragmentation have probably reduced democratic accountability—but such weakness also damaged the capacity of incumbents to impose authoritarian rule. National divisions often undermine peaceful democratic development; yet this analysis also shows that divisions may thwart authoritarianism. Although state weakness in Russia and elsewhere in the early 1990s did little to promote democratic consolidation, it also made it harder for autocrats to shut down legislatures and manipulate elections.

This disjuncture between the factors that promote competition and those that facilitate stable democracy help us to better understand why a number of countries experienced multiple electoral turnovers—including Albania (3), Bangladesh (3), Madagascar (3), Mali (2), Malawi (2), Moldova (3), Ukraine (4), and Zambia (2)—but failed to see the emergence of stable or consolidated democracy. As this research shows, even peaceful electoral turnovers—contra Huntington[107]—may be more the product of institutional dysfunction than of strong democratic institutions or elite democratic consensus.

Applying the Argument

This book explores the sources of pluralism in countries with weak democratic prerequisites through an examination of post-Soviet regime trajectories. In particular, I offer an in-depth analysis of Belarus, Moldova, and Ukraine. All three countries witnessed high competition at the beginning of the 1990s but later exhibited profoundly divergent regime trajectories: Moldova and Ukraine were on average the most pluralist countries in the former Soviet Union; while Belarus was among the most closed regimes in the region. I seek to explain differences across these cases as well as changes in competition in each over time (see table 1.1).

Historically parts of the "Soviet west" and now the "new Eastern Europe," these countries were chosen because they provide analytical leverage to understand the sources of post–Cold War regime competition: they are similar across a range of factors considered important for regime outcomes but exhibited key variations in identity and party and state capacity.[108] At the start of the transition process, Belarus, Moldova, and Ukraine had similar levels of economic development[109] and shared Soviet legacies unfriendly to democratic development—including weak civil societies, undeveloped rules of law, and high degrees of state economic control. None of the three countries had experience with democracy prior to 1991, and all were dominated by mostly undemocratic former high-level apparatchiks. Each initially had democratic oppositions of roughly comparable strength,[110] adopted semi-presidential constitutions in the early 1990s,[111] and had relatively weak ties to the West.[112] Finally, in contrast to their Eastern European counterparts, they were never seriously considered for membership in the European Union; but in contrast to Central Asia, they were "borderland" states geographically proximate both to Russia on the one side and to Western Europe and newly democratic Eastern Europe on the other.

At the same time, these countries varied in critical ways—both across time and case—that give us the opportunity to explore the impact of identity divisions, and party/state power (table 1.1). First, Moldova and Ukraine had national identities that were significantly more divided than in Belarus—differences that were largely grounded in variations in the historical timing of mass literacy and national schooling.[113] Moldova and Ukraine were riven between regionally concentrated populations in the west that were more Europeanist (Romanianist and Ukrainophile) on one side and those in the east that were more Russophile or Eurasianist on the other; while Belarusians were relatively unified around a Russophile conception of Belarusian identity.

Party and state capacity also diverged across time in each of the cases. In each case, state capacity was weak in the early 1990s but increased over the course of the 1990s. Party capacity also varied significantly over time: relatively

Table 1.1 Organizational Capacity, National Unity, and Regime Closure in Belarus, Moldova, and Ukraine

	Early/mid-1990s	Mid-1990s–early 2000s	Mid-late 2000s	Early 2010s
Belarus				
Leader in power	Kebich	Lukashenka	Lukashenka	Lukashenka
Party and state capacity	Low	Medium	Medium	Medium
National identity	Low split	Low split	Low split	Low split
Average political closure	Medium	High	High	High
Moldova				
Leader in power	Snegur	Lucinschi	Communist Party	AEI
Party and state capacity	Low	Med-low	Medium	Med-low
National identity	High split	High split	High split	High split
Average political closure	Low	Low	Medium	Low
Ukraine				
Leader in power	Kravchuk	Kuchma	Yushchenko	Yanukovych
Party and state capacity	Low	Medium	Med-low	Medium
National identity	High split	High split	High split	High split
Average political closure	Low	Medium	Low	Medium

Note: Definitions/operationalization of variables provided in appendix A. Detailed justifications of scorings provided at the beginning of each case study chapter.

weak in certain periods (in Ukraine under Kravchuk and Yushchenko, in Moldova under Snegur and Lucinschi) and stronger in others (Ukraine under Yanukovych and in Moldova under the Communists).

In the chapters that follow, we see how the evolution of political competition in each of these cases was the product of national identity and changes in incumbent state and party capacity. In a nutshell, shifts in organizational capacity best explain changes in competition over time, while differences in identity account for differences across cases. First, early pluralism by default was facilitated by the sudden dissolution of the Soviet party-state in 1991 that deprived incumbents of the organizational resources to maintain power and concentrate political control. The demise of the Communist Party and the decision by leaders in each country to forego party building made it harder to prevent prime ministers, vice presidents, or other key allies from going into opposition. Weak incumbent control over the economic and coercive arms of the state complicated efforts to impose political control through the distribution of resources, electoral manipulation or the use of force. Partly as a result, each case exhibited dynamic and competitive politics in the early and mid-1990s, resulting in electoral turnover.

Over the course of the late 1990s and early 2000s, leaders built more effective states with greater central control. Yet, far from promoting democratic consolidation, state building in the absence of consistent Western pressure instead facilitated more effective repression of opposition and electoral manipulation. In Lukashenka's Belarus, greater regime closure was further facilitated by weak national divisions and by the leader's success in centralizing control over the economy. By contrast, in Moldova and Ukraine, national divisions and weaker economic control undermined authoritarian consolidation as oppositions mobilized Russophile and non-Russophile national identities against successive incumbents. The result was regimes that alternated repeatedly between democratic and competitive authoritarian rule—depending in part on the strength of the organizational assets that leaders brought with them to power.

Theoretical Implications

The central aim of this book is to convince readers to rethink the origins of pluralism as well as the relationship between political competition on one side and governance and democratic consolidation on the other. Particularly in the absence of other factors supporting democracy, competitive politics have often been the product of authoritarian weakness, which has in turn threatened both governance and longer term democratic consolidation.

My analysis runs counter to several standard perspectives from the democratization literature. First, studies of democratization have frequently emphasized the importance of civil society.[114] In particular, observers of Ukrainian politics have commonly argued that a strong civil society was behind the country's repeated and often successful episodes of mass mobilization (including four different instances—in 1990, 1993, 2004, and 2014—when protests led to the ouster of the country's chief executive).[115] Yet a closer examination of these cases suggests that organized civil society played a relatively minor role in stimulating successful mass action and pluralism. Not only were groups organizing protests mostly formed during or just before protest actions, but there is little evidence that such groups played a significant role in bringing people to the demonstrations.[116] Instead, participation in mass protest can better be explained by national identity. Indeed, Belarusian groups in the early 1990s were about as well organized as their Moldovan and Ukrainian counterparts— they just lacked the broader popular support that identity provided in the other cases.

Next, studies of postcommunism have been dominated by attention to institutional design.[117] Indeed, as we see in subsequent chapters, design has clearly shaped contestation at key moments. There is a reason why political actors have fought so strenuously over constitutions. Yet scholars have pointed to several limitations of this perspective. First, laws are often widely ignored in post-Soviet and other developing countries.[118] How can institutional rules be important if those rules are not followed? Indeed, as we see in chapter 5, when Lukashenka was elected in 1994, he established fully closed authoritarian rule not by taking advantage of provisions in the constitution but by simply ignoring it. While not all constitutions are disregarded to such an extent, the fact that they are obeyed so irregularly means that we need to focus not just on the rules themselves but on the factors determining their efficacy.

In a sophisticated response to this critique, Henry Hale argues that, while particular laws are often ignored, constitutions nevertheless powerfully shape elite perceptions of the balance of power.[119] Yet constitutions may themselves be a *reflection* rather than the *cause* of the balance of power.[120] Instead of simply shaping elite perceptions of the balance of power, constitutions have often been the product of intense conflicts whose outcome has been determined by the balance of political forces.[121] Focusing only on the impact of institutional design begs the key question of why some leaders—for example, Lukashenka in 1996, Kuchma in 1996, and Yanukovych in 2010—were successful in strengthening presidential powers; while others—like Lucinschi in 1999, and Yushchenko in the late 2000s—were not.

Further, the *implementation* of the same constitutions has diverged dramatically under different presidents. Putin in Russia was able to concentrate power to a much greater degree than Yeltsin despite operating under the same constitution. Moreover, while pluralism under Kravchuk and Yushchenko in Ukraine are often seen as products of weak presidential powers, both Kuchma and Yanukovych were able to concentrate power despite being constrained *by identical constitutional rules* as their immediate predecessors. Indeed, as we see in subsequent chapters, the effects of a particular institutional design often hinge on the organizational resources of the incumbent.

This book also challenges views of the transition process that focus primarily on democratic values. Country specialists have frequently pointed to the existence of a democratic or anti-democratic political culture—such as a tradition of "Cossack democracy" in Ukraine from the fifteenth to the eighteenth centuries and a "patriarchal" political culture in Belarus—to explain differences in regime outcomes.[122] In fact, however, opinion surveys provide little evidence that support for democracy was significantly greater in Moldova and Ukraine than in Belarus. Indeed, preferences for democracy in Belarus appeared to be *higher* than in Moldova or Ukraine.[123] Instead, we find that regime outcomes are best explained by the different constraints on abuse confronting different leaders.

Observable Implications of the Argument

This book draws on in-depth case studies to assess the causal mechanisms that promote political competition. The analysis focuses on the ways in which identity, organizational capacity, and other explanatory variables do or do not shape the levels of political competition during each period in a country's history since 1990. This is a data-hungry exercise involving information about informal processes that are often hidden from public view and that generally cannot be found in datasets. Thus, I concentrate on just three countries—Belarus, Moldova, and Ukraine—drawing on over 150 in-depth interviews of local politicians, observers, bureaucrats, and activists; direct observation; analysis of memoirs and local newspapers in four languages; U.S. diplomatic cables; as well as Western and in-country secondary accounts.

I have relied on several strategies to assess whether authoritarian weakness accounts for political competition. At the broadest level, my theory suggests that political competition may result from failed attempts to concentrate or abuse power. Thus, along each dimension studied, I need to show that efforts were made to centralize control or suppress opposition, but that party/state weakness or identity divisions undermined such endeavors. The absence of such evidence would suggest that something other than authoritarian weakness (e.g., institutional design, leadership) was behind regime competitiveness.

The analysis also draws on several observable implications of my argument. First, party cohesion should only matter where the incumbent and his or her allies have at least nominal access to significant resources and sufficient allies to dominate the government or parliament—a reality that I must demonstrate in each discussion of parliamentary or opposition strength. Weak cohesion resulting from underdeveloped party structures can only be decisive where incumbents could plausibly monopolize control *absent defections*. Along similar lines, another key indicator of pluralism by default is whether opposition consists primarily of former associates of the incumbent. By contrast, where incumbent forces are small and opposition parties from *outside* the regime have a strong majority in the legislature or lead a powerful opposition challenge, it will be harder to argue that weak ruling-party cohesion per se explains the failure to control the legislature or suppress opposition challenges.

A second set of observable implications relates to state weakness and pluralism. State weakness can only be a factor promoting pluralism where the state is weak and sufficiently politicized to be a potential source of authoritarian abuse, and where incumbents make efforts to use the state to abuse power by manipulating elections or harassing opposition. We should find evidence that abuse was attempted but failed as a result of insubordination by state officials. By contrast, a strong rule of law and absence of a politicized state would suggest that strong *democratic* rather than weak *authoritarian* institutions are facilitating pluralism.

In the case of protest, pluralism caused by state failure as opposed to "people power" will be clearest where (1) the state is demonstrably weak; (2) there is evidence of open disobedience by state officials in response to demands to repress; and (3) demonstrations succeed even though they are not larger or more sustained than in many other cases of authoritarian survival. In instances where regimes fall in the face of powerful protest and the state remains more or less cohesive throughout (e.g., Ukraine in 2004), it will be harder to argue that state failure per se is the main explanation for regime breakdown.

Third, we can point to several observable indicators of whether or not national identity divisions are central in explaining competition. There should be ex ante evidence of relatively equal and salient divisions in national identity. National divisions should generally divide the main opposition from incumbent power. Where opposition is successful, it should mostly mobilize identity claims in opposition to incumbent power. By contrast, the frequent emergence of a powerful opposition unconnected to this divide would suggest that splits in identity have less to do with political competition.

Overview of the Book

To understand the sources of democratic or semi-democratic political competition in inhospitable conditions over the last quarter-century, we need to examine more closely the challenges of building institutions to maintain power and control dissent. By temporarily abandoning our normative biases and putting ourselves in the shoes of an autocrat, we often find sources of democracy or its rough equivalent in surprising places. The heroes of this book are not democratic activists or emerging civil society but rapacious opportunists too weak to centralize political control and passionate fanatics willing to take the risks necessary to throw autocracies into crisis. State and party weakness and divided identities—factors typically thought to undermine democracy—may in certain circumstances facilitate democratic or semi-democratic political competition.

The rest of this book lays out the origins and dynamics of pluralism by default in the former Soviet Union. Chapter 2 explores the roots of post-Soviet pluralism by default in Gorbachev's decision to reform and weaken the Communist party-state. Subsequent chapters provide detailed case analyses of regime evolution in Belarus, Moldova, and Ukraine. Process tracing of individual cases over time allows us to assess how authoritarian weakness interacts with other causal variables—including institutional design and leadership—in generating (or not generating) political competition.

Chapter 3 explores the impact of divided identity and party and state weakness in Ukraine since 1989. While identity divisions have almost entirely been seen as an obstacle to democratic change, splits in Ukraine regularly bolstered opposition mobilization and hampered authoritarian collusion at the top. But such divisions were also the source of serious dysfunction. Indeed, in 2014 polarized divisions both undermined authoritarian rule under Yanukovych and created conditions for social conflict. At the same time, shifts in party and state strength help account for changes in the level of competition over time. Next, chapter 4 demonstrates the ways in which identity divisions bolstered pluralism in Moldova. Here party and state weakness, together with severe and violent identity conflicts, undermined organizational capacity for authoritarian abuse and exposed leaders to Western democratizing pressure. As in Ukraine, the degree of party organization under different incumbents had an important impact on the extent of competition over time.

Then, in chapter 5, we see how a relatively unified national identity and increased organizational capacity in Belarus facilitated regime closure. In the mid-1990s weak splits in national identity hampered opposition efforts to mobilize opposition to Lukashenka's ham-fisted efforts to monopolize political control—despite opposition to such measures by enormous sections of the Belarusian elite. Subsequently, a combination of Russian support and Lukashenka's construction of a highly centralized system of economic control severely hampered the growth of viable opposition challenges.

Chapter 6 offers an initial investigation of pluralism by default in the rest of the former Soviet Union. Indeed, this book represents one of the first monographs to formulate and apply a theory of regime variation across case and time in the former Soviet Union.[124] I provide an overview of how organizational strength and splits in national identity help us to understand variations in political competition across cases and time in the Caucasus, Central Asia, and Russia. Finally, chapter 7 summarizes the evidence for pluralism by default and contrasts it with rival approaches to regime transition. I suggest ways in which my theory throws light on the origins of democracy in the West as well as pluralism in contemporary Sub-Saharan Africa.

2

Perestroika and the Origins of Post-Soviet Pluralism by Default

Decades of Soviet rule left new autocrats in the 1990s with a mixed legacy. On the one hand, leaders were weakly constrained by the rule of law, nominally commanded vast coercive and economic infrastructures, and confronted weak independent civil societies. On the other hand, long-term institutional decay combined with reforms by Mikhail Gorbachev in the 1980s created a system that initially made it much harder for leaders to prevent defections at the top or to cope with opposition from below. Gorbachev's reforms dismantled the Communist Party and deprived leaders of key mechanisms of social and economic control—necessitating serious efforts at authoritarian state building in all but a few cases in the 1990s. Simultaneously, leaders in the different republics confronted divergent levels of popular mobilization that were largely the product of precommunist patterns of national identity formation.

The Soviet System of Control

Until the late 1980s, Soviet leaders had at their disposal one of the world's most effective and extensive systems of control. The Communist Party lay at the center of Soviet power. "One of the Bolsheviks' greatest inventions" and a model for numerous authoritarian leaders in the twentieth century, the Party asserted control over a vast range of economic and societal activity and had an extraordinarily well-developed organizational culture of Party discipline.[1] The Party was extensive—penetrating virtually every public institution in the country with cells that monitored activities in each educational institution, factory, office, collective farm, and military unit with three or more Party members.[2] It was also highly centralized and disciplined. Party members were "obliged to carry out all Party directives," while "the threat of expulsion from the Party for failure to carry out orders" gave "officials the most powerful incentive not to challenge orders from above."[3] A central mechanism of Party control was the *nomenklatura*—a list of personnel deemed politically reliable by Party leaders to hold positions of authority. Nomenklatura positions included an extremely wide range of jobs—from head surgeon in a hospital, to factory director, to state administrator. This system allowed Party leaders to "fire any director and appoint a new one, or instantly change the social status of any senior official, all of whom were Party members."[4]

A key source of the Party's power lay in its ability to distribute economic resources. Until the late 1980s, economic activity—from large industrial plants to street cafes—was directly controlled by a vast state bureaucracy. Prices, inputs, investment levels, and distribution were determined by an enormous series of ministries and central planners.[5] The Party, in turn, included departments that paralleled each state economic ministry and dictated the distribution of resources across the economy. Overall, this system provided an important source of social control, since livelihood hinged less on a set salary than on the distribution of in-kind goods—from hard-to-find foodstuffs to rooms at vacation sanatoria—that could be taken away at will. The selective and particularistic distribution of goods strongly limited collective action.[6]

Finally, authoritarian control in the Soviet Union was built on a vast and cohesive system of coercion. The Soviet security services were founded in 1917 by Felix Dzerzhinsky shortly after the October revolution to cope with emerging threats to Bolshevik rule. Under Lenin and then Stalin, the security services regularly engaged in violence against broad swaths of the population through mass executions, manmade famines, population transfers, and the imprisonment of hundreds of thousands in prison camps. After Stalin's death in 1953, repression declined significantly. Under Nikita Khrushchev (1954–1964), thousands of political prisoners were released and large numbers of Party officials were rehabilitated. In turn, the transition from Khrushchev to Leonid Brezhnev marked a further reduction in the use of large-scale violence against protesters.[7] Mass shootings became extremely rare under Brezhnev.[8] While the regime was no less restrictive in permitting protest, responses to such actions grew more flexible and the regime relied increasingly on preemptive measures.[9] During this same time, the KGB shifted its focus from large-scale repression to information gathering and analysis.[10]

At the same time, the KGB expanded enormously in the 1960s and 1970s.[11] In 1990, there were more KGB officials in Moscow alone (47,000) than all of the employees of the FBI and CIA.[12] The KGB spent enormous resources to conduct surveillance on the population and had informants in virtually every apartment block.[13] KGB officials throughout the country were responsible for reading every piece of international mail sent by Soviet citizens and for conducting spot checks on domestic mail.[14]

Together, the Party hierarchy, economic control, and the vast network of security services were extraordinarily successful at suppressing public or organized dissent. By the mid-1950s, virtually no organized opposition existed in the Soviet Union, and the regime confronted almost no serious protest. Thus, in the thirty years after Stalin's death in 1953, there were only 45 non-state mass actions (including riots at sports events) of a thousand or more participants.[15] Resistance to the regime consisted almost entirely of small groups of dissident intellectuals encompassing "at most several thousand individuals" in a country of over 200 million.[16] Indeed, Communism left a long-term impact on the level of societal activism. Thus, Marc Howard pulls together an array of survey evidence to show that postcommunist civil society in the 1990s was "distinctively weak" as compared to other post-authoritarian countries.[17]

Perestroika and the Collapse of the Soviet System

By the 1970s, the Party began exhibiting notable signs of decay that ironically stemmed from new-found stability in the system. No longer facing any serious internal challenges, Brezhnev instituted a policy of "trust in cadres" that significantly reduced turnover of Party and states elites at both the central and local levels. Officials became "practically unremovable."[18] As a result, Ken Jowitt argues, interests of individual cadres gradually came to dominate. Cynicism became rampant throughout the elite and society. In 1987, Yeltsin complained of Party weakness when he lamented that "any decision could be left unimplemented, shifted, postponed, drowned in endless examinations, consultations, and clarifications."[19]

Then, between 1987 and 1990, Mikhail Gorbachev singe-handedly dismantled this vast, complex, and stunningly successful system of social and political control. By 1991, many of the individual elements of authoritarian control remained—including a vast infrastructure of surveillance, a nominally state-controlled economy, and a weak civil society. Yet the sources of cohesion holding this system together were gone. Gorbachev had transformed one of history's most cohesive autocratic systems into a disorganized collection of highly atomized actors competing for short-term power and rents.

Gorbachev's approach to reform changed radically over the course of the 1980s. Until 1987, Gorbachev sought to reduce the formalism in intra-Party relations and to encourage more open debate and a freer flow of information. He replaced editors of many key Soviet publications, ended press censorship, and encouraged the airing of much more extensive criticism of Soviet past and present than had been allowed previously. Articles detailing Soviet social problems and Stalinist crimes were published, and Gorbachev began a process of rehabilitating victims of Stalinist repression. In late 1986, he released Andrei Sakharov and other dissidents from detention.

Then, in response to opposition to reform from within the Party, Gorbachev began a much more fundamental program of reform—*Perestroika* (restructuring), which touched on core elements of the Soviet system. During this period, Gorbachev successfully led the Party to dismantle the central institutions of supremacy over both the economy and society and to destroy the decades-old traditions of Party discipline. After a prominent attack on Perestroika in a major Soviet newspaper (the famous "Nina Andreeva letter"), Gorbachev fundamentally undercut Party authority over the economy and society at the nineteenth Party conference in June 1988. In Gorbachev's words, the conference effectively severed "the umbilical cord tying [the Party] to the command-administrative system."[20] First, under pressure from on high, the conference agreed to a radical restructuring of the Central Committee that resulted in a sharp reduction in the Party's control over the economy. The Central Committee Secretariat that was responsible for enforcing central directives and managing the Party on a day-to-day level was replaced by a much weaker set of Central Committee commissions. "The Party was deprived of an operating staff for its leaders" and virtually all mechanisms of influence over economic enterprises.[21] Party committees "were forbidden to pass resolutions containing direct orders to government, economic, or public organizations."[22] Subsequently, in the fall of 1988, 1,064 departments and 465 sectors were eliminated in the Central Committees of the Union Republics.[23]

The nineteenth Party conference also took the momentous step of approving the creation of a new bicameral legislature that was intended to sideline the Party as the main center of power in the country. A USSR Congress of People's Deputies (CPD), consisting of 2,250 delegates, would be chosen through semi-competitive elections and would elect a much smaller Supreme Soviet that would function as a permanent legislature. The conference dictated that Party secretaries at all levels would head the corresponding council, but that if they were not elected to the council, they would have to resign their party post as well.[24] This measure in effect gave the population a veto over local and regional Party leadership. In turn, the March 1989 elections to the CPD resulted in the defeat of several highly placed functionaries, including the head of the Leningrad Party organization, and the victory of key proponents of reform—including Boris Yeltsin and Andrei Sakharov.

Elected by the Supreme Soviet as president of the USSR, Gorbachev sought to use the Supreme Soviet as his new base of power. He began transferring property from the Communist Party to the state and ceased to rely on the Party to implement key policies.[25] The Party Politburo that had long been the center of power met less and less frequently and no longer included major government power holders—the Chairmen of the Council of Ministers, KGB, or Foreign Affairs. With virtually no ties to the state, the Politburo was reduced to a secondary advisory committee.[26] Key policies—such as the future of East Germany and the government's 1989 economic plan—were not even discussed at meetings.[27] Instead, Gorbachev either made decisions alone or in consultation with advisors outside the Party leadership.

Under Gorbachev, the Party was in a bind. While Gorbachev showed little interest in leading the Party, he also refused to step down as its head—fearing that absent his leadership, the Party would become a threat to his rule. As he told an aide, "Seventy percent of the apparatus of the Central Committee and of the Central Committee itself are against me and hate me. . . . You mustn't let go of the reins of a mangy, mad dog!"[28] Thus, while Gorbachev created a fundamentally new, open, and competitive political environment, he simultaneously put the brakes on any effort by the Party to adapt to these new conditions. The Party was told not to interfere in the elections to the USSR Congress of People's Deputies. Subsequently, Gorbachev dictated that Party members, who constituted close to 90 percent of deputies, were not bound to a Party line.[29] "Communists at the local level waited in vain for directions from Moscow."[30] The Soviet leader even opposed efforts to create a more unified reformist movement—the "Democratic Platform"—within the Party.[31] As a result, confusion reigned in the late 1980s. In early 1990, the Party's "leading role"—prescribed in the 1977 Soviet constitution—was formally abolished, and Primary Party Organizations began disbanding in state ministries.[32] By early 1991, the party had largely ceased to control the economy.[33] "The Party's control over the state had finished."[34]

Catalyzed by Gorbachev's weakening of top-down controls, powerful nationalist movements emerged in the late 1980s that fundamentally challenged Soviet power. Benefitting from dramatically reduced efforts to curtail dissent, protests exploded in Armenia, Azerbaijan, Georgia, Moldova, Russia, and Ukraine. As Mark Beissinger demonstrates conclusively, ethnonationalism became the main vehicle for liberalizing demands.[35]

While some form of nationalist mobilization took place in most of the country, it was primarily centered in those areas where national identity had established itself prior to the territory's incorporation into the USSR. In particular, as Keith Darden shows, the strength, content, and unity of national identity in the late 1980s was heavily influenced by the national content of schooling when mass literacy was introduced.[36] In Armenia, the Baltics, Georgia, Moldova, and Ukraine, the inculcation of previous generations with non-Russian nationalism contributed to the construction of well-organized national movements drawing on precommunist myths, symbols, and rituals that directly challenged Soviet power in the late 1980s. Indeed, "one of the most striking aspects of anticommunist opposition was its fusion with nationalism."[37] By contrast, Belarus and the Central Asian republics experienced "little or no exposure to literate culture prior to communism" that resulted in weaker movements from below against Communist rule.[38]

The nationalities crisis had a doubly negative impact on Soviet state capacity. Besides reducing central control, unsuccessful and often half-hearted efforts to suppress nationalist protest demoralized the armed forces.[39] Morale in the armed forces was in particular undermined by the perceived failure of political leaders such as Gorbachev to take political responsibility for high-intensity coercion.[40] For example, many officials resented efforts to make officers take the fall for civilian deaths that resulted from military actions against demonstrators in Tbilisi in April 1989, and Vilnius in January 1991—concluding that it was risky to carry out repression "because, regardless of the facts, the military was bound to be blamed for any negative outcomes."[41] Thus, the military commander, Alexander Lebed, noted that "experience with innumerable inquiries by prosecutors and investigators had long ago taught me to make sure [all orders] were written down."[42] This lack of trust within the repressive apparatus ultimately constituted an important legacy from the Perestroika period that would hamstring leaders seeking to engage in high-intensity coercion in the 1990s and 2000s.

In turn, the election of republican legislatures in the spring of 1990 led to a decisive hemorrhaging of power from the Soviet center. Most momentously, in

June 1990, Boris Yeltsin was elected as chairman of the Russian Supreme Soviet. Yeltsin used this position as a platform to challenge Gorbachev's rule. The Russian Supreme Soviet declared political sovereignty and the preeminence of Russian legislation over all-union laws. Russia's avowed sovereignty forced the hand of other republics where domestic support for independence from the Soviet Union was relatively weak. As a result, a "war of laws" began in which republics throughout the USSR passed laws that contradicted all-union ones—that "in turn induced federal bodies to respond with countering laws, resolutions, or decrees intended to nullify those of the republics."[43] The consequence was a severe breakdown in central state authority.[44]

The Collapse of the USSR

Following a failed coup by hardliners within Gorbachev's government in August 1991, the system finally collapsed. That month, negotiations on a new union treaty came to a close. Azerbaijan, Belarus, Russia, and the Central Asian republics agreed to create a new federation of independent republics with a common president, military, and foreign policy. In an effort to prevent a treaty that they felt would destroy the Soviet Union, on August 18 hardline members of Gorbachev's administration flew to Foros, Crimea, where Gorbachev was vacationing, to demand that he sign a declaration of emergency. Gorbachev refused. The KGB shut down all communications lines from Foros and placed guards at the gate to prevent anyone from leaving. On August 19 at 6:00 a.m., a committee of top Soviet ministers declared a state of emergency throughout the country. Tanks rolled into Moscow, and independent newspapers and broadcast media controlled by the Russian republic were banned.

However, both indecisive leadership and a breakdown in central state control doomed the coup to failure. After Gorbachev refused to support the declaration of emergency, Defense Minister Dmitry Yazov admitted that they had no plan as to what to do next.[45] Coup leaders had also failed to undertake the most basic actions to thwart opposition mobilization. Phone lines remained open in Boris Yeltsin's summer home as well as in the Russian White House, thus permitting the Russian government to send out statements denouncing the coup. Never arrested, Yeltsin was able to leave his house and set up with thousands of supporters in and around the Russian White House.[46]

Throughout the coup attempt, security officials, beset by "careerism and hypocrisy," took a wait-and-see approach.[47] A plan to secure the White House before Yeltsin could get there was never carried out. Then, on the nights of

August 19 and 20, the military, police, and KGB surrounded the White House but failed to attack. Ordered to be ready for attack, "none of the assault forces were fully in position . . . numerous officers were reluctant and waiting to be pushed, or convinced that the operation was not seriously intended."[48] In response to such widespread insubordination, Yazov, the coup leader most committed to the use of force, was compelled to back down and call off the attack at the last minute.

The failed coup effectively destroyed what was left of the Soviet system. On August 24, Gorbachev resigned as General Secretary of the CPSU and urged the Central Committee to dissolve itself. Yeltsin, in turn, transferred all Party property to the state and banned the CPSU from Russia. The Party either dissolved or was banned in all republics except for Uzbekistan and Turkmenistan, where leaders rapidly reconstituted it under a new name. On December 8, Yeltsin, Stanislau Shushkevich of Belarus, and Leonid Kravchuk of Ukraine met in a forest in Belarus to replace the Soviet Union with a much weaker Commonwealth of Independent States (CIS).

The Fate of Pluralism after 1991

This is where our main story begins. The rest of this book explores how different leaders coped with the mix of challenges and opportunities for regime closure presented by the legacy of Soviet rule and its collapse. In most respects, autocrats continued to have the upper hand. Civil society—even after four years of relative openness—remained weak, under-institutionalized, and unstable. Thus, even in countries such as Moldova, Russia, and Ukraine, where significant mobilization occurred, civil society groups quickly divided and disintegrated after the fall of the Soviet Union. In most cases, government leaders were left to confront a weak and fragmented opposition. Additionally, the leadership almost always consisted of recent top-level nomenklatura with ties to a wide range of other economic and bureaucratic elites in their republics. With a few exceptions, leaders sat atop massive state economic and coercive infrastructures that mostly remained intact from the late Soviet period.[49]

Yet, as we saw above, four years of Perestroika and state collapse had severely weakened the organizational mechanisms that held political elites, economic structures, and the state together in an authoritarian whole. By late 1991, the Communist Party had ceased to function. While the economy in most countries remained nominally under state control, Perestroika-era reforms resulted in the eradication of state economic control in all but a few republics. Most leaders confronted the choice of either privatizing the economy or rebuilding new mechanisms of central rule.

Finally, coercive state power in the post-Soviet era was generally characterized by the existence of extremely extensive[50] but weakly cohesive institutions of repression. In the early 1990s, state elites throughout the former Soviet Union were beset by regular and flagrant disobedience by lower-level ministers and local and regional prefects as well as by police, soldiers, and other state officials on the ground. Local governments often refused to carry out central policies and deliver tax revenues to the central government. In extreme cases, local or regional governments threatened to secede.[51]

Such weakness was partially the result of the absence of clear lines of state authority following the disappearance of the Soviet center. The dissolution of the Communist Party and other mechanisms of control left presidents and prime ministers with few means to punish recalcitrant subordinates. Simultaneously, agencies such as the KGB that had been under Moscow's direct control were often reluctant to subordinate themselves to new masters in the republican capitals. Such weakness was further exacerbated by the severe fiscal and economic crises that hit post-Soviet countries in the early 1990s. Persistent wage arrears and underfunding destroyed morale and encouraged disobedience within state bureaucracies. In the absence of adequate financing or established systems of rule, subordinates were often reluctant to follow any orders that involved personal risk—a fact that made open coercive action especially difficult to carry out.

Subsequently, in almost all cases state power increased over time. Throughout the mid- and late-1990s, leaders institutionalized new mechanisms of central rule, while improvements in the state's fiscal health significantly decreased wage arrears and bolstered financing of state agencies overall. As a result, leaders generally confronted fewer problems of insubordination and possessed far more robust economic and coercive institutions of power and control. While such state building improved the lives of many, it also made it easier for leaders to repress media, sideline the opposition, and manipulate elections. In the absence of other checks on central power—civil society or a robust and independent judicial system—state building often reduced or eliminated key sources of contestation. Indeed, as detailed in subsequent chapters, regime closure increased in almost all post-Soviet cases by the late 1990s. As of the early 2010s, all but a few post-Soviet countries had become less rather than more democratic since 1992. Chapters 3–6 provide evidence that increased authoritarianism can partly be explained by expanded state and party capacity in much of the former Soviet Union over time.

As this book argues, competition was also significantly affected by very different national identity dynamics in the various republics—dynamics that influenced the degree of state and party collapse during the Gorbachev years as well as the extent and character of popular mobilization in subsequent decades.

The strength of anti-Russian/Soviet nationalism profoundly shaped the character of the exit from Soviet rule. At one extreme, the Baltic countries—where democracy was bolstered by their interwar history as independent democratic states—experienced a sharp break from Soviet rule. All three countries witnessed the rise of overwhelmingly powerful national movements in the late 1980s that forced local elites to make a fundamental break with the old system.[52] In Latvia, for example, the Party was essentially forced underground by 1989.[53] After the fall of Communism, significantly greater economic development, combined with extensive EU integration, put the Baltics on a democratic path.[54]

The rest of the former Soviet Union was less economically developed than the Baltics and received far less attention from the European Union. Because other constraints on authoritarianism in the region were so weak, the extent of competition depended heavily on the weakness of authoritarianism—which in turn was shaped by the degree to which national movements succeeded in dismantling the Soviet infrastructure of totalitarian control during the late Gorbachev period. In Georgia, the rise of a powerful national movement and ethnic conflict resulted in the "near total institutional collapse" of the Party as it was swept away by nationalist forces in 1990 and 1991.[55] Similarly, in Armenia a highly mobilized Armenian National Movement (ANM) emerged in 1988, demanding Armenian control over the Nagorno-Karabagh territory in neighboring Azerbaijan. In the ensuing conflict with Azerbaijan, the ANM rapidly replaced the Communists as the center of power. As we will see in chapter 6, this conflict also severely weakened the Soviet party-state in Azerbaijan, leading directly to the departure of two presidents in the space of a year.

By contrast, populations in Belarus and Central Asia, where anti-Soviet nationalism was weaker, the collapse of the Soviet Union was generally less disruptive. Elites in these countries usually[56] had an easier time preserving preexisting authoritarian institutions. In most of these cases, opposition could do little to prevent leaders from monopolizing control.

Finally, in Moldova and Ukraine, relatively entrenched identity divisions between Europeanist and Russophile groups provided robust structural impediments to the consolidation of authoritarian rule. In both cases, such divisions were strengthened by the fact that populations in the west gained significant literacy in Romanian and Ukrainian before entry into the Soviet Union, while populations in the east, gaining literacy under Soviet rule, "were schooled to believe . . . that they were part of a broader Russian nation."[57] Moldova and Ukraine emerged as the only post-Soviet states that included significant territorial units with populations that had been schooled in both Russian and non-Russian languages and identities. This fact infused divisions with geopolitical content absent in most other republics.[58] Such divisions meant that autocrats were unable to use nationalism in the classic autocratic fashion to unify the country, justify repressive actions, and bludgeon the opposition. Instead, nationalism tended to have the opposite effect of strengthening opposition challenges.

The chapters that follow explore in detail how leaders confronted different legacies of state power and national identity. I focus on the neighboring countries of Belarus, Moldova, and Ukraine, which exhibited similar institutional legacies of Soviet rule but profoundly divergent historical legacies of national identity from the late nineteenth and early twentieth centuries. Chapters 3 and 4 examine regime trajectories in Ukraine and Moldova, where leaders confronted highly divided identities. Chapter 5 explores the case of Belarus, where identity was less divided. Finally, chapter 6 applies this argument to the rest of the former Soviet Union.

3

Pluralism by Default in Ukraine

After gaining independence in 1991, Ukraine confronted profound obstacles to democratic development. State economic control and massive rents from an extensive gas transit network gave incumbents the resources to buy off potential enemies and monopolize political control.[1] Simultaneously, "a profound disregard for the rule of law" and a "weak and politicized criminal justice system" made it easy for autocrats to bring the full weight of the state against their adversaries.[2] Ukraine also emerged from the Soviet era with an "enfeebled" civil society, while opposition faced a "fundamental imbalance in raw political power."[3] Finally, like other countries in the former Soviet Union, Ukraine was never offered full EU membership—a fact that considerably weakened Western democratizing influence.[4] For all of these reasons, many expected that democracy would "not be attained until far in the future."[5]

Yet Ukraine became the most competitive and democratic country in the Commonwealth of Independent States (CIS) over the post–Cold War era—experiencing four electoral turnovers, a vibrant media, and repeated mass movements for political change. Ukraine's post-Soviet political trajectory raises two puzzles that are the focus of this chapter. First, why did pluralism flourish to such a degree in the face of the obstacles cited above? Why was authoritarian rule never consolidated as in neighboring Belarus and Russia? Second, what explains the notable shifts in political contestation over time? What explains the country's vibrant pluralism under Kravchuk (1991–1994) and Yushchenko (2005–2009), but greater regime closure under Kuchma (1995–2004) and Yanukovych (2010–2014)?

Ukraine's pluralism has been less the result of a "struggle to develop a democratic political system"[6] and more the product of failed efforts to create an

Table 3.1   Regime Closure and Party and State Capacity in Ukraine 1991–2014

		Party and state capacity			
	National identity	Party	State coercive capacity	State economic control	Overall capacity score
Kravchuk (1991–1994)	High split	Low	Med-low	Med-low	Low
Kuchma (1994–2004)	High split	Med-low	Medium	Medium	Medium
Yushchenko (2005–2009)	High split	Low	Medium	Medium	Med-low
Yanukovych (2010–2014)	High split	Medium	Medium	Medium	Medium

Note: For coding rules, see appendix A.

authoritarian one. The central heroes in this story are not died-in-the-wool democrats but oligarchs and ex-nomenklatura who lacked the organization to centralize political control. These actors facilitated regime competition not because they supported democracy but because their mutual distrust prevented the consolidation of authoritarian rule. Activists and protesters on the ground were also central. But as we shall see, their unity and passion generally derived less from shared democratic values and more from commitment to competing and polarized conceptions of the nation.

Attention to these dynamics highlights a central but frequently ignored characteristic of regime evolution in Ukraine and other "new democracies": the factors facilitating pluralism have often been identical to the ones creating dysfunction, corruption, and sometimes violent polarization. The contradictory character of pluralism by default in Ukraine was most clearly exemplified in early 2014 when authoritarian weakness and national polarization led to the downfall of an autocrat but also set the stage for violent state breakdown.

Ukraine's surprising pluralism was rooted in underdeveloped ruling parties, a weak authoritarian state, and national divisions between eastern and western Ukraine. Overall, leaders had little capacity to keep allies in line, manipulate the electoral process, starve opponents of resources, and violently suppress opposition challenges. Simultaneously, divisions facilitated pluralism by providing key mobilizational resources to each side when it was out of power and by complicating Russian efforts to support authoritarian rule. By framing resistance in terms of identity, opposition was able to tap into a committed voter and

Electoral manipulation	Media control	Regime closure		Overall regime closure
		Subordination of parliament	Subordination of opposition	
Low	Medium	Low	Low	Low
Medium	Medium	Medium	Medium	Medium
Low	Low	Low	Low	Low
Medium	Medium	Medium	Med-low	Medium

activist base even in the face of incumbent repression and resource advantages. Thus, each of Ukraine's four turnovers (1994, 2004, 2010, 2014) came about because the opposition was able to mobilize strong regional support—alternately Russophile and Ukrainophile—to overcome incumbent advantages.

At the same time, splits in identity made it virtually impossible for Russia to be an effective authoritarian black knight in Ukraine. When anti-Russian governments were in power, the Russian government fostered pluralism by aiding opposition, but when pro-Russian governments were in charge, Russian intervention generated a strong counter-reaction among the country's significant Ukrainophile population—thus undermining efforts to consolidate authoritarian control.

Simultaneously, shifts in the level of political competition over time reflected changes in organizational strength (see table 3.1). In particular, regime closure under Kuchma and Yanukovych was bolstered by relatively powerful party or party substitute organizations (including well-developed regional and economic patronage networks). By contrast, greater pluralism was fostered by organizational weakness under Kravchuk and Yushchenko, who rode to office almost entirely on ephemeral clouds of popularity.

National Identity

To the extent that national divisions are considered "one of the major threats to any democracy,"[7] Ukraine should have been in trouble. According to some, Ukraine was "not and cannot be a 'nation state' "[8] and was "a country of regions that evolved under different political, cultural, and even linguistic traditions."[9] Based on key historical and ethnolinguistic differences, Ukraine can roughly be separated into three separate regions—west, center, and east—that encompassed distinct blocs of political attitudes and became a highly attractive political resource for politicians and activists seeking to mobilize support. While western Ukraine had a much smaller share of the population than the east, it could win elections with support from the center.[10]

First, western Ukraine, long considered "the least Soviet area in the USSR,"[11] was not incorporated into the USSR until World War II and was dominated by Ukrainian-speaking ethnic Ukrainians. In particular, the area of Galicia, under Austrian control in the nineteenth and early twentieth centuries, became the center of Ukrainian nationalism. The Austrian government actively promoted the expansion of mass schooling in the Ukrainian language—a measure that Keith Darden shows created an extremely durable and passionate support for Ukrainian nationalism.[12]

By contrast, eastern/southern Ukraine, incorporated into the Russian empire in the seventeenth and eighteenth centuries, was historically closer to Russia, attained mass literacy under Soviet rule, and possessed a relatively weak Ukrainian identity.[13] While ethnic Ukrainians constituted the majority in every province but Crimea, most spoke Russian at home.[14] Surveys in the 1990s and 2000s identified significant cultural differences between east and west Ukraine. Western Ukrainians celebrated different holidays,[15] and expressed greater support for the European Union and NATO and less support for Russia and the CIS than did their counterparts in the east.[16]

Finally, central Ukraine was the country's swing region. Under Russian domination since the seventeenth and eighteenth centuries, central Ukraine lacked the history of nationalist mobilization found in Galicia but was more dominated by Ukrainian-speaking Ukrainians than eastern and southern Ukraine.[17] In the early 1990s, central Ukraine tended to support Russophile political forces, but it gradually shifted over to the Ukrainophile side by the mid-2000s.

This division between western and eastern Ukraine was central to Ukrainian politics until 2014. While not immutable, the divide often dominated because it provided politicians with an easy way to mobilize supporters that leaders found difficult to ignore (even if politicians periodically shifted sides). Indeed, the most enduring post-Soviet Ukrainian parties were built upon highly regionalized bases of support—including the Ukrainophile Rukh, the Russophile Communist Party, and the Party of Regions. Given the organizational and mobilizational advantages of taking one side or the other on the national question, few politicians were able to gain power without choosing sides. In the end, national differences helped generate some of the most regionally polarized elections in the world. Thus in 2010, Viktor Yanukovych won 77 percent of the vote in the east—compared to 8 percent in Galicia and 16 percent in the west as a whole.[18] The electorate was similarly polarized in 1994 and 2004. (At the same time, the 2014 crisis substantially reduced polarization in what was left of Ukraine—a development discussed briefly at the end of this chapter.)

As we see below, polarization was a critical force in facilitating pluralism in Ukraine. In particular, Ukrainophile identity was a powerful tool against authoritarian consolidation less because it reflected greater commitment to democratic values[19] than because it engendered passionate activism aimed at what were perceived to be Russophile power structures. (Indeed, the best available data shows that even "democratic" protesters in 2004 were not, in fact, unified by support for multi-party democracy.[20]) Further, as this chapter shows, both Ukrainophile and Russophile identities were used at different points to mobilize against incumbent power. Most notably, strikes by eastern Ukrainian miners against Kravchuk helped bring down his government in 1993–94. Simultaneously, regionally polarized voting blocs in both western and eastern Ukraine hampered efforts by either side to monopolize control.

Party and State Strength

Beginning with the collapse of Ukraine's Communist Party in the early 1990s, disorganization became another key source of pluralism in post-Soviet Ukraine. Following the resignation of Soviet coup leaders on August 21, 1991, the Communist Party in Ukraine confronted a massive wave of popular hostility for its role in the putsch. Deeply implicated, the Party was barred from all public institutions, its headquarters sealed, documents impounded, and assets seized. On August 31, it was banned. Party membership was suddenly treated like "a contagious disease."[21]

At this stage, abandoning the Communist Party was widely seen as the only way for top-level elites such as Leonid Kravchuk to remain in power.[22] Yet the dissolution of the Party also destroyed an extensive and well-institutionalized organization more than half a century in the making. The absence of a well-established party structure created serious structural challenges for virtually all post-Soviet leaders. Their capacities to meet these challenges were in turn affected by the strength of formal and informal organizational resources each president brought with him to power.

First, Kravchuk, who had spent his entire career in the Communist Party but rose to the top by rejecting Communism, had little time or opportunity to create a party. By abandoning the Party and taking an active role in the destruction of the Soviet Union, Kravchuk deprived himself of strong support from the old apparatus. At the same time, he lacked any effective party substitutes or regional patronage networks.[23] Indeed, Kravchuk had long abandoned his home province of Chernivtsi and thus lacked the kind of regional support that his successor, Leonid Kuchma, would use so successfully after coming to power. Kravchuk was left with "no political team."[24] He was instead backed by a loose, regionally diverse, and non-ideological "party of power"—a network of "pragmatically oriented and de-ideologized" elites that had no formal organization and was held together solely by self-preservation and "the idea of maintaining power."[25] Although many of the *people* remained the same from the Soviet era, the hierarchical *organization* of the elite had totally disappeared. Government functionaries like Evheniy Marchuk, Kravchuk's head of security, functioned as loosely knit "free agents." Marchuk was not the president's "subordinate, but his ally. Not a vassal but an equal."[26]

Leonid Kuchma (1994–2004), by contrast, came to power with a highly developed regional network from Dnipropetrovsk and was deeply embedded in a network of "red directors" who helped get him elected. Kuchma's strong regional and economic ties, which he retained after the collapse of the USSR, provided him with an initial base that he was able to leverage into new forms of political support. Ultimately, he relied on a centrally coordinated but highly fragmented "multi-party ruling party" that consisted of competing political parties and patronage networks that all depended for their survival on the president's support. This structure, combined with an increasingly effective state, allowed Kuchma to centralize power much more successfully than had Kravchuk. But as we see below, the fragmented character of his coalition also contributed to mass defections during crisis.

Next, Viktor Yushchenko (2005–2009) came to power backed by a more decentralized coalition of parties within a multi-party coalition. Before coming to power, Yushchenko and his party, Our Ukraine—formed in 2002 as a bloc of ten parties—was forced to create a relatively equal alliance with his competitor, Yulia Tymoshenko, who agreed in the summer of 2004 to sit out the presidential election in exchange for her appointment as prime minister. The coalitional structure of Yushchenko's regime—in stark contrast to that of Kuchma—forced the president to share power from the start. Endemically riven by factional struggles, the Orange coalition faced considerable constraints in centralizing control.

Finally, Viktor Yanukovych (2010–2014), backed by an extremely wealthy and tightly controlled regional network in Donetsk, made an explicit decision in the mid-2000s that "it is better to be a strong party, than a weak bloc."[27] In stark contrast to other political forces, including Our Ukraine, the Party of Regions was centered in one province and was not a coalition of multiple parties. Yanukovych's ruling coalition was far better organized and less fragmented than any that had existed in Ukraine since Communist rule. After taking power in 2010, Yanukovych became the first "party president" with a prime minister, Mykola Azarov, from the same party. Backed by powerful and wealthy regional interests, the party created a more unified basis for consolidating authoritarian control than had previously existed in Ukraine.

Simultaneously, Ukrainian leaders inherited a vast but weak state in 1991. On the one hand, they were left with an enormous coercive apparatus from the Soviet era, including a 700,000-strong army.[28] On the other hand, Ukraine's coercive apparatus in the early 1990s had little discipline and suffered from persistent wage arrears.[29] Furthermore, many SBU (former KGB) officers maintained "unbroken connections" to Moscow, which was thought to retain "significant influence" over security forces in Ukraine, thus undermining Kyiv's central control.[30] Simultaneously, fiscal crisis and institutional disarray severely weakened central control over state enterprises and local governments. President Kravchuk was often forced to issue decrees that reiterated powers already spelled out in the constitution.[31] Regional presidential prefects, established in March 1992 to increase central executive power, simply added to the confusion and became "the most defenseless structures" in the state.[32]

The Kuchma period saw a marked strengthening of state power. Eyewitness to the chaos of the Kravchuk era, Kuchma set out to create a "strong vertical of executive power."[33] He increased controls over local appointments of security officials and oversaw a proliferation of new police structures.[34] Simultaneously, an improved economy and the end of inflation meant that state structures were no longer wracked by wage arrears. By the late 1990s, security services were well funded and regional rebellions had ceased.[35] At the same time, the state possessed no special source of cohesion (ideology or revolutionary tradition). By the metric used in this book, coercive state strength, which remained more or less constant from the late 1990s until early 2014, was "medium": the center no longer faced rampant problems of insubordination, but it also lacked strong non-material sources of cohesion. At the same time, authoritarian state power was undermined in the 1990s by a move away from state ownership over the economy, which declined from 90 percent in 1992, to 50 percent in 1996, and to 40 percent in 2000.[36] Unlike in Belarus, little effort in Ukraine was made to rebuild institutions of central economic control.

National divisions and evolving state and party power had a powerful impact on political competition during the Ukraine's first decades of independence. In the late Soviet period, nationalist-led opposition stimulated the breakdown of Soviet rule. Then, after Ukraine became independent, the collapse of the party-state left Kravchuk virtually powerless in all areas except the media, where, as former ideology secretary, he retained ties from the Soviet era. Under Kuchma (1994–2004), increased state power and a top-down "multi-party ruling party" coalition helped the president to consolidate greater control. However, national divisions and elite splits engendered by privatization and a fragmented party structure left the regime highly vulnerable to defection and collapse. Under Yushchenko (2005–2009), an even more decentralized and divided governing coalition, and regional and oligarchic fragmentation combined to create democracy. Yanukovych (2010–2014), bolstered by an incredibly wealthy, regionally concentrated, and centralized party structure, was able to monopolize much greater political control. However, Yanukovych's blatantly pro-Russian behavior stoked regional divisions that contributed to the massive Euromaidan demonstrations and the stunning collapse of his regime in 2014. The regionalized character of the protests directly contributed to the violence and state breakdown in eastern Ukraine that followed Yanukovych's sudden exit from power.

National Divisions, Weak Organization, and Pluralism by Default under Kravchuk, 1989–1994

Ukraine's political trajectory in the early 1990s was wrought both by splits in identity and by an extraordinarily weak party and state. Divisions between east and west had infected elite politics since the 1960s and 1970s[37] and ultimately contributed to a fundamental weakening of the Party and the Soviet state itself. In Ukraine, as elsewhere in the Soviet Union, "the democratic movement acted under the slogan of national revival."[38] Demands for cultural rights—including the Ukrainianization of education and the state apparatus[39]—facilitated the swift mobilization of Ukrainian speakers in the Gorbachev period.[40] Western Ukraine became a "hotbed of nationalist dissent" and "by far the most politicized region of Ukraine."[41] Witnessing demonstrations of 30,000 to 100,000 in the summer of 1989, Lviv in Galicia was "spontaneously explosive in its emotions."[42] This mobilization culminated in the formation and rapid growth of *Rukh*, a predominantly western Ukrainian movement that focused initially on the promotion of Ukrainian language rights.[43]

Heightened mobilization in western Ukraine played a critical role in stimulating the rise of a reform wing in the Ukrainian Communist Party—something that never emerged in Belarus.[44] Kravchuk, who became head of parliament in 1990, responded to increased nationalist mobilization by dropping his earlier opposition to Ukrainian independence. He became a forceful spokesman for Ukrainian interests—a fact that ultimately alienated a number of erstwhile supporters in the east. In 1990 and early 1991, he boldly resisted efforts by Gorbachev to conclude a new union treaty.

At the same time, Communists still far outnumbered opposition activists, while "the overwhelming majority of state resources remained in communist hands."[45] Thus, to understand the opposition's success during this period we also need to look at cohesion within the ruling Party, which was profoundly weak and demoralized by 1990. The Party was "fractious and undisciplined." Members "had no faith in the Party's ability to overcome Ukraine's economic and social problems."[46] In 1990 and early 1991, the party suffered "massive" defections.[47] Low morale bolstered national democrats who exercised influence "out of proportion to their numbers."[48]

The party's disorientation also hampered its capacity to cope with mass protest. On September 30, 1990, hundreds of thousands protested in Kyiv against Ukraine's accession to a new Moscow-led, union treaty.[49] In a pattern of Ukrainophile opposition protest that was to be repeated in 2004 and 2014, about 150 students set up tents in the center of the city and declared a hunger strike, calling for the rejection of a union treaty until the ratification of a Ukrainian constitution, the posting of Ukrainian soldiers only in the republic, and the resignation of Prime Minister Vitalii Masol.[50]

In principle, the Party could have held out. Calls for a general strike failed, and the Communists still controlled a majority of the legislature.[51] Yet an insufficient number of pro-government deputies bothered to show up to back Masol's government.[52] Party leader Stanislav Hurenko grumbled that party members "decided to simply stand around. . . . More and more we are overtaken by a mood of nervousness and internal discord."[53] According to a widespread rumour at the time, Kravchuk turned to Gorbachev with a request that that he introduce martial law in Kyiv, but Gorbachev refused.[54] As a result, in a "moment of madness" that marked a "major shift" in Ukrainian landscape, the legislature voted for Masol's resignation and agreed not to consider a new union treaty.[55]

Five months later, national-democratic dissident Viacheslav Chornovil was elected to head the Lviv provincial administration—a move that further dismantled the Soviet authoritarian state. Reversing reform at this point would have required massive coercive capacity that the Ukrainian state simply did not have.

Subsequently, in the wake of the failed Soviet coup, Kravchuk put an end to the USSR. Resisting efforts by Gorbachev and Yeltsin to reanimate the Union, he orchestrated a referendum for Ukrainian independence that passed by an overwhelming 90 percent in December 1991. On the same day, he captured 62 percent of the presidential vote in the first round. A week later, Kravchuk, together with Boris Yeltsin and Belarusian leader Stanislav Shushkevich, founded the Commonwealth of Independent States (CIS).

Pluralism by Default under Kravchuk, 1992–1994

Elected by the widest margin ever in post-Soviet Ukraine and facing a feeble and divided opposition, Kravchuk came to power in late 1991 in a seemingly strong position to consolidate control. The establishment had backed Kravchuk's candidacy for president, and his hand-picked parliamentary speaker, Ivan Plyushch, was a "close ally."[56] While his ultimate failures led some observers to view Kravchuk as an incompetent and passive leader,[57] Kravchuk had been widely considered a skilled politician who maneuvered "like a fish in water" in power and was so cunning that he could "slip between the raindrops."[58] Given Kravchuk's prominent role in stalling the union treaty in 1990/1991, it can hardly be said that he was particularly passive. Nor was he especially democratic.[59]

Some have attributed Kravchuk's ultimate weakness to the presidency's weak formal powers.[60] Yet the constitution, which was amended more than 220 times between 1991 and 1995, was more of a "register of shifts in the political balance" than an independent determinant of the balance of political power.[61] Indeed, President Kuchma was subsequently able to consolidate much greater control despite initially possessing the same weak formal powers. Furthermore, lacking "a clearly defined role within the state" and the most basic mechanisms for coordinated action such as parties or factions, parliament possessed few sources of power.[62] "Directionless and reactive," the legislature would seem to have been extremely vulnerable to manipulation[63] by a president backed by a large state.[64] Despite the lack of some formal powers, Kravchuk—in principle at least—possessed more than enough administrative and material resources to bend the legislature to his will.

But of course the state itself barely functioned, and Kravchuk had minimal capacity to assert control. Kravchuk also lacked any organized base of support. His central role in destroying the USSR, combined with his rapid shifts in position—first opposing then supporting Ukrainian independence—alienated large numbers of his former colleagues in the nomenklatura, who were willing to support the president only so long as they had no choice.[65] In stark contrast to Kuchma, Kravchuk also lacked a strong regional network. Having spent most of his professional life in Kyiv, Kravchuk was virtually unknown in his home province, Chernivtsi, where he was defeated in the election for USSR People's Deputy in 1989.[66] The Ukrainophile Rukh movement, which might have helped him, split up within months of independence and gave Kravchuk only "selective support."[67] As a result, Kravchuk had no political force in parliament.[68] One commentator described the first year of Kravchuk's presidency as "365 days of solitude."[69]

State weakness and the absence of virtually any party or party substitute organization in the legislature meant that chaos in parliament translated into general powerlessness and stalemate rather than presidential dominance as we might expect. Kravchuk was repeatedly forced to switch allegiances, buy off individual opponents, and "play on the contradictions of various political movements."[70] Given the weakness of presidential power, former supporters suffered few costs for ignoring the president when interests diverged. The parliamentary speaker, recently a close presidential ally,[71] quickly became "one of the most serious critics of the President."[72] Partly as a result, power shifted to the parliament, and the "majority of laws and resolutions adopted by the parliament stemmed from its own initiative" rather than the president's.[73] After mid-1992, Kravchuk lost almost all political battles with the legislature. Ministers able to get approval from the fractious parliament were generally independent actors with their own bases of support and had little to gain by backing Kravchuk. For example, Evheniy Marchuk, the head of security, was "tied to no one."[74] In late September 1992, the parliamentary speaker, Plyushch, forced the resignation of Prime Minister Vitold Fokin, who was considered to be too close to Kravchuk.[75] After meeting with heads of major industrial enterprises, Plyushch proposed Leonid Kuchma, the head of the country's largest missile factory. Kravchuk had no choice but to support Kuchma, who had voted for Kravchuk to be head of parliament in July 1990 but was barely known to Kravchuk before Kuchma's appointment.[76]

One exception to Kravchuk's weak control was in the media, where Kravchuk maintained organizational ties from the 1980s when he was in charge of ideology. While parliament and president formally had equal power over television, Kravchuk was able to rely on support from his previous association with Mykola Okhmakevich, the head of Ukrainian television and radio in the early 1990s.[77] While the print media often escaped the president's control, central television gave him consistently positive coverage.[78]

Pluralism was also bolstered by divisions in Ukrainian identity. In the late 1980s and early 1990s, Kravchuk had ridden to power by promoting Ukrainian independence from the USSR. Once in power, Kravchuk promoted Ukrainian language and culture and took measures to distance Ukraine from Russia.[79] While such policies initially reflected the public mood, they generated an enormous backlash when the Ukrainian economy went into free fall in 1992 and 1993. In particular, Kravchuk's close identification with the Communist collapse made him highly unpopular among many ex-nomenklatura in the industrial east.[80]

The Ukrainian authorities were then buffeted by protests on both sides of the divide in 1993 that led to early elections and the fall of Kravchuk. Eastern Ukraine, where many felt that the crisis was rooted in the president's decision to break ties with Russia, experienced a massive wave of strikes by coal miners in Donbas demanding regional autonomy, higher wages, and a referendum on early parliamentary and presidential elections.[81] Demanding greater autonomy and closer ties to Russia,[82] mine directors warned that they would seek help from Yeltsin if they did not get what they wanted.[83] (By contrast, mines in western Ukraine where independence was "worth a very high price" experienced little strike activity.[84]) Affecting about 80 percent of mines in the east, the strikes terrified government officials, who agreed to hold a referendum on confidence in parliament and the president.

However, in response thousands of pro-Ukrainian activists descended on the capital, fearing that the referendum would be used to rescind pro-Ukrainian policies on language and national symbols. As "growing polarization of nation-alists and unionists" presented "the real danger of instability in Ukraine,"[85] Kravchuk "lost the ground under his feet and was unable to influence the course of events."[86] The one thing that the two sides *did* agree on was the need for early elections.[87] Confronted by protests from both sides and spooked by growing confrontation between president and parliament in Russia at the time, Kravchuk and the legislature agreed to cancel the planned referendum and to hold early legislative and presidential elections in 1994—a move Krav-chuk hoped would "bring peace to our society."[88]

But the compromise was a "sorry defeat" for Kravchuk, forcing him to go up for election almost three years before his term was up.[89] Indeed, Kravchuk quickly reconsidered his decision and engaged in a "lengthy behind-the-scenes battle to delay the elections"—arguing that a vote should not occur in the midst of economic crisis and before the passage of a constitution.[90] In early January 1994, he ordered the Ministries of Security, Interior, and Defense to suppress parliament and delay the elections.[91] However, the security services were underfunded and demoralized; moreover, cabinet officials had no organi-zational or partisan ties to Kravchuk and thus little reason to take any risks to keep Kravchuk in power. Many could expect to keep power under a new admin-istration. As a result, Kravchuk tells us that the heads of Security (Marchuk) and Interior (Andrii Vasilishin) expressed their reluctance to go along.[92] With-out the support from these critical agencies, Kravchuk was forced to rescind his initial plan and let the elections go forward.

Given an economic decline of 38 percent since 1990 and hyper-inflation in 1993, Kravchuk was clearly vulnerable. Yet his electoral vulnerability is less obvious when we consider that blame for Ukraine's economic crisis could also be laid at the doorstep of Kravchuk's main opponent, Leonid Kuchma, who had greater effective power than Kravchuk during the worst of Ukraine's inflation-ary spiral in June 1993.[93] Kuchma, however, was able to escape blame because Ukraine's economic problems were seen as rooted in Ukraine's break with Russia and the Soviet Union—an event that was indelibly tied to Kravchuk.[94] Kuchma sidestepped responsibility for the economic crisis simply by taking a strong pro-Russian stance in the elections.[95] Indeed, with economic problems viewed through the lens of interregional relations, "the relationship with Rus-sia was the primary issue in the Ukrainian presidential elections."[96] Kuchma "capitalized on the resentment over the influence of western Ukrainian elites on

Kyiv's policies and called for an end to 'the reign of Galician nationalism.' "[97] In the end, "ethnolinguistic and geopolitical factors not economic issues decided the presidential contest."[98]

Kuchma also benefitted concretely from tense relations between Kravchuk and the Russian government. Most importantly, Russian television, better funded than its Ukrainian counterpart and widely available in Ukraine,[99] greatly undermined Kravchuk's capacity to monopolize the flow of information. Thus, while Kravchuk successfully shut down the pro-Kuchma station Gravis, and Ukrainian state TV heavily favored Kravchuk,[100] Russian TV reflected a "complete bias in favor of Kuchma."[101]

Simultaneously, Kravchuk's weak control over regional governments undermined efforts to manipulate the vote. Kravchuk notes that prior to the election, local leaders "promised everything," including fraud, to facilitate Kravchuk's reelection.[102] But in fact, local officials and even Kravchuk's own appointees often directly undermined the president during the election. While some manipulation seems to have occurred in central and western Ukraine,[103] many election commission workers and Kravchuk appointees in eastern and southern regions openly supported Kuchma[104] and sometimes even campaigned against the president.[105] During the election, key officials played both sides. In particular, SBU head Marchuk "put eggs in multiple political baskets," holding "secret and separate negotiations with Kuchma."[106] Kravchuk complained that during the elections the SBU "shut its eyes . . . to crude violations." Even as president, he "was deprived of the ability to address violations of electoral law."[107]

Thus, the 1994 presidential election ended up being competitive, not because democratic institutions were strong or because leaders were committed to democracy, but because no single group was strong enough to monopolize political control. Kravchuk's seemingly enormous incumbent advantages were effectively neutralized by a weak central state and identity divisions that motivated opposition within a significant portion of the elite and the general public. Relying overwhelmingly on Russian speakers in the east, Kuchma was able to beat Kravchuk 52 to 45 percent.

In sum, the Kravchuk period provides a particularly clear illustration of the various ways in which identity divisions and state and party weakness can create the basis for robust pluralism by undermining the capacity for any single group to monopolize political control. During this period, both Russophile and Ukrainophile forces were able to use identity claims to undermine incumbent power—sometimes relying, as in 1994, on external support. Next, party and state weakness, which seriously undermined economic governance, also made it nearly impossible for Kravchuk to control parliament, manipulate elections, or prevent the rise of opposition from within his own ranks.

Rapacious Individualism and the Rise and Fall of Leonid Kuchma, 1994–2004

"Political cynicism is not the exception but the rule in Ukraine."[108]

The Kuchma era witnessed a significant strengthening of the authoritarian state. Building in part on regional and economic networks he had maintained from the Soviet period, Kuchma dominated parliament and created a state that had greater capacity to repress dissent and carry out electoral fraud than had existed under Kravchuk. Yet Kuchma built this regime on unstable foundations. Kuchma's tenure strikingly demonstrates the difficulties of preserving power by relying on political opportunists absent any overarching party organization. By distributing organizational and economic resources to a wide range of oligarchs and officials who lacked any kind of ideological or other stake in his survival, the president made it much easier for allies to defect when the going got tough. As evidenced by Kuchma's choice of successor, this organizational structure gave him only indirect control over his own ruling coalition. In this context, exceptional economic growth and access to substantial material resources did little to bolster Kuchma's regime.

Authoritarian State Building under Kuchma 1994–2001

Following his election in 1994, Kuchma became "President *de jure*," but "had to fight to become President *de facto*."[109] To do this, Kuchma had significant resources at his disposal. As head of the largest missile factory in the USSR, Kuchma was considered the informal leader of a still-powerful industrial sector in Ukraine in the early 1990s.[110] In contrast to Kravchuk, Kuchma was not forced to abandon his existing organizational base in order to gain power. Furthermore, as head of the dominant enterprise in Dnipropetrovsk, Kuchma established a loyal regional network in his home province that Kravchuk lacked. Support of fellow *Dnipropetrovtsy*, industrialists, and other business actors was important to Kuchma's selection as prime minister in September 1992 and provided the organizational basis of his campaign for president in 1994.[111]

Kuchma ran for president on a Russophile platform. However, after becoming president, he dramatically shifted gears and built a coalition of pro-

Ukrainian nationalists and oligarchic business interests. While initially pro-Russian, business interests became open to Ukrainophile views by the late 1990s. The rise of large financial industrialists in Russia in the mid-1990s generated fear among Ukrainian elites that Russians would grab valuable properties and out-compete Ukrainians in such vulnerable sectors as banking and finance.[112] At the same time, Kuchma's interests as president came into direct conflict with the pro-Russian Communist Party (created in 1993 from the remnants of the disbanded Soviet party),[113] which fought to weaken the presidency that was seen as "responsible for the demise of the USSR under the leadership of the 'traitor nationalist Kravchuk.'"[114]

Partly as a result, Kuchma quickly abandoned plans for closer economic and cultural ties to Russia and pushed for Ukrainian autonomy.[115] In turn, Kuchma opened his regime to a much greater degree to Western finance than did Lukashenka in Belarus, borrowing heavily on the international market.[116] Kuchma's shift in support for Ukrainophile identity allowed him to build a pro-presidential coalition consisting of nationalists, who feared a pro-Russian parliament, and newly pro-Ukrainian business-centrist deputies, who desired the material benefits of Ukrainian autonomy.[117] As we see below, this decision later forced Kuchma to appoint Viktor Yushchenko, who would lead the Orange Revolution that toppled his regime in 2004.

Backed by Ukrainophile groups, significant patronage, and a core base of 80 oligarchic deputies (20 percent of elected deputies), Kuchma pushed for Lukashenka-style powers over the legislature.[118] The president's draft constitution, which included the right to dissolve the legislature and a bicameral legislature, met significant resistance, however, and Kuchma was only able to get a constitution passed after threatening the deputies with a popular referendum that would have given him even greater power. Motivated to act, deputies passed a constitution in a 23-hour marathon session in June 1996 that substantially increased presidential powers.[119] The legislature subsequently ceased to dominate as it had through much of Kravchuk's tenure.

Nevertheless, the constitution that emerged was—in stark contrast to that in Belarus or Russia—a "compromise."[120] The formal powers given Kuchma were weaker than in most CIS countries—weak enough that he was subsequently motivated to seek greater powers in the early 2000s.[121] In particular, Kuchma failed to divide the legislature into a senate and a lower house, and parliament was able to preserve "the widest privileges for deputies," including immunity from prosecution.[122] The president's failure to secure more power was rooted first in the fact that a bicameral parliament "evoked the most zealous and uniform resistance" from Kuchma's oligarchic supporters and others,[123] while *all* parliamentary factions supported parliamentary immunity, which was a central reason why many business oligarchs joined parliament in the first place.[124] Simultaneously, in stark contrast to Belarus (see chapter 5), polarization in Ukraine meant that increased presidential powers were virulently opposed by a well-organized left, which was strongly Russophile and dominated the legislature. The powerful Socialist and Communist parties—at that point the largest and most cohesive parties in Ukraine—forced Kuchma to compromise on the constitution.[125] While it is impossible to know whether Kuchma might have gotten a more presidentialist constitution had he pushed harder, it is clear that he faced greater obstacles than did Lukashenka in Belarus.[126] Thus, better organization under Kuchma than under Kravchuk facilitated increased presidential power; but identity divisions created more impediments to full-scale presidential domination in Ukraine than existed in Belarus.

In turn, Kuchma built an authoritarian regime rooted in strengthened state power and competing oligarchic cliques. Setting out to create more centralized coercive power, Kuchma expanded security forces to the point where they were larger than the army.[127] With the help of Mykola Azarov, a former coal engineer from Donetsk, Kuchma also built an informal authoritarian state apparatus "consisting of a ten thousand strong network of tax inspectors and tax police spread across the country."[128] In 1996, the tax administration was transformed into an "organ of repression"—targeting regime dissenters with mass audits that often paralyzed their firms.[129] By the late 1990s, security services were well funded, and regional rebellions had ceased.[130] As suggested in the introduction, such well-financed police would be expected to maintain high levels of cohesion in most cases; nonetheless, absent non-material ties, such units should be reluctant to engage in risky, large-scale coercion.

Next, a key component of Kuchma's authoritarian state-building strategy was the promotion of competing oligarchic clan networks in the late 1990s. In exchange for support of Kuchma, "loyal members of the economic elite gained privileges in the redistribution of economic resources, while the president was promised steady support in parliament."[131] As in Russia under Yeltsin, the number and wealth of oligarchs exploded in Ukraine in the 1990s.[132] This system gave Kuchma rents and property to buy support as well as access to state sanctions to punish opposition.[133]

Kuchma's organizational base was relatively centralized—in that all groups pledged loyalty to Kuchma—but also highly fragmented. Instead of building a single pro-presidential party, Kuchma, like Yeltsin, relied on support from a variety of parties led by competing oligarchs—or what commentators referred to as a "multi-party ruling party."[134] With Kuchma's encouragement, a series of well-organized parties developed around specific government officials and regional elite groupings–Fatherland, headed by Yulia Tymoshenko; the Social Democratic Party (United), headed by Viktor Medvedchuk; and the Party of Regions, headed by Mykola Azarov and Viktor Yanukovych.

Like Yeltsin, Kuchma essentially outsourced the organization of political support to these groups. Oligarchs backed Kuchma in parliament and via oligarch-controlled television networks and newspapers as well as through direct mobilization of workers in their firms. At the same time, Kuchma refused to tie himself to any single group. By keeping his allies mutually antagonistic and competitive, the president was said to remain "the uniting, cementing force that keeps all of his allies together."[135]

What emerged under Kuchma, then, was a system that was much more authoritarian and centralized than Kravchuk's Ukraine but was also one that was vulnerable to elite defection. Indeed, non-ideological "centrist" and non-affiliated deputies (who were widely seen as the most corruptible) frequently failed to support the president between 1994 and 1998.[136] At least part of this failure to control deputies resulted from the fact that the president, who wanted greater central control, and his supporters, who wanted the autonomy to pursue their commercial interests, had long-term goals that were "in opposition to one another, if not antagonistic."[137] The lack of trust inherent in Kuchma's multi-party ruling party made it more difficult to overcome these differences despite the president's overwhelming access to state resources.

Polarization further constrained Kuchma's power over the legislature. The Russophile Communist Party (recreated in 1993) became the largest and best-organized party in Ukraine in the 1990s. As a result, despite repeated attempts throughout the mid-1990s, the president failed to unseat Oleksandr Moroz, the leftist head of parliament who became Kuchma's most powerful and vocal opponent.[138] Indeed, Kuchma was only able to place a direct ally as parliamentary speaker in 2002 (see below). The Communists also were able to block large-scale privatization in Ukraine until the late 1990s and impose a mixed proportional and majoritarian electoral system that favored the Communists.[139] Kuchma's successful efforts to assert greater presidential authority came only with extraordinary effort and arm-twisting.

The character—and potential pitfalls—of this system can be seen in the history of Ukraine's "first oligarch," Pavlo Lazarenko, and his protégé, Yulia Tymoshenko.[140] Restaffing the executive with his allies from his native Dnipropetrovsk,[141] the president appointed Lazarenko, the former governor of Dnipropetrovsk, as prime minister in May 1996.[142] Lazarenko quickly accumulated enormous power and became extremely wealthy through Tymoshenko's United Energy Systems (UES), which at the time monopolized gas imports from Russia to the industrial east of Ukraine.[143] Tymoshenko, known as the "eleven billion dollar woman," reputedly controlled 20–25 percent of Ukraine's economy at the time.[144] Fearing Lazarenko's accumulation of power in the run-up to the presidential election in 1999, Kuchma replaced Lazarenko in mid-1997 with Valery Pustovoitenko, a Kuchma loyalist, and deprived UES of the right to distribute gas to major enterprises. While it was relatively easy for Kuchma to cut off Lazarenko's source of income, it was harder for the president to take back the huge amount of income that Lazarenko and Tymoshenko had already accumulated—much of it in foreign bank accounts outside Kuchma's reach. Simultaneously, Tymoshenko and many of her associates (although not Lazarenko) were saved from prosecution by parliamentary immunity, which the legislature refused to lift despite demands from the state prosecutor.[145] Lazarenko and Tymoshenko then strengthened the *Hromada* [community] Party, initially formed to support Kuchma, and turned it against the president. Built in part out of the organizational structure of UES,[146] Hromada won almost as many seats in the 1998 parliamentary elections as the pro-presidential National Democratic Party (NDP).[147]

Kuchma, however, ultimately squashed Hromada and gained greater control over oligarchic deputies in the 1998–2002 parliament.[148] He was also able to pull together enough parliamentary support to thwart the reelection of Moroz as speaker. After two months of haggling, parliament elected Oleksandr Tkachenko. While he was not Kuchma's first choice, Tkachenko was too obviously corrupt and unpopular to pose a serious challenge to the president.[149]

In turn, Kuchma garnered enough elite and popular support to win reelection. With her bank accounts frozen, Tymoshenko was convinced to return to Kuchma's fold in January 1999.[150] After agreeing to back Kuchma's reelection, her assets were returned and she created the pro-presidential Fatherland party with assistance from the presidential administration.[151] Then, just as Yeltsin had done in 1996, Kuchma was able to utilize anticommunism to facilitate his reelection in 1999, despite relatively low levels of public support. Although he won only 36 percent of the first-round vote, Kuchma used a combination of patronage, harassment, media bias, and fraud to prevent the most viable electoral contenders—most notably former head of parliament Oleksandr Moroz—from qualifying for the runoff.[152] Instead, he faced hard-line and unelectable Communist Petro Symonenko.[153] In stark contrast to the 1994 election under Kravchuk, this contest was marked by "widespread, systematic and coordinated" fraud.[154] "Practically all high level officials, a large portion of lower level budgetary workers, [and] masses of enterprise directors actively supported Kuchma's campaign."[155] Increased state power under Kuchma directly translated into greater electoral manipulation. Kuchma won with 56 percent of the vote.

This period would witness the height of Kuchma's power. After the new head of parliament Tkachenko "began to pursue his own agenda," pro-Kuchma deputies walked out of parliament and formed a pro-presidential majority of 255–270 deputies.[156] Nevertheless, even during this period, signs of Kuchma's vulnerability emerged. First, in late 1999, Kuchma's dependence on Western financing forced him to appoint as prime minister the man who would ultimately take down Kuchma's regime. As already noted, Kuchma had opened Ukraine to Western finance to a much greater degree than had Lukashenka in Belarus. By 1999, however, Ukrainian National Bank reserves had declined precipitously, and the government faced serious danger of default on payments coming due in 2000. In order to gain financial support from the IMF to avoid default, Kuchma withdrew his support from the loyalist prime minister Pustovoitenko and appointed Viktor Yushchenko, the head of the National Bank, instead. Highly regarded in the West, Yushchenko was well positioned to lead negotiations with the IMF to resolve the crisis.[157] But Yushchenko also had an independent power base in western Ukraine and a clean reputation—factors that made him a serious rival.

Then, despite a pro-presidential majority in parliament, Kuchma proved unable to strengthen presidential powers. In April 2000, Kuchma orchestrated a referendum to bolster his powers and eliminate parliamentary immunity that, with significant fraud, passed overwhelmingly.[158] However, the courts insisted that the president obtain 300 votes from parliament for the referendum to become law. Kuchma felt that his parliamentary "majority would be able to gather sufficient votes to implement the results of the referendum."[159] Actually, the majority faction was itself "riddled by serious tensions," had "no united position" on presidential power, and remained deadlocked "over all bills in the sphere of executive-legislative relations."[160] While cronyism tied oligarchic deputies to the president, these deputies were reluctant to give up their own prerogatives—in particular, immunity, which guaranteed the safety of many oligarchic deputies.[161] Lacking a single ruling party that could guarantee future access to patronage, Kuchma's supporters had little reason to back greater presidential power. Simultaneously, the Communists, strengthened by identity polarization, strongly opposed the president's measure. As a result, despite "intense activity by the Presidential Administration," the president was only able to bring 251 deputies to his side in July 2000—far below the required 300.[162] By the middle of September—two months before a major crisis nearly swept Kuchma from power—a stable pro-presidential majority in the legislature had "ceased to exist."[163]

The Tapes Crisis and the Hemorrhaging of Kuchma's Coalition

Then, in late 2000, the whole edifice of Kuchma's rule nearly collapsed. At a dramatic press conference on November 28, Moroz revealed the presence of secretly recorded tapes of Kuchma that seemed to suggest that he had ordered the murder of journalist Georgi Gongadze, whose headless body had been found months earlier. The tapes exposed a striking level of presidential corruption and abuse in the 1999 election.[164] While supporters of the president shut off the electricity in parliament in a desperate effort to halt the press conference, news quickly got out, and on December 14, the legislature held a special session devoted to the tapes and charges against Kuchma, who narrowly escaped impeachment proceedings.

Public support for Kuchma declined precipitously, and the tapes sparked a mass movement in Kyiv against Kuchma—"Ukraine without Kuchma." After Tymoshenko was ousted from her position as deputy prime minister and briefly imprisoned, she joined the opposition. Fatherland, which had been formed with Kuchma's blessing as a pro-presidential party, was (like Hromada) turned against Kuchma. (One of its leaders, Oleksandr Turchynov, had been the "main brains" behind Kuchma in 1992/1993.[165]) Activists led by Tymoshenko, Moroz, and Yuriy Lutsenko (a leader in the Socialist Party) built a tent city in the center of Kyiv, and thousands demanded Kuchma's resignation. After the protests grew violent on March 9, however, demonstrations gradually petered out. The failure of 'Ukraine without Kuchma' may be related to the fact that national identity played a far less prominent role in this protest than it did in successful protests in 1990, 1993, 2004, and 2014.[166]

At the same time, the tapes scandal forced another shift in Kuchma's geo-

political orientation. Before the release of the tapes, Kuchma was seen by Western leaders as a bulwark against Communism in Ukraine. Afterwards, he became a pariah. In turn, Russia remained virtually Kuchma's only ally on the
international stage. Putin, who had visited Ukraine more than any other country, backed Kuchma with highly publicized economic concessions.[167]

Kuchma was enormously weakened after the crisis. In particular, Prime
Minister Viktor Yushchenko, lucky enough to take charge during a period of
economic growth, became "Ukraine's most popular politician" and the likely
winner of the 2004 presidential election.[168] Kuchma's worst nightmare about
Yushchenko had become true. In April, the legislature voted to oust Yushchenko. Yet this action did nothing to temper discussions of Yushchenko's prospects in 2004.

Simultaneously, opposition forces began scoring critical victories—ousting
presidential ally Viktor Medvedchuk as deputy head of parliament and thwarting efforts by Kuchma to fire Grigoriy Omelchenko, the mayor of Kyiv. While
Kuchma was able to impose an ally, Volodymyr Lytvyn, as head of parliament
in 2002, the former head of the presidential administration "gradually took an
absolutely independent position"—blocking attempts to deprive Tymoshenko
of her parliamentary immunity.[169] All talk of strengthening the presidency
ceased. Instead, fearing that he would lose control over the presidency in 2004,
Kuchma's team switched course and began pushing for constitutional reform
that would increase parliamentary powers. Yet the president failed again. Despite "huge efforts and expenditures," Kuchma was unable to gain the necessary
support after 16 deputies abandoned him in the last minute before a critical
vote in the legislature.[170]

At the same time, the highly fragmented "multi-party ruling party" left
the president with few options for dealing with challenges that had emerged
from within his own ranks. In the absence of an institutionalized ruling party,
Kuchma could not credibly guarantee that short-term losers in power struggles
(Tymoshenko and Yushchenko in 2001) would gain "a share of power and the
spoils of office over the long run" by remaining loyal to the president.[171] As a
result, these figures quickly joined the opposition once they had left office. And
while the president could halt the hemorrhaging of resources to potential competitors by firing them, he had a much harder time taking back those financial
and organizational assets that had already been distributed. The opposition
also benefitted from the fact that oligarchs—like businesspeople everywhere—

tended to distribute resources widely among any and all groups that might be influential.

All of this set the stage for the emergence of "Our Ukraine," a coalition of Yushchenko supporters created to contest the 2002 parliamentary elections. Seen as a serious contender for the upcoming presidential elections, Yushchenko became a magnet for a variety of pro- and anti-government elites in 2001–2002. Our Ukraine was initially created as an alliance of presidential allies and national democrats. The main organizer was Roman Bessmertnyi, Kuchma's official representative in the legislature. Petro Poroshenko, the head of Our Ukraine's election campaign (and future president), was leader of the pro-presidential "Solidarity" party. Poroshenko also helped to organize a powerful network of business support within Our Ukraine—including oligarchs from the energy sector, banking, and food production. As a result, Our Ukraine had "more than enough financial reserves."[172]

A "permitted opposition,"[173] Our Ukraine had an ambiguous relationship with opponents of Kuchma. On the one hand, Yushchenko was seen as a natural leader of the anti-Kuchma movement and hostile to many large-scale oligarchs—especially the energy interests threatened by Yushchenko actions as prime minister. On the other hand, Yushchenko repeatedly expressed strong support for Kuchma,[174] included key Kuchma allies in Our Ukraine's leadership, and actively distanced himself from the opposition—refusing to form an alliance with the more stridently oppositional Moroz and Tymoshenko. Indeed, the bloc's ties to the president gave it far greater access to large audience media in 2002 than other opposition parties. Thus, in contrast to Tymoshenko and Moroz, Our Ukraine was able to run ads on all but one national Ukrainian TV station. Partly as a result, the party won 24.5 percent of the proportional vote—gaining a plurality of the legislature in 2002.

National Divide, Rapacious Individualism, and the Orange Revolution

The death-knell for Kuchma's regime came with the 2004 Orange Revolution that resulted in the victory of Yushchenko, backed by millions of protesters. The Orange Revolution has been seen by many as the manifestation of "authentic democratic values" and a "vibrant civil society."[175] Yet, such a focus on democratic values and civil society leaves key aspects of the Orange Revolution unexplained. It does not account for the emergence of most of the key groups behind the revolution or for their access to significant organizational and material resources. It also tells us nothing about why incumbents responded to the crisis in such a confused and fragmented way despite access to substantial resources and active support from Russia. Perhaps most importantly, such a perspective cannot explain why so many people supported Yushchenko in 2004, while similar crowds failed to back opposition in 2001 or after fraudulent elections in Belarus in 2001 or 2006. To understand both the opposition's strength and the incumbent's weaknesses during the Orange Revolution, we have to look at Kuchma's organizational base and the impact of national polarization.

In the run-up to 2004, Kuchma possessed significant advantages, including vast patronage resources and the dedicated support of Russia's Putin. The Ukrainian economy was booming, with growth increasing from 5 percent in 2002 to 12 percent in 2004.[176] The incumbent campaign to win the election was awash in cash.[177] And in contrast to Kravchuk or Shevardnadze in Georgia, Kuchma also benefitted from a well-funded coercive apparatus.

However, Kuchma commanded a relatively weak party structure, which severely limited his choice of successor in 2004.[178] Indeed, one of the enduring mysteries of the Orange Revolution is why Kuchma picked Yanukovych—a corrupt official with a criminal past whose close association with the Donetsk "clan" made him a highly polarizing figure. While Kuchma claims that he did not know of Yanukovych's past transgressions,[179] a more plausible explanation relates to the fragmented, "multi-party" character of the president's ruling coalition, which ultimately limited his discretion. Yanukovych was the natural choice as successor not because he was the candidate most likely to appeal to the broadest number of Ukrainians but because he possessed the strongest and best-funded organization among the competing pro-Kuchma "clans." Five years earlier, during the 1999 presidential elections, Yanukovych had engineered a victory for Kuchma in Donetsk, where the opposition Communists had previously dominated. Yanukovych "consistently demonstrated the ability to control the situation" and had strong support from the local economic elite.[180] The other pro-government candidates with broader electoral appeal— Serhiy Tyhypko and Volodymyr Lytvyn—lacked the combined financial and organizational resources that Yanukovych possessed as leader of the largest and most important industrial center in Ukraine. In the absence of a single party with the capacity to impose discipline on its constituent groups, Kuchma "had no choice" but to pick Yanukovych—lest the president lose access to those key resources.[181]

Kuchma's weak party structure also encouraged defections. Indeed, since Yushchenko's emergence as Ukraine's most popular politician in 2001, a wide array of Kuchma allies had migrated into Yushchenko's camp. Most notably, just four months before the 2004 election, Alexander Zinchenko, the head of a pro-government TV channel, joined the opposition after a conflict with the head of the presidential administration.[182] In the end, almost all of the central figures in Yushchenko's campaign and the Orange Revolution were recent defectors from Kuchma's administration. Had Kuchma been able to maintain greater cohesion, there would likely have been no viable opposition in Ukraine in the early 2000s.

At the same time, national divisions allowed opposition leaders to distinguish themselves from the incumbent regime despite their close association with Kuchma—just as pro-Russian appeals had allowed Kuchma to distance himself from Kravchuk in the early 1990s. Yushchenko had long been identified with the Ukrainian national cause, and Tymoshenko, a native of Dnipropetrovsk in the east, inaugurated her shift to opposition in 2001–2002 by adopting a pro-Ukrainian image—assuming a hairstyle reminiscent of the Ukrainian national poet Lesia Ukrainka and wooing Soviet-era nationalist dissidents to her side.[183] Ukrainophile identity helped ex-Kuchma allies claim that the battle for the presidency in 2004 was not just a fight for power but a "conflict among two worldviews, two moral systems."[184] By contrast, weaker divisions in Belarus and Russia made it harder for former insiders to gain credibility.

Fearing that Yushchenko would win free and fair elections, Yanukovych then sought to carry out a meticulously planned and extremely well-financed program of electoral fraud in which he was to win by a plausible 3 percent.[185] Simultaneously, Russian president Vladimir Putin offered large economic concessions to Ukraine and provided millions of dollars to the Yanukovych campaign.[186]

Yet Kuchma's authoritarian state—which lacked non-material sources of cohesion—was ill-suited to carrying out risky actions in the face a serious opposition. Indeed, despite intense planning and resources, Kuchma faced "silent opposition from a significant part of the government in the localities."[187] In Lviv, for example, police and tax authorities refused to distribute absentee ballot certificates to be used for multiple voting. In some cases, local authorities may have facilitated fraud in Yushchenko's favor.[188]

Even parts of the country where support for Yanukovych was high witnessed a breakdown of autocratic control. As evidenced by secretly taped conversations, Yanukovych campaign officials expressed frustration that local officials in the otherwise pro-Yanukovych province of Kharkiv accepted money from the regime but "just refus[ed] to follow our orders" to carry out fraud.[189] Indeed, a comparison of the provincial distribution of votes in the highly fraudulent November 21 round and the relatively clean repeat election on December 26 suggests that the regime failed to steal many votes in Kharkiv or Zaporizhzhia in eastern Ukraine.[190] In some cases, as I witnessed firsthand as an OSCE election observer, seemingly conscientious officials simply refused to go along with abuse in Zaporizhzhia.[191] Other officials feared punishment for fraud, which, according to Ukrainian law, could result in multiyear prison terms. One poll worker in Zaporizhzhia explained: "Even if you are paid off . . . who wants to sit in prison so that some candidate can win?"[192] While a well-institutionalized national party machine credibly protecting such officials from retribution could probably have overcome such fears, the fragmented and weakly developed political structure left many subordinates exposed.

Ultimately, Yanukovych was able to steal the election, but he was forced to do so in an utterly transparent and ham-fisted manner. Because fraud was so weak in key parts of eastern/southern Ukraine, the government was only able to steal the vote on November 21 by adding significant numbers of stolen votes at the last minute in parts of the country—most notably Donetsk—that were securely controlled by the government. Such actions gave Yanukovych an official victory over Yushchenko of 49.46 to 46.91 percent but made the vote theft utterly obvious to all but the most ardent Yanukovych supporters. Had fraud been more evenly distributed and thus less obvious, Yanukovych's "victory" might not have sparked such an immediate and widespread uproar in Ukraine and in the West.

Blatant electoral fraud led to an explosion of protest in support of Yushchenko. Surveys suggest that as many as 13 percent of Ukrainian adults (4–5 million people) took part in pro-Yushchenko demonstrations in the three weeks after November 21.[193] What explains this massive protest? While many observers saw these demonstrations as evidence of "authentic democratic values,"[194] there is considerable reason to doubt that support for democracy per se explains the protests. Mark Beissinger's close examination of several surveys of pro-Yushchenko demonstrators finds that protesters possessed "weak commitment to democratic ends"—just 34 percent of those who took part in the Orange Revolution protests said they favored a multiparty system for Ukraine: "More participants actually opposed a multi-party system than favored it."[195] While many individual protesters no doubt came out in support of democracy, there is little evidence that this was a dominant value.

Next, the massive protests have been seen as the product of a strong and emerging Ukrainian civil society.[196] Civic groups—most notably the youth movement Pora—played an active role in the protests. At the same time, much of the organizational and financial muscle behind the protests was provided not by any kind of democratic civil society but by recently pro-government and oligarchic forces (Alexander Zinchenko, Petro Poroshenko) who had transferred their loyalties to Yushchenko—in some cases just months before the election.[197] Oligarchic contributions helped to pay both for the election campaign and for the protests in late 2004.[198] Key leaders of the protests—including Roman Bessmertnyi—had very recently been Kuchma insiders.[199]

Most importantly, civil society cannot explain why the protests were so large. As Beissinger notes, "The overwhelming majority of revolution participants had never participated in any civil society organizations," while those *opposed* to the protests "were actually more heavily involved in civil society associations."[200] Furthermore, sizable protests arose in some regions where the youth movement Pora was well organized—Lviv, Kyiv, and Sumy—but mostly failed to emerge in others where Pora was also quite active—Kharkiv and Odesa.[201] While groups like Pora helped organize protesters that arrived in Kyiv, there is little evidence that their activity explains why millions came out against the government in the first place.

Rather than yearnings for "democratic renewal,"[202] or an awakened civil society, the key source of the protests can be found in the dynamics of Ukrainian identity conflicts. The election tapped into widely shared anti-Russian nationalist sentiments dominant in the west of the country, where an overwhelming share of the protestors came from in late 2004. While the opposition did not make nationalist demands or even use Ukrainian national symbols, the government actively encouraged polarization around national issues—repeatedly tieing Yushchenko to extremist Ukrainian nationalism.[203] Yanukovych stoked anti-Russian passions by running an overtly pro-Russian campaign, even bringing Russian president Vladimir Putin to Ukraine, where he held a nationally televised press conference.[204] By insulting their national pride, the blatantly stolen election likely convinced many hitherto inactive individuals in the west of the country to challenge the regime.

Indeed, surveys of protesters in 2004 suggest that participants predominantly "wanted to see Ukraine as Ukrainian rather than as an appendage of Russia."[205] In a survey undertaken by the Kyiv International Institute of Sociology (KIIS) during the Orange Revolution, identity shows up as a powerful predictor of participation in the protests even when we control for a range of nonidentity demographic variables. Speaking Ukrainian increased the odds of demonstrating by 382 percent.[206] Similarly, Mark Beissinger's analysis of a different survey of Ukrainian protesters shows that Ukrainian identity was a powerful predictor of participation.[207]

Protesters came disproportionately from western Ukraine. According to KIIS, 37 percent of adults in western Ukraine (including 50 percent of those in Lviv) protested in favor of Yushchenko in late 2004 as compared to just 3 percent of adults in eastern and southern Ukraine.[208] While populations in both central and western Ukraine voted for Yushchenko, western Ukrainians provided a significantly larger share of demonstrators in late 2004.[209] In fact, the epicenter of Ukrainian nationalism, Galicia, which made up about 10 percent of Ukraine's population, accounted for about 36 percent of all pro-Yushchenko protesters—more than double the share of protesters (14 percent) from the capital, Kyiv, where the main demonstrations took place.

Although the backing of liberals in Kyiv was also key to the success of the Orange Revolution, there is little evidence that support for democracy in Kyiv was much higher than in other capitals of the post-Soviet region. Thus, populations in the capitals of both Belarus and Ukraine gave significant support to regime opponents. But in contrast to activists in Minsk, opposition liberals in Kyiv were also able to rely on the support of sizable numbers of passionate regional activists who were willing to withstand almost three weeks of subfreezing temperatures on the streets of the capital.

At the same time, Kuchma's weak authoritarian organization played a central role in the ultimate success of these demonstrations. First, the mayor of Kyiv, Omelchenko, whom Kuchma had failed to get rid of, gave the demonstrators access to city services—including water, electricity, and garbage collection that were arguably critical in supporting the massive influx of demonstrators.[210] Even before the election, in mid-September, parliamentary speaker Lytvyn, who had earlier headed the pro-presidential faction in parliament, publicly broke with Kuchma, bringing about 40 other deputies with him. Shortly after protests began, Tyhypko, Yanukovych's campaign manager, resigned and left the country. Then, five days after protests began, the parliament under Lytvyn declared the second-round results invalid and demanded that a repeat second round be held on December 26. It was thus Kuchma's erstwhile allies who gave the opposition its first base within central institutions as Lytvyn "effectively became Yushchenko's ally and guarantor."[211]

Perhaps most critically, Kuchma himself demonstrated strikingly weak support for Yanukovych before and during the crisis. Even after choosing Yanukovych to be his successor, Kuchma continued to hint that he might run for a third term.[212] Yanukovych thus contested the presidential election not only with Yushchenko but with Kuchma. As a result of Kuchma's reticence, Yanukovych "did not have consistent support from the governors [appointed by the president]. They awaited orders from the President, often receiving them at the very last minute."[213] After protests were in full swing, Kuchma opposed the use of large-scale force and actively cooperated in negotiating with the opposition—thus making it nearly impossible for Yanukovych to ride out the crisis.[214]

Finally, the coercive apparatus was far too divided to carry out the large-scale repression. Most critically, the SBU quickly broke from the regime—releasing taped phone conversations proving fraud. Simultaneously, the military came out against the use of force.[215] According to at least one account, the minister of internal affairs was ordered by Yanukovych to crack down but backed away after it became clear that such an action would be resisted by the military.[216]

But if opposition was so strong and Yanukovych so weak, why did Yushchenko decide to negotiate with Kuchma—agreeing to a reduction of presidential powers in exchange for a rerun of the fraudulent second round? Why did Yushchenko not immediately seize power as Saakashvili had done in Georgia in 2003 after the ouster of President Eduard Shevardnadze? In Georgia, such a seizure of power had a detrimental impact on democracy—weakening opposition and concentrating power in the presidency. Indeed, Yushchenko initially had himself sworn in as president a day after protests began and was "categorically opposed" to any kind of reform that would weaken the presidency.[217]

Ultimately, however, Yushchenko lacked the power to impose unilateral victory. Above all, Ukraine's divided national identity significantly raised the costs of unilateral seizure of power. The revolution exacerbated regional divisions in a way that bolstered support for pro-government forces in the east, thereby forcing the Orange forces into a compromise. Opposition leader Yuriy Lutsenko noted that a Georgian-style seizure of power "would have been interpreted by the east as an aggressive seizure of Kyiv by western Ukrainians." "Fear of splitting Ukraine" dissuaded activists from seizing power and encouraged them to negotiate a settlement with Kuchma forces to weaken the presidency in exchange for a rerun of the second round.[218] (By contrast, as we shall see, the breakdown of negotiations in 2014 contributed to the dismembering of Ukraine.) As a result of a constitutional agreement in mid-December 2004, the legislature became responsible for selecting the prime minister and approving most cabinet members nominated by the prime minister. Such reforms would help spur significant competition in the Yushchenko era.

In sum, the Orange Revolution was less the product of "democratic renewal" or the "triumph of civil society"[219] than the outgrowth of organizational failure and regional divisions. The absence of a well-established ruling party facilitated massive defections and gave the opposition critical resources and leadership. It also severely limited Kuchma's capacity to choose the most electable successor. Furthermore, the softness of the authoritarian "vertical" hampered electoral fraud in key eastern provinces and forced the regime to engage in blatant vote theft in Yanukovych's home region. Such transparent fraud combined with Russia's overt backing of Yanukovych stimulated unprecedented numbers of highly motivated protesters from the capital and western Ukraine to challenge the regime. Without strong support from the security forces—or even from Kuchma himself—Yanukovych was forced to back down in a humiliating defeat.

Party Weakness and Democracy under Yushchenko, 2005–2009

Even after agreeing to constitutional reform, pro-Orange forces emerged in 2005 in a seemingly strong position. Yushchenko had successfully mobilized one of the largest protests in recent European history and, in early 2005, was supported by about 70 percent of Ukrainians—far greater support than was ever enjoyed by Yanukovych.[220] Such a clear signal of his "raw political superiority" might have enabled Yushchenko to reverse constitutional reforms and centralize political control—just as Yanukovych was to do five years later.[221] Simultaneously, Yushchenko's main opponent, Yanukovych, seemed utterly discredited in early 2005, with his supporters "demoralized" after their humiliating defeat.[222] Deprived of key state resources, and disgraced by extensive negative media coverage and a criminal record, Yanukovych seemed destined for history's dustbin.[223] Sixty thousand left the Party of Regions, and even Yanukovych's Donetsk allies "began to gradually dismiss him."[224]

Indeed, in their first months of power, Yushchenko and Tymoshenko actively assaulted the Party of Regions' financial base—a move that could have effectively defanged a major source of opposition. The government annulled the earlier sale of Ukraine's largest steel company, Kryvorizhstal, to Rinat Akhmetov and Viktor Pinchuk. Putting heavy pressure on the Ministry of Interior to find negative material on Donetsk oligarchs, Yushchenko publicly questioned Akhmetov's purchase of a major iron ore plant, Ukrrudprom, and threatened jail time for oligarchs.[225] In turn, the police arrested the former governor of Transcarpathia, Ivan Rizhak, as well as Boris Kolesnikov, the head of the Party of Regions in Donetsk.[226] In April, Akhmetov fled the country. Backed by public support and the same formal authority as Kuchma, Yushchenko was poised to sideline the opposition's main backers.[227]

Nevertheless, politics under Yushchenko's regime was the most competitive, chaotic, and democratic in Ukraine since the early 1990s. Rather than seeing the final defeat of Yanukovych, the first year of Orange rule witnessed the unprecedented expansion of the Donetsk clan and the Party of Regions.[228] Under Yushchenko, incumbent control over the legislature, media, elections, and opposition was far weaker than it had been under Kuchma. Despite continued corruption and outside interference, the media exhibited "wide-ranging pluralism."[229] Electoral manipulation declined dramatically, and parliament became enormously powerful. Finally, opposition led by Yanukovych became quite strong—gaining the prime ministership in 2006 and winning the presidency in 2010.

Such competition cannot simply be explained by the democratic inclinations of the Orange coalition. Both Yushchenko and Tymoshenko demonstrated a willingness to repress opposition and abuse political power.[230] Indeed, Yushchenko introduced several new autocratic practices that were in turn developed by Yanukovych.[231] Given Yushchenko's decision to skirt the constitution and shut down parliament in 2007 (see below), it can hardly be said that Yushchenko was especially "confrontation-averse" as some have argued.[232]

Undeniably, a key source of pluralism under Yushchenko was the constitutional reform of late 2004—itself a product of Ukraine's regional polarization—that divided power more or less equally between president and prime minister. As a result, the government changed hands in 2006 and 2007, while divided control over the state significantly hampered efforts by either side to monopolize political control.[233] Yet the constitution alone cannot account for the high degree of political competition in the late 2000s. As we shall see, evidence of pluralism by default emerged *before* the constitutional changes took effect in 2006. More importantly, the pluralizing effects of the constitution hinged on the failure of one political force to control both the presidency and the parliament[234]—an outcome made virtually inevitable by the fragmented nature of the Orange forces. By contrast, a single political force controlling both branches would face relatively few obstacles monopolizing power as Yanukovych successfully did for eight months in 2010 under the 2004 constitution. Indeed, constitutional rules cannot explain the shift toward greater authoritarianism after 2010. Yushchenko came to power with extensive formal powers but was unable consolidate control; whereas Yanukovych took the presidency in 2010 with much weaker formal powers but was able to monopolize power for four years.

Rather than institutional design, Yushchenko's inability to consolidate control can most directly be traced to party weakness and national divisions. First, Yushchenko was forced to rule as the head of one party within a relatively equal coalition of political elites and parties—Our Ukraine together with Tymoshenko and the Fatherland Party. The Orange alliance between Yushchenko and Tymoshenko emerged in 2003 after polls showed that Tymoshenko was unlikely to beat Yushchenko in the 2004 election. After "protracted and extremely difficult" negotiations between Tymoshenko and Yushchenko, Tymoshenko agreed to back Yushchenko in the 2004 presidential election in exchange for the promise that Tymoshenko would become prime minister.[235] Tymoshenko then played a major role in organizing protests in 2004. While Yushchenko sought to create a single party uniting the various pro-Orange factions in early 2005, he faced enormous resistance from Tymoshenko and other allies.[236] Thus, a new ruling coalition arose in early 2005 that was about equally divided between two political heavyweights.

While the Orange coalition obtained higher levels of support than Yanukovych in parliamentary elections in 2006 and 2007, organizational fragmentation (much more severe than under Kuchma) critically undermined efforts to consolidate political control. Indeed, days after Tymoshenko became prime minister, Poroshenko was appointed the head of the powerful National Security and Defense Council to combat Tymoshenko's influence—an appointment that contributed to an "intense competition for power" within the new Orange government and "the collection and distribution of mutual *kompromat* [compromising material]" concerning leaders in the Orange Revolution.[237]

In turn, divisions within the coalition undermined the prospects of reversing the 2004 constitutional changes. Thus, Tymoshenko, whose support would have been critical in any effort to dial back reform, was highly ambivalent about reversing reforms and repeatedly threw her support behind greater parliamentary powers in the late 2000s.[238] The fragmentation of the Orange camp made it extremely difficult for Yushchenko to fire judges, who "almost always found protection from rival political forces."[239] Thus, "despite all his efforts," Yushchenko "was unable to assemble a loyal composition" of the Constitutional Court.[240] In contrast to the Kuchma and later Yanukovych eras, when judges "knew whom to be afraid of, judges now faced multiple political forces."[241] Yushchenko lacked the requisite support in the Court to affect increased presidential powers.[242]

Simultaneously, conflicts within the Orange coalition strengthened Yanukovych as Yushchenko and Tymoshenko used him to neutralize each other's influence. First, in the summer of 2005, Yushchenko obtained Yanukovych's support to oust Tymoshenko as prime minister in exchange for an amnesty for 2004 electoral fraud and a promise to "stop political repressions" against Yanukovych.[243] As a result, attacks on Yanukovych supporters ceased and Yanukovych's enormous financial base was allowed to remain intact—giving him the resources to later challenge the Orange coalition.

The easing of attacks on eastern oligarchs in mid-2005 unleashed a period of highly corrupt but also relatively pluralistic media. While editorial autonomy was extremely low, media pluralism was bolstered by competition between media oligarchs.[244] In the language of one commentator, media transformed from a "harem" devoted to a single power center under Kuchma to a "bordello" in which access was sold to anyone with the money to pay.[245] With different oligarchs supporting different groupings, this system generated a relatively equal playing field among the major parties.[246] It became very hard for Yushchenko to impose a single official line on the media.

Divisions in the coalition also critically undermined Yushchenko's capacity to use the state to manipulate elections in his favor. Competition among allies for votes in the same areas served "as a check on each other's [electoral] shenanigans in the west and center."[247]

At the same time, identity divisions gave Yanukovych a strong political base despite his humiliation in 2004. While the Kuchma regime's polarizing, anti-Ukrainian rhetoric failed to undermine support for Yushchenko in late 2004, it did consolidate support for Yanukovych in the east. In stark contrast to the early 2000s, Yanukovych consistently garnered sizable majorities in the east in the mid- and late 2000s.[248] By comparison, different parties in the Orange coalition competed for the same votes in the west. Yanukovych's support in the east also bolstered unity within the Party of Regions itself—despite a high degree of factionalism—by guaranteeing oligarchs a share of power.[249] As a result, Yushchenko, unlike Saakashvili in Georgia, was forced to confront a popular, well-organized opposition after coming to power.

Over the next four years, a combination of incumbent fragmentation, national divisions, and constitutional rules generated a rough balance of power between the Party of Regions on one side and representatives of the Orange coalition on the other. First, disorganization and national divisions fatally undermined several efforts by Yushchenko and Yanukovych to unify the presidency and legislature under a single political force—a move that would have reduced the pluralizing effect of the 2004 constitutional changes. As a coalition of six different parties, Our Ukraine had difficulty maintaining the unity necessary for a stable alliance with the Party of Regions.[250] Simultaneously, the history of intense, identity-infused polarization between the Party of Regions and the Orange coalition raised the political costs of such an alliance. Key members of the Our Ukraine coalition strongly opposed a coalition with the "alien," "anti-Ukrainian and anti-state" Yanukovych.[251] Identity divisions significantly complicated efforts at political collusion.

After the 2006 parliamentary elections, splits in the Orange coalition allowed Yanukovych to gain sufficient support to capture the prime minister's office.[252] Yanukovych in turn began to consolidate control in his hands. Using bribery and other tactics, Yanukovych nearly gained the 300 parliamentary votes necessary to unilaterally amend the constitution.

Yet President Yushchenko still retained sufficient administrative power to thwart this effort. He responded by issuing a decree on dubious constitutional grounds that dissolved parliament and called for early parliamentary elections. Subsequently, he fired three judges from the Constitutional Court in order to prevent it from ruling against his decision. Tymoshenko, feeling threatened by Yanukovych's power grab, backed this effort. After Tymoshenko's bloc (BYuT) and Our Ukraine deputies resigned from the legislature, the parliament was dissolved. New elections were held on September 30, 2007, resulting in a renewed alliance between Tymoshenko and Yushchenko that voted Tymoshenko again into power as prime minister.

Yet the president again fell out with Tymoshenko, and in October 2008 he issued a decree dissolving the legislature and calling for early elections. In turn, a Kyiv administrative court quickly declared the decree unconstitutional.[253]

While Yushchenko responded by liquidating the court itself, his *own* party rebelled, and a majority 37 of 72 members of the faction voted to remain in Tymoshenko's coalition—thus preserving Tymoshenko's power.[254]

At this point, Yanukovych and Tymoshenko came "as close as ever" to creating a "grand coalition" that would have created a "kind of cartel . . . to monopolize power in Ukraine."[255] According to one proponent of the coalition, the agreement would have made the 2010 presidential election "so quiet 'you would hardly know it was happening.' "[256]

Yet two key factors intervened to undermine such a coalition. Above all, "fear of betrayal on both sides ultimately doomed the coalition deal."[257] In particular, Akhmetov, who strongly distrusted Tymoshenko, claims to have scuttled the agreement.[258] As earlier, political cynicism and mutual distrust fatally undermined efforts at political collusion and greater political closure.

Simultaneously, regional polarization increased the costs of political union. Both sides worried that the union was "a violation of the preelection promises" and might split both parties.[259] Many within the Orange coalition expressed concern that an alliance with the Party of Regions would fundamentally undermine Tymoshenko's image with her base, while key figures in the Party of Regions considered the union to be a "betrayal of voters," who were strong opponents of Tymoshenko.[260] Thus regional polarization raised the costs of collusion across identity lines, reducing the chances that any alliance would remain stable.

Then in early 2010, the Orange coalition lost power in presidential elections to Yanukovych. Prime Minister Tymoshenko and Yanukovych made it to the second round, while Yushchenko, whose campaign was wracked by defections, severe underfunding, and disorganization, obtained just 5 percent of the vote.[261] Yanukovych then beat Tymoshenko 49 to 45 percent. While this outcome is hardly surprising, given that Ukraine's economy had declined by 15 percent in 2009, disorganization of the Orange coalition also played a role. Thus, Yushchenko actively organized against Tymoshenko, encouraging his supporters to vote "against all" in the second round.[262] As one scholar argues, "Yanukovych did not win the election; instead, the Orange Coalition lost it because of Yushchenko and Tymoshenko's inability to work together."[263]

In sum, national divisions and severe disorganization at the top made pluralism under Yushchenko virtually inevitable. While the 2004 constitutional reforms gave parliament dramatically more power,[264] such contestation could have been avoided if a single cohesive party had taken control over both the presidency and the legislature. Instead, rampant tensions within the Orange coalition guaranteed that different forces would control the different branches of government, undermined efforts to reverse constitutional changes, and provided key openings for Yanukovych to regain power. Simultaneously, national divisions bolstered Yanukovych and prevented the utter destruction of the opposition that occurred in Georgia in 2003. This divide also undermined repeated efforts to create "grand coalitions" that might have significantly reduced political uncertainty in the late 2000s. The result was highly dysfunctional democracy.

The Rise and Fall of Authoritarianism under Yanukovych, 2010–2014

The early 2010s saw the remarkable rise and catastrophic fall of authoritarian rule under President Viktor Yanukovych. Despite coming to power with relatively weak formal powers, Yanukovych used his party's control over the legislature to rapidly consolidate a greater monopoly of power than had existed before him. In late 2013, Yanukovych was in a strong position to secure re-election in 2015. However, Ukraine's split identity and Yanukovych's failure to understand the limits of Ukraine's authoritarian state contributed to a crisis that ultimately led to the collapse of his regime in 2014 and violent conflict. These events highlight a key theme of this book: the same factors promoting contestation often foster severe dysfunction and even the breakdown of social order.

Between 2010 and 2013, Yanukovych rapidly concentrated power and put an end to democratic rule under Yushchenko. Press freedom declined and electoral fraud increased, while parliament took on "a largely rubber-stamp role."[265] In late 2010, Yanukovych successfully pushed through a reversal of the 2004 constitutional reforms. Finally, Yanukovych's tenure witnessed "the dramatic and sudden increase in criminal prosecutions of high-level politicians"— including Yuriy Lutsenko and Yulia Tymoshenko.[266]

Certainly, key aspects of regime closure—most notably the unprecedented jailing of major political figures—can only be explained with reference to Yanukovych's authoritarian proclivities. Yet other changes—including increased pressure on journalists and expanded executive powers—were in sync with the aims of Yushchenko and Tymoshenko during their tenure.[267] Furthermore, to understand why Yanukovych was *capable* of jailing major opposition leaders, we need to look beyond Yanukovych's authoritarian inclinations.

Increased regime closure after 2009 was greatly facilitated by Yanukovych's access to a much more cohesive and better-organized party than had previously existed in independent Ukraine. Backed by Ukraine's "first party in power" that dominated both the presidency and the legislature, Yanukovych was able to overcome the formal fragmentation of power, utilize the legislature to concentrate control, and pressure the judiciary to a much greater degree than had been possible in the Yushchenko era.[268] Increased control over the judiciary, in turn, facilitated both the reversal of the 2004 constitutional reforms and the jailing of major political opposition leaders.

Yanukovych concentrated power in part by learning from "fatal mistakes" of Kuchma and Yushchenko, who organized pro-government forces around multi-party coalitions.[269] "Any bloc is knowingly temporary and unstable formation," Yanukovych commented. "The party is created for long-term work."[270] Thus, unlike Our Ukraine, the Party of Regions dictated that all allies must dissolve their other parties and join the Party of Regions as individuals.[271] Given the Party's strong position and domination of eastern Ukraine, established politicians—including Evheniy Kushnarev and Serhiy Tyhypko—complied.[272] The Party of Regions had "more money at its disposal" and was "more organized" than other parties in Ukraine.[273] It was also less personalized than other Ukrainian parties, had the largest network of primary organizations in the country, and, in stark contrast to Our Ukraine, "retain[ed] strong voting discipline."[274] The Party of Regions also invested heavily in strengthening their presence in local councils and mayoralties.[275]

Perhaps most importantly, Party cohesion was bolstered by the fact that it was based on a well-oiled, tightly disciplined political machine in a single province, Donetsk, the largest industrial region of Ukraine. Yanukovych had "consistently demonstrated the ability to dominate" the province since 1999 when he displaced the Communist Party in the presidential election.[276] Yanukovych deeply infiltrated the state apparatus in Donetsk—a fact that likely contributed to the utter breakdown in social order in the province when he suddenly fled the country in late February 2014. Building from this powerful base, Yanukovych, in contrast to Kuchma in the early 2000s, did not have to pull together a regionally diverse coalition. Yanukovych was able to attract the support of outsiders such as Tyhypko on his own terms. As of September 2013, officials from the Donbas area controlled half of all government ministries, including the ministries of energy and the interior, and "occupied high-ranking positions in two-thirds of the country's provinces."[277] Finally, like Kuchma, Yanukovych benefitted from the support of the country's richest oligarchs, who were mostly concentrated in the east—a fact that gave the Party of Regions enormous wealth.[278]

The combination of a relatively cohesive party structure and immense material resources provided Yanukovych with critical capacity to transcend the presidency's relatively weak formal powers in early 2010 and seize control over both the legislature and executive. Flush from its electoral victory, the party attracted the support of about 260 deputies to oust Tymoshenko as prime minister.[279] Key politicians such as Volodymyr Lytvyn, the head of parliament under Kuchma, "put their eggs in Yanukovych's basket," and numerous Tymoshenko supporters defected to the Party of Regions.[280] Then, in a "critically important decision," the party pushed through a change in parliamentary rules that permitted a majority to be made up of deputies rather than factions— thereby allowing the party to poach deputies from opposition groups.[281] "Not losing any time," the legislature voted Party of Regions stalwart Mykola Azarov in as prime minister—the same Azarov who had helped to build Kuchma's authoritarian state in the late 1990s.[282] In stark contrast to Tymoshenko, the Orange coalition's first prime minister in 2005, Azarov was in the same party as the president and too unpopular to be a political threat.

With a rare level of coordination between prime minister and president, and a "stable majority" that had never existed under Kuchma, parliament became "a branch of the presidential administration" even *before* the subsequent reversal of the 2004 constitution.[283] In just 40 minutes in April 2010, the legislature approved a highly controversial agreement with Russia extending Russia's lease over the Black Sea Fleet.[284] The legislature then rapidly passed a series of laws that facilitated the Party's concentration of power. In just ten minutes, the legislature liquidated rayon councils in Kiev that "hit the opposition hard" in the capital.[285] It later pushed through a return to a mixed proportional, majoritarian system of electing the legislature—a system that greatly benefitted the Party with its local patronage machines.[286]

Critically, the Party was able to use its dominance of the legislature to cow the courts to a degree that was impossible under Yushchenko. In the summer of 2010 (before the reversal of constitutional reforms), the Party adopted "major revisions" to the Law on the Judiciary that amounted to an "institutional attack" on the Supreme Court and that created a new High Court for Civil and Criminal Cases, which was then filled with pro-Party cronies.[287] By the fall of 2010, five of the Constitutional Court's anti-Yanukovych justices had been forced out, while the rest either supported the Party or were intimidated into submission.[288] Judicial subordination was almost certainly facilitated by the radical shift in the perceptions of the balance of power, which often influence judicial decision making in authoritarian regimes.[289] In stark contrast to the Yushchenko era, judges now "knew whom to be afraid of" and were remarkably compliant.[290] By late 2011, the party had successfully removed "the last [judge] in power not allied with president."[291]

Subordination of the judiciary greatly enhanced Yanukovych's capacity to monopolize political control. Such dominance likely facilitated the regime's highly controversial prosecution of Tymoshenko.[292] And perhaps most importantly, control over the courts helped Yanukovych to quickly reverse the constitutional reform of 2004. Under Yanukovych's thumb, judges bluntly cut through a morass of legal problems standing in the way of constitutional reform and voted overwhelmingly in late September 2010 for a return to the 1996 constitution.[293] Yanukovych's government and a "loyal" parliament quickly sponsored and passed legislation to make these changes effective.[294]

Euromaidan, Yanukovych's Fall, and Ukraine's Descent into Violent Conflict

Then, in the space of just five months between December 2013 and April 2014, Ukraine was transformed from a peaceful, stable, and seemingly consolidated authoritarian regime to a country with a new president wracked by war. At one level, this outcome constituted a highly unpredictable "Black Swan" event that was heavily shaped by a range of contingent choices. At the same time, key factors stressed in this book—Ukraine's national divide and the limits of the country's authoritarian state power—provide a necessary (if hardly sufficient) explanation for the downfall of Yanukovych and Ukraine's slide into chaos. The same factors that promoted pluralism and hampered Yanukovych's consolidation of authoritarian rule also helped spark violent conflict.

In late 2013, Yanukovych was in a fairly strong position. While zero economic growth in 2013 had damaged his popularity, Yanukovych retained a majority of the legislature and faced a weak and divided opposition. His major challenger, Tymoshenko, was in jail and seemed there to stay. However, trouble began on November 21, when Yanukovych unexpectedly shifted course and announced his decision to refrain from signing an association agreement with the European Union that had been negotiated over several years—a decision that came as a surprise even to many within the Party of Regions.[295] Within days, "Euromaidan" demonstrations on the central square (*maidan*) in Kyiv increased from about a thousand on November 22 to about 100,000 on November 24.[296]

From the beginning, the government was hampered in its ability to respond to the protests. Thus, the regime failed to shut off the electricity on the main square—apparently to avoid disrupting business in high-end stores nearby. Surprisingly, several major television stations, including 1+1, covered the protests in a balanced manner. To be sure, significant and often brutal low-intensity coercion later took place (including several reported kidnappings and vigilante assaults on activists). However, for the first two months, public assaults on protesters were infrequent (though sometimes bloody), inconsistent, and sporadic. This "staccato repression" was precisely the kind typically thought to encourage greater mobilization.[297]

Indeed, while Yanukovych's regime was well funded and better organized than any that had existed since independence, it still lacked the kind of ideological or pervasive familial ties that could engender the intra-elite trust necessary for sustained, large-scale violence in the face a well-mobilized opposition. Instead, the regime was backed by oligarchs willing to support Yanukovych only as long as there were no viable alternatives but unlikely to stick their necks out to save the regime.

The first serious effort at coercion took place in the early morning of November 30, when police attacked about 80 protesters in an effort to clear out the Maidan.[298] Yet the government promptly backed off. While no one was killed, Yanukovych and other top regime officials immediately distanced themselves from these actions. Yanukovych claimed he was "deeply disturbed" by the attacks and demanded an investigation, while Azarov apologized for the actions.[299] Two prominent members of the ruling faction—David Zhvania and Inna Bohoslovska—defected; Yanukovych's chief of staff, Serhiy Lyovochkin, threatened to resign.[300] The crackdown stimulated more intense protest. What had been a relatively modest protest camp on the Maidan[301] suddenly became much larger as tens of thousands, "fuel[ed] by rage," protested on Sunday.[302] After that, surveys of protesters in December showed that protesters were united by the failure to join Europe (54 percent) but even more by the police beatings on November 30 (70 percent).[303]

These demonstrations were also bolstered by Ukraine's regional divide. Yanukovych had come into power as an extremely pro-Russian candidate—agreeing immediately to extend Russian Black Sea Fleet access to Crimea. Both his refusal to further European integration and his very public (if limited) assault on protesters tapped into Ukrainophile identity. Deputies from the nationalist Svoboda Party, which captured 38 seats and 10 percent of the vote in the 2012 parliamentary elections, offered important leadership on the ground in December. Svoboda was arguably the most active political party in the protest.[304] They controlled the Kyiv city administration building and initially provided the opposition with its most "fearsome demonstrators," who "led some of the more provocative efforts to occupy buildings and block government offices."[305] Nationalist symbols, including portraits of the World War II anti-Soviet leader Stepan Bandera and the red and black flag of the Organization of Ukrainian Nationalists proliferated. Although these symbols alienated Russophile Ukrainians, they likely inspired numerous Ukrainophile activists. Indeed, while initially about half of the protesters in Kyiv were from the capital, western Ukrainians (representing 20 percent of the population) accounted for about half of the protesters in Kyiv by late January.[306] Across the country, a disproportionate share of protests were concentrated in western Ukraine.[307] According to one survey, 53 percent of western Ukrainians participated in the protests as compared to 17 percent of central Ukrainians and 2–4 percent of southern and eastern Ukrainians.[308]

Yet by late December, protest momentum seemed to die down. As Western countries had begun to lose interest, a promised infusion of Russian financial assistance of $15 billion bolstered perceptions of Yanukovych's strength. In stark contrast to the Orange Revolution, there appeared no plausible short-term route to power for the opposition—outside of the already-scheduled 2015 presidential election two years away.[309] The opposition's fragmentation between three small parties, its weak chances of success, and a highly disciplined ruling party discouraged open defection from the regime.[310] If Yanukovych had simply avoided provoking the protesters, the demonstrations might have died out of their own accord.

However, Yanukovych again overplayed his hand—using his parliamentary majority to force through a series of "dictatorship" laws on January 16 that appeared to forbid any form of protest. But this again generated even more protest. In mid-January, Kyiv saw its first serious violence. Right Sector, a radical nationalist group created at the start of the protests, responded by violently attacking the police with Molotov cocktails and burning tires. The group, which saw Svoboda as too "liberal and conformist," quickly rose in prominence and actively organized violent measures against the regime.[311] Simultaneously, in late January and early February, protesters seized provincial administration offices throughout western Ukraine[312] and several provinces in central Ukraine.[313] But again the regime responded inconsistently. In response to the unrest, the regime did not intensify coercion but chose to back down. The Party of Regions agreed to partly rescind the autocratic January 16 laws, and Yanukovych's loyalist prime minister, Azarov, resigned.

Up to this point, Yanukovych's regime still remained intact. The top leadership of the security services (SBU) and the Ministry of Interior (although not the military) appeared loyal.[314] Simultaneously, the Party of Regions had managed to limit outright defections to a few individuals. The regime did not witness anything like the flood of early defections suffered by Kuchma in the first days of the Orange Revolution.

Then, quite suddenly, the Yanukovych regime collapsed. On February 18, violent protests erupted in reaction to parliament's refusal to consider curbs on Yanukovych's power. The regime responded with a concerted attack on the Maidan, and it was widely expected that the government would successfully clear the square.[315] But the flood gates burst after February 19–20, when the government apparently made the fateful decision to do something that no leader in post-Soviet Ukraine had ever done: order security personnel to kill protesters in public. On February 20, snipers fired on protesters in broad daylight in the centre of Kyiv, killing about 70 people[316]—a clear example of high-intensity coercion that set in motion the stunningly rapid collapse of the regime. Early in the afternoon, as violence was raging on the streets, Tyhypko called on the legislature to elect a new head of parliament from the opposition. A group of government allies, shocked by the bloodshed, beseeched the armed forces to disobey "criminal orders" to shoot people and demanded an emergency session of the legislature.[317] Decrying the violence as a "tragedy of all the Ukrainian people," the mayor of Kyiv resigned from the Party.[318] In response to government attacks, the U.S. and European powers announced a range of sanctions targeted at high-level members of the Yanukovych regime involved in the crackdown. Regime supporters began to flee the country in droves.[319]

Increasing cracks emerged in the authoritarian state. Police and security divisions from various parts of western Ukraine announced their support for the protesters, and about a hundred arrived the next morning from Lviv to defend the Maidan against government attack.[320] Security forces were "thrown into panic" by rumours that a large cache of weapons seized by protesters in Lviv were on their way to the capital.[321] The Kyiv metro, as well as a number of trains and bridges that had been blocked to prevent protesters from coming to the demonstration were now allowed to operate.[322] The authoritarian state ceased to function in significant parts of the country. Then, in the first clear indication that the ruling Party had lost its parliamentary majority, 236 deputies (including at least 34 from the Party of Regions) voted to end the violence against protesters in the capital, while a majority voted to remain in session until the crisis was resolved.[323] Volodymyr Rybak, pro-government the head of parliament, reportedly sent his family to Budapest.[324]

That night Yanukovych met to negotiate with opposition leaders and representatives of France, Germany, Poland, and Russia. At noon on Friday, February 21, Yanukovych and opposition leaders announced a major deal whereby Yanukovych agreed to early elections at the end of 2014 and to a reversion to the 2004 constitution within 48 hours. But then the authoritarian state dissolved in plain sight. According to Radoslaw Sikorski, the Polish foreign minister, "Within minutes of us signing the agreement, the protection, the security forces, started leaving the vicinity of the presidential palace, which they didn't need to do, and the decompression of the regime started very quickly."[325] According to one opposition leader, about 800 of 1,100 police guarding the presidential administration defected.[326]

From the moment it was announced, the agreement between Yanukovych and the opposition was doomed. The agreement was highly unpopular among protesters, who booed opposition leaders when they attempted to explain it. Right Sector, among others, announced that it would continue their actions until Yanukovych resigned.[327] Then in the late afternoon, parliament voted to reinstitute the 2004 constitutional changes, while large sections of the Party of Regions essentially went over to the opposition—contributing to significant majorities for a range of anti-Yanukovych actions, including the freeing of Yulia Tymoshenko and the firing of the minister of interior and close Yanukovych associate, Vitalii Zakharchenko.[328] By early evening on Friday, at least 40 deputies were reported to have left the Party in the previous two days.[329] Just before 10:00 p.m., the SBU announced that it had ceased the anti-terror operation against protesters that had been announced on February 19.[330] Then, at 10:40 p.m., Yanukovych fled Kyiv, leaving his large mansion outside the capital unguarded.[331] The next day, parliament voted to dismiss Yanukovych and elected Oleksandr Turchynov, Tymoshenko's close ally, as parliamentary chair and acting president. For the first time since independence, Ukraine experienced a leadership turnover completely outside the electoral process. Power was not transferred. It dissolved.

In turn, large sections of the Ukrainian state collapsed. Police and special forces "disappeared from the streets." The new authorities in Kyiv lacked any effective means of imposing order—outsourcing security functions to local oligarchs and opposition paramilitaries.[332]

Having suddenly come to power on the backs of protests in Kyiv, opposition leaders worried most about responding to the demands of activists on the Maidan. Thus, the new cabinet included no pro-Russian leaders and was presented before the protesters for "approval." The nationalist (and electorally marginal) Svoboda Party was given five posts in the cabinet—including the powerful Ministry of Defense and the Procuracy.

The problem was that the protests were not, in fact, supported by a clear majority of Ukrainians. Just under 50 percent supported the protests in February—with support starkly divided between east and west.[333] While those in western and central Ukraine saw the events as a democratic revolution, half of the population in the south and east—and 70 percent of Donetsk and Luhansk—viewed the new government as illegal.[334] Opposition to the new government in the east was far higher than it had been following Yushchenko's accession to power in 2005.

This hardly made the subsequent fragmentation of Ukraine and descent into war inevitable. Absent Putin's extraordinarily aggressive behavior following Yanukovych's exit, Ukraine would almost certainly have ridden out the transition in a peaceful manner. However, Yanukovych's sudden disappearance, state collapse, and transfer of power to leaders that were widely viewed as illegitimate in the east created an opening for Putin. The wide use of highly polarizing Ukrainian nationalist symbols in the demonstrations (including the black and red flags and portraits of Bandera) made it easy for Russian media to plausibly (but incorrectly) portray the new government as fascist. In fact, the new government was quite moderate—agreeing to keep a pro–Russian language law passed by Yanukovych, publicly committing to decentralization, and promising not to seek NATO membership. But these moderate steps were easily drowned out by widely proliferated images of nationalist violence and polarizing WWII-era symbols.

In March, Putin's government forcibly annexed Crimea. Then in late March and early April, separatist militias began seizing government buildings in Donetsk and Luhansk. By April, these two regions descended into chaos. At the end of May, voters overwhelmingly chose a new president, Petro Poroshenko, in an election that was widely seen as free but that occurred without the participation of voters in Crimea, Donetsk, and Luhansk, representing almost 20 percent of the electorate. Ukraine had nearly transitioned to democracy but had not survived as a single country.

In sum, Ukraine's national divide and the state's limited authoritarian power contributed to both the fall of autocracy and Ukraine's descent into violent conflict. These two factors were critical to Yanukovych's downfall. Yanukovych's aggressively pro-Russian behavior and sudden refusal to sign the European Association Agreement stoked Ukrainophile mobilization in Kyiv and western Ukraine. While divisions in Ukraine did not make the protests inevitable (after all, few protests occurred in response to Yanukovych's earlier controversial agreement with Russia on the Black Sea Fleet), they almost certainly made the protests more likely and much more powerful than they would have been otherwise. Ukrainophile activists disproportionately from western Ukraine also provided the protests' most committed activists—helping to prevent the demonstrations from petering out. Indeed, a disproportionate share of protesters who died in Kyiv during the crisis came from western Ukraine.[335] Strong regional opposition to Yanukovych also led to the breakdown of Yanukovych's authoritarian state in western Ukraine. Even if Yanukovych had managed to put down protesters in Kyiv, he would almost certainly have lost half the country. Thus, while many democratically minded activists in the capital played a key role in the crisis, it is hard to imagine that the protests would have succeeded without committed support from western Ukraine. Indeed, this regional dimension most clearly separates Ukraine from countries like Belarus or Russia, where authoritarian rule has been more stable.

Simultaneously, Yanukovych's party and state, while more robust than those of previous Ukrainian incumbents, lacked the cohesion to carry out highly visible and risky acts of repression that attract international and domestic sanctions. As discussed in chapter 1, such high-intensity violence creates risks for a regime's allies, who may not want to take responsibility for its illegal actions. Given Yanukovych's almost sole reliance on patronage, many within the ruling coalition—especially those outside a tiny core of Yanukovych relatives (the "family")—tended to be risk averse. United mainly by their desire to make money and enjoy the fruits of their corruption, most regime supporters were not willing to risk their vacation homes in Europe or the United States—much less jail time—so that Yanukovych could hang on. As a result, they were reluctant to support aggressive and public repression—retreating after attempts to crack down generated a public backlash in late November and again in mid-

January. While the absence of clear alternatives and party discipline kept the president's allies in line for three and a half months of crisis, the government's unprecedented step of shooting protesters in broad daylight radically increased the costs of loyalty, motivating open defection. Within 24 hours, Yanukovych's party and state disintegrated before the world, forcing him to flee.

At the same time, these same national divisions and limited authoritarian power created a critical opening for violent conflict. By feeding polarization, national divisions—stimulated by Yanukovych's aggressive behavior—discouraged activists from accepting the brokered agreement on February 21 that would end up being the last chance for a negotiated transition. Divisions also encouraged activists to use an array of symbols inimical to half the country and made it extremely easy for Putin to tag the new power structure as fascist (something that Kuchma and Putin failed to do against Yushchenko in 2004). Most importantly, Yanukovych's sudden exit created a power vacuum, destroyed the state, and damaged legitimacy in the east—creating an opportunity for Putin to sow unrest. Feeling threatened by a new government in Kyiv widely perceived to be illegitimate, the population and local power structures in Donbas did little to counter aggression by pro-Russian militias. The result was violent state collapse.

Conclusion: Pluralism by Default in Ukraine

This chapter has sought to explain two puzzles. First, why, despite Ukraine's weak democratic prerequisites—historically impotent civil society, high concentration of economic assets, weak rule of law, and relative international isolation—did Ukraine maintain the most democratic polity in the CIS over the last quarter century? Even at its most authoritarian under Kuchma and Yanukovych, Ukraine was significantly more open than Lukashenka's Belarus or Putin's Russia. Second, what explains Ukraine's notable variation over time: greater pluralism under Kravchuk and Yushchenko and less democracy under Kuchma and Yanukovych? In a nutshell, I have argued that changes in organizational capacity best account for shifts in pluralism over time, while national divisions best explain Ukraine's greater pluralism relative to other post-Soviet cases.

National divisions and state and party weakness—factors typically thought to undermine democracy—were central to Ukraine's dynamic and competitive trajectory. Ukraine's persistent pluralism was created less by institutional design or a vibrant civil society, and more by opportunistic oligarchs and government officials who lacked the mutual trust and organization to collude successfully. Party and state weakness hindered attempts to repress opposition, manipulate elections, and maintain elite cohesion; while national polarization bolstered opposition mobilization and impeded collusion among political elites. This is not to deny the bravery of many genuinely democratic activists. However, absent incumbent disorganization and national division, such leaders would have likely faced the same fate as their numerous counterparts in Belarus, Russia, and other post-Soviet states.

The story of Ukraine's political evolution begins in 1988 with Gorbachev's decision to weaken the Soviet Communist Party—a move that created a critical opening to national dissidents in western Ukraine. Demands for cultural rights led to the "rapid politicization of the Ukrainian-speaking population" and split the Ukrainian Communist Party.[336] Such nationalist mobilization quickly led to a breakdown of the authoritarian state in western Ukraine that would have required massive coercive capacity to reverse. In the wake of the failed Soviet coup of 1991, Kravchuk rode a wave of anticommunism by destroying the Party and pushing for the destruction of the Soviet state. These events represented the political "big bang" that created the basis for pluralism by default in Ukraine over the next quarter century.

The sudden dissolution of Ukraine's party-state would have created significant challenges for any leader. In the institutional void that existed in the former Soviet Union in the early 1990s, strengthening the state and rebuilding patronage networks necessarily involved some amount of time. However, Kravchuk's background—his lack of any regional networks and the destruction of the Party where he had spent his entire career and had his strongest ties—meant that Kravchuk rode to power almost solely on the fleeting strength of his popularity. Lacking a strong state and any political party or party substitute, Kravchuk was unable to control a parliament dominated by a close ally, suppress opposition, or manipulate elections—despite his widely acclaimed political skills. In the wake of a wave of strikes in eastern Ukraine against Kravchuk's anti-Russian policies, Kravchuk lost power to his former prime minister, Kuchma—even though Kuchma had been in charge of the economy during its worst crisis. Ukraine's first electoral turnover occurred not because democratic institutions were particularly strong or Ukraine's leaders particularly democratic but because the state and ruling party were too weak to monopolize control.

Then, building in part on regional and economic networks he had maintained from the Soviet period and the creation of a system of competing oligarchic parties, Kuchma secured greater control over parliament and created a state that had far greater capacity to repress dissent and carry out electoral fraud than had existed under Kravchuk. Yet, by distributing organizational and economic resources to a wide range of officials with few stakes in his survival, Kuchma undermined his ability to control his coalition and made it easier for allies to defect when the going got tough. Thus, despite unprecedented economic growth and access to substantial material resources, Kuchma's regime fell after opposition consisting of former allies mobilized Ukrainophile supporters in massive demonstrations that culminated in the Orange Revolution in late 2004. At the same time, opposition, faced with significant support for the old regime in eastern Ukraine, was forced to agree to constitutional reforms that weakened the presidency.

In turn, the Orange coalition, which came to power divided between two political heavyweights—Yushchenko and Tymoshenko—who split support in the west and were too fragmented to suppress Yanukovych's political machine. Political divisions also made it much more difficult to reverse the constitutional reform of 2004. The result was highly democratic but equally dysfunctional rule.

Then, with strong support in eastern Ukraine, Yanukovych won the 2010 presidential elections. Supported by Ukraine's "first party in power" that dominated both the presidency and the legislature (as well as some of Ukraine's richest oligarchs), Yanukovych was able to concentrate political control to a much greater degree than in the Yushchenko era.[337] But the regime still had significant vulnerabilities. First, Ukraine's divided identity made the strongly Russophile Yanukovych susceptible to Ukrainophile mobilization. His sudden decision to withdraw from negotiations over the European Association Agreement—seemingly part of an attempt to build a Lukashenka-style Russian-backed regime—generated a massive popular backlash. Second, Yanukovych's authoritarian state—while relatively well-funded and organized—lacked the nonmaterial sources of cohesion necessary to carry out consistent and sustained high-intensity repression. As a result, the regime collapsed in late February 2014.

This analysis has important implications for how we understand political transitions. The factors facilitating pluralism have been deeply intertwined with those that have created dysfunction and corruption in Ukraine. Parliamentary immunity, which protected corrupt oligarchs from criminal accountability,[338] also provided key protection to opposition leaders in the late 1990s and early

2000s. Political paralysis created by party fragmentation and polarization repeatedly undermined reform efforts throughout Ukraine's period of independence but also made it more difficult for incumbents to monopolize political control. Polarization and incumbent weakness both damaged governance and promoted pluralism by default—a fact that was tragically manifested in early 2014 when Ukraine got rid of an autocrat but descended into violent conflict.

The 2014 crisis altered key variables in this analysis that likely affected the future of pluralism. First, as indicated above, the crisis severely undermined organizational capacity, dramatically weakening state power. The new president, Petro Poroshenko, came to power backed by a loose coalition of parties and personalities. (His party at the time of his election was referred to as a "myth with no website, unknown phone numbers, and nonexisting addresses."[339]) At the same time, the crisis reduced the salience of regional cleavages within what was left of Ukraine. The exit of Crimea and the Donbas resulted in the departure of a highly Russophile 20 percent of Ukraine's electorate. War with Russia also made it substantially harder for politicians to mobilize Russophile support. The pro-Russian population in 2014 was demoralized, weakly organized, and substantially smaller—all of which seemed to augur the rise of a dominant Ukrainophile identity. Indeed, presidential and parliamentary electoral results in 2014 reflected far less significant regional divisions than in the past—in part because many in the east refrained from voting.[340]

Such changes had potentially contradictory implications for Ukrainian democracy. On the one hand, changes in identity seemed to create new opportunities to undermine pluralism. The combination of war and a more unified Ukrainian identity allowed leaders to exploit nationalism to unite the population around a common threat, discourage opposition, and justify repression. Indeed, Poroshenko used the conflict to threaten the imposition of martial law in early 2015.[341] War with Russia also made it harder for Russophile forces to mount a serious bid for power within Ukraine. At the same time, Ukraine's fragmented state and weak ruling party created obstacles for any leader to consolidate control—undermining efforts to prevent defections and crack down on dissent. Simultaneously, war with Russia significantly heightened Ukraine's dependence on Western support—a fact that likely created a check on any authoritarian behavior by the Ukrainian government. Such factors seemed to augur the persistence of Ukrainian pluralism. Indeed, as we see in the next chapter, such vulnerability to Western pressure bolstered democracy in Moldova.

4

Pluralism by Default in Moldova

"Nothing is coordinated in this country."

PETRU LUCINSCHI, PRESIDENT OF MOLDOVA 1996–2000

Moldova represents one of the most puzzling cases of persistent pluralism in the postcommunist world. A poor and rural country, wracked by ethnic tensions and with no serious dissident movement or democratic history, Moldova had a weak civil society and "stood out as a backwater within the Soviet system" when it emerged as an independent state in 1991.[1] Moldova initially seemed destined for dictatorship. Yet after the Soviet collapse, Moldova was one of the most democratic countries in the CIS. Elections were mostly free, and incumbents confronted enormous difficulties controlling the legislature, opposition, and the media. Between 1992 and 2014, Moldova experienced three turnovers in power—in 1996, 2001, and 2009. During that time, presidents were held in check by a powerful parliament and Constitutional Court. Even the more authoritarian Communist Party of Moldova (PCRM) (2001–2009) was "noticeably more pluralist" than other governments in the former Soviet Union.[2]

What explains Moldova's democratic success? It is not that Moldova had particularly tolerant leaders. Even "democratic" politicians like Moldova' first president, Mircea Snegur (1991–1996), and the subsequent Alliance for European Integration (AEI) (2009–2013) sought to shut down opposition media and exclude opposition from elections.[3] Moreover, few argue that the PCRM, with its pro-Russian, Communist ideology, was particularly democratic. A stronger argument can be made for the importance of institutional design, which had a clear and important impact in 2009. Yet design offers little explanation of Moldova's overall democratic trajectory. After all, given that almost all of Moldova's leaders sought to concentrate executive power, focusing on constitutional rules simply begs the question of why they failed.

Instead, Moldova, like Ukraine, provides a clear illustration of the ways in which weak organization and divided national identity facilitated pluralism in the post–Cold War era. A combination of party weakness, state collapse, and deep national divisions heightened vulnerability to Western democratizing pressure and generated political chaos that no single side could control (table 4.1). Moldova's "bipolar" society did not simply "complicate" democratization but was instead a wellspring of political dynamism and competition that has distinguished Moldova from most of its post-Soviet counterparts.[4]

National Identity

Moldova's "cleft,"[5] "confused,"[6] and "bipolar"[7] national identity was divided between Russophile and more pro-European, Romanianist identities. This division had its origins in Moldovan history. Most of present-day Moldova (known then as Bessarabia) was annexed by Russia after the 1806–1812 Russo-Turkish war but taken over by Romania during the 1920s. Romanian rule witnessed a steep increase in literacy and the rapid growth of pro-Romanian and anti-Russian identity.[8] In response to Romanian efforts, the Soviet regime created the Moldavian Autonomous Republic (now Transnistria) just east of the Bessarabian border, which retained a significant Slavic population and was untouched by Romanianization efforts.[9] After World War II, Bessarabia was re-incorporated into the Soviet Union and united with the Moldavian republic to create a single Moldavian Union Republic—with the eastern Transnistria region that had always been under Russian/Soviet control and a western region previously governed by Romania. Fearful of Romanian claims on Moldovan territory, Soviet authorities engaged in an active effort to promote a separate "Moldovan" identity distinct from Romanian. The Latin alphabet, which had been introduced after World War I, was abandoned and replaced by Cyrillic. At the same time, the Russian language was heavily privileged in the media, schools, and bookstores.[10] Russian language came to be viewed as essential for upward mobility.[11] By the 1980s, Moldovan speakers felt disadvantaged in competition for skilled employment and housing due to perceived preferences for Russian speakers. As a result, the language issue became a "particularly sensitive problem" in the late Soviet era.[12] With Moldovan speakers representing about 65 percent of the population, such resentment became the source of a powerful anti-incumbent identity in the late 1980s.

Table 4.1   Regime Closure, Identity, and Organizational Capacity in Moldova 1992–2014

	National identity	Party	Party and state capacity		
			State coercive capacity	State economic control	Overall capacity score
Snegur (1991–1996)	High split	Low	Low	Med-low	Low
Lucinschi (1996–2000)	High split	Med-low	Med-low	Medium	Med-low
PCRM (2001–2009)	High split	Medium	Med-low	Medium	Medium
AEI (2009–)	High split	Low	Med-low	Medium	Med-low

Note: For coding rules, see appendix A.

In the early 1990s, conflicts over language and national identity provoked a brief civil war that resulted in the de facto independence of Transnistria. Because the exit of Transnistria eliminated large numbers opposed to separation from the Soviet Union, the war created a stable "right-bank consensus" around the necessity of Moldovan independence from both Russia and Romania.[13] Nevertheless, the country retained a "deep"[14] divide over Moldova's geopolitical orientation—with about a third supporting closer ties to Russia, a third opposed to Russia, and a third who were neutral.[15] Moldova's leaders were "equally split" over whether to pursue pro-European or a pro-Russian policies, and "the identity question remained one of the few clear ideological issues that distinguished one party from another."[16]

Ultimately, as in Ukraine, this divided identity facilitated Moldovan pluralism in three ways. First, in the late 1980s, identity issues stimulated massive mobilization and counter-mobilization that pushed the Communist Party aside and contributed to the dismantling of the old authoritarian state. Conflicts in the early 1990s helped to gut the coercive apparatus in a way that fundamentally hampered the consolidation of authoritarian rule. Subsequently, divisions over Moldova's geopolitical orientation provided relatively stable bases for competing parties in the 1990s and 2000s. Second, as in Ukraine, identity polarization created a barrier to collusion across identity lines. In particular, polarization bolstered opposition unity in 2009 in the face of enormous pressures by the ruling Communist Party to coopt a single opposition vote in parliament that would have allowed the PCRM to retain the presidency.

		Regime closure		
Electoral manipulation	Media control	Presidential power over parliament	Opposition subordination	Overall regime closure
Low	Low	Low	Low	Low
Low	Low	Low	Low	Low
Low	Medium	High	Medium	Medium
Low	Medium	Low	Low	Low

Third, civil war, which emerged from Moldova's divided identity, created enduring tensions between Moldova and Russia that increased Moldova's vulnerability to Western pressure. The legacies of this conflict made it very hard for Moldovan incumbents to garner the kind of large-scale Russian black knight support[17] that (as we see in chapter 5) largely immunized Belarus from Western sanctions. Confronted with persistent Russian hostility, Moldovan leaders remained highly dependent on Western support and thus extraordinarily vulnerable to Western democratizing pressure. As a result, authoritarian behavior was curbed to a greater extent than in most other CIS countries.

Party and State Strength

Ruling party and state strength was extremely low after 1989. Petru Lucinschi, who took over as Moldovan Communist Party leader in 1989, reduced the Party's Central Committee nomenklatura fourfold and actively discouraged local leaders from defending their power and prerogatives.[18] Party discipline collapsed.[19] Then, following the failed Soviet coup in August 1991, the Party disappeared—its assets were seized, press was banned, and presence in the workplace was forbidden.[20] For the next decade, presidents were unable or unwilling to create a new ruling party to replace the old—resulting in a string of short-lived, weak, and "embryonic" parties.[21] Moldova's first president, Mircea Snegur (1991–1996), maintained only tenuous relations to parties throughout his tenure. In early 1990, he established an alliance with the Moldovan Popular Front, "a collection of disparate and frequently incoherent organizations" that had been created to support Soviet reform in 1989.[22] In the 1990 republican legislative elections, the Front garnered an estimated 145 of 380 seats—but it was quickly abandoned by 80 percent of those supporters by the end of 1991.[23] Subsequently, Snegur supported the Agrarian Democratic Party (ADP), an alliance of agricultural directors created to counter the Front in 1991.[24] The ADP, a non-ideological "collection of regional fiefdoms and personal cliques," lacked a developed organization or established identity.[25] In 1994, the party gained a majority 56 of 104 seats in parliament, but it began to fragment within just over a year. In 1998, the ADP disappeared after it was unable to cross the four-percent threshold in parliamentary elections.

In turn, the former Party leader, President Lucinschi (1997–2001), fearing the rise of a competitor, tried to prevent the institutionalization of any single political faction. While he was backed by a pro-government Bloc for a Democratic and Prosperous Moldova (BDPM), the president divided his support among competing pro-presidential parties and groups.[26] As one former ally remarked, "Lucinschi liked to break up any group—whether it backed the president or not—that was becoming too powerful."[27] By contrast, the Communist Party (2001–2009), founded in 1993 as a successor to the Soviet Moldovan Communist Party, drew the support of many hardline communists and had a far more extensive and institutionalized party structure than had existed in Moldova since independence.[28] Finally, the Alliance for European Integration (AEI)/Pro European Coalition (2009–)—loose coalitions of different anti-communist parties—governed Moldova in various guises from 2009 through the early 2010s.

At the same time, the Moldovan state was extremely weak. In the early 1990s, the country's armed forces consisted of "lightly armed" and underpaid policemen, a "hastily assembled" army, and nationalist volunteers with farm implements who were mobilized to fight separatists in the eastern region of Transnistria.[29] Moldovan nationalists were "successful at destroying much of the authoritarian state apparatus" after the Russian-dominated KGB apparatus largely deserted western Moldova during the conflict with Transnistria.[30] Discipline was also compromised by large-scale wage arrears and pervasive low morale.[31] While the situation improved after the country's brief civil war in Transnistria in 1992, the military remained under-equipped, with a smaller number of troops than most other post-Soviet armies.[32] The security forces continued to be "extremely poorly funded,"[33] and per capita military expenditure was the lowest in Europe.[34] Finally, authoritarian state power was undermined in the 1990s by a move away from state ownership in the economy. First Snegur and then Lucinschi undertook significant privatization, and the non-state sector increased from 10 to 50 percent of GDP between 1992 and 1998.[35]

Pluralism by Default in Moldova, 1989–2000

After the collapse of the Soviet Union, Moldova hovered on the border between democracy and competitive authoritarianism. The 1990s were characterized by relatively free elections, a high degree of media pluralism, weak presidential power, and strong opposition. After independence, electoral manipulation was low. While President Snegur was the only candidate in the December 1991 presidential election,[36] Moldova witnessed little serious electoral manipulation in the years that followed.[37] Next, despite its vulnerability to government interference, media pluralism was "highly developed in Moldova."[38] For example, in the 1996 presidential elections, state TV and the country's two major newspapers were actually biased *against* the incumbent Snegur.[39] Next, the president, widely seen as a "decorative figure,"[40] had little power over the legislature in the 1990s. In 1994, for example, Snegur was powerless in the face of efforts by parliament to create a semi-presidential system with a weak presidency—even though his own allies in the ADP dominated parliament. Snegur was also forced to cede control over key institutions—including state media and the Ministry of Defense—to the legislature.[41] Then in 2000, parliament reacted to efforts by President Lucinschi to create a stronger presidency by voting to eliminate the post of a popularly elected president altogether.

The great irony of Moldova's trajectory is that many of the same factors typically seen as sources of democratic failure—a weak party and state, splits in national identity—were in fact central to understanding the emergence and persistence of pluralism. Weak organizational capacity promoted elite defection and undercut efforts to crack down on opposition. Simultaneously, splits in identity facilitated opposition mobilization and—perhaps most importantly—made Moldova extremely susceptible to Western democratizing pressure.

Pluralism in Moldova emerged out of identity conflicts in the late 1980s. While initially opposition groups refrained from articulating nationalist demands, activists quickly realized that such calls could mobilize significant support, and they began calling for Moldovan (Romanian) language rights.[42] By mid-1989, opposition leaders demanded increased use of Moldovan in higher education, state-language status for Moldovan, and the reintroduction of the Latin alphabet.[43] In turn, popular discontent over language policy "galvanized political opposition" and "provided a substantially more viable vehicle for popular mobilization" than earlier demands focusing solely on democratization and reform.[44] From January to March 1989, protest increased "dramatically" as thousands came onto the streets calling for an end to "colonization" and brought business in central Chişinău to a standstill several times throughout the winter and spring.[45] In late August 1989, the Popular Front organized a "Grand National Assembly" demonstration of up to 500,000 in support of language reform that helped convince Mircea Snegur, then chair of the Moldovan Supreme Soviet, to introduce a law making Moldovan the official language of the republic.[46]

Nationalist-inspired mobilization also facilitated the ouster of Moldova's conservative Party First Secretary Semyon Grossu, the last republican leader appointed by Brezhnev.[47] On November 10, 1989, crowds of Popular Front supporters armed with rocks and Molotov cocktails attacked the Ministry of Interior demanding the release of activists who had been detained several days earlier.[48] In the wake of these riots, Grossu was replaced by Petru Lucinschi, a more liberal member of the Soviet Central Committee.[49] Under Lucinschi's tutelage, the Party sought accommodation with the opposition and began to reorient itself to the introduction of a multiparty system.[50]

Yet Lucinschi's efforts to revitalize the Party were quickly outpaced by events that spun out of the Party's control. In February 1990 legislative elections, the Popular Front "soundly defeated" numerous Communist candidates and formed a governing alliance with Snegur and his supporters.[51] A Front leader, Mircea Druc, was made prime minister. In turn, Snegur's alliance with the Front allowed him to ignore the Communist Party, which was transformed into a fragmented "opposition party" without a coherent program.[52] The government eliminated "Soviet Socialist" from the name of the republic and exempted Moldovans from the Soviet military draft.[53] Druc began a campaign to "nationalize" the education system, initiated a purge of non-Moldovans from cultural institutions, and began to press for Moldova's unification with Romania.[54]

At the same time, the Front's support for unification with Romania and its aggressively anti-Russian rhetoric contributed to increasing polarization between Moldovans in the west and Slavic and Gagauz populations in the east and south.[55] In response to the pro-Moldovan language law passed in August 1989, strikes in the east spread to over 150 factories and shut down the country's rail system.[56] Fearing Moldovan unity with Romania, the Transnistrians and Gagauz declared their regions autonomous in September and August 1990, and Transnistrian officials "stopped taking orders from Chişinău."[57] In early 1991, parliamentary deputies from the east began boycotting parliament. Central control disintegrated as armed clashes began between Moldovan troops and Transnistrian armed units backed by Russian Cossack forces.[58] After several months of low-intensity fighting in early 1992, Transnistrians captured nearly all of the Left Bank in Eastern Moldova. "Moldovan police, outgunned and outnumbered, generally yielded without resistance."[59] In response to emerging ethnic tensions, the Russian-dominated KGB almost completely deserted western Moldova.[60]

In turn, Moscow instituted a de facto economic blockade of Moldova.[61] Acceding to nationalist pressure, Snegur declared a state of emergency in March 1992 in an attempt to disarm separatist units—but this backfired when the pro-Russian 14th army responded by distributing weapons to Transnistrians. At the end of the summer, Snegur and Yeltsin agreed to a ceasefire to a conflict that had led to 300 deaths and more than 1,000 wounded. Thrown into disarray, most of the government resigned in July.[62] The Popular Front's membership in parliament dramatically declined from about 145 to 30.

In the wake of this disaster, Snegur shifted his support to the anti-Romanian ADP, which quickly became the dominant political force in the country.[63] With Snegur's support, Andrei Sangheli, a leader in the ADP and former agriculture official, became head of a new government of "national consensus." The ADP captured 43 percent of the vote and 56 of 104 seats in the 1994 legislative elections—significantly outpacing the nationalists, who won a combined 17 percent of the vote and 20 seats. Understaffed and weakly institutionalized,[64] the parliament should have been no match for the Snegur, who commanded an extensive (if weakened) bureaucracy and sought to make Moldova a presidential republic.[65]

Yet polarization and Snegur's lack of strong party support translated into exceptionally weak control over the legislature—even over his own allies.[66] Conflict between Russophile and Romanianist forces had left Snegur almost totally isolated. On the one hand, the nationalists remained suspicious of Snegur because he refused to support unification with Romania. Thus, during the debate over the Moldovan constitution, Snegur failed to gain the backing of nationalists, who controlled about one-fifth of parliamentary seats, in his fight for greater presidential power.[67] On the other hand, the ADP distrusted Snegur because of his early association with the Front and his role in the civil war.

Thus, Snegur had few strong supporters in the ADP, which essentially dictated a constitution that maximized the power of the prime minister and the legislature.[68] The result was a constitution, passed by an overwhelming majority in the summer of 1994, that gave the president few powers compared to his counterparts in the rest of the former Soviet Union.[69]

In an effort to overcome such weakness, Snegur used older tactics from the Soviet era to assert central control. He sought to control subordinates by supporting the promotion of "his" people into key positions in the government—expecting that these officials would remain loyal to their "patron" in the future. For example, Snegur supported the nomination of Andrei Sangheli as prime minister in mid-1992 following the disastrous war over Transnistria. In the absence of a well-established party, however, such informal ties did nothing to prevent defection. Despite benefitting from Snegur's support, Sangheli challenged Snegur for the top job. The memory of this "betrayal" was still fresh nearly ten years later when I interviewed Snegur in 2002. Snegur angrily complained that the prime minister had betrayed him even though Snegur had been the one to advance his career [*"Ia ego tianul!"*].[70] Simultaneously, head of parliament Lucinschi, also a nominal ADP ally, broke away to challenge Snegur for the presidency.

Confronted by opposition from both Sangheli and Lucinschi, who were considered pro-Russian, Snegur abandoned the ADP and again shifted back to the right—securing the support of nationalists by proposing to replace the Soviet era wording "Moldovan language" with "Romanian language" in the constitution.[71] In the run-up to the 1996 election, he concluded an alliance with the Popular Front forces.[72]

By 1995, the state was torn asunder by a tug of war between the "three whales"[73]—Lucinschi, Sangheli, and Snegur—who each sought to use "their" part of the state against one another. This resulted, first, in highly contested control over coercive forces (such as they were) and made it hard for any single force to use coercion to monopolize control. For example, after Snegur attempted to fire the head of the military, General Pavel Creanga, a Snegur ally who had begun to side with Sangheli, Creanga refused to comply.[74] The army itself was split between supporters of Snegur and Sangheli,[75] and Snegur was only able to remove Creanga from his office by using "his" people in the army.[76] The conflict went to the Constitutional Court, which ruled that the president could not unilaterally dismiss the defense minister.[77] Yet parliament was also unable to dictate military policy: three years earlier the prime minister had been prevented from firing a top military official without the president's consent.[78]

Pluralism by default also extended to the media. Despite several draconian laws instituted in 1992,[79] media was quite open and independent of government control throughout the 1990s. Because many pro-Romanian intellectuals had infiltrated state media in the 1990s, state broadcasting often took an anti-Snegur slant, and "government policies [were] regularly challenged in the government media."[80] Even more importantly, Moldova's divided identity exposed the country to rival media systems favoring different incumbents. Situated between competing powers, Moldova became host to "two separate autonomous media subsystems"—one dominated by Romanianist and the other by Russophile forces[81]—that were difficult for any government to control. Thus, during the height of the civil war, the Moldovan government was unable to halt the influx of anti-Moldovan Russian press.[82] Simultaneously, Russian TV channels, still widely available in Moldova, presented events from a distinctly Russian point of view—overtly opposing Snegur in 1996.[83] Finally, Snegur was unable to control his own appointees. Thus, the head of state media, Adrian Usatii, whom Snegur had appointed in 1989, had a falling out with Snegur in 1995 and openly backed Lucinschi in the 1996 election.[84] As a result, even as an incumbent, Snegur received generally negative coverage on state television—the only television to reach many rural areas.[85]

Snegur also faced significant difficulties controlling local governments—a fact that largely precluded serious vote fraud. Instead, Prime Minister Sangheli, as head of the ADP with the most direct administrative power over regional leaders, was widely expected to use "administrative" tactics to influence the election.[86] Yet, confronted with severe splits in the ADP and opposition from both the president and the parliamentary chair, Sangheli effectively had little power. He could hardly deprive Snegur or Lucinschi of access to meeting halls, as the ADP had sometimes done to the opposition in 1994.[87] Indeed, Sangheli finished third behind Snegur and Lucinschi, who went on to the second round. Hurt by his association with pan-Romanian nationalism, Snegur then lost to Lucinschi 46 to 54 percent. As in Ukraine in 1994, Russophile opposition defeated a nationalist-backed incumbent.

In sum, a combination of incumbent weakness and intense identity polarization facilitated the destruction of Communist Party rule and fatally undermined efforts by Moldova's first president to concentrate political control or impose any kind of order—authoritarian or otherwise. In the late 1980s and early 1990s, nationalist-inspired mobilization contributed to the overthrow of the Brezhnev-era leadership, while Moldova's short and disastrous civil war led to the partial dismantling of the Russian-dominated KGB. Then, in the early 1990s, Snegur was forced to shift back and forth between Romanianist and Russophile groups—which in the end completely isolated him from any organized political force. Simultaneously, disorganization at the top deprived any political force of reliable administrative resources, creating a highly competitive and democratic political regime.

Moldova's next president, Petru Lucinschi (1997–2001), was in many ways well-placed to monopolize political control. An experienced apparatchik and former Politburo member, Lucinschi was partially successful at creating more effective authoritarian state institutions. Thus, upon taking office in 1997, he created a "Department for Organized Crime and Corruption Prevention" that was widely believed to target political opponents.[88] Simultaneously, Lucinschi's allies gained increasing control of parliament. Just after his election, many ADP deputies defected to the president,[89] and a pro-presidential party, the Bloc for a Democratic and Prosperous Moldova (BDPM) gained substantial seats in elections in 1998.[90] The elections resulted in an initially pro-presidential Alliance for Democracy and Reform (ADR), which constituted 61 of 101 seats in the legislature. On April 21, Lucinschi's close ally, Dumitru Diacov, who had worked with Lucinschi since 1995, was elected speaker of parliament.[91] Observers widely expected that "Lucinschi would be able to dominate the legislative process."[92]

Yet party weakness fundamentally undermined Lucinschi's efforts to concentrate political control. The problem was not that Lucinschi lacked sufficient allies in the legislature but that—in the absence of a well-institutionalized party—the president quickly lost control over the supporters he had. Party weakness encouraged Lucinschi to engage in divide and rule behavior that alienated those close to him. Fearing the rise of a competitor, Lucinschi dispersed support across a wide range of political organizations while preventing the concentration of power in any single group.[93] Thus, while the BDPM had been created as a pro-presidential party, Lucinschi openly promoted a number of competing groupings (the "Furnica" electoral bloc and the Social Democratic Bloc "Speranta") and independent deputies in the 1998 parliamentary elections, which his allies felt undermined the electoral chances of the BDPM.[94] Such actions, though motivated by a desire not to tie his political fortunes to a new and untested party, alienated key supporters and contributed to the perception that he was a "bad-payer of political bills."[95]

As a result, despite his strong starting point, Lucinschi was unable to concentrate political power. To begin with, the legislature deprived the president of control over the media. In response to Lucinschi-inspired attacks against deputies on state television, parliament fired Usatii, a key Lucinschi supporter in 1996, and reduced the president's formal role in appointing media heads.[96] Subsequently, according to informal rules, control over different parts of the government media complex was distributed among different parliamentary factions,[97] promoting pluralism in the media.

Most critically, Lucinschi's efforts to strengthen presidential rule were overturned by those closest to him. Beginning in February 1999, Lucinschi proposed to dramatically increase the power of the president.[98] In response to severe opposition from the legislature, including Diacov and the BDPM (which ironically had run on a platform of *strengthening* presidential power), Lucinschi organized a national referendum. Although it garnered majority support, it failed to attract sufficient turnout to make it binding.[99] While Lucinschi actively sought Western support, the Venice Commission, a European advisory body on constitutional law, concluded that the proposed changes were "contrary to European democratic principles."[100] Most critically, Diacov "responded promptly" to Lucinschi's efforts "by launching a campaign to transform Moldova into a parliamentary republic."[101] This proposal to have the president elected by parliament rather than popular vote was supported early on by over half of the erstwhile pro-presidential ADR coalition. Diacov told the author that while he was "not particularly supportive of a parliamentary system," Lucinschi was "totally unreliable" and that strengthening parliamentary power was the only way to defeat him: "I had always supported uniting democratic forces [into the BDPM]. But Lucinschi feared us and refused to support us. So I saw no reason to back his efforts to strengthen the presidency. Quite the opposite was required."[102]

Diacov successfully led efforts in mid-2000 to change the constitution and eliminate the popularly elected presidency, which passed on July 5, 2000, with support from 92 of 101 parliamentarians. Thus, as in Ukraine, the president's efforts to disperse resources among competing groups generated unreliable allies who directly and successfully challenged executive power. While it may be tempting to view his failures as a function of incompetence or bad leadership, Lucinschi, with extensive experience in the Soviet elite, was among the most seasoned politicians in Moldova. His "mistakes"—like those of Kuchma in Ukraine—were a direct response to challenges created by the absence of a robustly institutionalized party. Leaders during these early years were caught in a Catch-22. On the one hand, new political forces were too weak to rely on. On the other hand, efforts to diversify allies away from these forces often alienated existing supporters.

In the wake of constitutional change, the legislature had to elect a new president supported by 61 deputies. The ADR, originally supported by 61 deputies,[103] was too fragmented to push through its own candidate, and new elections were called for February 2001.[104] The Communist Party (PCRM), which had been out of power since independence and therefore could not be blamed for the economic crisis, was in a very good position. In addition, the Party had built an extensive network (by Moldovan standards) of 4,000 activists to mobilize voters across the country.[105] Finally, the party was able to draw on overwhelming support from Moldovan Russophiles[106] that helped it to garner just over half of the vote. In part because many parties were unable to pass the six-percent threshold, the Communists gained a commanding 71 of 101 seats in the legislature.[107]

The Rise and Fall of Communist Authoritarianism

Following the victory of the Communist Party in early 2001, Moldova experienced a noticeable decline in pluralism. The Communists immediately translated parliamentary power into greater control over the press by firing the previous directors of radio and television.[108] State-run television was censored and grew increasingly biased; independent talk shows were taken off the air.[109] Beginning in 2004, Freedom House categorized Moldova's media as "not free." Yet, in contrast to Belarus, state-run television continued to air opposition voices, and large independent media (such as Pro TV) did not stop operating—giving the population significant access to non-government controlled sources of information.[110]

Simultaneously, parliament was severely weakened as a source of opposition. In the 2000s, President Vladimir Voronin tightly controlled the legislature through the Communist Party, which now became the main locus of decision making.[111] Furthermore, in elections in 2005 and 2009, opposition faced increasing difficulties finding sites for meetings, and public employees were discouraged from attending pro-opposition rallies.[112] Opposition found it increasingly hard to attract donations from businesses and other sources.[113] Nevertheless, the opposition was able to mount serious national campaigns and garnered critical success in elections—including a victory in the mayoral election in the capital. Simultaneously, outright electoral fraud was minimal in the 2000s.[114] Thus, in elections in 2005 and July 2009, international observers noted many problems but identified few clear violations in the vote count or tabulation—concluding that "procedures were mostly followed."[115] While serious accusations were made in regard to voter lists in the April 2009 elections, evidence was unclear and the vote process in other respects was assessed positively.[116]

To an important extent, increased regime closure under the Communists can be attributed to the rise of a much more organized and cohesive party than had existed in Moldova previously. Decision making within the party was "orchestrated," "predictable," and characterized by "unanimous voting" according to the wishes of the top leadership.[117] Such organization eliminated key sources of contestation and contributed to much greater stability than had existed in the 1990s. Absent the rampant elite defection that had characterized the 1990s, Moldova was "marked by tight presidential control over the legislature, executive, and judiciary."[118] By the mid-2000s, the Party became "omnipresent in all public institutions, which [made] it difficult to speak about effective checks and balances on the power of the ruling party."[119] Party dominance meant that the government could largely ignore complaints from the opposition. A single cohesive group now dominated the judiciary and media.[120] The Party successfully packed the judiciary with pro-Party judges[121] and did not lose a single libel case against journalists in the early 2000s.[122] "In these conditions, the division of power was destroyed."[123]

In the first years of his presidency, Voronin appears to have envisioned a Belarusian scenario by which he would impose pro-Russian policies and in return garner significant black knight support from Russia.[124] Following its victory in 2001, the PCRM attempted to shift Moldova's orientation towards Russia—seeking to include Moldova in the Russian-Belarusian Union, reviving Soviet-era holidays, and eliminating Romanian aspects from the school curriculum that had been introduced in the 1990s.[125] Reciprocal Russian support would have greatly bolstered authoritarian stability in Moldova by protecting the regime from Western democratizing pressure.

Yet, Moldova's polarized history made such reciprocity very difficult. Above all, the dispute with Transnistria prevented Moldova's leaders from forming any kind of lasting relationship with Russia. Russian leaders, partly in response to domestic pressures, were unwilling to abandon Transnistria for the sake of good relations with Moldova. Despite Snegur's support for Yeltsin during the 1993 crisis in Russia, Yeltsin refused even to meet with Snegur in 1993 for fear of alienating conservatives in Russia—even though the Transnistrians had backed Yeltsin's enemies during the Russian leader's conflict with parliament.[126] Such hostility left Moldova extremely exposed. Moldova was "too dependent on outside support" to ignore criticisms by the EU or Council of Europe.[127]

Similarly in the 2000s, despite Communist overtures, the Russian government refused to give Voronin any serious concessions in gas deals and completely sidestepped Moldova in discussions of a Single Economic Space with Belarus, Kazakhstan, and Ukraine in 2003.[128] Most critically, Russia would only agree to back a Transnistria settlement that demanded heavy concessions from the Moldovan side. In 2003, the Russian government brokered a settlement— known as the Kozak Memorandum—that would have given Transnistrian authorities enormous power within a unified Moldovan state. While Voronin initially expressed support for this agreement, he was forced to back out, "under intense Western pressure" and widespread domestic opposition, just before Putin was due to visit Moldova.[129] The costs of close ties to Russia were simply too heavy to bear and relations with Russia remained "ambivalent" even with a "pro-Russian" Moldovan government in power.[130] Unable to gain concessions from Russia, Voronin was "much more willing to integrate more closely with West"—a fact that made him vulnerable to Western democratizing pressure.[131] Despite the fact that the Europe applied only "soft" pressure and mostly ignored Moldova, Western criticisms were given enormous weight, thereby constraining autocratic behavior.[132]

Moldova's external vulnerability was clearly evident in 2002 when the Christian-Democratic People's Party (PPCD)—a successor of the Front— organized series of demonstrations in the capital against the government's pro-Russian government education policies.[133] The Communists initially reacted to these protests by suspending the PPCD for organizing the protests, while rumours circulated that the government was about to declare a state of emergency.[134] The Council of Europe asked the government to explain its actions against the PPCD and urged it to annul the PPCD suspension.[135] Yet such pressure was extremely mild and the threat of actual sanction was merely "implicit." Simultaneously, the government enjoyed overwhelming popular support.[136] The PCRM should have therefore been in a good position to ignore European entreaties to halt repression.

Yet a lack of strong Russian backing and Moldova's consequent geopolitical vulnerability made it extremely difficult for Voronin to buck Western opinion. Indeed, the government was "quick to respond" and rapidly lifted the ban on the PPCD in direct "response to concerns expressed by the Council of Europe over the suspension."[137] Education reform was dropped, and due to external constraints, "nearly every element of the communists' political design was abandoned or sharply curtailed"—leaving in place textbooks that presented a distinctly Romanianist view of Moldovan history.[138]

The failure to sideline the PPCD as well as other parties can also be traced to the dispersal of economic power in Moldova in the 1990s. While Moldova mostly lacked the kind of flamboyant, quasi-independent oligarchs found in Russia (in the 1990s) and Ukraine, the private economy was consistently robust enough that parties had comparatively little trouble finding the resources to survive. For example, despite its strong opposition to the Communists and lack of power in the legislature between 2001 and 2003, the PPCD was able to operate through donations and profits from various side businesses—including a printing company and small bus company.[139]

Moldova's fraught relations with Russia then motivated Voronin to shift geopolitical allies. Improved ties with the European Union became "a central priority."[140] Voronin, like Snegur before him, was forced by the country's divided identity to shift back and forth between Russophile and Romanianist positions. As a result, the Russian government, stung by Voronin's rejection of the Kozak Memorandum, openly back opposition forces in the run-up to the 2005 parliamentary elections—lambasting Voronin on Russian-controlled ORT television in Moldova and allegedly funding opposition. The government responded provocatively—deporting Russians who had come to Moldova to observe the elections and arresting Russians suspected of giving cash to Communist opponents.[141]

In the run-up to the election, the government arrested four employees of the mayor's office in Chișinău on alleged corruption charges in what may have been the beginning of an orchestrated attack on Serafim Urechean, the opposition mayor of the capital.[142] However, given Moldova's tense relations with Russia and geopolitical vulnerability, Voronin could not afford to alienate the West by jailing a major opposition figure. Thus, after informal pressure from a diplomat based in Chişinău, Voronin backed down.[143] While the 2005 elections were marked by media bias and serious abuse of state resources,[144] the opposition was able to mount a serious national campaign for office. Urechean's Democratic Bloc of Moldova garnered nearly 30 percent of the vote. However, the Communists still captured a majority of 56 seats.[145] The PPCD, in a startling decision made easier by the Communist's geopolitical turn-around, agreed to ally with the Communists, and Voronin was re-elected president.[146]

Following their victory, the Communists were domestically in a strong position—much more united than any Moldovan government since independence and facing an opposition wracked by divisions. Moreover, the Moldovan economy was quite strong—having grown an average of 6 percent during the PCRM's tenure. Then, in the run-up to the 2009 parliamentary election, the Communists again sought to tighten the screws on the opposition. In late 2008, the government sought to push out the owners of the oppositional Pro TV station, whose license was about to expire. However, in the face of concerns expressed by the international community, the government again held back and agreed to allow the station to operate through the election.[147] The opposition also benefitted from significant oligarchic support.[148] In particular, businesses backed two of the most popular opposition parties—Mihai Ghimpu's Liberal Party and the Liberal Democratic Party (LDPM) of Vlad Filat, who had been director of the Department of Privatization under Lucinschi.[149]

At first the election—in which the Communists captured 60 of 101 seats (four more than in 2005)—appeared to mark a significant victory for Communist power. Opposition leaders, divided into three right-leaning parties,[150] immediately declared the election fraudulent[151] and organized demonstrations of 5,000–10,000 on April 6–7 in central Chişinău.[152] However, the opposition parties rapidly lost control over events,[153] and protesters stormed, ransacked, and set fire to the parliamentary and presidential buildings. Flags of the European Union and Romania appeared over parliament.[154]

Having by now improved his ties to Russia, Voronin responded to these riots by ratcheting up the national conflict.[155] Accusing Romania of instigating the riots, Voronin declared Romania's ambassador persona non grata, and banned Romanian journalists from entering the country.[156] The charges of Western interference were echoed by the Russian Foreign Ministry, who claimed that the unrest was part of a campaign by Romanian and Western secret services to destabilize former Soviet republics.[157] In turn, hundreds of activists were arrested and many Romanians were forced to flee the country.[158] International organizations such as Amnesty International faced increasing pressure from authorities.[159] At the same time, the Communists remained constrained. By late April, Voronin had amnestied most of those arrested, partly in response to EU pressure.[160] The government also agreed to continue allowing the opposition Pro TV to broadcast in the country.[161] Protests died down.

In mid-April, Communist hold on power seemed relatively assured. With 60 of 101 deputies, they only had to gain the support of a single deputy—the "golden vote"—from a highly fragmented and "often-quarrelsome"[162] opposition to secure the presidency. With a strong popular mandate and control over the state, the government was in a powerful position to secure the vote—just as it had secured opposition support in 2005. As one commentator noted, the PCRM had a lot to offer in return for support—including "the post of vice Speaker of Parliament, property guarantees," and the closure of criminal cases.[163]

Yet, shockingly, for two months, Moldova's three opposition parties "stood as a solid bloc against the dominant Communists."[164] By boycotting legislative votes for the president in May and early June, the minority opposition was able to deprive the Communists of the single vote and force new elections. Such unity cannot be explained by support from Europe. While top EU officials condemned government repression,[165] they refused to isolate Voronin and quickly recognized his victory.[166] The opposition's surprising unity has been attributed to a variety of factors—including efforts by opposition leaders to physically prevent deputies from entering the parliament building.[167] Yet it seems doubtful that regime opponents could have physically prevented defection by any deputy who really wanted to go over to the Communists.

To understand the opposition's remarkable display of unity, we also need to look at the ways in which the April events tapped into Moldova's legacy of polarized politics and created barriers to collusion. As Adrienne LeBas argues, intense polarization sharpens "us-them" distinctions and strengthens opposition unity.[168] Indeed, the April events, which were closely followed by over 90 percent of Moldovans, had an immensely polarizing effect on the Moldovan electorate and elite[169]—reigniting older divisions between Romanianist and Russophile forces. Thus, as citizens became more polarized in their views about Moldovan foreign relations,[170] parties such as the Liberals and AMN "began to push Romanian nationalism, NATO membership," and language issues.[171] Vlad Filat, the head of the opposition LDPM similarly criticized the Communists for "coordinating their internal and external policies with Moscow."[172] Opposition parties that had largely ignored identity or shown sympathy to Russia now openly attacked Moscow or allied themselves with Romania.

As in Ukraine in the 2000s (see chapter 3), polarization raised the costs of opposition defection and collusion. There was widespread consensus among Moldovan commentators (even in the Russian-language press) that in the polarized atmosphere, "any of the three parties who voted for a Communist candidate would lose their electorate."[173] A vote for the Communists would be considered a "moral defeat" and "treason."[174] "Due to the provocations of April 7, the opposition was put in a situation where any dialogue with Voronin's group would mean political death"—a message brought home by the PPCD's electoral failure in 2009 after its agreement with the Communists in 2005.[175] In contrast to 2005, the Communists now took a starkly pro-Russian position—thereby making it more costly for pro-European opposition to cooperate with the government. In addition, the total breakdown of trust between the sides also meant that any opposition deputy offering his or her support could not be sure that the Communists would not renege on a deal after the "golden vote" was cast.[176]

Partly as a result, the otherwise fragmented opposition maintained a "stubborn unity,"[177] and consistently boycotted votes for the president. "Neither threats nor bribes worked."[178] Voronin admitted defeat on June 3 and was forced to call early elections. In turn, Marian Lupu, the former speaker of parliament who had joined the Communist government in 2001 as a technocrat, broke with the PCRM and took leadership of Diacov's Democratic Party. Lupu's defection, which was facilitated by the support of the oligarch Vladimir Plahotniuc, was a serious blow to the Party.[179]

In turn, the election on July 29—held with minimal irregularities[180]—saw the Communists lose 13 seats, while opposition parties won a majority of 53.[181] The opposition subsequently cobbled together a coalition government—Alliance for European Integration (AEI)—consisting of the four non-Communist parties. Vlad Filat was chosen prime minister, and Mihai Ghimpu, speaker of parliament and subsequently acting president.[182] In turn, the Communists remained staunchly opposed to the new government—refusing to support any of the new government's candidates for president.[183]

The course of events in 2009 were hardly inevitable and hinged on several contingencies, including the rather stringent vote totals required for electing a president, Voronin's decision to stoke national conflict during the April riots, and finally Lupu's decision to defect. Nonetheless, the legacy of polarization created a series of hot-button issues concerning relations with Russia and Romania that primed actors on both sides to view events through the lens of identity and to frame political choices in indivisible terms. Once triggered, this polarization bolstered opposition unity, which allowed a minority of otherwise divided politicians to generate serious crisis in the system.

Yet even absent this rather contingent string of events, the regime would still have remained mildly authoritarian. The legacy of polarization continued to leave Moldova highly vulnerable to external pressure. If Voronin had succeeded in his efforts to secure strong Russian backing support for his regime, he would have (like Lukashenka in Belarus) been less constrained by Western pressure. But identity divisions and legacies of the Transnistr conflict made it extremely difficult for Russia and Moldova to maintain close ties similar to those between Belarus and Russia. As a result, Voronin remained exposed and was repeatedly thwarted in his efforts to suppress opposition.

Disorganization after 2009

Moldova became significantly more open after 2009. State-run media was more balanced and accessible to opposition. Overall, journalists faced less harassment.[184] After the Communists left power, the Central Electoral Commission was viewed as more impartial.[185] In addition, control over parliament became far less centralized. Such improvements do not seem to have been a function of democratically minded leadership. Indeed, the AEI shut down the pro-Communist NIT TV station on technical grounds and attempted some of the same pressure tactics used by the Communists—threatening criminal investigations of major Communist figures.[186]

Such pluralism can be traced less to democratic leadership and more to the obvious but important fact that the AEI came to power as a coalition of parties rather than as a single cohesive party. Indeed, the AEI was in a much weaker position than the PCRM to monopolize political control. As a fluid coalition of relatively equal political groups, the AEI was extremely weak by the metrics used in this book. The parties were "partners in a coalition" but also "political competitors."[187] After taking power, the AEI rapidly "decomposed into mutually hostile camps."[188] The regime incorporated strong "internal checks and balances" that made it nearly impossible for any one faction to monopolize control.[189] As in the 1990s, competing parties infiltrated different ministries and parliamentary committees, which created an enormous amount of default competition within the state and regime.[190] The government was no longer sufficiently unified to impose a single editorial line in the media.

Competition among the coalition partners, as in Ukraine under Yushchenko, created a highly rapacious and competitive political system in which leaders and parties repeatedly shifted alliances and corruption was rampant. In the spring of 2013, Prime Minister Filat from the Liberal Democratic Party came into open conflict with the Democrats, another member of the coalition, when Filat sought to limit the influence of the Democrat oligarch Vladimir Plahotniuc. In the end, Filat was forced to resign and was replaced by Iurie Leancă in May 2013. The AEI was dissolved in favor of a new "Pro-European Coalition." In the first four years after 2009, Moldova was led by three different presidents—Ghimpu of the Liberal Party (2009–2010, Lupu of the Democrats (2010–2012), and the independent Nicolae Timofti (2012–).

Conclusion

This chapter has sought to explain the remarkable resilience of pluralism in post-Soviet Moldova—the poorest country in Europe with a weak civil society, fragmented party system, severe ethnic divisions, and a failing state. As we have seen, polarization and state and party weakness—factors typically seen as impediments to democracy—were in fact critical to undermining the consolidation of an authoritarian (or virtually any) political order. The same forces that promoted dynamic political competition were also responsible for periodic violence and a dysfunctional situation in which "no actor was able to impose definitive decisions."[191]

Between 1989 and 1991, polarization around national identity contributed to significant opposition mobilization in a country with a history of political quiescence. Conflict led to civil war but also resulted in the weakening of Communist Party control and the partial destruction of key authoritarian state institutions. In the 1990s, the organizational void created by the destruction of the Communist Party contributed to severe elite conflict—as competing political forces dominated different parts of the governmental apparatus. Indeed, while students of postcommunist politics have emphasized the weakness of civil society, the collapse of the USSR left both the masses and elites highly atomized. Thus, despite efforts to strengthen the presidency, both Presidents Snegur and Lucinschi confronted recalcitrant legislatures dominated by former presidential allies.

In 2001, the victory of a much better organized and cohesive Communist

Party led, as this model predicts, to greater regime closure—despite the introduction of parliamentary rule. In the early 2000s, Voronin sought to garner Russian support that would insulate Moldova from Western pressure. Yet the legacy of conflict with Russia over Transnistria made it much harder for the pro-Russian PCRM to form a stable alliance with Russia. The government was left in the cold and forced to rely on the West for support. This made the PCRM highly susceptible to even modest Western pressure. As a result, the Communists were relatively constrained in their efforts to harass opposition, engage in electoral fraud, or eliminate independent media. Finally, polarization contributed to opposition mobilization in 2002 and bolstered opposition cohesion in 2009—which led to the PCRM's downfall.

Other factors do less well in accounting for competition in Moldova. First, it is tempting to trace pluralism to democratic leadership. However, Snegur, Lucinschi, the Communists, and the AEI all demonstrated a readiness to use extra-legal measures to stay in power[192] but were highly constrained. Next, Moldova's exposure to Western pressure cannot simply be explained by the country's small size, as some have suggested.[193] After all, Belarus is also quite small but was not vulnerable to Western pressure. As we shall see in the next chapter, Belarus's predominantly Russophile identity facilitated significant Russian assistance—thereby immunizing Lukashenka from Western influence. By contrast, divided identity in Moldova (as well as in Ukraine) made such a tight relationship with Russia nearly impossible—thereby exposing Moldova to much greater external pressure.

Others have traced Moldova's pluralism to the constitution.[194] Certainly, constitutional rules shaped regime outcomes in some critical instances—as in 2009 when the high vote requirement to elect a president gave a lifeline to an otherwise weak opposition. Yet to an important extent, both the design and implementation of institutions were shaped by organizational capacity and identity polarization. As we saw above, the combination of polarization and party weakness severely undermined efforts by Snegur and Lucinschi to garner sufficient allies in support of presidential power. Next, the emergence of a highly centralized and cohesive Communist Party resulted in a far more centralized and undemocratic system, despite the introduction of greater parliamentary power. And as events in 2009 amply demonstrated, parliamentary institutions did not significantly reduce polarization as March and Herd argued it would.[195] While the high vote requirement in 2009 is necessary to understanding why the PCRM fell, Moldova's external vulnerability—a partial outgrowth of its divided identity—had already created a much more liberal state than would have existed otherwise. In fact, the next case in this book, Belarus, reveals the ways in which an absence of relatively equal and polarized divisions can foster authoritarianism.

5

Authoritarian Consolidation in Belarus

In stark contrast to Moldova and Ukraine, Belarus witnessed the rapid consolidation of authoritarian rule after the fall of the Soviet Union. After coming to power in 1994, Alyaksandr Lukashenka shut down parliament and successfully sidelined opposition for more than twenty years. Belarus's trajectory raises three key puzzles. First, how did a republic that was so completely dominated by the old Soviet nomenklatura until 1994 witness the sudden rise to power of Lukashenka, a near-total outsider? Second, why was Lukashenka able to so rapidly transform Belarus into a closed authoritarian regime in the 1990s with so little violent repression? Finally, why, despite Belarus's vulnerable position near Western Europe, was Lukashenka able to consolidate power for so long in the face of enormous external hostility from the West and, to a much lesser extent, from Russia?

Discussions of Belarusian authoritarianism have focused largely on a supposedly patriarchal Belarusian culture[1] and on Lukashenka's charismatic and belligerent personality. Yet such perspectives offer a limited understanding of why a country so close to the West became Europe's "last dictatorship." Instead, I argue that three sets of factors account for Belarus's trajectory: (1) weak coercive capacity and elite disorientation in the early 1990s; (2) the dominance in Belarus of a single Russophile national identity; and (3) Lukashenka's coercive and economic state-building strategies.

First, Lukashenka's political instincts and ability to connect to the electorate certainly aided his rapid rise to power. Yet at the start of the 1990s, Lukashenka was a small-scale farm director and parliamentarian known to few beyond his electoral district. His innate political abilities almost certainly would have gone unnoticed had it not been for the weak central control and disorientation among Belarus's older nomenklatura elite that created key openings for Lukashenka in the early 1990s.

In turn, Belarus's unified Russophile identity cleared the way for Lukashenka to create and consolidate closed authoritarian rule. In contrast to its counterparts in divided Moldova and Ukraine, Belarusian opposition could not mobilize national cleavages to block the transition to autocracy. As a result, Lukashenka was able to shut down parliament and concentrate control without resorting to serious violence. Next, national identity and Lukashenka's authoritarian state-building efforts facilitated the consolidation of authoritarian rule in the late 1990s and 2000s. A relatively unified Russophile identity made it easier for Lukashenka to attract significant Russian support that was less accessible to leaders in divided Moldova and Ukraine. Finally, authoritarian state building by Lukashenka in the mid-1990s—asserting power over the coercive apparatus and rebuilding centralized economic control—allowed Lukashenka to preempt any serious challenges before they emerged in the late 1990s and 2000s. Thus, while Lukashenka (like his counterparts in Ukraine and Moldova) lacked the capacity to engage in sustained high-intensity coercion, a weakly divided national identity and economic control deprived the opposition of material or symbolic power to mount a serious challenge that would make large-scale violence necessary.

Now widely regarded as "the last dictatorship in Europe," Belarus in fact saw sharp changes in the levels of political competition in the 1990s (see table 5.1). Between 1990 and 1994, under Prime Minister Viacheslau Kebich, elections were marked by notable but limited manipulation; media was seriously harassed but nonetheless presented a wide range of opposition views; and the executive generally dominated the legislature but sporadically faced serious challenges.[2]

Table 5.1   Regime Closure and Party and State Capacity in Belarus 1991–2014

		Party and state capacity			
	National identity	Party	State coercive capacity	State economic control	Overall capacity score
Kebich (1991–1994)	Low split	Low	Med-low	Med-low	Low
Lukashenka (1994–2014)	Low split	Low	Medium	High	Medium

Note: For coding rules, see appendix A.

Finally, Kebich was unable to prevent the emergence of a strong opposition. Despite facing unequal access to resources, opposition was allowed to freely operate in the country and seized power in presidential elections in 1994.

In stark contrast to Moldova and Ukraine, however, Belarus witnessed the rapid consolidation of authoritarian rule in the 1990s. Between 1994 and 1996, the media faced increasing harassment as several opposition newspapers, including *Svaboda*, were closed. After unilateral changes in the constitution in 1996, parliament became a "rubber stamp for presidential decrees."[3] Almost all domestic independent media outlets were shut down, and opposition was deprived of access to press, television, or radio. Elections were also reduced to a mere "ritual" by 2000.[4] After 1999, the opposition failed to mount any serious challenges. Only three opposition candidates were elected to the legislature in 2001, and no opposition candidates gained seats in 2004, 2008, or 2012.

While both Kebich and Lukashenka benefitted from a relatively unified Russophile national identity, state coercive and economic power increased dramatically in the mid-1990s—a fact that directly contributed to the consolidation of Lukashenka's rule in the 2000s (table 5.1).

National Identity

Belarusian national identity has mostly lacked the high degree of polarization found in Moldova and Ukraine. Russophile attitudes have dominated, while strong support for anti-Russophile Belarusian identity has been limited to a small minority centered mostly in the capital. In contrast to Ukraine, Belarusian nationalism was "a conspicuously weak movement" prior to the creation of the Soviet Union.[5] The vast majority of Belarusian speakers lived in rural areas, and literacy lagged significantly behind other linguistic groups.[6]

		Regime closure		
Electoral manipulation	Media control	Executive control over parliament	Opposition subordination	Overall regime closure
Medium	Medium	Medium	Low	Medium
High	High	High	High	High

In turn, the most salient contemporary myths have been intimately tied to the history of the Soviet Union in Belarus. In particular, stories surrounding Belarusian partisan activity against the Nazis in World War II constituted *"the central trope of postwar Belarusian culture."*[7] The popular resonance of such myths was strengthened by an enormous growth in literacy, industrialization, and urbanization under Soviet rule. In the 1950s–1970s, Belarus was transformed from an overwhelmingly peasant society into an advanced industrial society.[8] Belarusian language use declined, and the population became increasingly Russified.[9]

Belarusian national identity has thus been intimately tied to Russia. All Belarusians speak Russian, and most have viewed themselves as part of the same nation as Russia rather than as "representatives of different peoples."[10] An overwhelming share of voters supported a return to Soviet-era symbols and Russian language in the relatively free referendum of May 1995.[11] Until the early 2000s, integration with Russia was widely associated with "improved economic prospects and standards of living."[12] In the 1990s, Lukashenka and Yeltsin carried out highly publicized, but ultimately ill-fated, efforts to unite the two countries.

Indeed, what most distinguishes Belarus from its neighbors is the absence of a significant or regionally concentrated population of anti-Russian Belarusian nationalists. Belarus was not as sharply divided into east and west as was Ukraine.[13] While anti-Russian Belarusian nationalists garnered greater support in the capital and on the border with Poland, they lacked a majority in any part of the country—a fact that deprived them of any kind of stable base of operations equivalent to Galicia in Ukraine.[14] In contrast to Moldova or Ukraine, the country's main electoral fault lines did not typically reflect these identity divisions. Thus, in the presidential elections of 1994 and 2001, the top two candidates supported close ties to Russia.[15] Partly as a function of such attitudes, Russia was more closely tied to Belarus than to any other post-Soviet state.[16]

Certainly, anti-Soviet Belarusian nationalism has been a factor in Belarus. Founded in late 1988, the anti-Russian Belarusian Popular Front (BPF), led by Zenon Pazniak, garnered significant attention in the late Perestroika era for its strident opposition to Soviet rule. Nevertheless, the highly anti-Russian nationalism propounded by Pazniak lacked significant popular support and instead represented what Andrew Wilson calls a "minority counterculture."[17] In the March 1990 parliamentary elections, the party gained only 8 percent of seats in the legislature and was unable to gain any seats in the still relatively free 1995 elections—far less than nationalist groups in Moldova and Ukraine (not to mention the Baltics) in the early 1990s.[18] The BPF was "too weak to take power on its own, or even to threaten to take power."[19]

In the mid-2000s public opinion began to turn against shared statehood with Russia.[20] Indeed, increasing antagonism between Putin and Lukashenka encouraged Lukashenka to promote Belarusian independence and autonomy from Russia—actively criticizing Russian attempts at domination and even providing declarative support for Belarusian language. Nevertheless, Lukashenka's rhetoric was strongly Russophile—anti-Western and pro-Soviet.[21] A strong majority continued to regard Russia positively, with an overwhelming majority viewing themselves as ethnically closer to Russia than to Europe.[22] Anti-Russian nationalism may at some point gain a strong foothold in Belarus. However, such an identity would almost certainly emerge as an outgrowth of opposition to the president rather than as an independent force for change as in Moldova and Ukraine.

Party and State Strength

Both Prime Minister Kebich (1990–1994) and Lukashenka relied primarily on state power to assert political control—foregoing any serious efforts at party building.[23] The big difference lay in the nature of state power. The 1990s witnessed the evolution from a relatively weak, effectively decentralized state under Kebich to a highly personalistic and centralized state under Lukashenka.

State Power under Kebich

More than in Moldova or Ukraine, "Belarus's political landscape remained stable to the point of immobility" in the late 1980s and early 1990s.[24] Due in part to the weakness of Belarusian nationalism, the Belarusian Communist Party did not witness the emergence of a powerful pro-reform wing in 1989–1991 as occurred in the Baltics, Moldova, and Ukraine. With the notable exception of Stanislau Shushkevich, who became head of state in 1991 but was largely powerless by early 1992,[25] the Belarusian state and government was staffed with holdovers from the late Soviet era. For example, in contrast to Moldova, the security services retained their entire structure and suffered almost no loss of personnel after the Soviet collapse— largely due to the absence of ethnic tensions in Belarus.[26]

As a result, the Belarusian state under Prime Minister Kebich penetrated much of society but possessed weak cohesion. On the one hand, post-Soviet Belarusian leaders had at their disposal a vast coercive and economic state apparatus, including the Belarusian KGB (BKGB) that infiltrated major media and other state institutions.[27] Simultaneously, Kebich opposed large-scale privatization, and the government maintained de jure control over most of the economy.[28]

On the other hand, fiscal crisis and the elimination of Soviet-era mechanisms of central economic control—including central planning and the Communist Party—severely undermined effective control over the economy (see chapter 2). In August 1991, parliament voted to dissolve the Party—a move that, in Kebich's words, destroyed the government's only remaining "organizational structure of influence over the population."[29]

What emerged was a system kept largely intact by inertia. While there was a widespread assumption at the time that Kebich effectively controlled the appointment of local officials,[30] he in fact lacked formal authority over local state personnel and was effectively powerless when openly challenged.[31] Weak central control was further enhanced by Kebich's retention of the Brezhnevian norm of "trust in cadres," whereby ministers and other officials were only fired for serious misconduct rather than bad performance.[32] As a result, key state agencies—including agencies formally subordinate to Kebich such as the army and police—functioned with a fair degree of de facto autonomy.[33] In particular, the BKGB, which retained strong ties to Moscow, frequently took positions independent of the government.[34] By early 1994, Kebich had begun to centralize his control over the security apparatus and, with great difficulty, succeeded in replacing the heads of the police and BKGB with Kebich loyalists.[35] Yet such measures were only partially effective. Thus, officials who worked in the BKGB at that time report that many officers in the service did little to support Kebich.[36]

Authoritarian State Building under Lukashenka

In the 1994 presidential election, Lukashenka beat Kebich by a stunning 80 to 14 percent margin. Yet as an outsider, Lukashenka faced significant challenges building an authoritarian state. Before 1993, he had been the head of a small collective farm and an unknown deputy with few ties to the establishment. Ultimately, he chose a very different strategy from those discussed in previous chapters. While Yanukovych in Ukraine, and the Communists in Moldova (as well as Putin in Russia) used single parties to enhance coordination and to give allies a clear stake in incumbent success, Lukashenka made no effort to create a ruling party. Rather than giving allies a long-term interest in his incumbency, Lukashenka increased the costs of opposition by depriving opponents and allies of resources outside the president's direct control. The president generated compliance mostly by "scaring government officials" and depriving the nomenklatura of any "mechanisms to lobby its own interests."[37]

Immediately upon taking power, Lukashenka focused on rebuilding a powerful authoritarian state. He personally travelled to numerous locales to pressure local state officials into resigning in favor of other officials deemed more loyal to the new president.[38] He also began to infiltrate key central ministries. As an outsider lacking an established network, Lukashenka feared being outflanked by established forces within the security bureaucracy. After purging the leadership of the armed forces,[39] Lukashenka created a Security Council headed by his close associate Viktor Sheiman that centralized control over security appointments at all levels—often bringing in outsiders over the protests of older BKGB officials.[40]

In October 1994, Sheiman created a new department, the Office for the Protection of the President (later the Security Service of the President), out of the BKGB's Alpha unit and the General Directorate within the Ministry of Internal Affairs.[41] Lukashenka then rapidly expanded the armed forces. The government's share of expenditures on coercive agencies doubled between 1994 and 1996, becoming one of the largest items in the budget.[42] By the late 1990s, the Ministry of Internal Affairs had grown to over 120,000 officers, making Belarus "one of the most militarized countries in the world."[43]

At the same time, expanding the state and lavishing resources on the security services was insufficient to ensure their absolute loyalty. In the first years of his rule, Lukashenka had "failed to put the KGB under his complete control."[44] In response, Lukashenka created and strengthened a range of agencies to monitor and control the state bureaucracy and economic enterprises. Shortly after taking power, he founded the Presidential Control Service to audit local governments and enterprises.[45] Central control over the state increased. While administrators under Kebich were only replaced in cases of "serious misconduct," officials under Lukashenka could be let go simply for "not pleasing the official above him," and "new hires emerged from no one knew where."[46]

Thus, the coercive state in Belarus was palpably stronger by the late 1990s than it had been under Kebich. Yet it was no stronger than in Ukraine under Yanukovych or Kuchma (both scored as medium coercive capacity[47]). Well into the 2010s, it was not clear that the coercive apparatus would be willing to engage in risky, high-intensity violence to save the regime.[48]

What did distinguish Lukashenka from his counterparts next door was his decision in the mid-1990s not to privatize but instead to rebuild a highly centralized system of economic control. In contrast to leaders such as Kuchma in Ukraine and Snegur in Moldova (as well as Boris Yeltsin), Lukashenka never undertook large-scale privatization and instead renationalized significant parts of the economy.[49] More than two decades after the collapse of Communism, the private sector in Belarus still accounted for just a third of its GDP, while estimates from 1999 suggest that under 20 percent of the population was employed in the private sector—a degree of state control matched only by Turkmenistan in the former Soviet Union.[50]

In fact, these figures likely *under*estimated Lukashenka's control over the economy. Power over both private and state enterprises was enhanced by agencies such as the Committee for Government Control (KGK) that provided "the main instrument for control over the economy." Appointed by the president, the KGK was given wide powers in the 1996 constitution to monitor the implementation of Belarusian law. It was made responsible for auditing and collecting fines from a vast array of government agencies, private enterprises, opposition NGOs, and individual politicians.[51] With access to extensive compromising material on officials (*kompromat*) and a range of administrative sanctions, the head of the KGK "supervised the nomenklatura" and was considered the third or fourth most powerful official in the country.[52]

Lukashenka also armed his subordinates with a vast array of regulations giving them extraordinary capacity to interfere in the operation of nominally private companies, including the ability to threaten private company heads with dismissal.[53] From 1998 until 2008, the government instituted a "golden share" rule that gave the government significant control over enterprises in which it had any ownership share, rules that in 2004 were spread to all previously government-owned enterprises.[54] Along similar lines, Lukashenka introduced a system of short-term employment contracts in 1999 that quickly became "omnipresent."[55] This system greatly enhanced Lukashenka's capacity to target and punish individual activists, dramatically raising the costs of opposition.

Finally, Lukashenka's economic control was enhanced through the creation of a network of commercial enterprises and funds that gave the president access to enormous patronage. The most important commercial center was the Presidential Business Administration (UDP). Created in 1994, the UDP rapidly became a "biggest commercial enterprise in the country," benefitting from broad tax and customs privileges that brought in hundreds of millions of dollars—all under Lukashenka's "private control."[56] The UDP quickly took control over a vast number of hotels and other state properties throughout the country and became the "biggest landlord in the country," leasing space to thousands of commercial enterprises.[57] The UDP also benefitted from monopoly import and export of a wide range of consumer products and was responsible for selling property confiscated in criminal cases.[58] Its subsidiaries were involved in industries ranging from shopping malls to construction, food production, and the resale of oil.[59] The president also accumulated significant resources in a special off-budget Presidential Fund that reportedly received profits from a range of arms sales carried out by the administration.[60]

In sum, while Lukashenka came to power in 1994 as an outsider with little effective control over the state, he rapidly built up and expanded agencies of coercion (the police, BKGB) and economic control (KGK, UDP). By the mid- to late-1990s, Lukashenka possessed significant coercive and economic power that (with a weakly divided national identity) would contribute to the consolidation of his rule in the 2000s.

As I will argue below, increased organizational capacity helps to explain why authoritarian stability under Lukashenka was greater than under his predecessor, Viacheslau Kebich.

Weak Authoritarianism under Kebich, 1990–1994

In the early 1990s, Belarus was widely considered the "Vendée of Perestroika" and "one of the most resistant to reform," with both government and the legislature dominated by hardline Communists.[61] Thus, in contrast to Moldova and Ukraine, no serious reform Communists emerged in the late 1980s or early 1990s, while pro-Communist deputies overwhelmingly dominated the new legislature elected in 1990.[62]

Yet Communist Party influence in 1990–1991 was surprisingly weak. Following the 1990 parliamentary elections, a relatively small contingent of anti-Party forces was able to push through the election of a relative outsider, Stanislau Shushkevich, a former professor of physics, to the post of first vice-chair of parliament. Shushkevich, in turn, frequently took de facto lead of parliament. For example, Shushkevich spearheaded a resolution condemning Soviet attacks on Lithuania in January 1991 and headed a government delegation to negotiate with strikers in April 1991.[63] The Party, despite its nominal parliamentary majority, was left largely on the sidelines.[64] By contrast, the BPF, with a tiny contingent of deputies, had outsized influence—helping to push the legislature toward a declaration of autonomy.

As in Moldova and Ukraine, such weakness can be traced to the passivity of top Communist Party officials who, under Gorbachev's direction, were unwilling to actively defend the Party's power. Inaction in Moscow was deadly in the strictly top-down organizational culture of the CPSU. Without clear direction from above, the party turned into "a poorly organized crowd, which was only ruled by an instinct for self-preservation."[65] Much of the top Belarusian leadership "had a panicked fear of talking to crowds" and therefore was often inclined to rely on non-Party leaders in the legislature such as Shushkevich to cope with opposition challenges.[66] One Party official complained that "as historically critical decisions are made in the Supreme Soviet, the first Secretary of the Party [Malofeev] maintains a proud silence."[67]

Then, in late August 1991, the failed Soviet coup shook the Belarusian leadership and ushered in a four-month period in which otherwise conservative politicians supported radical measures to destroy the Soviet system. Images of crowds tearing down the statue of Soviet secret police founder Felix Dzerzhinsky in Moscow terrified many Communists, who assumed that they would soon be put on trial. "Shuddering from fear, party leaders closed down the Party."[68] Government leaders exited the Party en masse, and the Party ceased to exist as a political force. Kebich, selected as prime minister in 1990, called on deputies to support independence because "a functional center does not exist"; and the Belarusian Soviet Socialist Republic was officially renamed the "Republic of Belarus."

Radical changes in the neighboring Baltic states generated a widespread expectation that the nationalist Pazniak would take power as chair of parliament—a remarkable belief, given the BPF's small level of support.[69] Many otherwise conservative deputies decided to throw their support behind Shushkevich—despite his lack of ties to the Communist establishment—as a way to avoid the more radical Pazniak's selection.[70] As a result, despite Belarus's otherwise conservative history and lack of strong opposition, a non-Communist succeeded in taking power during a critical period in Belarusian history. In December, Shushkevich, Kravchuk, and Yeltsin signed the Belovezhskaia Accord that ended the Soviet Union.

However, this period of "extraordinary politics" did not last long. As "fear subsided" over time, the conservative majority quickly adapted to the new conditions and began reasserting control.[71] Shushkevich rapidly lost effective power. While formally the head of state, he had virtually no mechanisms to monitor or control the government, and in 1992 there was a "gradual concentration of all power in the hands of Kebich."[72]

By early 1994, Kebich had eliminated most major threats to his power by replacing the head of parliament, the Ministry of Interior, and BKGB with loyalists.[73] Unlike its counterparts in divided Ukraine (in 1994) and Moldova (in 1996), the opposition in more unified Belarus was unable to draw on a widely popular competing national identity to mobilize support. As a result, neither Shushkevich nor Pazniak presented a serious danger to Kebich. Thus, in stark contrast to Kravchuk in Ukraine or Snegur in Moldova, Kebich had seemingly uncontested control over all major state and government institutions.

Yet, as discussed above, Kebich's control over the state was demonstrably soft—a fact that directly contributed to pluralism in the early 1990s. For example, the bureaucratic autonomy described above initially gave judges enough job security to ignore government efforts to suppress opposition. A former justice in the Constitutional Court, Mikhail Pastukhov, reported: "The Party [in the old system] provided the main means of control. After the Party left, however, judges felt much more secure in their positions. They were almost never fired. As a result, many felt safe in applying the law even when that meant helping the opposition."[74] According to Pastukhov, judges were able to thwart several efforts by the government to punish journalists with libel suits.[75] In addition, parliament as well as ministers in the Kebich government maintained sufficient autonomy to weaken government efforts to muzzle the press.[76]

In addition to weak central control, Kebich's own mistakes contributed to his demise in 1994.[77] Selected as prime minister by the Belarusian Party leadership in 1990, Kebich was the only executive in the former Soviet Union who had never run in a nation-wide election in the early 1990s. "No one had any kind of experience with elections in the new conditions."[78]

Such inexperience contributed directly to the rise of Lukashenka. First, Kebich's lack of familiarity with polling led him to misjudge his own support as he discounted polls in early 1994 suggesting he would lose.[79] Kebich "thought that he was at the peak of his popularity."[80] Kebich's nominal domination of the state and the weakness of his most obvious opponents—Pazniak and Shushkevich—gave him the confidence to call presidential elections in 1994.

At the same time, until early 1994 few top leaders considered Lukashenka to be a viable candidate for the presidency.[81] As the mere head of a small state farm, Lukashenka lacked the credentials considered necessary to become head of state by those Belarusian leaders accustomed to the slow-moving, seniority-based Soviet nomenklatura system. According to several participants and close observers, many in the leadership could not imagine that "someone so uneducated and so low down in the nomenklatura hierarchy could become a serious contender for the presidency."[82] As Kebich himself noted, it had been "simply impossible to jump from 'pauper to prince' [*popast' iz gryazi v knyazi*]" under the old system.[83] Many, including Kebich, wrongly assumed that these old rules still applied.

The leadership's underestimation of Lukashenka led them to permit Lukashenka, widely viewed as a wild card at the time, to take charge of a parliamentary anticorruption commission formed in mid-1993.[84] Pro-government leaders, who had gained power under the old system, "had no clue that the commission might be important."[85] Lukashenka, in turn, took full advantage of this opportunity to make a name for himself. The commission spent months interviewing officials and brought in a number of investigators from the Ministry of Interior and BKGB. According to several BKGB sources, the head of the agency at the time—unbeknownst to the prime minister—fed Lukashenka material aimed at undermining Kebich's reputation.[86] Following a widely publicized speech on December 14, 1993, Lukashenka, virtually unknown before, became a household name. Even after the speech, the government allowed Lukashenka to use state-controlled offices in the center of Minsk free of charge.[87] Kebich also made little effort to ensure that the constitutional age limit for those running for president was 40 or older (the minimum age in many democracies)—a provision that would have disqualified the 39-year-old Lukashenka.[88]

In the run-up to the election, Kebich appeared to have the entire state apparatus behind him.[89] A large majority of local and regional officials and enterprise managers signed on to Kebich's campaign and the head of the electoral commission was a Kebich loyalist.[90] Kebich was assured that "the majority of local executives" were on Kebich's side.[91]

Yet such officials often failed to support Kebich in practice—a degree of disobedience that would become unimaginable under Lukashenka. For example, the deputy mayor of Gomel city recalled that pro-Kebich leaflets dropped off at the city council were never distributed because of widespread support for Shushkevich there.[92] Another former local official from Mogilev reported that many from his region would "go to [the capital] and report to Kebich 'we support you 100 percent'—but then fail to do the most basic activities to support his candidacy."[93] Such insubordination was made possible by the fact that Kebich had not developed new mechanisms to monitor officials and punish those who disobeyed orders. As a result, Kebich was like a pilot sitting at the controls of a downed airplane—pressing buttons and pulling levers that no longer had any effect.

In turn, Kebich reaped a stunningly low 17 percent of the vote in the first round compared to 45 percent for Lukashenka—a result that Kebich says he had "not imagined even in [his] nightmares."[94] Weak support for Kebich turned into large-scale open defection in the run-up to the second round. There was "panic as in an earthquake" among Kebich officials, and Lukashenka noted that suddenly everyone was extremely cooperative.[95] By the time of Lukashenka's astonishing 80 percent victory in the second round, most elites had thrown their support behind the new president.

In sum, Belarus's weak authoritarian state and Kebich's inexperience with open political competition led to the prime minister's downfall four years after taking power. While weak identity polarization initially created few apparent challengers, a series of avoidable mistakes led to the rise of Lukashenka, a pro-Russian candidate who presented a uniquely serious threat to incumbent power. As a result, Kebich fell after just one term in office.

Closed Authoritarianism under Lukashenka

"The end of anarchy has arrived."

ALYAKSANDR LUKASHENKA, 7 OCTOBER 1994[96]

Following his overwhelming victory in presidential elections in July 1994, Lukashenka rapidly consolidated authoritarian control—eliminating free media, harassing opposition, and severely weakening parliament. By the early 2010s, Lukashenka had stayed in power longer than any other post-Soviet leader outside of Central Asia without ever facing a serious opposition challenge.

What explains Lukashenka's ability to monopolize political control? Analysts have focused on Belarusian political culture and the personality of Lukashenka. First, a number of authors argue that democracy in Belarus has been undermined by a rural and "lingering collectivist mentality," by a "patriarchal and traditionalist consciousness," and by a population "with a social order rooted in strict, authoritarian power" whose "majority were ready to sacrifice 'freedom' for 'order.'"[97]

It is hard to completely disprove that an aspect of Belarusian "patriarchal culture"—somehow conceived—might account for part of Lukashenka's popular appeal. However, it is worth pointing out that there is little evidence that Belarusians as a whole are less supportive of democracy than their counterparts in other parts of the former Soviet Union. First, the republican legislative elections of 1990s brought about the same share (one third) of self-proclaimed democrats as in Moldova, Russia, and Ukraine. Public opinion surveys in the 1990s and 2000s also show little that distinguishes Belarus from its neighbors. In fact, data from the 1990s suggested that "desire for a strong leader instead of a pluralist democracy [was] lowest within the Belarusian population" compared to other post-Soviet cases including the Baltic states.[98] "Support for democracy [was] higher than in Ukraine, Russia, or Moldova."[99] Furthermore, the World Values Survey conducted in Belarus in 1999 suggested a level of interpersonal trust—considered an important source of stable democracy—that was in line with the Baltic republics.[100] In the mid-2000s, available survey evidence suggested that 65 to 70 percent of Belarusians supported free and fair elections and ending harassment of opposition.[101]

Second, almost all analyses of Belarus focus on the personality of Lukashenka. Such an emphasis is understandable. Lukashenka's innate political abilities—his public speaking skills and populist instincts—were likely important to his political success. The president's extraordinarily aggressive political style and desire for personal power have undeniably defined Belarusian regime politics for the last twenty years. Indeed, the president regularly engaged in exceptionally provocative behavior—arresting high-level Belarusian officials, detaining a Russian journalist in 1997 in the middle of negotiations for a political union with Yeltsin, and illegally evicting Western diplomats from their residences in 1999.

Yet Lukashenka's highly belligerent style does less to explain his success than make his consolidation of control even more puzzling. Indeed, while the Belarusian elite initially sought to cooperate with Lukashenka, his aggressive behavior antagonized almost everyone—rapidly turning allies into sworn enemies.[102] Lukashenka's needlessly aggressive posturing "threatened" his hold on power.[103] Why, despite such polarizing actions—undertaken before the regime became highly repressive and consolidated—was opposition so passive?

Weak splits in Belarusian national identity enabled the transition to closed authoritarianism by depriving the opposition of mobilizing appeals to attract popular support at a moment when state cohesion was still relatively low and authoritarian rule had not been fully established. Facing little mobilized opposition, Lukashenka was able to suppress parliament and create fully closed authoritarian rule relying on a minimum of repression. Subsequently, the consolidation of authoritarian rule under Lukashenka was facilitated by extensive Russian support and Lukashenka's decision to concentrate economic control. Russian assistance, made possible by Belarus's overwhelmingly Russophile identity, gave Lukashenka access to significant patronage and bolstered the economy in the late 1990s and early 2000s. Simultaneously, Lukashenka's tight control over the economy significantly raised the costs of opposition activity.

Belarus's Transition to a Closed Regime

Immediately after coming to power, Lukashenka aggressively censored state media, closing Belarus's only independent radio station and several independent newspapers, including *Svaboda*, the main nationalist paper that had been operating since 1990. Nevertheless, during this period, Lukashenka lacked full control over key institutions, giving opposition important opportunities to resist his efforts to monopolize power. The courts maintained autonomy, and "the machine of mass falsification and administrative pressure had not yet been fully constructed."[104] In addition, state cohesion was still relatively low, and opposition continued to have some access to television. With no organization of his own or experience in government, Lukashenka was forced to appoint ministers with whom he had very weak ties.[105] Lukashenka had limited capacity to engage in high-intensity coercion and therefore was vulnerable to any serious opposition threat.[106] Indeed, Lukashenka openly admitted in a speech before officers in 1995 that he did "not trust the central apparat of the KGB."[107]

What saved Lukashenka during this period was the absence of a powerful anti-incumbent identity that deprived the opposition of sufficiently passionate and widespread support to make large-scale coercion necessary. Lukashenka instead used Belarus's unified national identity to bludgeon opposition. In 1995, Lukashenka called a referendum to make Russian an official language, replace the new Belarusian national flag with older Soviet-era symbols, and strengthen economic integration with Russia. Belarusian nationalists strenuously opposed such measures, which touched on the core of BPF anti-Soviet identity. Announcing that they were "ready for any radical action," about fifteen BPF politicians called a hunger strike and holed themselves up in parliament. "The opposition demonstrated its moral strength."[108]

The problem was that while anti-Russian nationalism motivated a small core of activists, it lacked sufficiently broad support to threaten the government. Lukashenka "could not have chosen a better disagreement over which to fight the opposition."[109] Supporters of the hunger strike were few enough in number that Lukashenka was able to quickly evacuate them from the parliament building on the pretext of a bomb scare—physically attacking some parliamentarians in the process.[110] The comparatively mild violence "scared the rest of parliament to such a degree" that deputies quickly decided to support the president's referendum.[111] In turn, Lukashenka's pro-Russian/Soviet referendum passed overwhelmingly—with 83 percent supporting closer ties to Russia and making Russian an official language, and 75 percent in favor of the replacement of the Belarusian national emblems with the Soviet-era symbols.

Even more critically, not a single BPF politician won a seat to the new legislature in elections that were widely considered to be free of serious fraud.[112] Advocating a national position unacceptable to most Belarusians, the BPF suffered a "profound defeat."[113]

The legislature, consisting of just a few die-hard opposition members, was dominated by leftist deputies and overwhelmingly sought peaceful cooperation with the president (a stark contrast to Moldova and Ukraine at that time). The new speaker, Semion Sharetskii, a "cautious" former collective farm chairman, initially did "everything so as not to antagonize Lukashenka."[114]

Yet Lukashenka did not reciprocate—refusing to show minimal deference to the legislature and openly violating the law. By late 1996, the Constitutional Court had declared 16 of Lukashenka's executive decrees unconstitutional, but he ignored these rulings. Such polarizing behavior forced Sharetskii and other conservative leaders into opposition.[115] Simultaneously, nationalist activism against Lukashenka heated up. The BPF led a series of opposition protests—a "Minsk spring" in April against the union with Russia—including a demonstration of up to 50,000 on the tenth anniversary of Chernobyl.

In mid-1996, opposition parties began to call for Lukashenka's impeachment. Lukashenka responded by organizing a referendum in November to dissolve parliament and approve a new constitution that would reduce parliament to a "rubber stamp for presidential decrees."[116] The proposed changes in the constitution would create a two-tier parliament, extend the presidential term, and eliminate parliamentary control over the composition of the government. Lukashenka ignored a Constitutional Court ruling that the referendum was nonbinding. When Election Commission head Victor Hanchar questioned the referendum's legality, he was illegally sacked. Seventy legislators, led by Sharetskii, began formal impeachment proceedings against the president.[117]

Lukashenka was simultaneously made vulnerable by weak support within his own government. His blatant power grab motivated his prime minister, Mikhail Chigir, to resign on November 18, while many others expressed their quiet opposition to Lukashenka's actions.[118] Simultaneously, Lukashenka still lacked firm control over the armed forces. It was widely believed that he could not count on their support if forced to storm parliament as Yeltsin had done in Russia in 1993.[119]

Yet regime opponents were highly divided. Above all, the separation of nationalist activists from any formal base of power significantly weakened regime challenges. The BPF was relatively successful at bringing people onto the streets in the capital in April, but these activists "were not supported by any of those with positions in power." Thus, "the parliamentary majority quietly condemned the 'mass unrest,'" and the spring protests failed to produce any changes.[120]

The legislature remained uncommitted in its response to Lukashenka's overt assault on its power. While many deputies supported impeachment, over half of them were willing to back Lukashenka, despite the fact that his reforms would seriously weaken their positions. In contrast to Russia or Ukraine, where leftists spearheaded opposition to presidential rule, the left in Belarus had a much harder time mobilizing opposition against the ideologically aligned Lukashenka.[121] Ideological proximity "strongly limited" the Communists' willingness to go into opposition.[122] Indeed, the events of 1996 created a crisis in the Communist Party, which underwent two splits in the space of a month. While some Communists went into opposition, a number of them sided with Lukashenka.[123]

A group of deputies led by Sharetskii continued to push for impeachment but lacked the commitment or support to generate a viable challenge to the regime. The parliamentary opposition was led by former high-level nomenklatura who were "scared . . . and not ready to call on the people."[124] The absence of BPF deputies in the legislature meant that "no one had the capacity to organize street protests."[125] The recently fired head of the Electoral Commission, Viktor Hanchar, called for more radical resistance. "But there were not enough people around him. He could not do it alone."[126] One opposition deputy from the period commented that "at the time, it was less clear what we were fighting for . . . we felt isolated . . . there was no obvious deep basis of conflict."[127] Indeed, many of the opposition had recently been closely allied with Lukashenka—making it harder for the general public to believe that anything was at stake.

In late November, a high-level delegation from Moscow, including Egor Stroev, the chair of the Russian Council of Federation, and Prime Minister Chernomyrdin, arrived to broker negotiations between Sharetskii and Lukashenka. Sharetskii's long experience in the Soviet system made him particularly susceptible to their influence. As one former Lukashenka official recalled, "Stroev in particular was well known to Sharetskii from their work in the Soviet Communist Party apparatus. When both Chernomyrdin and Stroev insisted that the referendum go ahead, Sharetskii had a hard time refusing."[128] Sitting with Chernomyrdin and Stroev, Sharetskii "sipped champagne and surrendered everything that could be surrendered."[129] Under Russian pressure, Sharetskii agreed to halt impeachment proceedings and told thousands of demonstrators gathered outside parliament to go home.[130] In stark contrast to Russia in 1993, the parliamentary opposition refused to fight to the end, leaving the parliament quietly. Thus, the opposition never tested Lukashenka by forcing him to engage in large-scale coercion.[131] While much of the elite and many within Lukashenka's own administration were opposed to the president's power grab, "the weakness and indecisiveness of the opposition forced officials to work with the president."[132]

Subsequently, the referendum, marred by "massive violations of election law," passed overwhelmingly.[133] Parliament was disbanded and replaced by a body filled with hand-picked supporters.[134] Officials from the United States, OSCE, France, Germany, Italy, and Great Britain reacted sharply—condemning Lukashenka's actions and restricting visas from Belarusian government officials.[135] After these events, Western leaders consistently refused to meet with Lukashenka; meanwhile, U.S. assistance declined dramatically, from $59 million in 1995 to a mere $1.8 million in 1997.[136]

Consolidation of Authoritarian Rule 1997–2014

In the years that followed, Lukashenka continued to face significant external challenges. As a number of scholars have argued, geographic proximity to democratic countries creates key challenges to authoritarian rule.[137] Indeed, Belarus's regional neighborhood gave opposition far greater access to resources and support (financing, places to meet) than was available to opposition in countries in Central Asia further from Western Europe.[138]

Yet not only was Lukashenka able to hold onto power longer than any post-communist leader outside of Central Asia, but he faced no serious challenges over multiple elections in the face of tremendous pressure from the West and periodic hostility from Russia. Even during the various trade wars with Russia in the 2000s and the economic crisis of the early 2010s, when his approval rating dropped precipitously, no opposition force was ever able to gain traction.

The sidelining of opposition can most immediately be traced to the creation of a highly effective system of electoral fraud, media control, and repeated violations of civil liberties. Indeed, within the first two years of Lukashenka's tenure, he had created a strictly controlled electoral system in which everyone "in the regions understood that they must do what the center tells them."[139] By the 2000s, the regime had developed "detailed" and institutionalized systems for ensuring overwhelming victories in elections—including quotas of signatures to be collected for Lukashenka in "every region, state enterprise and university."[140] Lukashenka demonstrated consistent ability to engage in massive fraud in elections in 2000, 2001, 2004, 2006, 2008, 2010, and 2012.[141]

By the 2000s, state media operated in "close cooperation with the BKGB and other security services."[142] Opposition activists faced significant harassment from the police and security services. Most notably, it has been widely alleged that Lukashenka was responsible for the death of four people with ties to the opposition in 1999.[143] According to one estimate, more than 4,000 people had been detained at one point or another for political reasons through 2005.[144]

By themselves, however, such authoritarian measures would seem insufficient to explain the consolidation of Lukashenka's rule. As we saw in chapter 3, Kuchma and Yanukovych also constructed highly centralized systems of electoral falsification and invested considerable effort into censuring the media and harassing journalists. Moreover, it is not clear that Lukashenka was much more violent than his counterparts nearby. Thus, the number of those killed for political reasons—four by most estimates—is not much higher than the number who died under Kuchma and far lower than the 187 killed when Yeltsin's government stormed parliament in 1993 and the nearly a hundred activists killed under Yanukovych in January and February 2014. Certainly, the extent of Lukashenka's assault on businesspeople was, as we see below, unique. Yet the president's success in institutionalizing such measures only begs the question of why he was able to so completely sideline independent business actors, while others were not. Indeed, Lukashenka "was hardly original" among post-Soviet leaders in his ceaseless "battles for more power" and efforts to prevent businesses from contributing to opposition.[145]

Instead, to better understand authoritarian consolidation after 1996, it helps to examine those factors that most clearly distinguish Lukashenka's Belarus from its neighbors: Lukashenka's success in attracting uniquely large amounts of Russian assistance, and his imposition of strict economic control.

Most strikingly, Belarus received an array of Russian subsidies totaling billions of dollars in the 1990s and 2000s that were not matched anywhere else in the former Soviet Union.[146] First, Belarus paid the lowest prices for Russian gas of any country supplied by Gazprom—on average almost a third less than in Ukraine, 40 percent less than in Moldova, and three to five times less than in Western Europe.[147] Second, Belarus was allowed to buy Russian oil at subsidized prices and resell it on the world market—deals that generated millions of dollars in annual export revenue.[148] Third, the resale of Russian arms generated $1.1 billion in revenue in the late 1990s.[149] Finally, as Margarita Balmaceda argues, the unique, incomplete, and largely virtual efforts to formally unite Belarus and Russia in the 1990s "stimulated growth" in Belarus and enabled Russian oil subsidies.[150]

Overall, Russian assistance accounted for a startling 10 to 30 percent of GDP and a third of government revenue in the late 1990s and 2000s.[151] It was a "tremendous boost to the Belarusian economy"—contributing to relatively high growth rates during Lukashenka's tenure.[152] Perhaps more importantly, the vast sums from the resale of arms and oil were channeled through the Presidential Fund and directly controlled by Lukashenka. Such income was a key source of cohesion within the state—providing loyal officials with bribes and foreign cars (as well as a range of other benefits to certain "loyal" social groups).[153]

The enormous size of Russian subsidies also inoculated Lukashenka against Western democratizing pressure, allowing him to avoid dependence on Western financing that in Ukraine in 1999 forced Kuchma to appoint Viktor Yushchenko, who toppled the regime in 2004 (see chapter 3). The Belarusian government was in fact able to use its relationship with Russia to dissuade Western actors from more severe democratizing pressure, which many argued would simply push Belarus further into Russia's arms.[154]

What explains Lukashenka's success in attracting such massive assistance? One approach, best exemplified in Balmaceda's impressive study of this issue, has been to focus on Lukashenka's skilled negotiating tactics—overcoming his country's weak bargaining position vis-à-vis Russia. She emphasizes Lukashenka's "crafty bargaining" and impressive "rhetorical abilities" in allowing Yeltsin in the 1990s to appear as a "collector of [Russian] lands" while tapping into Russia's "collective self-esteem" as Russia's "last ally" and the "last defender of the USSR" in the 2000s.[155]

Balmaceda makes a convincing case that Russian nationalism and domestic politics are central to understanding the scale of Russian subsidies.[156] Alliance with Belarus tapped into the Russian population's "enduring Soviet pride." It is hard otherwise to understand why both Yeltsin and Putin would provide the unreliable Lukashenka with billions of dollars in resources.[157] But Balmaceda's emphasis on Lukashenka's leadership seems misplaced. Few would doubt that Lukashenka was a good negotiator. But it is far less clear that his finesse as a statesman was that much greater than that of other post-Soviet leaders—Kravchuk and Kuchma in Ukraine; Lucinschi in Moldova—who were also widely seen to be wily tacticians.[158]

What *is* clear is that Belarus's unified Russophile identity allowed Lukashenka to offer Russian leaders domestic and foreign policy benefits that Moldovan and Ukrainian presidents could not provide. For example, other leaders were more constrained in publicly supporting formal union than was Lukashenka in the 1990s. In fact, as we saw in chapters 3 and 4, divided identities motivated Snegur (in 1989–1990) and Kravchuk (1992–1993) to undertake anti-Russian language and economic policies that provoked Russian economic isolation and support for opposition, triggering crises in both countries. In Ukraine in 2004, Russian intervention also provoked severe counter-reaction by anti-Russian Ukrainophiles in the west. The legacies of civil war in Moldova also undermined Voronin's efforts to garner black knight support in the 2000s. Finally, Yanukovych discovered in 2014 that splits in identity created profound structural obstacles to a Lukashenka-style strategy rooted in rejection of the West and the promotion of Ukraine as Russia's die-hard ally.

At the same time, Russian influence on regime development in Belarus should not be exaggerated. Indeed, in the 1994 presidential elections, Lukashenka beat Kebich despite Russian support for the prime minister.[159] Nor did significant Russian assistance to Yanukovych in Ukraine in 2004 and 2013/14 help his efforts to hang onto power. Furthermore, as we shall see, Lukashenka survived severe tensions with Russia in the late 2000s. Russian assistance certainly bolstered Belarusian growth. Yet autocrats in Georgia in 2003 and Ukraine in 2004 fell despite extremely high growth rates. Good economic performance helps but hardly immunizes autocrats against challenges. Indeed, both Kuchma and Yanukovych were flush with cash when their regimes collapsed in the 2000s.

Lukashenka's survival was rooted not just in a stronger economy or Russian material support, but in the particularly centralized system of economic control that (together with increased coercive capacity and weak anti-Russian identity) allowed Lukashenka to completely sideline opposition and to promote the general perception that the opposition was "disengaged from the wider population."[160]

First, Lukashenka's system of economic control allowed him to prevent the emergence of oligarchs with independent sources of income outside his control.[161] A large share of wealthy individuals in Belarus were directly employed by the state or state companies.[162] Simultaneously, Lukashenka used his control over the police and courts to prosecute and jail enterprise directors on a scale seen in few other countries. In 2001 alone, more than 20,000 individuals, including 400 enterprise directors, were charged with "economic crimes." In 2003, an estimated 8,500 entrepreneurs and enterprise directors—including heads of some of the country's largest and most profitable companies—were in jail.[163] In the 2000s, Lukashenka regularly had major enterprise directors arrested on corruption charges—such as the head of the state petrochemical holding company *Belneftekhim* (a major source of the Lukashenka regime's income), who was arrested after contradicting Lukashenka in public.[164] In the mid-2000s, an estimated 20 percent of prison inmates in Belarus were former heads of state and private enterprises.[165] The treatment of enterprise directors, combined with near constant turnover and arrests of major government officials suspected to be working with opposition[166] made it nearly impossible for an even quasi-independent business class to emerge that might provide opposition with resources to challenge Lukashenka.

The Presidential Business Administration's (UDP's) control over property gave Lukashenka yet another indirect lever over private enterprises, civil society, and opposition groups leasing its ubiquitous properties.[167] Relying increasingly on "astronomical rent increases or termination of leases," the regime made it nearly impossible for many oppositional organizations to function effectively in the mid- and late 2000s.[168] In April 2008, for example, the government raised the rent for NGOs by ten times—a move that brought nearly a thousand organizations "to the edge of closure."[169] Given the extent of state economic control, activists faced almost impossible challenges finding landlords willing to rent space at an affordable price.

Lukashenka's coercive and economic system dissuaded all but the most dedicated activists to engage in opposition activity. While there were relatively few long-term political prisoners, consistent and extensive police harassment often made it nearly impossible for the opposition to function. For example, during the 2006 election, activists attempting to distribute opposition leaflets (a completely legal action according Belarusian law) would be detained for several hours and then released late at night.

Lukashenka's extensive control over employment further increased the costs of opposition activity. "The placement of all government employees on one-year contracts limit[ed] those persons' willingness to provide political support to anyone outside the regime."[170] Threats not to prolong work contracts "forced activists and their relatives employed by state enterprises to work 'underground' in order not to lose their jobs."[171] As of 2008, it was estimated that a thousand activists had been fired for opposition political activity.[172] The dominance of state employment and the contract system meant that "individuals risk[ed] their livelihood" for opposition activity and forced many activists to work outside the formal sector.[173]

Deprived of any resources to survive and forced to live on the margins of Belarusian society, the opposition was beset by a mutually reinforcing dynamic between repression, economic control, and identity politics that pushed regime opponents further into a minority counterculture. The privations required to engage in opposition activity meant that only the most committed activists were willing to take part. Partly as a result, Belarusian nationalists increasingly dominated the opposition as one of the only groups prepared to undertake significant sacrifice for their views. Such nationalism helped motivate other activists but was largely foreign to most Belarusians.

In 2006, for example, the main opposition candidate, Aliaksandr Milinkevich, relied on a stridently pro-European message, the anti-Soviet white-red-white flag, and support from members of the Belarusian Popular Front. Such messages and symbols drew significant support from many in Minsk. As many as 20,000 demonstrated with white-red-white banners on October Square against the regime for several days. The size and length of the demonstrations—while modest by most standards—surprised many observers, given the opposition's total lack of access to media.[174]

Yet it is not clear that the nationalist appeals that helped bring activists into the streets in 2006 had broader public appeal in Belarus as a whole. (Indeed, Milinkevich never came close to winning in 2006.) Polls conducted in the

2000s suggested that a stable 40 percent did not see a difference between Belarusians and Russians, while a vast majority identified themselves as ethnically closer to Russians than Europeans.[175] Close to 80 percent did not consider the border with Russia to be a foreign border.[176]

As tensions with Russia heated up in the late 2000s, a decreasing share of the Belarusian population supported outright union with Russia.[177] However, Russophile attitudes remained "preponderant," and there was little evidence that nationalist or anti-Russian sentiments—in contrast to Ukraine—motivated a significant section of the Belarusian population to make the sacrifices necessary to engage in opposition activity.[178] Most Belarusians continued to see Russia "as an integral part of Belarusianess."[179] Partly as a result, Belarusians did "not recognize themselves" in an opposition that was strongly tied to anti-Russian nationalism.[180]

Because the opposition was so marginalized, Lukashenka appears to have remained the most popular politician in the country even as his popularity declined significantly in the 2000s. There are obviously significant limitations to polling in a country like Belarus.[181] However, available data from the mid-2000s show that Lukashenka had consistently higher support than that of all opposition figures combined—with support for Lukashenka ranging from 40 to 58 percent, while combined support for all opposition figures ranged from about 15 to 30 percent.[182]

The relegation of opposition to a minority counterculture likely explains why Lukashenka was able to survive an increasingly hostile external environment in the late 2000s. Low-level tensions between Russia and Belarus had existed under Yeltsin. But relations radically worsened under Putin, when ties became characterized by "scandals, demarches, and mutual jabs."[183] The Russian government began to chafe at providing large energy subsidies—insisting that Belarus transfer ownership of *Beltranshaz* pipeline connecting Russian gas supplies to Europe in exchange for assistance. By 2005, the Russian government was widely rumored to have considered replacements for Lukashenka.[184]

Then tensions became even worse in 2007.[185] In a "body blow to the Lukashenko regime," Gazprom doubled gas prices from $46 to $100 per thousand cubic meters in 2007, then to $165 by 2012.[186] Belarus was forced to agree to the transfer of 50 percent of its ownership of *Beltranshaz* and a gradual increase in gas prices to European market prices. Simultaneously, Putin introduced export tariffs on Russian oil, which caused a significant reduction in Belarusian revenues.[187] Russian media in the late 2000s increasingly highlighted problems in Belarus[188]—negative media attention that in Kyrgyzstan contributed to the collapse of the Bakiyev regime in 2010.

Such pressure from Russia, combined with Western sanctions against *Belneftekhim*, encouraged the Belarusian government to seek improved relations with the West.[189] This trend was amplified by Russia's invasion of Georgia in the summer of 2008. "Terrified" by the prospect of complete Russian domination, Lukashenka tried to break from his Russian ally—refusing to recognize the independence of Abkhazia and Ossetia in the face of enormous Russian pressure. There ensued a series of mini trade wars—a "milk war" in the summer of 2009, and gas and oil "wars" in 2010.[190]

While Russia ultimately relented and continued to provide major subsidies,[191] Belarus suffered significant economic problems in the late 2000s. Facing a "risk of serious economic shock"[192] due to reduced access to cheap energy, the government was forced to cut social benefits, affecting a large majority of Belarusians.[193] Belarus then experienced near-zero growth in 2009 and 53 percent inflation. Real wages were cut in half in 2011, and surveys suggested that a large majority of citizens felt that the economy was in crisis.[194] Lukashenka's approval rating dropped from 53 percent in December 2010 to 21 percent in September 2011.[195] Following the 2010 election, Lukashenka was "in panic mode."[196]

Yet the marginalization of opposition partly inoculated Lukashenka from the effects of such downturns. Indeed, while polls in September 2011 suggested the president's approval had sunk to its "lowest ever," there was "no corresponding rise in the ratings of opposition leaders."[197] Despite the fact that public support for Lukashenka was "not overwhelming," he was "far ahead" of any other opposition figure.[198] Thus, even when Lukashenka faltered, no politician or groups existed to take advantage of his misfortune.

Conclusion

In sum, this chapter has sought to reframe our understanding of the rise and consolidation of authoritarian rule in Belarus. Many approaches have focused either on the supposedly non-democratic or patriarchal Belarusian political culture on the one hand, or on Lukashenka's political skills and aggressive style on the other.[199] Both approaches are incomplete or misleading.

First, we saw that there is, in fact, little available evidence that Belarusians are less democratic than their counterparts nearby. Next, while indisputably important for understanding the overall character of the regime, Lukashenka's political style and personality provide only a partial understanding of his success at transitioning to and consolidating non-democratic rule. Few would have ever heard of Lukashenka had it not been for the weak authoritarian state under Kebich and the incompetence and disorientation of the old ruling elite that encouraged them to underestimate Lukashenka. Moreover, Lukashenka's aggressive style motivated the creation of centralized rule but also seriously antagonized an otherwise pliable and accommodating nomenklatura. Lukashenka's personality, rather than explaining his success, makes his victory even more puzzling.

To understand Lukashenka's domination of Belarus, it is worthwhile recalling Adam Przeworski's famous observation that support for an autocratic regime hinges on the existence or absence of a viable and preferable alternative.[200] Even weak autocrats may survive for a long time if there is no political force ready to replace them. Lukashenka was able to establish and maintain autocratic power in the face of significant external and nomenklatura resistance by using national identity and economic and coercive power to prevent the emergence of any serious alternative to his rule. As Vitali Silitski notes, Lukashenka thrived mainly by preempting significant opposition before it emerged rather than by putting down serious challenges.[201] The question left largely unanswered by Silitski is why Lukashenka was able to do this when the other autocrats nearby were not. I have suggested two major sets of factors.

First, the weak support for anti-Russian Belarusian identity and the overwhelmingly pro-Russian attitudes of the population in the 1990s allowed Lukashenka to marginalize opposition and divide high-level regime opponents from the most passionate nationalist opposition. As in Moldova and Ukraine in the 1990s, opposition to incumbent rule rapidly emerged from within the ranks of the ruling coalition. However, the weakly polarized Belarusian national identity meant that former regime insiders—in contrast to their counterparts next door—had a much harder time distinguishing themselves from the existing regime. Lukashenka faced little mobilized opposition in his efforts to monopolize political control. Thus, Lukashenka was able to put down opposition without resorting to large-scale repression and violence.

Mine is certainly not the only discussion of Belarusian authoritarianism to focus on national identity. In particular, several accounts have argued that Belarus's "denationalized" and "weak national consciousness" undermined democratic development.[202] But such a focus on the weakness of identity is not particularly illuminating. While Belarus certainly lacked a strong independent national identity in the early 1990s, such identity was not obviously weaker than Moldovan national consciousness, which had been invented just fifty years prior. Moreover, a similarly low share of both Ukrainians as well as Belarusians (37 percent) spoke their national language at home in the 1990s.[203] Indeed, "weak national identity" is often understood to reflect the presence of severe conflict among subnational ethnic or other groups—which did not exist in Belarus.[204] In fact, as we saw above, it was not the *weakness* of national identity, but the *strength* of a widely shared (Soviet) identity that most directly facilitated authoritarianism in the 1990s. Furthermore, it is not clear that weak identity per se always undermines pluralism. Strengthened support for Belarusian independence in the 2000s did little to promote democracy. As we will see in the next chapter, strong national identity in Armenia and Russia facilitated authoritarianism in those countries. Instead, this book argues that the lack of *divisions* in the titular identity have hampered pluralism.

Second, authoritarian consolidation was affected by a uniquely centralized system of economic control. As we saw in chapters 3 and 4, Ukrainian and Moldovan presidents in the 1990s built their ruling coalitions by using privatization and the creation of a loyal group of oligarchs. Once they did this, it was very hard to put the genie back in the bottle and prevent the opposition from gaining access to economic resources. In Belarus, by contrast, no serious effort at large-scale privatization was made in the 1990s—either by Kebich or Lukashenka. Lukashenka, in fact, immediately built an economic system that gave him enormous power over the distribution of wealth in the country. Given Lukashenka's wide capacity to punish business or political dissidents at the elite and mass level, only the most committed activists were willing to engage in open opposition activity. The result was highly consolidated authoritarian rule.

At the same time, identity politics and economic control did not doom Belarus to indefinite domination by Lukashenka. Indeed, the framework offered in this book points to the sources of Lukashenka's regime survival but also draws our attention to potential sources of vulnerability. While Lukashenka's authoritarian system gave him enormous capacity to prevent challenges from emerging, there are many reasons to think that Lukashenka's regime would collapse rapidly should a viable challenge nevertheless emerge—either because of sustained economic crisis or extensive pressure from Russia.

Above all, we would expect the absence of an established ruling party to facilitate defection during crisis. In addition, the lack of non-material sources of cohesion in the coercive apparatus should make it harder for autocrats (like

Yanukovych in 2014) to engage in sustained, large-scale coercion. More broadly, the regime was almost certainly very unpopular with large sections of the ruling elites, who can hardly have appreciated a system in which they were so vulnerable to Lukashenka's whim. As a result, we would expect that, if given the opportunity, elites would defect and that the security forces would resist high-intensity coercion. Few around Lukashenka would seem likely to try very hard to maintain the regime in the face of serious opposition. Thus, if the regime falls, it would likely do so quite quickly with relatively little violence.

6

Consolidated and Unconsolidated Authoritarianism in the Former Soviet Union

The last three chapters have investigated the sources of pluralism in inhospitable conditions through an in-depth investigation of Belarus, Moldova, and Ukraine. We have seen that pluralism is sometimes better explained by authoritarian weakness (polarized identities and weak ruling parties and states) than by more standard factors discussed in the recent literature on democratization—civil society, democratic values, and institutional design. My conclusions have emerged out of extensive fieldwork over many years and a wide range of primary and secondary sources in five languages. However, the reader may wonder whether the causal processes uncovered are unique to these three cases or can help us to understand pluralism in other countries.

A glance at post-Soviet regime trajectories since the collapse of Communism provides clues about the relative importance of theories rooted in democratization versus those grounded in authoritarianism. A democratization perspective would lead us to expect an increase in regime competition and democracy over time. As we saw in chapter 2, Soviet rule had effectively decimated virtually all forms of organized opposition. Soviet power also left several generations isolated from the outside world and deprived them of any experience or understanding of multiparty elections or democratic institutions. If civil society, democratic values, and democratic institutions were the driving forces behind regime outcomes, we might expect regimes to become *more* democratic and competitive over time as civil society developed and grew more effective in the absence of totalitarian repression and as the population and leadership gained greater experience with elections and democracy. Along these lines, Staffan Lindberg argues that experience with even problematic multi-party institutions bolsters democracy by stimulating activism in society and heightening popular expectations about the need for democracy.[1]

On the other hand, if pluralism in the CIS emerged primarily from weak authoritarianism, we would expect the opposite—that democracy would decrease over time as leaders became better organized, states became stronger, and leaders grew more adept at manipulating democratic institutions. In the institutional void created by the Soviet collapse, some amount of time was required to strengthen the state, rebuild patronage networks, and institutionalize new party structures. Furthermore, accumulated experience with multiparty rule often gave leaders greater capacity to undermine competitive elections, co-opt rivals and independent media, control the private sector, and starve civic and opposition groups of resources.

In fact, while individual trajectories vary, all but a few post-Soviet regimes became *more* authoritarian over the course of the post-Soviet era.[2] Indeed, the first competitive legislative elections in 1990—when abuse was widely constrained by severe disorganization within the ruling Communist Party (chapter 2)—ended up being the most democratic election in the majority of CIS countries.[3] Furthermore, where there was leadership turnover, the majority of politicians who took office after the first incumbent demonstrated greater capacity to hold onto power. With the exception of Kyrgyzstan, later incumbents held on either as long as or longer than the first leader.[4]

The role of weak authoritarianism in fostering regime competition is more directly suggested from a brief examination of regime trajectories in Russia, the Caucasus, and Central Asia. Table 6.1 measures the cases along two sets of variables. The first is national identity: cases where the titular national identity was highly split (Moldova and Ukraine), moderately split (Kazakhstan, Kyrgyzstan, Tajikistan), or not split (the rest of the CIS). I also distinguish between cases of higher and lower organizational capacity. Organizational capacity describes the incumbent's access to organizational mechanisms to suppress popular dissent and promote elite cohesion. Low-organizational-capacity cases include those in which incumbents initially lacked any established ruling party or even party substitutes[5] (e.g., Ukraine under Kravchuk, Moldova under Snegur), suffered from severe state weakness including civil war (e.g., Azerbaijan under Mutalibov, Georgia, Tajikistan) and/or did not possess established means of central economic control (e.g., Belarus under Kebich, Russia under Yeltsin, Kyrgyzstan). Cases of higher organizational capacity include cases in which incumbents possessed an established ruling party or highly effective security

Table 6.1 Organizational Capacity, National Divisions, and Political Competition in the Former Soviet Union

	Party-state capacity during first incumbent term	National identity	Political competition	
			Total turnovers 1992–2014	Average Freedom House score 1991–2014
Post-Soviet West				
Belarus	Low	Low split	1	5.9
Moldova	Low	High split	3	3.5
Ukraine	Low	High split	4	3.3
Russia				
Russia	Low	Low split	0	4.7
Caucasus				
Armenia	Medium	Low split	0	4.3
Azerbaijan	Med-low	Low split	2	5.5
Georgia	Low	Low split	3	3.9
Central Asia				
Turkmenistan	Med-high	Low split	0	6.9
Uzbekistan	Med-high	Low split	0	6.7
Kazakhstan	Medium	Med split	0	5.4
Tajikistan	Low	Med split	1	5.9
Kyrgyzstan	Med-low	Med split	2	4.7

Note: Scorings based on coding rules described in appendix A. Full scorings of all incumbents in each country can be found in appendix B.

apparatus, did not suffer from severe state breakdown, and/or retained the means of central economic control (Armenia, Kazakhstan, Turkmenistan, Uzbekistan).

Given the different domestic starting points and external constraints in these cases, we should not expect my variables to have the exact same impact on all cases (indeed, Central Asian cases were, as a whole, less democratic than the rest of the CIS). However, an approach focusing on authoritarian weakness elucidates critical differences in the levels of pluralism across time and across cases within the different regions of the former Soviet Union. Below, we find concrete (though preliminary) evidence that the approach explains increased regime closure in Azerbaijan, Kazakhstan, Kyrgyzstan, and Russia (as well as

Belarus) from the 1990s to the 2000s as well as divergent regime trajectories within Central Asia and the Caucasus. At the same time, expanding the analysis to a broader range of cases offers some important lessons about the dynamics and limits of my theory. In particular, the cases of total state collapse (Azerbaijan, Georgia, and Tajikistan in the early 1990s) highlight the importance of distinguishing coercive *weakness*, in which state agencies suffer from severe underfunding but where the national state remains more or less intact, from a more fundamental *collapse* of the state and social order.

Russia

Russia is a case of unified national identity and increasing organizational capacity. Russia was dominated by a single national identity that pitted small numbers of ethnic separatists against a large majority of Russians. Simultaneously, the country witnessed a sharp increase in organizational capacity over time—a shift that was attended by a precipitous decline in pluralism. In the early 1990s, under President Boris Yeltsin, the Soviet collapse led to a severe weakening of central state control.[6] Simultaneously, Yeltsin refrained from investing his initially high popularity into party building—relying instead on personal ties and a variety of competing pro-government groups.[7]

By the early 2000s, organizational capacity had increased significantly. First, Yeltsin sought to strengthen central control by appointing a large numbers of security officials "accustomed to military discipline" to key positions in hopes that they would provide a "steel rod" to bring order to the state.[8] Simultaneously, state fiscal health improved dramatically due to rising energy prices. As a result, bureaucratic discipline increased, subnational rebellion declined sharply, and Putin re-imposed the Kremlin's power over key coercive and fiscal levers of the state.[9] In contrast to Yeltsin, Putin also began his tenure by creating a single governing party: Unity/United Russia.[10] United Russia ultimately incorporated smaller parties and regional patronage networks into a tightly disciplined, well-financed, and extensively organized "dominant party" by the mid-2000s.[11]

At the same time, Russian politics were marked by a sharp shift from dynamic pluralism in the 1990s to closed authoritarianism in the 2000s. In the late 1980s and early 1990s, Boris Yeltsin challenged the Soviet Communist Party from within and then dismantled the Soviet Union in late 1991. In turn, the 1990s witnessed extraordinarily high regime competition: a powerful legislature, extremely competitive elections, strong opposition challenges, and a vibrant independent media. By the 2000s, after Yeltsin's resignation and the rise of Vladimir Putin, the situation had radically changed. The legislature ceased to challenge executive power; elections became much more fraudulent and media more closed. Opposition was almost completely sidelined.

The divergent personalities of Russia's two presidents partly explain this change. Most notably, Yeltsin's willingness to permit public criticism (as long as it did not "mortally" endanger his power) bolstered a dynamic and contentious independent media.[12] Thus, the stifling of NTV and other independent media in 2001 under Putin can most directly be traced to Putin's intolerance of dissent rather than any shift in organizational capacity.

At the same time, other key dimensions of pluralism under Yeltsin can more easily be explained by the president's extraordinarily weak organizational capacity rather than any support for democracy. On the face of it, for example, the Russian legislature should have presented few challenges to Yeltsin in the early 1990s. Yeltsin's hand-picked ally (Ruslan Khasbulatov) was put in charge of the legislature, while the president's supporters initially had a majority. Furthermore, Yeltsin's vast array of economic and coercive ministries, his patronage appointments, and his control over most major media outlets would seem to have given him a decisive advantage.

Yet, like Kravchuk in Ukraine and Snegur in Moldova, Yeltsin was undermined by a weak ruling party and authoritarian state. First, Yeltsin had neither sufficient time nor inclination to create a new institutionalized ruling party. His heavy reliance on personal friendships in the absence of a party or more established patronage networks encouraged the defection of key allies to the opposition in 1992 and 1993. Lacking a clear stake in Yeltsin's survival, deputies and other associates defected the minute they did not get what they wanted from the president. For example, Yeltsin's chosen successor, Khasbulatov, went into opposition after he was not chosen as prime minister.[13] Second, state weakness severely hampered Yeltsin's capacity to cope with Khasbulatov's open challenge to his presidency in late 1993. Thus, Yeltsin ultimately convinced the armed forces to storm the legislature and arrest the opposition in October 1993, but only in the face of significant resistance from the Defense Minister and Alpha security units.[14]

On a more subtle level, the absence of compliant state agencies "forced Yeltsin into frequent concessions."[15] For example, Yeltsin's strenuous objections could not prevent his own appointees from releasing Khasbulatov and others from prison shortly after the 1993 crisis.[16] State weakness directly undermined efforts to suppress opposition as "orders to stop extremist behavior, to close openly fascist publications" were ignored. "His strict commands to the power ministries . . . did nothing but disturb the air."[17]

The Yeltsin government continued to face crises through the end of the decade. In 1996, the Communist leader Gennady Zyuganov seriously challenged Yeltsin in presidential elections. Fearing he might lose the election, Yeltsin considered delaying the vote—but backed down after the head of the police refused to go along.[18] While he ultimately beat Zyuganov, the president again faced powerful challenges following the 1998 financial crisis, when Yeltsin's erstwhile parliamentary allies blocked his efforts to reappoint loyalist Viktor Chernomyrdin as prime minister and pushed him instead to select Evgenii Primakov, with whom Yeltsin had few ties. After Primakov quickly emerged as a likely successor, many former allies and regional leaders—including Moscow Mayor Yurii Luzhkov—deserted Yeltsin for Primakov to create a new party, Fatherland-All Russia, in opposition to Yeltsin. The opposition's control over large sections of the Russian state undermined government opportunities for fraud. Thus, during the 1999 parliamentary elections, widely seen as a precursor to the 2000 presidential elections, competing factions were able to use vote manipulation in different regions to support their candidates, resulting in a "pluralism of falsification."[19]

At the end of 1999, however, Russia's single dominant national identity bolstered the regime. In Ukraine and Moldova, demands for autonomy and secession mostly split the countries, mobilizing large numbers of Russophiles against anti-Russian parts of the population. In Russia, by contrast, separatism in Chechnya pitted a small, visible minority against the dominant ethnic group. As a result, Putin was able to use the issue to bolster his support and bludgeon the opposition. In September 1999, following a series of bombings in Moscow blamed on Chechen forces, Russian forces invaded Chechnya and regained effective control over the breakaway region. Military success and economic growth generated a surge in public support for the government.[20] The issue isolated liberals such as Grigorii Yavlinskii, who supported negotiation with Chechen forces.[21] Despite its inconsistent capacity for electoral fraud, the progovernment Unity coalition finished a close second (23 percent) behind the Communists (24 percent) and well ahead of Fatherland-All Russia (13 percent). Then, portraying himself as the "defender of the homeland," Putin easily won the presidential election in 2000.[22] (Fifteen years later, Putin would again use

Russia's unified national identity to bludgeon domestic opposition when he annexed Crimea in March 2014.)

Shortly after taking power, Putin began to attack oligarchs who might present a threat. In contrast to oligarchs in Ukraine such as Tymoshenko, who used Ukrainian identity to build support against Kuchma in 2002–04, oligarchs in Russia had no cleavage that they could use to mobilize public support against the government. Simultaneously, greater organizational capacity under Putin facilitated further regime closure. First, a more institutionalized ruling party—United Russia—effectively eliminated parliament as a major source for opposition challenges—even though Putin operated under the same constitution as Yeltsin.[23] In addition, Putin's greater central control deprived regional leaders of key resources and permitted him to undermine regional power centers that had been a core threat to Yeltsin in the 1990s. This control also facilitated much more consistent and one-sided electoral fraud than had existed in the 1990s. Opposition no longer had the capacity to garner administrative resources from rogue regional governments as in 1993 and 1999. Thus, the 2004 presidential election was "the most explicitly rigged contest" in Russia since Soviet rule.[24] After that, Putin essentially took unilateral control over the national regime—giving Dmitri Medvedev the presidency in 2008 and taking it back in 2012.

In sum, a glance at the Russian case uncovers evidence that shifts in organizational capacity may partly explain increased regime closure over the last quarter-century. While Yeltsin was certainly more of a democrat than Putin, key elements of contestation can most easily be traced to the first president's lack of access to robust party and state institutions rather than to any democratic tolerance. For example, there is little reason to think that early parliamentary challenges were a product of the president's support for democracy. On the other hand, while the Putin era was certainly influenced by his autocratic character, the president's efforts to suppress opposition would have been much harder without increased state and party capacity in the 2000s.

The Caucasus

A comparison of trajectories in the Caucasus also illustrates the impact of state strength on regime competitiveness. Armenia, Azerbaijan, and Georgia were small, underdeveloped states that emerged from violent ethnic conflict in the early 1990s. At the same time, they each experienced divergent patterns of state building that can partly be traced to differences in the cohesion of national movements in the early1990s. By the metrics of this book, none of these countries had a divided national identity: no case emerged with the stable and polarized cleavages in the titular national identity found in Moldova or Ukraine. Nonetheless, national movements were demonstrably less unified in Azerbaijan and Georgia than in Armenia at the start of the 1990s. In Armenia, the battle over the exclave of Nagorno-Karabagh unified the national movement and bolstered state-building efforts by tapping into salient anti-Turkic sentiment.[25] By contrast, in Azerbaijan and Georgia, conflicts against separatist movements in the late 1980s fostered divisions within these two republics that greatly hindered early state building.[26] These patterns of state building fundamentally influenced regime trajectories—helping to explain why incumbents in Armenia were consistently able to resist powerful outside opposition challenges, why Azerbaijan was initially quite competitive but much less so over time, and why Georgia was the most consistently competitive of the three countries.

First, Armenia demonstrates how a highly unified national identity and powerful coercive apparatus may help to maintain authoritarian control in the face of serious opposition challenges. Armenia's post-Soviet authoritarian regime emerged out of a strong nationalist movement—the Armenian National Movement (ANM), which led a series of large-scale protests demanding Armenian control over the ethnically Armenian Nagorno-Karabagh territory in neighboring and Turkic-speaking Azerbaijan. The Karabagh issue unified Armenians because it tapped into widespread resentment toward Turkey grounded in the 1915 Armenian genocide.[27]

In the face of ethnic conflict between Armenians and Azeris, the ANM built up a powerful coercive apparatus. After taking power in 1990, the ANM, led by Levon Ter-Petrosian, created a national army and brought irregular paramilitary forces under central state control, rapidly establishing a "monopoly of the means of coercion."[28] The army possessed extremely high esprit de corps and became the center of power in the republic.[29] As a result of such state-building efforts, Armenia conquered Nagorno-Karabagh and seized 20 percent of Azerbaijani territory. The regime's repressive capacity was further strengthened by *Yerkrapah* (Defenders of the Land), a paramilitary organization consisting of thousands of Karabagh war veterans.

The regime's repressive capacity played a central role in pushing back numerous opposition challenges. The regime faced its most serious threat in the 1996 presidential election when Ter-Petrosian was challenged by former prime minister Vazgen Manukian.[30] While massive fraud allowed officials to declare Ter-Petrosian a winner in the first round, electoral abuse sparked protest by about 120,000 opposition supporters who attacked the parliament.[31] In response, the government declared martial law that was implemented by Yerkrapah paramilitary agents.[32] Security forces surrounded the capital, Yerevan, to prevent more protesters from entering the city. Public squares were shut down, hundreds of opposition activists were detained, and opposition headquarters were raided.[33]

Despite its success in facing down such challenges, disagreements within the regime over Nagorno-Karabagh forced Ter-Petrosian to resign in favor of his prime minister, Robert Kocharian, who was elected president in 1998.[34] In 2003, Kocharian won reelection in part through significant ballot stuffing and other vote fraud. As in 1996, fraud sparked substantial opposition demonstrations of between 25,000 and 100,000 people.[35] But just as in 1996, the regime's powerful security forces quickly suppressed the protests—arresting hundreds of opposition leaders and crushing protests before they could grow.[36] Again in 2004, thousands of protesters, inspired by the Rose Revolution in Georgia (see below), came onto the streets against the regime. Yet the Armenian security services were better financed and more motivated than those in Georgia, and in contrast to their counterparts next door, they successfully sealed off the capital from further protesters.[37] Finally, in 2008, Serge Sarkisian, Kocharian's successor, was able to beat back a challenge from Ter-Petrosian and again won reelection in 2013. While coercive capacity hardly accounts for all aspects of the country's trajectory, authoritarian state power appears to have bolstered the regime's repeated success in putting down highly mobilized opposition challenges.

Compared to their counterparts in Armenia, Azerbaijani leaders were at first far less unified and confronted greater difficulties establishing effective state power. Due in part to the relative weakness of Azerbaijani national identity, political forces in Azerbaijan were initially split between the nationalist Azerbaijani Popular Front, which wanted to build a strong, independent Azerbaijani army, and the Communist leadership, who felt they should rely on Soviet forces instead. As a result, Azerbaijan carried out the war against Armenia via disparate and locally controlled paramilitaries that functioned more or less as "extended families" and often did as much fighting with each other as with the Armenians.[38] Simultaneously, Azerbaijan's first president lacked a party. In the wake of the failed Soviet coup, the Communist leader Ayaz Mutalibov ran uncontested in a snap presidential election. However, the Azerbaijani Communist Party dissolved itself a few days later and was not replaced with a new structure as in Turkmenistan or Uzbekistan (see below).

With no powerful state or ruling party, Azerbaijan was "enveloped in political turmoil" for the first months of its existence as an independent state in 1992.[39] Following Armenian military victories, Mutalibov was forced to resign and was replaced by Yaqub Mamedov, who took over as acting president. Effectively, however, there was "no leadership" in the capital.[40] Then, on May 14, following another major Armenian victory, the Popular Front easily captured the parliament and state TV. Pro-government forces, lacking any reliable security forces to back them, "gave up the fight and fled."[41] In June 1992, Abulfaz Elchibey, the leader of the Front, won election as president with 59 percent of the vote.

Under Elchibey, however, chaos within the armed forces continued—riven by an open conflict between Defense Minister Rahim Gaziev and Interior Minister Iskander Hamidov, who operated his own "Grey Wolf" militia. Unable to control them, Elchibey fired both in the spring of 1993—a move that "ironically undermined his authority because [the] men with guns who could prop him up disappeared from the scene."[42] Surat Husseinov, a military commander in Ganja who had refused to integrate his forces into the national army, marched on Baku. Elchibey was forced to flee in June 1993, and Heidar Aliev was installed as acting president. Elchibey's fall can thus be directly attributed to state weakness and his "failure to secure a monopoly of the means of coercion on the territory of the country."[43]

Aliev came to the presidency in a far better position to consolidate authoritarian control than his predecessors. He had access to significant party substitutes. He was well connected, having been a Politburo member and head of the Azerbaijani KGB and Communist Party before being sidelined by Gorbachev. Drawing on extensive networks and critical support from former subordinates in the apparatus, he rapidly created a "powerful political machine, which no other political group in the country [could] match."[44] By 1995, Aliev "had eliminated the last vestiges" of the independent militias that once dominated the country. Most significantly, he signed an oil agreement—the "deal of the century"—which allowed him to firmly consolidate his rule.[45] Controlling vast resources, Aliev was "able to reward and punish his clients by appointing them or removing them from lucrative income-generating official positions."[46] He simultaneously secured his power through the New Azerbaijan Party, which was formed before he came to power in early 1993. Membership in the Party, which controlled the legislature by 1996, "became an important factor in administrative appointments and promotions" and exercised "near complete" control over the higher echelons of the state.[47] By the early 2000s, Aliev had achieved nearly total personal control over Azerbaijan and passed power to his son, Ilham, who was elected president in 2003. Subsequently, the regime faced no serious challenges to its power.

Finally, Georgia confronted the most serious obstacles to authoritarian state building. From the beginning of Perestroika, the Georgian national movement was highly divided—in part over how to deal with secessionists in the regions of Abkhazia and Ossetia.[48] The movement lacked a salient unifying issue akin to Karabagh in Armenia. Partly as a result, the movement splintered into rival paramilitaries. After independence, government forces "were just another militia."[49]

Following the collapse of the USSR, efforts to consolidate authoritarian political control were fundamentally undermined by Georgia's weak state. Zviad Gamsakhurdia, a nationalist dissident who became the country's first president, led Georgia to independence in 1991. While Gamsakhurdia governed in an openly autocratic manner—arresting opponents and censoring media—his regime rapidly collapsed. In the wake of the failed August coup in Moscow, warlords surrounding Gamsakhurdia abandoned the president, leaving him without an effective state.[50] Protected by only a ragtag collection untrained militiamen,[51] Gamsakhurdia was forced flee into exile in early 1992—a mere seven months after winning the presidency in a landslide.

By the early 1990s, Georgia had descended into all-out civil war. Following Gamsakhurdia's exit, the victorious warlords invited Eduard Shevardnadze, a former Georgian Communist Party Secretary, to lead the country. By the mid-1990s, Shevardnadze had sidelined Georgia's independent paramilitary forces and reestablished a modicum of central-state control in the country.[52] However, Shevardnadze did not have the capacity to maintain power, and despite a healthy economy, the regime collapsed in 2003. As in Ukraine, former regime insiders played a central role in facilitating authoritarian breakdown. In mid-2001, Shevardnadze allies—including Justice Minister Mikheil Saakashvili—broke with the government. The president then faced a serious challenge in the 2003 legislative election when fraud triggered a regime crisis. Opposition groups led by Saakashvili organized demonstrations in the capital that ultimately culminated in the storming of parliament by protestors and Shevardnadze's resignation.

Images of protesters storming parliament led many observers to view the "Rose Revolution" as a clear example of "people power."[53] Yet most studies have shown that the demonstrations were in fact relatively small.[54] The largest demonstration, on November 22, attracted just tens of thousands of protesters—no larger than numerous failed protests that had taken place in Armenia, Azerbaijan, and Belarus in the late 1990s and 2000s.[55] Indeed, the fall of Shevardnadze can be attributed less to the size of protests and more to the degree of state weakness. Not having been paid in months, the police simply let the protesters walk into parliament.[56] When Shevardnadze attempted to declare a state of emergency, the military refused to go along, and he was forced to resign. In January 2004, Saakashvili was overwhelmingly elected president.

Saakashvili ruled through a relatively well-disciplined United National Movement. Simultaneously, reforms by Saakashvili increased the coercive capacity of the police, and key regions—such as Ajaria—were brought under central control.[57] Partly as a result, Saakashvili became "the unchallenged master of Parliament," and "the judiciary became his rubber stamp."[58] He was able, for example, to move the parliament to a provincial town of Kutaisi, 150 miles by winding road from the capital. After putting down opposition protests in late 2007, Saakashvili called early presidential elections in 2008, which he won easily.

Saakashvili ultimately left power peacefully after losing parliamentary elections in 2012—resulting in Georgia's first democratic transfer of power. Like Kuchma in Ukraine in 2004, Saakashvili fell at the hands of oligarchs who had previously supported him. In the run-up to the 2012 parliamentary election, the billionaire businessman Bidzina Ivanishvili, whose net worth amounted to more than Georgia's annual revenues and about a quarter of the country's GDP, created the "Georgian Dream," a coalition of six opposition parties.[59] The Saakashvili government responded by aggressively monitoring Ivanishvili, harassing his supporters, and imposing enormous fines on Ivanishvili and his allies.[60] In August, the government declared that Ivanishvili's coalition would be barred from taking part in the elections due to violations of spending laws— but it "flinched" in the end, fearing foreign disapproval.[61] Saakashvili handed over the reins of government to Ivanishvili and did not attempt to run for a third term. In 2013, Giorgi Margvelashvili, supported by the Georgian Dream coalition, won presidential elections with 62 percent of the vote.

In sum, incumbent weakness clearly contributed to turnovers in 1992 and 2003. After 2003, increased party and state capacity enhanced Saakashvili's power over the legislature and courts. At the same time, Saakashvili gave up power without much of a fight—an outcome that is not predicted by my theory. In part, Saakashvili's exit can be explained by his weak economic control: an oligarch such as Ivanishvili could never have arisen if the Georgian state had retained greater discretionary control over the economy. Yet Saakashvili's actions may also be explained by factors outside my theory—namely, the West's significant leverage over Georgia due to Georgia's small size and hostile relations with Russia.[62] With few allies outside the United States, Saakashvili was susceptible to external democratizing pressure.

Central Asia

Central Asia arguably faced the least propitious external and domestic conditions for democratic rule in the former Soviet Union. Far from Western Europe but close to regional conflicts in Afghanistan to the south and a "muscular" and authoritarian China to the east, Central Asia's regional neighborhood was far less friendly to democratic development than that of Belarus, Moldova, or Ukraine.[63] Furthermore, most Central Asian leaders had access to particularly strong and well-institutionalized party substitutes in the form of informal networks or "clans," which tended to be less fluid, more broadly recognized, and more entrenched than informal networks in the western former Soviet Union.[64]

At the same time, Central Asian countries exhibited striking differences in their organizational capacity and national divisions (see table 6.1). On the one hand, Turkmenistan, Uzbekistan, and, to a lesser extent, Kazakhstan emerged from the Soviet collapse with relatively powerful states.[65] Turkmenistan and Uzbekistan were the only post-Soviet states to retain the existing Communist Party intact. By contrast, Kyrgyzstan and Tajikistan arose after 1991 with relatively weak and underfunded states led by incumbents without a ruling party. Furthermore, Kyrgyzstan and Tajikistan (as well as Kazakhstan) each possessed moderately divided national identities;[66] whereas Turkmenistan and Uzbekistan lacked such clear cleavages. A brief analysis of these cases suggests that differences in organizational capacity contributed to divergent regime trajectories in the region.

Strong Organizational Capacity in Turkmenistan, Uzbekistan, and Kazakhstan

First, as "one of the most isolated Soviet republics" with a "high degree of [national] homogeneity," Turkmenistan experienced the least institutional disruption of any post-Soviet state during late 1980s and early 1990s.[67] Saparmurat Niyazov, appointed to head the republic's Communist Party in 1985, was the only leader to remain in office throughout the Perestroika years, and he retained core state and party structures from the Soviet era virtually intact.[68] In late 1991, the Turkmen party "agreed to disband . . . went to lunch together and reconvened afterward to establish the People's Democratic Party of Turkmenistan."[69] Thoroughly dominated by Niyazov, the Party inherited the Communist Party's membership and retained the "primary cells in factories, enterprises, and institutes."[70] More importantly, the country's vast gas and oil reserves remained "tightly in state hands."[71]

Backed by Soviet institutions of control and vast energy wealth, Niyazov asserted near total control over Turkmenistan—including all media, elections, and the legislature. Facing "very tight societal controls," opposition consisted almost entirely of "small groups of dissidents, most of whom live outside the country."[72] It is obviously quite difficult to disentangle questions of institutional capacity from leadership in assessing regime origins in Turkmenistan. Clearly, the emergence of quasi-totalitarian dictatorship and Niyazov's flamboyant brand of personality cult cannot be separated from the leadership of Niyazov himself, who failed to offer even rhetorical commitment to democracy. At the same time, highly concentrated resource wealth, the absence of regional divisions, and the continued efficacy of Soviet political and economic institutions meant that there were few obstacles to Niyazov's efforts to monopolize political control. It seems unlikely that Niyazov could have centralized power to such an extent without these key sources of economic and organizational power. Indeed, the regime remained stable even after the death of Niyazov and the transfer of power to Gurbanguly Berdimukhamedov in 2006.

Similarly in Uzbekistan, concentrated control over extensive resource rents and the preservation/expansion of Soviet era repressive and political institutions likely facilitated regime stability and closure. Islam Karimov, who became the republic's Party Secretary in 1989, maintained strict state control over income from cotton as well as "large endowments of natural gas, coal, gold, and uranium."[73] Because significant wealth "could only be generated by having access to state resources," an independent business class failed to emerge.[74] In turn, Karimov utilized these rent-seeking opportunities to maintain power over regional governments and encourage the "rapid growth" of the security apparatus throughout the country.[75] And like Niyazov but in contrast to Kazakhstan's Nazarbayev, Karimov "retained the infrastructure of the Communist Party in the form of the President's People's Democratic Party," which was formed in November 1991 to replace the previous ruling Party.[76]

Backed by centrally controlled natural resources and relatively "intact" Soviet-era repressive institutions,[77] Karimov created "one of the most stable authoritarian regimes in the world."[78] While Uzbekistan witnessed the emergence of a sizeable nationalist/Islamist movement, *Birlik*, in the early 1990s, Karimov forbade the movement from taking part in the 1991 presidential elections, and *Birlik* lost steam. In 2005, Uzbekistan exhibited signs of instability as protests erupted in Andijan in response to the demotion of a local official. However, these were rapidly suppressed.[79]

It is worth stressing that, despite the preservation of the (renamed) Communist ruling parties in Turkmenistan and Uzbekistan, the parties themselves became substantially weaker and more personalized than they had been in the Soviet era. Indeed, as I argued in the introduction and in chapter 5, a high degree of discretionary economic control allows incumbents to starve opposition out of existence with or without an established ruling party. Nevertheless, party preservation in the two Central Asian cases may have provided an important signal to other elites that existing power hierarchies would remain intact. By contrast, the abandonment or breakdown of ruling parties in the early 1990s in Kazakhstan, Kyrgyzstan, and Tajikistan likely made power distribution less clear in the legislature and other institutions—thus encouraging greater early defection.

By contrast, relative to his counterparts in Uzbekistan and Turkmenistan, President Nursultan Nazarbayev in Kazakhstan emerged with somewhat weaker mechanisms of control—initially choosing to abandon the old Communist Party structure and privatizing significant economic assets.[80] Moreover, prior to the rise in oil prices in the late 1990s, Kazakhstan confronted problems in central control over the state.[81] Simultaneously, divisions between a more Russian north and a Kazakh south increased the potential for opposition mobilization.[82] At the same time, Nazarbayev benefitted enormously from access to significant natural resources, which accounted for about 40 percent of Kazakhstan's GDP by the 2000s.[83] While much of the oil sector was privatized in the 1990s, Nazarbayev retained a "high degree of discretion" over such revenues.[84] Nazarbayev, like Lukashenka in Belarus, took advantage of vast off-budget funds to pay off supporters and starve opponents.[85] In turn, such monies helped to bolster state strength in the late 1990s. Thus, in the 1990s and 2000s, Kazakhstan had the highest per capita military spending in the region and possessed between two and three times the per capita armed personnel of Kyrgyzstan.[86]

At the start of the 1990s, privatization and the absence of any single pro-presidential party weakened Nazarbayev's capacity to control key institutions such as parliament, which was initially "an important obstacle" to the president's personal rule.[87] Similarly, privatization of the media promoted a relatively open media environment in the early 1990s.[88] In the medium run, however, Nazarbayev's "exclusive decision-making authority" over "seemingly limitless" patronage resources allowed him to secure control over the state and to systematically eliminate any serious opposition challenges.[89] Furthermore, immense patronage "dampened ethnic radicalism" as the Russian factor failed to have a serious impact on Kazakhstani politics in the 1990s and 2000s.[90] By the late 1990s, parliamentary elections "were primarily a contest among pro-regime groups," and Nazarbayev had attained near "total control."[91]

Low Organizational Capacity in Kyrgyzstan and Tajikistan

Relative to Kazakhstan, Turkmenistan, and Uzbekistan, Kyrgyzstan and Tajikistan faced far greater barriers to centralized political control. First, Kyrgyzstan under Askar Akaev (1990–2005) lacked a single ruling party, had a weak and underfunded state, and carried out significant privatization of the economy in the 1990s.[92] While more particularistic and less ideologically polarized than in Ukraine, regional divisions between the northern and southern Kyrgyzstan were widely viewed as significant.[93]

After the collapse of the Soviet Union, Kyrgyzstan was widely seen as an "island of democracy,"[94] and witnessed greater pluralism than any other Central Asian state.[95] In the early 1990s, media was quite free, and the legislature "assumed real authority to draft, debate, and adopt legislation."[96] To explain such openness, observers have mostly started from the premise that Akaev was "ideologically committed to pluralism" and set out to "build" a "new democratic political order" but was thwarted in this effort by local clan networks, who demanded anti-democratic prerogatives in exchange for their support.[97]

The argument in this book suggests a quite different perspective—focusing instead on the serious obstacles to authoritarian consolidation created by a weak ruling party, privatized economy, and weak and underfunded state. According to this perspective, early democratic contestation in Kyrgyzstan was caused as much by Akaev's weakness as by any kind of genuine commitment to democracy. Indeed, Akaev's devotion to democracy was "not always . . . clear": he maneuvered to be the sole candidate in the 1991 presidential elections and began appointing hardliners to the security services almost immediately after independence.[98] But in stark contrast to his counterparts in other Central Asian states, Akaev came to power as a near-total outsider—elected in a close vote by the legislature after the two major contenders (both political insiders) were unable to gain majority support. A former professor of physics, Akaev had "neither significant political experience nor solid political backing at the republican level"[99] and, like Kravchuk in Ukraine, was forced to confront parliament without any serious party support. Partly as a result, Akaev's first term was "repeatedly shaken by elite defection and conflict." This fact—rather than any liberalism on his part—probably best explains Akaev's inability to control the legislature in the early 1990s.[100]

Yet in stark contrast to Kravchuk, Akaev did possess access to party substitutes in the form of northern "clan" networks. Thus, in response to parliament's obstruction of his power, Akaev met with leaders of local power structures (*akims*) in the summer of 1994 and gained their support to shut down the legislature and impose a more presidentialist constitution through referendum.[101] In turn, the northern *akims* became "the only reliable source of institutional support for the President" and the "backbone of authoritarian power" in Kyrgyzstan as increasing restrictions were placed on the media, while parliament was sidelined.[102] Yet Kyrgyzstan's state remained weak. In exchange for their support, Akaev gave *akims* significant autonomy, which imposed "limits on Presidential authority."[103] Simultaneously, Kyrgyzstan's security forces remained highly fragmented and "lacked training and equipment."[104]

Such weakness made Akaev vulnerable. Indeed, authoritarian breakdown in Kyrgyzstan in 2005 and 2010 was in large part the outgrowth of Kyrgyzstan's weak state and regional divide. In the wake of parliamentary elections in 2005, southerners who had been excluded from power mobilized what Scott Radnitz calls "subversive clientelistic networks" to take over regional governments.[105] Overall these demonstrations were much more sporadic and far smaller as a share of population than those in Ukraine in 2004.[106] Yet Kyrgyzstan's much weaker coercive apparatus made it possible for a fragmented opposition backed by relatively few protestors to capture key state institutions and overthrow the regime. Thus on March 18, a few hundred protestors were able to seize the regional government in Jalal-Abad in southern Kyrgyzstan. Confronting small and underfunded police forces, protestors took about half the country within a week. Finally, on March 24, Akaev abandoned power as about ten thousand rallied in the capital and stormed the government headquarters. Kurmanbek Bakiyev from the south took power. However, just five years later, Bakiyev's regime fell after a few thousand lightly armed protestors overwhelmed police and took over government buildings in the capital.[107] As Scott Radnitz notes, "the Kyrgyz state was still so weak that a protester could drive a truck through the front gates of the White House, opening the way for mobs to flood into the building."[108]

In sum, leadership moderation may have played a role in promoting Kyrgyzstan's pluralism—particularly in the early 1990s. However, key elements of political competition—most notably legislative power in the early 1990s and the subsequent ouster of both Akaev in 2005 and Bakiyev in 2010—are much easier to understand as a function of authoritarian weakness than any normative tolerance. Furthermore, it is worthwhile considering the possibility that Akaev's initial moderation may itself have been a *product* of his perceived vulnerability. Some form of soft authoritarianism was the easiest regime to impose in the absence of robust party or state institutions. Political tolerance may sometimes be endogenous to authoritarian weakness.

Finally, Tajikistan, like Kyrgyzstan, emerged as a weak state and divided society in the early 1990s. Regional divisions in Tajikistan centered around tensions between the politically and economically dominant Khujand (Leninobad) region in northern Tajikistan and groups in the south—especially Pamiris and Gharmis—who perceived themselves as being excluded from the fruits of power. As in Kyrgyzstan, regional divisions primarily reflected particularistic competition among clientelistic networks for resources rather than broader ideological cleavages as in Ukraine or Moldova.[109]

Tajikistan faced a significant test to its survival immediately after gaining independence. Regional tensions between Khujand in the north and groups in the south were fed by total fiscal collapse and spreading conflict (including an influx of weapons) from neighboring Afghanistan.[110] In the wake of the failed Soviet coup of August 1991, Tajikistan's unreformed Communist party was suspended and presidential elections were held in September.[111] Rahmon Nabiev, the Communist leader from Khujand won with 57 percent of the vote against 33 percent for Davlat Khudunozar, who was supported by Pamiri groups in the south.[112] While the opposition accused the government of fraud, this election was highly contested by the standards of Central Asia, where elections were typically won with 80–99 percent of the vote.

Yet Nabiev was unable to hold onto power for even one year. In response to anti-government demonstrations in the capital and the defection of key generals in the south, Nabiev distributed Kalashnikov rifles to his supporters in May 1992—a move that helped to transform the regional tensions into a civil war.[113] In August, armed opposition units seized the presidential palace, and Nabiev was forced to resign. Akbarshoh Iskandarov, the head of the Supreme Soviet, took over an interim government. Then, under the direction of Emomalii Rahmon from the (southern) Kulobi region, a pro-government alliance of Khujandis and Kulobis recouped in Khujand and, in November 1992, retook the capital, Dushanbe.

At this point, Russia and Uzbekistan gave critical financial and military support to Rahmon, which allowed him to retake the country and reconstitute the central government "with remarkable ease."[114] Rahmon quickly sidelined his Khujandi allies, and the Kulobis became "the mainstay of the new regime."[115] In November 1994, Rahmon beat Abdumalik Abdullajanov from Khujand by 59 percent to 35 percent—a much closer election than in other Central Asian states. In turn, the government "substantially strengthened" the police and security forces, relying in part on numerous "battle-hardened" Kulobis, who had played a critical role in the civil war.[116] While the Tajik state remained quite weak and fragmented,[117] the Russian government provided critical military and financial aid to the Tajik government that helped to prop up the Rahmon regime.[118] After the mid-1990s, Rahmon and his Kulobi allies retained power in a series of shifting alliances with groups in the south. Uzbek and Russian support likely explains why, contrary to the expectations of my theory, Rahmon remained in power for so long.

Pluralism by Default in the former Soviet Union

While this synopsis of post-Soviet politics since 1992 is far too brief to address other potential explanations for regime trajectories, this summary (together with chapters 3–5) provides evidence for a causal chain linking organizational strength and national divisions to levels of pluralism in the region. In particular, we saw how weak coercive capacity in Azerbaijan, Georgia, Kyrgyzstan, and Tajikistan (as well as Ukraine and Moldova in the 1990s) directly contributed to the rise of successful opposition challenges, while more robust coercive capacity in Armenia allowed incumbents to repeatedly suppress powerful threats. Furthermore, party weakness in Kazakhstan, Kyrgyzstan, and Russia (as well as Moldova and Ukraine) in the 1990s appears to have facilitated greater parliamentary power. This account also provides evidence that increased organizational capacity fostered greater regime closure over time in a range of post-Soviet countries—particularly Azerbaijan, Belarus, Kazakhstan, and Russia.

Next, state weakness elucidates the rather puzzling cases of "people power" in Georgia in 2003 and Kyrgyzstan in 2005 and 2010 (as well as in Ukraine in 1993) when autocrats fell in the face of modest crowds—mass actions that were no larger than failed protests in Armenia in 1996, Azerbaijan in the 2000s, or Belarus in 2006.

Organizational capacity also appears to account for variation within the different regions of the former Soviet Union. Differences in authoritarian state capacity may help explain why Georgia was more competitive than Armenia and Azerbaijan (after 1993) in the Caucasus and why Kyrgyzstan, and to a lesser extent Tajikistan, were more competitive and unstable than other countries in Central Asia. Finally, as argued in chapters 3–5, my theory helps explain why Moldova and Ukraine were more pluralist than Belarus in the post-Soviet west.

A comparison of post-Soviet cases also highlights the role of national identity in shaping authoritarian closure. In those post-Soviet cases where national identity has arguably been most unified (as well as salient)—Armenia and Russia—nationalism (absent EU-style external pressure) served the classic authoritarian function of unifying the population around a common threat, discouraging opposition and justifying repression.[119] By contrast, where national identity has been more divided in Moldova and Ukraine, nationalism tended to have the opposite effect of *stimulating* opposition challenges.

The significance of authoritarian weakness to post-Soviet regime trajectories most directly reveals itself in the incidence of incumbent turnover since 1992. Comparing the fate of all post-Soviet leaders (appendix B), we find that 9 of 11 incumbents with relatively high organizational capacity and united national identities survived for more than two terms or passed power to someone within the regime. By contrast, just 3 of 16 incumbents with weak organizational capacity or a highly divided identity accomplished this feat.[120]

Next, Freedom House scores (appendix B) suggest that strong incumbents in relatively unified republics exhibited more authoritarianism than did incumbents with weak organizational capacity or a highly divided identity.[121] Not surprisingly, a closer examination of these numbers suggests that the levels of democracy also reflect regional environment—Central Asian states had the most authoritarian scores, followed by the Caucasus, Russia, and finally the post-Soviet west. Nonetheless, *within* these regions we find a rough correlation between authoritarian weakness and democracy.[122] Weaker and more divided

Moldova and Ukraine were less authoritarian than more unified and generally stronger Belarus in the west; in the Caucasus, weaker Georgia was on average less authoritarian than Armenia and Azerbaijan, which had both created powerful authoritarian states by the late 1990s. And in Central Asia, weaker Kyrgyzstan was on the whole less authoritarian than stronger Kazakhstan, which was consistently less authoritarian than the even more powerful and unified Turkmenistan and Uzbekistan. The one clear exception here is Tajikistan, which had greater regime closure than my theory would predict.

We also find that with the exception of Georgia, the level of authoritarianism generally rose or fell in line with changes in organizational capacity across different incumbents. In Azerbaijan, Belarus, and Russia, Freedom House shows an increase in authoritarianism as better-organized incumbents came to power. Similarly, in Moldova (after 1996[123]) and Ukraine, Freedom House scores rose and fell depending on the organizational capacity of different incumbents. When coupled with the case studies, these relationships suggest that authoritarian weakness explains key aspects of post-Soviet regime evolution.

At the same time, the additional post-Soviet cases highlight important dynamics that were less apparent in the comparison of Belarus, Moldova, and Ukraine—namely, the importance of distinguishing between coercive *weakness*, in which agencies suffer from severe underfunding but where the national state remains more or less intact (e.g., Russia and Ukraine in the early 1990s and Kyrgyzstan), and state *collapse* characterized by a more fundamental breakdown of social order. A weak coercive state mostly facilitates greater political competition only so long as such weakness does not devolve into complete state breakdown and civil war. State collapse (as in Azerbaijan and in Tajikistan in the early 1990s) often contributes to incumbent turnover but can, of course, undermine pluralism by fostering widespread violence.

An analysis of the entire region also provides insight into which aspects of organizational capacity had greater or lesser impact. In particular, ruling parties, which were weaker in the former Soviet Union than in other parts of the world, played a less central role in fostering authoritarian consolidation than state power. Relative to many of their counterparts in Africa and Asia, post-Soviet ruling parties were too new and too personalized to function as an institutionalized and stable source of elite cohesion. Furthermore, no parties in the region were grounded in a tradition of revolutionary violence that could unify the elite.[124] Thus, in no cases were parties strong enough to compensate for weak state structures (e.g., Georgia and Kyrgyzstan) or highly divided identities (e.g., Moldova and Ukraine). Nor were parties sufficiently institutionalized to prevent top-level defections—which explains why presidents sometimes chose to put nonparty officials in the highest positions within the administration.[125]

But this hardly means that we should ignore party strength as some suggest.[126] First, party breakdown at the start of the 1990s fostered enormous elite fragmentation and competition in all but two post-Soviet republics. The explosion of pluralism in the early 1990s is obviously incomprehensible without reference to the collapse of the Communist Party's tightly disciplined organization. Second, shifts in party strength over time in Moldova, Russia, and Ukraine resulted in significantly different levels of competition—as evidenced most strikingly in Ukraine by the extremely rapid reduction of parliamentary power following the rise of the Party of Regions in 2010. In such cases, ruling parties provided a much more effective means of organizing rank-and-file support within the legislature than had existed before.

My point here is not to deny that a range of other factors also shaped regime trajectories. First, leadership tolerance likely accounts for certain outcomes—such as relative press freedom in Russia under Yeltsin. But there is little reason to believe that open-mindedness does much to explain other important outcomes, such as legislative power in Russia (or Kazakhstan and Kyrgyzstan) in the early 1990s. In these cases, weak state and party capacity would seem to provide a more straightforward explanation. Furthermore, as suggested above, leaders may sometimes be tolerant *because* they lack the capacity to monopolize control. Support for democracy may be endogenous to authoritarian weakness. At the other end of the spectrum, no one can deny that Belarus, Russia under Putin, Turkmenistan, and Uzbekistan have been heavily influenced by the autocratic proclivities of their leaders. Yet in each of these cases autocrats would have had a much harder time consolidating control without powerful coercive apparatuses and highly concentrated economic control (a point that failed autocrats such as Yanukovych in Ukraine, Nabiev in Tajikistan, or Gamsakhurdia in Georgia would heartily confirm).

Second, as suggested by the ultimate fate of Saakashvili in small, geopolitically weak Georgia, regime trajectories are also shaped by a country's leverage or vulnerability to Western democratizing pressure.[127] Yet a comparison of Armenia, Belarus, Georgia, and Moldova—all small countries—suggests that the degree of external vulnerability is not just a function of size but may be heavily shaped by national identity and the strength of domestic authoritarian institutions. These factors explain why small states such as Georgia and Moldova were heavily exposed to Western pressure, while other small states, such as Belarus and Armenia, were not.

Finally, this analysis confirms extensive research suggesting that regional context heavily shapes regime outcomes.[128] It is hard to deny that Central Asia's less democratic neighborhood has influenced its more authoritarian trajectory or, in particular, that Tajikistan's long border with Afghanistan rapidly transformed pluralism by default into civil war. For this reason, I have been careful to compare post-Soviet countries in the same regional neighborhood—the post-Soviet west (Belarus, Moldova, Ukraine); the Caucasus; and Central Asia. Controlling for region reveals most clearly the significant impact of authoritarian weakness on regime trajectories.

7

Conclusion

The end of the Cold War era witnessed an explosion of democratic and semi-democratic regimes in countries where few thought democracy was possible—in conditions characterized by underdevelopment, weak civil societies, rampant corruption, and international isolation.[1] This analysis has centered on the diverging trajectories of three such cases: Belarus, Moldova, and Ukraine. All are in the same regional neighborhood, had similar levels of economic development and corruption,[2] possessed equally nondemocratic histories, and experienced nearly democratic rule in the early 1990s. Yet Belarus rapidly consolidated authoritarian rule by the late 1990s, while Moldova and Ukraine fluctuated between democracy and competitive authoritarianism throughout the post–Cold War era.

This book proposes a theory rooted in authoritarian weakness to explain variation across these and other post-Soviet states. At the same time, studies of democratization and postcommunism suggest alternative explanations for post-Soviet regime outcomes. In particular, most scholarship on democratization has focused on the pressures, institutions, and social forces that directly promote long-term democratic development. Such a democratization perspective includes classic studies pointing to the ways in which high economic development facilitates mobilization for democratic change,[3] as well as examinations of more recent transitions highlighting the importance of democratic leadership, civil society, and institutions that facilitate power sharing.[4]

Economic development is an obvious place to start. Yet the post-Soviet space is populated entirely by middle- and lower-income economies not considered especially conducive to democracy. Furthermore, it is hard to identify any relationship between wealth and pluralism in the Commonwealth of Independent States (CIS).[5] Alternatively, the external environment might explain diverging regime outcomes. But in fact, none of the cases in this book faced particularly strong external democratizing pressure.[6] Simultaneously, all were beset by a lack of democratic history, undemocratic leadership, and heavy corruption. They all began the transition with economies concentrated in state hands.

What about civil society? A preoccupation of Eastern Europeanists since the decline of Communism,[7] civil society has been a visible part of several transitions, including the Orange Revolution in 2004 and Euromaidan in 2014 in Ukraine. Yet a closer look raises doubts about its real importance in the post-Soviet region. If the strength (or weakness) of civil society is central to understanding regime development, we would expect democracy to have gained strength over time as the relaxation of Soviet-era controls created room for independent activity. In fact, as discussed in the previous chapter, pluralism across the CIS was greatest in the early 1990s shortly after the collapse of Soviet rule, when civil society was arguably least developed. This is the opposite of what we would predict if civil society is a major driver of pluralism or democracy.

Indeed, the case studies suggest that independent groups played a minor role in promoting pluralism. Even in Ukraine, organized civil society was relatively weak and did little to stimulate protest. Organizations tended to be ephemeral and often emerged just before or during protest (e.g., the student movement Pora in 2004; Right Sector in 2013). While groups sometimes played a role in managing the protests that emerged, there is little evidence that they were important in bringing people onto the streets in the first place. For example, Mark Beissinger's analysis of the Orange Revolution demonstrates that those who *opposed* the protests in 2004 were "more heavily involved in civil society associations" than those who protested.[8] More recently, surveys of participants in the 2013–14 Euromaidan demonstrations suggest that an overwhelming majority (75 to 90 percent) came to the rallies on their own or with family and friends rather than as part of any organized group.[9] Instead, as I argue in chapter 3, the largest and most successful mass actions (in 1989–91, 1993, 2004, 2013–14) were rooted in national divisions.

At the same time, there is little indication that organized groups were especially weak in authoritarian Belarus. For example, the nationalist Belarusian Popular Front had sufficient capacity to collect 400,000 signatures calling for early parliamentary elections in 1994. The problem was not the level of organization but the lack of widespread support. Simply put, incumbents could afford to ignore these groups, which, in contrast to their counterparts in Moldova and Ukraine, lacked broad popular backing.

In a similar vein, some have pointed to the importance of popular support in shaping regime stability.[10] Unpopular autocrats would seem more vulnerable than popular ones. While intuitive, this approach has limitations. Above all, popularity is often endogenous to regime competitiveness. Thus, leadership approval in closed regimes is often bolstered by the suppression of public criticism or negative information. Furthermore, as Adam Przeworski has famously argued, regime support may be heavily influenced by the presence or absence of preferable alternatives to the existing power structure.[11] People may be willing to support a regime if there are no serious alternatives or if the existing opposition appears to be much worse. The existence of such alternatives is at least partly the result of the degree of democracy. More broadly, popularity is unlikely to explain country-level patterns of regime development—unless we are to believe, for example, that Moldova and Ukraine were consistently pluralist because they could only produce unpopular leaders.

Another approach focuses on popular democratic values. Ex post, it is tempting to search for particular "traditions" that might explain these countries' divergent trajectories. Thus, local observers frequently point to legacies of "Cossack democracy" in Ukraine as opposed to a "lingering collectivist mentality" in Belarus to explain divergent outcomes in these cases.[12] The explanatory challenge is that most countries have multiple and contradictory traditions, and it is not clear how to decide which "past" to select. Thus, we can just as easily argue that Belarus had a strong tradition of pluralism grounded in the eighteenth-century Polish-Lithuanian Commonwealth as we can claim that Ukraine had a democratic tradition from the eighteenth-century Cossacks. More to the point, there is little evidence that support for democracy was lower in the 1990s and 2000s in Belarus than in other parts of the CIS.[13] Indeed, the World Values Survey suggested a level of interpersonal trust—considered an important source of stable democracy—that was in line with the Baltic republics.[14] Finally, it is not clear that supporters of the "democratic" revolutions of 2004 or 2014 in Ukraine were particularly democratic. As Beissinger shows, more protesters in 2004 opposed than supported multiparty elections in Ukraine.[15]

Along similar lines, discussions of leadership have sometimes focused on leaders' support for democracy.[16] Yet even "democratic" leaders—Askar Akaev in Kyrgyzstan; Leonid Kravchuk and Viktor Yushchenko in Ukraine; Boris Yeltsin in Russia—engaged in serious and repeated efforts to abuse power in order to retain control: bombing and shutting down parliament, closing television stations, and excluding major candidates from elections. Such efforts should not be ignored simply because these leaders led relatively democratic countries and gave rhetorical support to democracy. In fact, the degree of abuse by *all* sides in power in the region suggests that it is rarely useful to view regime trajectories as the outcome of battles between "democratic" and "anti-democratic" forces.

At the same time, the cases reveal that leadership may be important in other ways that are largely ignored in the literature—including leaders' attempts to build authoritarian institutions such as parties and agencies of coercive and economic control. For example, chapter 5 suggested that Lukashenka's efforts to rebuild institutions of centralized economic control—such as the Committee for State Control (KGK)—was a more important source of authoritarian consolidation in Belarus than his aggressive personality or any "patriarchal" Belarusian political culture. Greater attention needs to be paid not simply to leaders' democratic inclinations but to the organizations they do or do not create to concentrate power.

Some readers may complain that I present an excessively cynical picture of political developments in the former Soviet Union, leaving out discussion of the many genuinely democratic activists in places like Georgia and Ukraine. My point is not to deny that democrats existed but to say that their presence cannot explain divergent regime outcomes in the region. After all, brave and democratic activists also existed in countries like Belarus and Russia, but they faced far more daunting structural conditions than did their counterparts in other countries.

Finally, formal institutionalism has arguably been the dominant approach to the study of post-Soviet democratization.[17] It is easy to see the appeal of this perspective: pluralism in Eastern Europe has often been strongest when formal institutions distributed power most equally among competing forces.[18] While we cannot entirely dismiss the importance of institutional design, my analysis suggests that formal rules have a weaker effect than some would suggest.

First, design itself has rarely been exogenous to the dynamics of political contestation.[19] A focus on formal rules begs the question of why some executives garnered greater formal power than others. Indeed, chapter 3 provides evidence that Kuchma and Yanukovych in Ukraine gained more constitutional power than their predecessors in part because they came to office with greater organizational assets. At the same time, chapters 3–5 provided evidence that the absence of serious identity divisions in Belarus facilitated the imposition of greater presidential control than was possible in highly divided Moldova or Ukraine.

Simultaneously, party strength directly affected the *implementation* of formal constitutional rules. Indeed, pluralism may be undermined more by disciplined and coherent ruling parties than by constitutional design. In Moldova, executive concentration of power increased in 2001 after parliamentary rule was introduced because the Communists were backed by a much more coherent party structure than were their predecessors or successors. Similarly, the 2004 Ukrainian constitution, often seen as the source of democracy in the late 2000s, only promoted pluralism when competing parties controlled the presidency and parliament—an outcome that was virtually inevitable under Yushchenko's multiparty ruling coalition (2005–2009). Indeed, Yushchenko's successor, Yanukovych, quickly established tight control over the legislature for eight months under the same constitution because a single, cohesive party (the Party of Regions) now controlled both bodies of government.

In this latter case, institutional design was certainly considered important enough by actors to undertake sizeable efforts to change it. Yet formal design did not generate the balance of power but instead reinforced already existing distributions of authority. While it is certainly possible to identify instances when institutions have independent effects on political outcomes, analysts need to pay greater attention to the ways in which both the design and the implementation of rules may be influenced by organizational and other factors affecting the balance of power.

In a similar vein, Henry Hale has argued that formal term limits have fostered competition and leadership turnover by creating uncertainty and opportunities for challengers among post-Soviet "patronal" systems characterized by high corruption and weak legal systems.[20] While term limits have likely been a factor in some countries, this approach accounts for a relatively limited number of cases. The large majority (11 of 16) of post-Soviet incumbents suffering turnover[21] did not confront impending term limits; while just 5 of 16 lost power in the immediate run-up to their mandated final term. Even in the 2000s, when more incumbents began to run into term limits, almost as many leaders fell with no impending term limits (4) as with such limits (5) (see table 7.1). By contrast, 14 of 16 post-Soviet leaders who suffered turnover between 1992 and

Table 7.1   Term Limits and Leadership Turnovers 1992–2014

Turnover with no impending term limit	Turnover with impending term limit
Gamsakhurdia (Georgia) 1992	Shevardnadze (Georgia) 2003
Nabiev (Tajikistan) 1992	Akaev (Kyrgyzstan)[a] 2005
Mutalibov (Azerbaijan) 1992	Voronin (Moldova) 2009
Elchibey (Azerbaijan) 1993	Bakiyev (Kyrgyzstan) 2010
Kravchuk (Ukraine) 1994	Saakashvili (Georgia) 2013
Kebich (Belarus) 1994	
Snegur (Moldova) 1996	
Lucinschi (Moldova) 2001	
Kuchma (Ukraine)[b] 2004	
Yushchenko (Ukraine) 2010	
Yanukovych (Ukraine) 2014	

[a] Third term
[b] Left power after second term but had obtained a court ruling allowing him to run anyway.

2014 possessed relatively weak organizational capacity or were in a highly divided country.[22] More importantly, term limits have repeatedly been circumvented or ignored in the post-Soviet context. Thus, between 1992 and 2014, more post-Soviet autocrats (7) sidestepped their constitutionally mandated term limits and were elected for an extra term than lost power in the run-up to their final term (5).[23] In other words, using term limits as an explanation simply begs the question of why certain incumbents failed to get around the constitution when so many others succeeded. Indeed, four of the five incumbents who fell to term limits were weak or in a divided country.[24] While several post-Soviet cases exhibited the highly fluid political dynamics described by Hale, my analysis suggests that this was more a product of authoritarian weakness than an essential characteristic of "patronalism" per se.

In sum, then, we need to look beyond the sources of democracy to understand the roots of post–Cold War pluralism and pay greater attention to the sources of authoritarianism. Pluralism by default describes a range of democratic, competitive authoritarian, and soft authoritarian regimes in which political competition emerges, not because leaders are especially democratic or because institutions or societal actors are particularly strong, but because the government is too divided and the state too frail to impose authoritarian rule. Such authoritarian weakness resulted in often dynamic—but also unstable and dysfunctional—political regimes.

My analysis suggests that two sets of factors help explain regime evolution: (1) state and party capacity, and (2) polarized splits in the titular national identity between relatively equal and politically salient groups. Poorly developed or nonexistent ruling parties and weak, underfinanced authoritarian states or states with little economic control have encouraged allies to defect and deprived incumbents of the means to repress or co-opt opposition. At the same time, national divisions have opened leaders to greater external pressures and made it easier for otherwise weak opposition to mobilize support. These two sets of factors have made it harder for incumbents to control political outcomes by threatening their capacity to create *any* kind of political order, whether democratic or authoritarian.

Among the three main cases in this book, differences in national identity most clearly account for divergent regime trajectories, while shifts in organizational capacity best explain changes within each case over time. First, fluctuations in competition over time emerged from the dynamics of Perestroika and the Soviet collapse, which destroyed a well-oiled party-state that was seventy years in the making. New leaders were suddenly forced to recreate state hierarchies without the Communist Party to impose top-down discipline. Security forces that had previously been answerable to Moscow resisted subordinating themselves to their new masters in the republican capitals. All of this occurred at the same time that severe fiscal crisis and underfunding destroyed morale and encouraged disobedience within state bureaucracies. Incumbents in each case initially had little capacity to use state power either to provide public goods *or* to steal elections.

Simultaneously, the disappearance of the Communist Party in all but a few post-Soviet states created an organizational void that deprived leaders of institutions to manage intra-elite conflict or mobilize support. Leaders were suddenly forced to create new political organizations from scratch—a process that often takes considerable time. As a consequence, executives initially had few means to prevent their allies from going into opposition. The result was highly dynamic political competition in the first part of the 1990s.

Over the 1990s, state capacity generally increased as fiscal conditions recovered and leaders had to time to institutionalize new state hierarchies. In turn, state building facilitated regime closure. In Belarus, Lukashenka built a system of highly centralized economic control. Increased coercive and economic state power both enabled greater fraud and gave Lukashenka the means to rob the opposition of necessary resources even without a ruling party.

In Moldova and Ukraine, where privatization weakened economic control, changes in party strength had an important impact on pluralism. Competition was greatest when ruling parties were highly fragmented or nonexistent, as under Kravchuk and Yushchenko in Ukraine, and Snegur and the AEI in Moldova. Coming to power without the support of *any* organization or backed by an evenly divided coalition, these officeholders faced enormous challenges in consolidating control. By contrast, other incumbents—the Communist Party in Moldova, Yanukovych in Ukraine—built relatively powerful parties on the basis of established organizational traditions (the Communists) or well-funded and tightly organized regional machines (Yanukovych). In the absence of other constraints on authoritarian rule, party discipline greatly bolstered regime closure.

While changes over time can best be accounted for by shifts in organizational capacity, divergent regime trajectories across cases can be traced to differences in *national identity*. In Moldova and Ukraine, polarized identities provided opposition with powerful appeals to mobilize passionate and consistent popular support both at the ballot box and on the streets. Thus, in all seven turnovers in Moldova and Ukraine since 1991, opposition ousted incumbents by mobilizing significant Ukrainophile/Romanianist or Russophile sentiment. Simultaneously, by tapping into broader geopolitical divisions, these splits opened incumbents to external pressure. On the one hand, identity divisions led to the rise of anti-Russian governments, which then faced heavy pressure from Russia. These governments found it impossible to obtain the kind of black knight support that bolstered regime stability in Belarus. On the other hand, Russian support for Russophile autocrats often stimulated a severe backlash from anti-Russian social forces. Overall, Russian intervention and hostility made these countries more dependent on Western diplomatic and material support, thus heightening their vulnerability to even modest Western democratizing pressure.

By contrast, the lack of serious divisions in Belarus made it very hard for opposition to tap into a broad and committed base to challenge Lukashenka. Wide-ranging support for Russophile identity also allowed Lukashenka to take advantage of significant Russian diplomatic and material assistance. In 1996, Russian intervention dissuaded parliamentary opposition from challenging Lukashenka's efforts to impose a highly authoritarian constitution. Then, in the late 1990s and 2000s, massive Russian subsidies insulated Lukashenka from Western pressure that was triggered by his autocratic behavior.

Overall, my approach is intended to highlight how, in the absence of strong democratic prerequisites, disorganization and identity polarization have been important—but largely ignored—sources of pluralism in the post–Cold War era. I do not intend to replace standard theories of democratization or to deny that a strong civil society, high levels of economic development, and strong institutions have been important to democratic transitions in many countries. Yet in numerous countries where such pro-democratic forces are underdeveloped, authoritarian weakness has played a central role. Rather than assume that pluralism in "new democracies" reflects especially tolerant leaders or an "emerging" civil society, analysts need to be sure that leaders have the *capacity* to suppress even modest opposition challenges.

Chapters 3–6 offer case-study evidence that post-Soviet pluralism was an outgrowth of authoritarian weakness. A glance at overall patterns of competition and democracy across the region provides further evidence for my theory. First, the importance of authoritarian weakness is suggested by an analysis of which post-Soviet incumbents survived and which did not (table 7.2). Contrasting the fortunes of all post-Soviet leaders since 1992, we find that an overwhelming majority (9 of 11) of incumbents backed by a relatively strong party/state and united national identity survived for more than two terms without a turnover or transferred power to someone in the regime. By contrast, a tiny minority (3 of 16) with weak organizational capacity or a highly divided identity endured as long.[25]

The distribution of Freedom House democracy scores provides additional evidence for the argument. As shown in the previous chapter, incumbents in relatively unified countries backed by stronger states and parties generally exhibited greater authoritarianism according to Freedom House than did their counterparts with weak organizational capacity or a highly divided identity. While a good deal of variation appears to be explained by regional context (e.g., Central Asia was more authoritarian than the rest of the CIS), we find a rough correlation between authoritarian weakness and democracy *within* the different regions.[26] Countries with weaker incumbents or highly divided identities were generally less authoritarian than their more unified and powerful counterparts in the Caucasus, Central Asia, and the post-Soviet west. Tajikistan, which had greater regime closure than my theory would predict, is an exception (see discussion in chapter 6). Simultaneously, the level of authoritarianism mostly rose or fell in line with changes in organizational capacity across different incumbents in Azerbaijan, Belarus, Moldova, Russia, and Ukraine (but not

Table 7.2   National Identity, Organizational Capacity, and Incumbent Survival

	Medium/high organizational capacity	Low organizational capacity
High split	Survival: **None**	Survival: **None**
	Turnover: *Communists;* *Kuchma; Yanukovych*	Turnover: *Snegur; Lucinschi;* *Kravchuk; Yushchenko*
Medium/low split	Survival: **Ter-Petrosian,** **Kocharian; H. Aliev;** **I. Aliev; Lukashenka;** **Nazerbayev; Putin;** **Niyazov; Karimov**	Survival: **Akaev;**[a] **Yeltsin; Rahmon** Turnover: *Mutalibov; Kebich;* *Gamsakhurdia; Shevardnadze;* *Bakiyev; Nabiev*
	Turnover: *Saakashvili; Elchibey*	

Note: Survival (**bold**) is coded as in power for more than two terms or transfer of power to a chosen successor/top regime official. Turnover (*italics*) is coded as survival for two terms or fewer and ouster by opposition from outside the regime (e.g., not a chosen successor or official with high position in regime at time of taking power).

[a]Experienced turnover but remained in power for 3 terms.

Georgia). Thus, as states in Azerbaijan, Belarus, and Russia became better able to pay state officials and created more reliable coercive structures, they also became less pluralist. Similarly, in Moldova and Ukraine, incumbents who came to power backed by more cohesive parties were generally more authoritarian than those who came to power without a ruling party or in an evenly divided coalition.[27] These numbers—together with case studies in the previous chapters—provide evidence that authoritarian weakness accounts for critical aspects of post-Soviet regime evolution.

Rethinking Authoritarianism

This study also offers new perspectives on theories of authoritarianism. First, authoritarian stability is widely seen as a product of economic performance, which affects leaders' popularity as well as their capacity to provide patronage to allies.[28] This book confirms that although economic performance is often important, its impact may be limited by interaction with other factors.[29] For example, even regimes benefitting from high growth—Georgia's Shevardnadze in 2003 and Ukraine's Kuchma in 2004—may collapse due to national divisions or authoritarian weakness.[30] Furthermore, as suggested in chapter 5, economic performance was itself partly endogenous to identity dynamics in Belarus, Moldova, and Ukraine.

In addition, the analysis shows how the impact of economic crisis often hinges on the apportionment of blame for the downturn. Thus, in the mid-1990s, Presidents Kravchuk and Snegur lost power to other government leaders (Kuchma and Lucinschi) who were arguably just as culpable for the crises in their countries. Despite sharing top power during economic decline, these opposition leaders were able to use identity splits and their support for Russian integration to deflect blame and bolster public support. By contrast, the absence of identity divisions in Belarus made it harder for opposition parliamentary leader Stanislau Shushkevich to avoid a share of the blame for economic decline.

This book has also drawn extensively on the authoritarian parties' literature focusing on the ways in which parties bolster authoritarian survival.[31] In line with these works, I argue that ruling parties are often central to the maintenance of elite cohesion. Focusing on authoritarian durability (in this case authoritarian parties) uncovers sources of pluralism where few observers of democratization have bothered to look. At the same time, this book examines the impact of weak parties beyond the narrow question of whether leaders survive in power. For example, weak parties in Kazakhstan, Kyrgyzstan, Moldova, Ukraine, and Russia in the 1990s contributed to relatively robust legislative power—even (as in Kazakhstan and Russia in the 1990s) when weak parties did not result in turnover. The case studies in this book suggest that scholars of competitive regimes need to pay greater attention to the structure and centralization of ruling coalitions that incumbents bring with them to power.

Finally, this analysis overlaps with the literature on the "resource curse" which argues that oil wealth bolsters authoritarian stability.[32] Indeed, it is hardly surprising that all five post-Soviet cases relying heavily on natural resources discussed in chapter 6—Azerbaijan, Kazakhstan, Russia, Turkmenistan, and Uzbekistan—ultimately created quite stable and closed authoritarian regimes. However, several points are worth emphasizing. First, we find significant variation among the majority (7 of 12) of post-Soviet cases that *lacked* natural resources—relative pluralism in Georgia, Kyrgyzstan, Moldova, and Ukraine; but higher regime closure and/or authoritarian stability in Armenia, Belarus (after 1996), and Tajikistan. Furthermore, oil cannot account for the quite different trajectories among the resource-based regimes. Thus, while Azerbaijan, Russia, and Kazakhstan experienced significant pluralism and instability in the early 1990s, Uzbekistan and Turkmenistan witnessed no such opening after the collapse of the Soviet Union. As argued in chapter 6, such variation is likely explained in part by differences in the strength of authoritarian institutions in the early 1990s. Azerbaijan, Russia, and to a lesser extent Kazakhstan, confronted serious problems of state failure in the early 1990s not evident in Turkmenistan or Uzbekistan.

My analysis also suggests the need to refocus our thinking about the impact of natural resources on authoritarian stability. While a number of causal mechanisms have been posited, studies of oil-based regimes have mostly drawn attention to the sheer extent of fiscal resources provided by natural resources—or what Michael Ross calls the "spending effect."[33] Such resources clearly provide incumbents with greater access to patronage and the means to strengthen state power. But, as illustrated most glaringly and repeatedly in Ukraine, those same resources can easily *strengthen* opposition if not controlled by the incumbent. Thus, even well-financed incumbents with relatively well-funded security services (e.g., Kuchma and Yanukovych in 2004 and 2014) may be vulnerable to defeat at the hands of semi-independent oligarchs with resources. As chronicled in chapter 3, key oligarchs in 2004 and 2014 openly backed opposition and/or kept their distance from incumbent power at critical moments, greatly facilitating regime breakdown. The contrasting case of Belarus illustrates that regime outcomes are heavily influenced not just by the *quantity* of resources but by *who controls them*. Resource rents such as oil and gas certainly provide autocrats with significant cash for patronage; but more importantly, they are relatively easy for even weak autocrats to monopolize. It is almost certainly simpler to centralize economic control if most wealth comes out of a few spigots than if autocrats have to seize a large numbers of factories, farms, or other enterprises.[34] Indeed, economic control likely explains why oil-based regimes tend to be especially robust in the face of economic downturns.[35] Crises may dramatically reduce the extent of regime spending, but they are unlikely to have much effect on economic control.[36]

Pluralism by Default beyond Eurasia

The argument laid out here emerged from a close examination of the former Soviet Union. Yet this approach has potential applicability to a wide range of transitions. Indeed, autocratic failure may have been one of the factors at play in successful transitions in much older, established Western democracies. For example, in the United States the absence of a standing army has been cited as a reason why the Federalists ultimately failed to implement the Sedition Act and suppress Republican dissent in the late eighteenth century.[37] Similarly, a number of authors have argued that the erosion of the English monarchy's monopoly over political power and the emergence of a democratic order in Great Britain was rooted not only in the rise of commerce but also in the fact that—unlike many of its continental counterparts in the seventeenth century—the country lacked a centralized standing army and an "effective administrative and legal machinery of its own that could force its will on the countryside."[38] As Barrington Moore notes, the crown could hardly repress the gentry when the gentry itself provided coercive order in much of the country.[39] While such weakness was certainly not the only or even most important cause of democratic success in the Western core, coercive capacity may have played a more important role than is often assumed.

In the contemporary era, authoritarian weakness also may account for variations in the level of pluralism in Sub-Saharan Africa. Like their counterparts in the former Soviet Union, countries in Sub-Saharan Africa emerged from the Cold War with generally weak democratic prerequisites but nonetheless saw the rise of a number of highly democratic regimes. As a whole, African states were quite weak, but they varied substantially in the strength and cohesion of specialized organs of repression in the early 1990s. On the one hand, countries such as Benin, Madagascar, and Zambia, as well as Botswana and Mauritius possessed relatively underdeveloped, highly fractious, and/or severely underfunded agencies of coercion;[40] while countries like Cameroon, Eritrea, Ethiopia, Zimbabwe, and Rwanda (after 1994) began the 1990s with massive and cohesive internal security services that were in part the product of long and successful violent struggles for power.

Such divergent legacies may be one factor shaping the degree of post–Cold War pluralism. Thus, it may not be a coincidence that the two most consistently democratic countries in Africa—Botswana and Mauritius—also possessed extremely undersized militaries for most of their existence as independent states.[41] The absence of cohesive and powerful security forces often increased the costs of repression and frequently made it harder for leaders to suppress opposition through force. The weakness of security services in Benin, Madagascar, Malawi, Mali, and Zambia in the early 1990s undermined efforts to crack down on opposition challenges and likely contributed to relatively open regimes in these countries.[42] Such weakness—most often accompanied by severe fiscal shortfalls and weak cohesion at the top—also made these countries vulnerable to even modest external democratizing pressures.

By contrast, highly cohesive and well-developed security forces that emerged from armed conflict in Cameroon, Eritrea, Ethiopia, and Zimbabwe allowed autocrats in these countries to stamp out even powerful opposition challenges and remain in power for a very long time in the face of post–Cold War democratizing pressures.[43] Comparing the range of cases in the region, we find that an overwhelming proportion of the most pluralist countries in Sub-Saharan Africa had fractious, underfunded, and/or weakly developed security services at the start of the 1990s; while most of the longest lasting and most repressive authoritarian regimes entered the 1990s with extremely well-developed coercive agencies.[44] Although it is certainly possible to identify African democracies with strong coercive states (South Africa, Namibia, and to a lesser extent Ghana), such cases do not appear to be representative of pluralist regimes on the continent. Further research may demonstrate that authoritarian state weakness is an important source of pluralism in the region.

Nevertheless, a glance at some of the African "success" stories—Benin, Madagascar, Mali, and Zambia—reminds us of the contradiction that is central to this book: where democratic prerequisites are weak, the same factors that facilitate democratic political competition may also critically undermine governance and longer-term democratic development.[45] On the one hand, weakened coercive control and national polarization may undermine leaders' ability to monopolize political control. On the other hand, such weakness may facilitate corruption, dysfunction, and, in extreme cases, fundamental breakdown in social order. For example, Mali, despite extreme poverty, was for years a "model of African democracy" partly because its leaders lacked the coercive or party capacity to impose political control.[46] Yet Mali's fragile state also contributed to the country's descent into chaos and civil war in 2012. Similarly, as discussed in chapter 3, national divisions in Ukraine helped bring Euromaidan protesters onto the streets and led to the ouster of the autocratic Yanukovych in 2014 but also directly contributed to violent conflict.

If we look beyond the dominant explanations of democracy, we can identify critical dynamics that have been largely ignored in discussions of political transitions. Where pluralism is primarily a function of authoritarian failure, electoral turnovers and the persistence of democratic or semi-democratic politics may do nothing to promote democratic consolidation[47] but may instead reflect weak institutions. Such cases of pluralism by default may exhibit flashes of democracy, stunning opposition victories, and inspiring examples of "people power." But they are also likely to face major crises in the future that will bedevil their people, their leaders, and the West for years to come.

Appendix A

Coding Rules for Main Variables

CODING RULES FOR REGIME CLOSURE

Scores for regime closure are broken up into four categories: electoral control, media control, parliamentary subordination, and opposition subordination. Each is scored high (2), medium (1), or low (0) and combined into a single composite "regime closure" score.

ELECTORAL CONTROL

Electoral manipulation describes the degree to which elections for the country's top executive are manipulated by the incumbent.

High electoral control indicates that manipulation—via banning opposition candidates, pervasive bans on opposition campaigning, invalidating opposition victories, or centrally coordinated electoral abuse (large-scale voter intimidation, ballot tampering, falsification of results)—is sufficiently high to effectively eliminate uncertainty in the electoral process in the eyes of most independent observers.

Score: 2

Medium electoral control means that elections are characterized by widespread abuse— serious partisan manipulation of voter rolls, large-scale voter intimidation or disruption of voting, ballot tampering, and/or some falsification of results. However, abuse is not sufficiently serious to make the elections uncompetitive.

Score: 1

Low electoral control indicates that elections are more or less free of serious abuse. In such cases, problems that exist do not seriously hamper the ability of opposition to compete.

Score: 0

MEDIA CONTROL

Media control reflects the extent to which opposition government critics are given access to large-audience electronic media, including national television and radio.

High media control indicates the almost total absence of opposition in large-audience electronic media such as national television and national radio available

to citizens in the country. In such cases, government critics either have virtually no access to any media or are limited to low-circulation print media.
    Score: 2

Medium media control indicates that the top executive uses its administrative authority to exercise effective partisan control over the content of large sections of the national media. As a result of government abuse, opposition faces serious obstacles in gaining access to national media. However, citizens continue to have access to large-audience media that openly criticize the government.
    Score: 1

Low media control indicates that opposition has widespread and relatively unimpeded access to large-audience media.
    Score: 0

PARLIAMENTARY SUBORDINATION

Parliamentary subordination describes the effective balance of power between the top executive and the legislature.

High parliamentary subordination indicates that the country's top executive manipulates the legislature at will to the extent that the body provides virtually no challenge to executive authority. In such cases, opposition within the legislature either does not exist or is extremely marginal and completely excluded from the policymaking process.
    Score: 2

Medium parliamentary subordination indicates that the balance of power heavily favors the executive, but parliament is able nonetheless to challenge the executive occasionally in a serious way or force compromise on important issues such as appointments or key policy decisions. In such cases, top executives generally dominate, but strong and vocal anti-incumbent parties present persistent and periodically effective sources of opposition.
    Score: 1

Low parliamentary subordination indicates that the balance of power between executive and parliament is widely perceived to be more or less equal or favoring parliament. In such cases, the top executive is regularly forced to make serious compromises on key issues such as selection of the prime minister, constitutional design, or major policies.
    Score: 0

OPPOSITION SUBORDINATION

Opposition subordination describes the degree to which opposition forces are marginalized as an effective threat to the incumbent's position as head of state. This aspect of regime closure is divided into two dimensions: (1) suppression of opposition capacity to mobilize; and (2) how long the leader is able to survive without being ousted by an opposition force. These two dimensions are scored and averaged into a single opposition subordination score.

High opposition subordination exists when incumbent power successfully marginalizes opposition to the extent that regime opponents have little or no de facto ability to operate openly. In such cases, opposition is widely perceived to be completely outside the political process.

Suppression of opposition mobilization:

A high score is given when opposition is effectively prevented (via physical attacks, repressive laws, political detentions, and/or frequent use of legal or tax system to harass critics) from openly mobilizing support on a national scale. In such a case, opposition is effectively forced to operate clandestinely or openly in just one or two parts of the country.

Score: 2

Incumbent survival:

A case of high incumbent survival exists when the opposition is prevented from coming to power for at least three terms or (when no terms exist) 15 years.

Score: 2

Medium opposition subordination exists when opposition faces serious harassment but is able to mobilize significant public support (as evidenced by frequent protest actions or significant electoral support[1]) to present a real threat to incumbent power.

Suppression of opposition mobilization:

A medium score is given when opposition faces serious harassment (via physical attacks, repressive laws, political detentions, and/or frequent use of legal or tax system to harass critics) that appreciably hampers its activity. However, opposition is nonetheless able to openly mobilize support on a national scale.

Score: 1

Incumbent survival:

A case of medium incumbent survival exists when opposition comes to power after two terms or (when no terms exist) 10 years.

Score: 1

Weak opposition subordination exists when opposition faces few obstacles and regularly and successfully challenges the incumbent's power and demonstrates the capacity to overthrow incumbent rule.

Suppression of opposition mobilization:

A low score is given when at least some opposition to incumbent rule faces few or no obstacles in mobilizing throughout the country.

Score: 0

---

[1] Only cases where electoral control is medium or low.

Table A.1   Regime Closure: Overall Scores

	Ukraine			
	Kravchuk	Kuchma	Yushchenko	Yanukovych
Electoral manipulation	0	1	0	1
Media control	1	1	0	1
Parliamentary subordination	0	1	0	1
Opposition subordination	0	1	0	0.5
Total (out of 8)	1 (low)	4 (medium)	0 (low)	3.5 (medium)

Incumbent survival:

A case of low incumbent survival exists when the opposition comes to power within the first term or (when no terms exist) within 5 years.

   Score: 0

Overall Scores for Regime Closure:

   6–8: High
   3–5: Medium
   0–2: Low

CODING RULES FOR INCUMBENT TURNOVER, DEMOCRATIC AND AUTHORITARIAN CONSOLIDATION

Incumbent turnover: Incumbent turnover occurs when the top executive is replaced by someone from outside the existing ruling coalition. Successors are considered to be part of the old ruling coalition when they are chosen by the incumbent or the incumbent ruling party or are a high-level official in the previous government immediately prior to gaining power.

Democratic consolidation: "Stable" or "consolidated" democracies are democratic regimes in which major rules regulating the structure and acquisition of power change very infrequently and are taken for granted by virtually all major regime actors. In "unstable" or "unconsolidated" democracies, regime change is frequent and powerful actors regularly seek to upend the fundamental rules of the game.

Authoritarian consolidation: "Stable" or "consolidated" authoritarian regimes are defined as authoritarian regimes in which no political force from outside the ruling coalition exists that is widely perceived by outside observers to be a serious threat to incumbent power.

	Moldova			Belarus	
Snegur	Lucinschi	PCRM	AEI	Kebich	Lukashenka
0	0	0	0	1	2
0	0	1	1	1	2
0	0	2	0	1	2
0	0	1	0	0	2
0 (low)	0 (low)	4 (medium)	1 (low)	3 (medium)	8 (high)

CODING RULES FOR ORGANIZATIONAL CAPACITY

Organizational capacity is divided into the dimensions of state coercive capacity, discretionary economic control, and party strength. Each of these dimensions is scored from high to low (with an equivalent numerical scoring 4 to 0) and combined into a single organizational capacity score (12 to 0).

STATE COERCIVE CAPACITY

Coercive capacity refers to the effective reach and cohesion of the state's coercive apparatus. The "coercive apparatus" is understood here broadly to include the army and police and intelligence forces as well as other state agents—local prefects, tax officials, and state enterprise directors—who may be mobilized to harass the opposition.

Low Coercive Capacity: Evidence of complete breakdown of central control/ social order (e.g., the presence of warlords) in large sections of the country. Unusually small/underdeveloped security apparatus. Severe deficits of funding, equipment, and training.
    Score: 0
Medium-Low Coercive Capacity: Representatives of central state maintain an effective presence across the national territory (as evidenced by the maintenance of elementary social order throughout the country), but there exists severe underfunding, persistent and substantial wage arrears to state officials, and/or prior evidence of significant insubordination by state security officials, including attempted coups, open rebellion, large-scale desertion, open refusal to carry out major executive orders.
    Score: 1
Medium Coercive Capacity: Representatives of central state maintain an effective presence across virtually the entire national territory (as evidenced

by the maintenance of elementary social order throughout the country). State apparatus is well funded, equipped, and trained; no recent defeat in national military conflict; little evidence of previous insubordination; no non-material sources of cohesion (see below).

Score: 2

High Coercive Capacity: Representatives of central state maintain an effective presence across virtually the entire national territory. State apparatus well-funded, equipped, and trained; no recent defeat in national military conflict; little evidence of previous insubordination. Evidence of non-material sources of cohesion including (1) sultanistic family ties (as evidenced by the extensive penetration of key state agencies by the top executive's extended family); (2) recent history of successful military conflict: large-scale external war (without defeat); intense and enduring military competition or threat; successful revolutionary or anticolonial struggle.

Score: 4

DISCRETIONARY STATE CONTROL OF THE ECONOMY

Discretionary state control of the economy describes the extent to which incumbents can unilaterally control economic resources for use in political battles.

Low discretionary economic control: Cases in which there is a significant private sector (above 50 percent of GDP as measured by EBRD) and there is perceived to be a strong rule of law that effectively protects property rights.

Score: 0

Low-Medium discretionary economic control: Cases in which there is a weak private sector (less than 50 percent of GDP as measured by EBRD) but weak central control/significant insubordination by local economic/state officials; no established mechanism of central control/planning.

Score: 1

Medium discretionary economic control: Cases in which there is a significant private sector (at least 50 percent of GDP as measured by EBRD) but in which there is a weak rule of law and relatively effective central control that gives incumbents significant capacity to harass and indirectly control private companies.

Score: 2

High discretionary economic control: Cases in which the incumbent enjoys a high degree of discretionary control over a state sector, accounting for at least 50 percent of GDP in a context of effective central state control; or in which natural resource rents account for at least 20 percent of the country's GDP.[2]

Score: 4

---

[2] As measured by World Bank World Development Indicators: "Total natural resources rents (% of GDP)."

PARTY STRENGTH

Party strength describes the cohesiveness and organization of the ruling coalition. Strength is determined by (1) the degree of centralization and organization of the ruling coalition; and (2) whether patronage-based exchange in the party is bolstered by non-material ties.

Low Party Strength: Incumbent comes to power with no party, lacks access to well-established regional patronage networks or other party substitutes

Or

Comes to power via a coalition of parties in which no party or politician overwhelmingly dominates the other members of the coalition.[3]

Score: 0

Med-Low Party Strength: Incumbent comes to power backed by centralized, multiparty coalition in which coalition parties are clearly subordinated to the incumbent party or politician.

Or

Incumbent comes to power as the clearly dominant figure in a well-established regional patronage network or other party substitute.

Or

Incumbent comes to power through one ruling party, which has not run in two elections.

Score: 1

Medium Party Strength: Incumbent comes to power through one party with a presence in a large share of the country's major cities that has run in at least two successive elections. No evidence of non-material sources of cohesion

Score: 2

High Party Strength: Incumbent comes to power (1) backed by one ruling party with a presence in a large share of the country's major cities that has run in at least two consecutive elections; (2) the party is backed by non-material sources of cohesion including sultanistic family ties (as evidenced by the extensive penetration of party by incumbent's extended family), founding in revolutionary or anticolonial struggle; highly salient shared ideology in a context in which this ideological cleavage is dominant.

Score: 4

Overall Scores for Organizational Capacity

10–12: High

8–9: Medium-High

5–7: Medium

---

[3] This is indicated if the incumbent has made a power sharing agreement with a major opponent prior to acceding to power or (in a parliamentary system) if no party has more than two thirds of the seats in a coalition.

Table A.2   Organizational Capacity Overall Scores

	Ukraine			
	Kravchuk	Kuchma	Yushchenko	Yanukovych
Coercive capacity	1	2	2	2
Economic control	1	2	2	2
Party strength	0	1	0	2
Total organizational capacity (out of 12)	2 (low)	5 (medium)	4 (med-low)	6 (medium)

3–4: Medium-Low
0–2: Low

CODING RULES FOR NATIONAL DIVIDE

Divided national identities exist when there are relatively equal and politically salient divisions in the titular national identity along ethnic, regional, cultural, or other lines.[4] Relatively equal means that each of the main competing identity groups has sufficient support either to gain national power by itself or as an equal member in a coalition with other groups. This definition excludes national divisions involving separatist minorities that do not seek national power (e.g., Abkhaz in Georgia, Chechens in Russia) as well as countries with minorities (e.g., Coptic Christians in Egypt) that are widely considered to be too small to ever gain national power.

High national divide

- Strong ex ante evidence of politically salient, easily identifiable, and relatively equal divisions in titular national identity along ethnic, regional, cultural, or other lines.
- Main opposition to incumbent rule mostly from the opposing identity group.
- Divide in part reflects highly salient, deep-seated ideological/cultural divide or competing worldviews.

---

[4] I define national identity as the conception of community that forms the basis and/or justification of claims for statehood. Such community may be defined by perceived common ancestry, language, physical characteristics, culture, values, religion, shared history, and/or conception of out-group.

	Moldova			Belarus	
Snegur	Lucinschi	PCRM	AEI	Kebich	Lukashenka
0	1	1	1	1	2
1	2	2	2	1	4
0	1	2	0	0	0
1 (low)	4 (med-low)	5 (medium)	3 (med-low)	2 (low)	6 (medium)

Medium national divide
- Strong ex ante evidence of politically salient, easily identifiable, and relatively equal divisions in titular national identity along ethnic, regional, cultural, or other lines.
- Main opposition to incumbent rule mostly from the opposing identity group, but not always.
- Divide reflects particularistic demands for resources but not broader and more deep-seated ideological/cultural divide or competing worldviews.

Low national divide
- No strong ex ante evidence of politically salient, easily identifiable, and relatively equal divisions in national identity along ethnic, regional, cultural, or other lines.

Appendix B

Table B.1 National Identity, Organizational Capacity, and Regime Outcomes among Post-Soviet Incumbents

Incumbent (years in power)[a]	National identity	Party score	State coercive score	State economic control score
Armenia				
Ter-Petrosian ('91–'98)	Low split	1	4	1
Kocharian ('98–'08)	Low split	0	4	2
Sarkisian ('08–)	Low split	0	4	2
Azerbaijan				
Mutalibov ('91–'92)	Low split	0	0	4
Elchibey ('92–'93)	Low split	1	0	4
H. Aliev ('93–'03)	Low split	1	2	4
I. Aliev ('03–)	Low split	2	2	4
Belarus				
Kebich ('91–'94)	Low split	0	1	1
Lukashenka ('94–)	Low split	0	2	4
Georgia				
Gamsakhurdia ('91–'92)	Low split	1	0	1
Shevardnadze ('92–'03)	Low split	1	0	1
Saakashvili ('04–'13)	Low split	1	2	2
Margvelashvili ('13–)	Low split	0	2	2
Kazakhstan				
Nazarbayev ('91–)	Med split	1	1	4
Kyrgyzstan				
Akaev ('91–'05)	Med split	1	1	1
Bakiyev ('05–'10)	Med split	1	1	2
Atambayev ('10–)	Med split	2	0	2

Overall organizational capacity	Overall organizational capacity	Terms in office[a]	Turnover?[b]	Average Freedom House score (1991–2014)[c]
		No leadership turnovers		4.3
6	Medium	<2	No	4
6	Medium	2	No	4.2
6	Medium	1+	No[d]	4.8
		2 leadership turnovers		5.5
4	Med-low	<1	Yes	5
5	Medium	<1	Yes	5
7	Medium	2	No	5.5
8	Med-high	2+	No	5.6
		1 leadership turnover		5.9
2	Low	<1	Yes	4
6	Medium	3+	No	6.2
		3 leadership turnovers		3.9
2	Low	<1	Yes	5.5
2	Low	2	Yes	4.1
5	Medium	2	Yes	3.4
4	Med-low	<1	No[d]	3
		No leadership turnovers		5.4
6	Medium	3+	No	5.4
		2 leadership turnovers		4.7
3	Med-low	2+	Yes	4.6
4	Med-low	<2	Yes	4.7
4	Med-low	<1	No[d]	5

(continued)

Incumbent (years in power)[a]	National identity	Party score	State coercive score	State economic control score
Moldova				
Snegur ('91–'96)	High split	0	0	1
Lucinschi ('97–'01)	High split	1	1	2
PCRM ('01–'09)	High split	2	1	2
AEI /Pro European Coalition ('09–)	High split	0	1	2
Russia				
Yeltsin ('91–'99)	Low split	0	0	1
Putin (2000–)	Low split	1	2	4
Tajikistan				
Nabiev ('91–'92)	Med split	1	0	1
Rahmon ('92–)	Med split	1	0	1
Turkmenistan				
Niyazov ('91–'06)	Low split	2	2	4
Berdimuhamedov ('06–)	Low split	2	2	4
Ukraine				
Kravchuk ('91–'94)	High split	0	1	1
Kuchma ('94–'04)	High split	1	2	2
Yushchenko ('05–'09)	High split	0	2	2
Yanukovych ('10–'14)	High split	2	2	2
Poroshenko ('14–)	Low split	0	0	2
Uzbekistan				
Karimov ('91–)	Low split	2	2	4

Note: Scoring is for the incumbent's first term in office.

[a] As of 31 December 2014; interim leaders excluded.
[b] Turnover coded if transfer of power to an official who was outside the regime at the time of power transfer.
[c] Average of civil and political rights. On a scale of 1–7 with 7 being the most authoritarian.
[d] Leader had not survived two terms as of December 31, 2014.

Overall organizational capacity	Overall organizational capacity	Terms in office[a]	Turnover?[b]	Average Freedom House score (1991–2014)[c]
		3 leadership turnovers		3.5
1	Low	1	Yes	4.3
4	Med-low	1	Yes	3.1
5	Medium	2	Yes	3.5
3	Med-low	1	Yes	3
		No leadership turnovers		4.7
1	Low	2	No	3.6
7	Medium	3+	No	5.4
		1 leadership turnover		5.9
2	Low	<1	No	5.5
2	Low	3+	No	6
		No leadership turnovers		6.9
8	Med-high	2	Yes	6.9
8	Med-high	1+	No[d]	7
		4 leadership turnovers		3.3
2	Low	<1	Yes	3.4
5	Medium	2	Yes	3.7
4	Med-low	1	Yes	2.5
6	Medium	<1	Yes	3.4
2	Low	<1	No[d]	3
		No leadership turnovers		6.7
8	Med-high	2+	No	6.7

Notes

1. These events are described in detail in Kravchuk's memoires (Kravchuk 2002: 227–28).

2. Huntington (1991).

3. In 1987, 17 percent of countries that the World Bank categorized as low- and lower-middle-income were ranked by Freedom House as "free"; by 2002, that share had increased to 31 percent. See World Bank (1995) and www.freedomhouse.org.

4. Diamond (2008).

5. The term *pluralism* is used throughout this book to describe political competition broadly understood rather than any kind of group theory of politics. See appendix A for coding rules used in the analysis. For a useful overview of the concept of pluralism, see S. Solomon (1983).

6. See appendix A for definitions of democratic and authoritarian stability/consolidation.

7. See Kohli (1990); Mainwaring and Scully (1996); McFaul (2001); Fish (2006). My focus here is on the strength of the governing party rather than the party *system*. Certainly, weak party systems unambiguously undermine democracy and pluralism.

8. Holmes (1997); see also O'Donnell (1993); Sperling (2000).

9. Glazer (2010: 5); see also Dahl (1971), Nodia (1994); Linz and Stepan (1996); Suny (1999/2000).

10. Fish (1998).

11. In line with convention, "post-Soviet" or "former Soviet" in this book refers to the twelve former Soviet republics, excluding the Baltic states.

12. See also Hale (2015).

13. This is reflected in both Freedom House (www.freedomhouse.org) and Polity (www.systemicpeace.org/polity/polity4.htm) democracy rankings.

14. Nodia (2002: 15).

15. On institutional design, see Linz (1990); Colton and Skach (2005); Fish (2005); Stepan (2005); Hale (2011, 2015). On economic development, see Lipset (1959), Przeworski et al. (2000). On parties, see Fish (2006). On strong states, see O'Donnell (1993); Holmes (1997).

16. For critiques along these lines, see Schedler (2006); Levitsky and Way (2010).

17. See in particular Holmes (1997, 2002); Sperling (2000); Grzymala-Busse and Jones Luong (2002); Fukuyama (2004); Colton (2006).

18. Taylor (2011).

19. See Diamond (2002); Levitsky and Way (2002, 2010); Schedler (2002, 2006); McGlinchey (2011).

20. See Geddes (1999); Ross (2001); Bellin (2004); Brownlee (2007); Gandhi and Przeworski (2007); Greene (2007); Gandhi (2008); Magaloni (2008); Svolik (2012).

21. O'Donnell and Schmitter (1986).

22. See, for example, Linz and Stepan (1996).

23. McFaul (2001); Fish (2005).

24. See "Opposition Leader Condemns One-Candidate Election in Kirgizia," *Associated Press,* 11 October 1991; Collins (2006).

25. Fish (1998).

26. Ferdinand (2000); Diamond (2010).

27. See, for example, Keck and Sikkink (1998).

28. Kelley (2012).

29. Diamond (2008).

30. Schimmelfennig and Sedelmeier (2005); Vachudova (2005).

31. Marinov and Goemans (2013).

32. Levitsky and Way (2010).

33. Kopstein and Reilly (2000); Levitsky and Way (2010); Levitz and Pop-Eleches (2011).

34. For example, Levon Ter-Petrosian in Armenia, Yeltsin in Russia, and Kuchma in Ukraine all continued to receive significant aid following serious democratic abuses in the mid- and late 1990s. See Bureau of European and Eurasian Affairs (2009).

35. Howard (2003: 1).

36. Darden (2008); Hale (2015); Popova (2012a); P. Solomon (2010).

37. See, for example, Dahl (1971); Moore (1954).

38. Lipset (1959); Dahl (1971); Rueschemeyer, Stephens, and Stephens (1992).

39. Dahl (1971); Boix (2003); Acemoglu and Robinson (2005).

40. Huntington (1968); O'Donnell (1993); Holmes (1997).

41. Dahl (1971); Rustow (1970: 350–51); Linz and Stepan (1996).

42. Levitsky and Way (2002, 2010).

43. See appendix A for definitions of consolidated and unconsolidated democracy/authoritarianism.

44. Political closure is defined as high, medium, and low along four dimensions: *electoral control, media control, parliamentary subordination,* and *opposition subordination.* See appendix I for coding rules. My definition of closure in this book heavily overlaps with but is not the same as regime type. Thus, while low closure (or high competition) cases are almost always democratic and vice versa, my conception of closure includes dimensions—opposition and parliamentary power/subordination—that are not typically included in procedural definitions of democracy.

45. Organizations, for Huntington (1968: 10), are characterized by "regularized, stable, and sustained coming together." Franz Schurmann (1966: 3) defines organizations as "structures of differentiated roles which require the ordered exercise of power."

46. See appendix A for full coding rules.

47. See, in particular, White (1993: 312); McFaul (2001: 316–17).

48. Huntington (1968); Geddes (1999); Magaloni (2006, 2008); Brownlee (2007); Svolik (2012).

49. See Jowitt (1992); Howard (2003).

50. Bienen and van de Walle (1991).

51. On party substitutes, see Hale (2006). These first presidents often initially viewed parties as unnecessary appendages needlessly limiting their discretion. For detailed discussions of why some leaders in the region failed to build new parties, see especially McFaul (2001); Hale (2006).

52. Brownlee (2007); Magaloni (2008).

53. Brownlee (2007: 13).

54. Examples include Ruslan Khasbulatov and Alexander Rutskoi in Russia; Leonid Kuchma, Yulia Tymoshenko, and Viktor Yushchenko in Ukraine.

55. Tarrow (1998: 71–90); also McAdam (1996).

56. Tarrow (1996: 56).

57. Way (2008).

58. McAdam (1996); Tarrow (1998: 79–80).

59. See, in particular, McFaul (2001); Andrews (2002).

60. For example, the Russian constitution was changed nearly 400 times between 1992 and 1993 (Filatov 2001: 180).

61. Kryshtanovskaya (2005: 160).

62. Bellin (2004); Levitsky and Way (2010); Slater (2010).

63. Sperling (2000).

64. Colton (2006: 8). See also Holmes (1997); Grzymala-Busse and Jones Luong (2002); Fukuyama (2004).

65. Way (2003: 460); Colton (2008: 259).

66. Wilson (2005a); Darden (2008).

67. See, for example, Tilly (1975, 1985: 182); Skocpol (1979); Mann (1984).

68. This concept is similar to Michael Mann's (1984) "despotic power" and Brian Taylor's (2011) "exceptional state power."

69. "Ukraine Leader's Allies Deserted Him as His Power Melted Away," *New York Times*, 4 January 2015.

70. As Russian Prime Minister Viktor Chernomyrdin reportedly told a subordinate, "If something is really necessary, I will tell it to you, not write it to you." Quoted in Baturin et al. (2001: 424).

71. Marinov and Goemans (2013).

72. McAdam (1996: 28).

73. Tarrow (1996: 54); also see Beissinger (2002: 152–53).

74. Lachapelle, Way, and Levitsky (2012).

75. Such non-material ties include a familial network that pervades most of the government and security sector (e.g., Syria under Assad), or origins in violent struggle (e.g., Zimbabwe under Mugabe). See Lachapelle, Levitsky, and Way (2012); Levitsky and Way (2012). Cases where the security sector is extensive and well-funded and have such ties are coded as high capacity; cases with well-funded security services *without* such ties are coded as medium (see appendix A).

76. Kulikov (2002: 394–402).

77. For example, former Belarusian parliamentary leader Stanislau Shushkevich reports that he was able to use personal connections with the head of police to countermand orders given by the prime minister, who formally controlled the police (interview with Stanislau Shushkevich, Minsk, 23 June 2004).

78. Myagkov, Ordeshook, and Shakin (2009).

79. Dahl (1971: 48–61); Fish (2005); McMann (2006); Greene (2007).

80. Fish (2005)

81. Moore (1954: 171).

82. McMann (2006); Greene (2007).

83. Radnitz (2010a).

84. See, for example, Freeland (2000).

85. Way (2005b).

86. Radnitz (2010a, 2010b).

87. For example, party strength is measured by whether or not the incumbent is backed by a single, dominant party when he/she takes power.

88. For example, coercive capacity is measured by the size of the coercive apparatus and by the presence or absence of warlords, state wage arrears, and recent history of military conflict.

89. I define national identity as the conception of community that forms the basis and/or justification of claims for statehood. Such community may be defined by perceived common ancestry, language, physical characteristics, culture, values, religion, shared history, and/or conception of out-group. See Calhoun (1993); Shulman (2005: 59); Mandler (2006).

90. Dahl (1971: 108); Lijphart (1977: 1); Suny (1999/2000: 176); Glazer (2010: 5); Lebas (2011).

91. Beissinger (2002: 79).

92. Berezin (2001: 86); see also Rothschild (1981); Barany (2002).

93. Aminzade and McAdam (2001: 17, 31).

94. Lipset and Rokkan (1990 [1967]: 138).

95. Beissinger (2002: 76).

96. Ahmed (2006).

97. Way (2012b).

98. Interview with Stevfan Mushi, Professor of Political Science, University of Dar Es Salaam, 23 November 2007, Dar Es Salaam, Tanzania.

99. LeBas (2011).

100. Black knights refer to counter-hegemonic powers whose economic, military, and/or diplomatic efforts may blunt the impact of U.S. or EU democratizing or other pressure. See Levitsky and Way (2010).

101. D'Anieri (1999).

102. Caraus (2004: 331).

103. Howard (2003); Levitsky and Way (2010); LeBas (2011).

104. Berezin (2001: 89, 87).

105. Neidhart (2003: 5).

106. Snyder (2000).

107. Huntington (1991).

108. Szporluk (1991); Plokhy (2011). This comparison has a purely heuristic value. It does not allow me to control for variables that are similar among my cases. Instead, causal factors are assessed through process tracing in the case study chapters.

109. Classified by the World Bank in 1993 as middle income.

110. As measured by the share of deputies in the first openly elected legislature. Thus, self-proclaimed democrats controlled about one-third of parliamentary seats in 1990 in all three cases. On Belarus, see Gerasiuk (1991: 49); on Moldova, Crowther (1997); on Ukraine, Wilson (1997: 120).

111. Thus, Belarus after 1994 and Moldova and Ukraine after 1991 were led by a prime minister approved by parliament and a president.

112. Levitsky and Way (2010).

113. Darden and Grzymala-Busse (2006); Darden (forthcoming).

114. By civil society, I mean the network of voluntary and autonomous organizations and institutions that exist outside the state, market, and family, and that are difficult for state leaders to eliminate or control. See Howard (2003).

115. Karatnycky (2005); Kuzio (2005, 2010); Diuk (2006); Onuch (2014).

116. Mark Beissinger (2013) makes this point in regard to the Orange Revolution of 2004.

117. See Colton and Skach (2005); Fish (2005, 2006); Hale (2011, 2015).

118. Levitsky and Murillo (2009); Levitsky and Way (2010).

119. Hale (2011; 2015).

120. Easter (1997); Levitsky and Way (2010).

121. Easter (1997).

122. Bekus (2010: 88); Karbalevich (2010: 438); see also Mihalisko (1997: 259); Shulman (2005); Kuzio (2009).

123. Haerpfer (2005: 177).

124. See also Hale (2015).

CHAPTER TWO: Perestroika and the Origins of Post-Soviet Pluralism by Default

1. Shlapentokh (2001: 84).

2. The Party had 441,851 primary Party organizations in 1987 (United States Library of Congress Country Studies, "Soviet Union: Primary Party Organization," http://lcweb2.loc.gov).

3. Hough (1997: 255, 257).

4. Yasin (1998: 168).

5. Ellman and Kontorovich (1998).

6. Walder (1986); Crowley (1997).

7. According to an unpublished survey of over 2,000 cases of mass unrest 1953–1983 by Liudmilla Alexeyeva and Valery Chalidze (1985: 352), shootings by officials occurred in six of the twelve cases between 1953 and 1964. By contrast, officers fired on demonstrators in just one instance (in Dneproderzhinsk in 1972) of the 21 times when special troops were called in 1965–1983, despite the fact that the scale of protests was roughly the same as in the Khrushchev period.

8. Alexeyeva and Chalidze (1985: 356–57).

9. Ibid.

10. Knight (1990); Murawiec and Gaddy (2002: 33).

11. Kalugin (1994: 257); Kryshtanovskaya (2005: 224).

12. Kalugin (1994: 109); Albats (1994: 23) estimates that the KGB had a total staff of 720,000.

13. Albats (1994: 68); Waller (2004: 336).

14. Kalugin (1994: 298).

15. Shelley (1996: 181–82).

16. Beissinger (2002: 70).

17. Howard (2003: 1).

18. Jowitt (1992: 142–43).

19. Quoted in Aron (2000: 199); also Jowitt (1992).

20. Quoted in Chernyaev (2000: 160).

21. Ligachev (1996: 109–10).

22. Mozhin (1998: 165).

23. Ellman and Kontorovich (1998: 197).

24. Brown (1996: 176).

25. Hough (1997: 268, 272).

26. Brown (1996: 274).

27. Hough (1997: 271).

28. Quoted in Brown (1996: 196).

29. Brown (1996: 191).

30. Ligachev (1996: 91–93, 110).

31. Ogushi (2008: 94).

32. Ogushi (2008: 71–73).

33. Belik (1998: 167).

34. Ogushi (2008: 73).

35. Beissinger (2002).

36. Darden and Grzymala-Busse (2006); Darden (forthcoming).

37. Darden and Grzymala-Busse (2006: 89).

38. Ibid., 96.

39. Beissinger (2002: 339).

40. Lebed (1995: 280, 297); Senn (1995: 138); Kryuchkov (1996: 28).

41. Taylor (2003: 29); see also Beissinger (2002: 352).

42. Lebed (1995: 396).

43. Walker (2003: 65).

44. Chernyaev (2000: 226).

45. Odom (1998: 312).

46. Dunlop (1995).

47. Odom (1998: 345).

48. Ibid., 320; see also Lebed (1995: 404–5).

49. Knight (1996).

50. Exceptions included Georgia, Moldova, and Tajikistan, where ethnic conflict encouraged Russians who often dominated the security services to flee the country, leaving these countries with particularly undersized and weak security structures.

51. See, for example, Kahn (2002); Stoner-Weiss (2006).

52. Lieven (1993, chap. 7).

53. Beissinger (2002: 98).

54. For example, Ukraine's GDP per capita was less than half that of the Baltics in the early 1990s (World Bank World Development Indicators).

55. Beissinger (2002: 100).

56. The notable exceptions are Kyrgyzstan and Tajikistan, where state and party weakness severely undermined authoritarian control. These cases are discussed in chapter 6.

57. Darden and Grzymala-Busse (2006: 97).

58. In Kazakhstan, Kyrgyzstan, and Tajikistan, regionally based identity divisions tended to be more localized and particularistic than in Moldova and Ukraine. See Collins (2006); Radnitz (2012); Markowitz (2013).

CHAPTER THREE: Pluralism by Default in Ukraine

1. Balmaceda (2013: 93–152).

2. Ryabinska (2011: 15); http://www.freedomhouse.org/report/nations-transit/nations-transit-2010.

3. Kubicek (2002: 618); D'Anieri (2006: 12).

4. Levitsky and Way (2010).

5. Holovaty (1993: 111).

6. Anderson and Albini (1999: 282).

7. Glazer (2010: 5).

8. Batt (1998: 57).

9. Solchanyk (2001: 6).

10. Western Ukraine accounted for about 20 percent of the population; eastern Ukraine just under 50 percent, and central Ukraine just over 30 percent.

11. Szporluk (1991: 475).

12. Darden (forthcoming: 101–2); see also Szporluk (1979: 78, 88).

13. Darden (forthcoming).

14. Arel and Khmelko (1996); Khmelko and Wilson (1998: 75).

15. Katchanovski (2006: 119).

16. Hesli (1995: 106); Khmelko and Wilson (1998: 69–70); Katchanovski (2006: 113, 114).

17. Burant (1995: 1127); Hesli (1995: 100).

18. Calculated from cvk.com.ua.

19. Thus, there is only mixed evidence that western Ukrainians support democracy more than their eastern counterparts. For evidence that western Ukrainians are more democratic, see Dowley and Silver (2002); Shulman (2005). For evidence of the lack of such a difference, see Arel and Khmelko (1996: 85); Miller, White, and Heywood (1998: 279–80); Miller, Klocubar, and Reisinger (2000: 225, 227); and, most recently, Norris (2014).

20. Beissinger (2013).

21. "Nationalists Send Party to Scrapyard as They Take Control," *The Times* (London), 31 August 1991.

22. Lytvyn (1997: 216).

23. Hale (2006).

24. Markov (1993: 34).

25. Holovaty (1993: 112); Whitmore (2004: 32).

26. Bondarenko (2003).

27. "Party of Regions to Run for Parliament on Its Own," *Ukrainian News*, 5 November 2005.

28. See Kramer (1992: 330); Pyskir (1993: 143); Olynyk (1994: 5–6).

29. *Nezavisimost'* (11 August 1993: 3); Anderson and Albini (1999: 288).

30. Anderson and Albini (1999: 286, 285); See also Kuzio (1994).

31. *Nezavisimost'* (18 June 1993: 1).

32. *Nezavisimost'* (17 June 1994: 4); *Nezavisimost'* (22 June 1994: 5).

33. Lukanov (1996: 119).

34. Harasymiw (2002: 185, 200). Beginning in 1994, police chiefs of each province were required to pass an interview with the president.

35. *Nezavisimost'* 17 August 1994: 1, 2; 10 February 1995: 5; Boichenko (2004); Sasse (2007: 175–80).

36. EBRD ND; Puglisi (2003).

37. See Solchanyk (1989); Kapto (1996).

38. Haran (1993: 62); see also Beissinger (2002: 192).

39. Kuzio (1989: 68).

40. Haran (1993: 62).

41. Marples (1990b: 15); Beissinger (2002: 192).

42. Solchanyk (1990a: 13); Beissinger (2002: 193); also Haran (1993: 16). A Ukrainian Politburo report in March 1989 reported that 60,000 informal groups undertook 1,200 meetings that included 13 million people throughout Ukraine (Lytvyn 1997: 146).

43. Haran (1993: 59, 50).

44. See Wilson (1997); also Haran (1993: 48).

45. Whitmore (2004: 30). Total membership in all noncommunist parties in 1991 was 35–40,000, compared to 2.9 million in CPU in December 1990 (Kuzio 2000a: 156).

46. Marples (1990a: 20).

47. Lytvyn (1997: 182, 177); see also Solchanyk (1990b: 13).

48. Wilson (1993: 8).

49. Pavlychko (1992: 78).

50. Pavlychko (1992: 76–98).

51. Marples (1990c: 16).

52. Lytvyn (1997: 196).

53. Quoted in Lytvyn (1997: 196).

54. Pavlychko (1992: 97).

55. Beissinger (2002: 196).

56. Lytvyn (1997: 236); McCauley (1997: 159). Kravchuk had earlier been elected chair of parliament by an overwhelming 239 votes.

57. Brooker (2004: 70; 2008: 295); Whitmore (2004: 33).

58. Lytvyn (1997: 67).

59. In 1994 he tried to forcibly shut down the legislature to avoid early elections and closed down the only Ukrainian TV station backing his main opponent.

60. In particular, the presidency lacked veto power (Whitmore 2004: 32).

61. Wolczuk (1998: 128).

62. Whitmore (2004: 33).

63. Whitmore (2004: 33).

64. Lytvyn (1997: 327); Whitmore (2004: 30)

65. See Kapto (1996: 102, 99); Lytvyn (1997).

66. Lytvyn (1997: 75).

67. Wilson (2000: 178–79).

68. Markov (1993: 34); Kravchuk (2002: 248).

69. Lytvyn (1997: 295).

70. Ibid., 293–94.

71. McCauley (1997: 159)

72. Lytvyn (1997: 318).

73. D'Anieri (1999: 188); see also Markov (1993: 33); Lytvyn (1997: 277, 282, 287).

74. Matviiuk (1994).

75. D'Anieri (1999: 188).

76. Kravchuk (2002: 198); Bondarenko (2007: 63).

77. *Nezavisimost'* (22 September 1993: 1); Hritsenko et al. (1995: 147).

78. For examples of failures to control print media, see *Nezavisimost'* (17 November 1993: 2; 22 June 1994: 1).

79. On Ukrainian language policies in the media and education, see Arel (1995); Khmelko and Wilson (1998: 76). On anti-Russian economic policies and their effects, see D'Anieri (1999, chap. 4).

80. Kapto (1996).

81. Bojcun (1995: 230); Lukanov (1996: 61); see also Wilson (1993); Solchanyk (1994: 59–61); Kubicek (2000: 77–78).

82. *United Press International,* 16 December 1993.

83. *Nezavisimost'* (4 August 1993: 1–2). On the Russophile identity components of the strike, see Wilson (1993).

84. D'Anieri (1999: 40).

85. *The Guardian,* 24 September 1993.

86. Lukanov (1996: 71).

87. See "Picketing of Supreme Council Building by 15,000 people," *UNIAN,* 21 September 1993.

88. "Presidential and Parliamentary Elections Set for Next Year," *AP,* 24 September 1993; *AFP,* 24 September 1993.

89. "Ukraine Schedules Early Elections," *UPI,* 24 September 1993.

90. Lytvyn (1997: 324); see also Lukanov (1996: 64–65); Kravchuk (2002: 227).

91. Kravchuk (2002: 228).

92. Ibid.

93. Lukanov (1996: 68, 62).

94. One deputy from Donetsk claimed that better relations with CIS countries could "solve 95 percent and possibly 100 percent of economic problems facing Ukraine" (Quoted in Lukanov 1996: 110).

95. Lukanov (1996: 86).

96. D'Anieri (1999: 117).

97. Wolczuk (1998: 139).

98. Wilson (2000: 193). 71 percent of Kravchuk voters in the election were primarily Ukrainian speakers, while 77 percent of Kuchma voters were primarily Russian speakers (Khmelko and Wilson 1998: 75).

99. Arel (1995: 611–12).

100. Lytvyn (1997: 326); Korzh (2004: 35).

101. Kuzio (1996: 124).

102. Kravchuk (2002: 238, 239); also Kuzio (1996: 132).

103. *Nezavisimost'* (29 June 1994: 1); *Foreign Broadcast Information Service-SOV* (12 July 1994: 37).

104. For example, local officials in Odesa and other cities prevented Kravchuk supporters from monitoring the vote (Kuzio 1996: 132–33).

105. *Foreign Broadcast Information Service-SOV* (3 August 1994: 38). Another election observation report noted that pro-Kravchuk fliers sent to Kravchuk-appointed representatives in eastern Ukraine went unused, while "anti-Kravchuk materials were distributed widely by local officials." Democratic Elections in Ukraine (1994: 14); Kravchuk (2002: 230).

106. Bondarenko (2003).

107. Kravchuk (2002: 229).

108. Bondarenko (2007: 316).

109. Lukanov (1996: 117).

110. Bondarenko (2007: 60).

111. Bondarenko (2007: 60–64, 58, 97). In December 1993, Kuchma became head of the Ukrainian Union of Industrialists and Entrepreneurs, which united about 100 industrial enterprises and helped organize Kuchma's campaign (Bondarenko 2007: 105).

112. Wilson (2000: 195); Puglisi (2003: 836).

113. The Party captured 90 out of 405 seats. Together with the Socialist and Peasant Parties, the left controlled 164 of 405 seats as of 1995 (Wolczuk 1998: 134).

114. Wolczuk (1998: 142).

115. Arel (1998: 342, 344).

116. Between 1998 and 2002, Ukraine's external debt as share of GDP was 30–44% as compared to 6–7% in Belarus (World Bank World Development Indicators).

117. Bondarenko (2007: 188, 189).

118. Wolczuk (1998: 198–99).
119. Wolczuk (1998); Whitmore (2004: 73). In particular, Kuchma gained powers of appointment that left the legislature severely weakened by the late 1990s.
120. Whitmore (2004: 78). See also Bondarenko (2007: 193); Haran (2011: 93)
121. According to Fish (2006), only Armenia, Georgia, and Moldova had weaker parliamentary power than Ukraine.
122. Bondarenko (2007: 194).
123. Wolczuk (1998: 200).
124. Personal communication Kataryna Wolczuk, June 2, 2011.
125. Korzh (2004: 47); Kulchytsky (2005: 22).
126. Thus, the threat of referendum that he used to get the constitution had no legal basis and would likely have sparked a major crisis (Korzh 2005: 47; Kulchytsky 2005: 22). While Yeltsin in Russia *did* push through a constitution in the face of leftist resistance, this action sparked a major crisis, barely succeeded, and forced Yeltsin to rely heavily on support from Western powers that Kuchma did not have (Levitsky and Way 2010: 192–93).
127. Lukanov (1996: 119); Kuzio (2000b: 29). By 1999, the number of police had quadrupled (Harasymiw 2003: 323).
128. Koshiw (2010: 78); see also Darden (2008).
129. Bondarenko (2007: 215–16).
130. *Nezavisimost,'* 17 August 1994: 1, 2; 10 February 1995: 5; Boichenko (2004); Sasse (2007: 175–80).
131. Puglisi (2003: 837).
132. In 2000, 386 of the 450 deputies in parliament controlled 3,954 businesses—accounting for 25 percent of imports and 10 percent of exports in Ukraine (Melnychenko 2002: 15).
133. Darden (2008).
134. Ishchenko (1996).
135. "Pyat' Istochnikov, Pyat' Sostavnykh Chastey Bloka 'Za Yedinuyu Ukrainu!'" *Zerkalo nedeli* , 23 March 2002, No. 11.
136. Overall, "centrist" and non-aligned deputies voted with the president about 80 percent of the time in 1998–2002, as calculated with data from Protsyk and Wilson (2003: 715) plus data on faction size from *The Ukrainian Weekly*, 21 January 1996, No. 3, Vol. LXIV.
137. *Zerkalo nedeli* (22–28 February 1997).
138. The legislature pushed back at least three attempts to remove Moroz (Whitmore 2004: 78).
139. Wilson (1997); Whitmore (2004: 88).
140. Bondarenko (2007: 223).
141. Whitmore (2004: 37).
142. Popov and Milshtein (2006: 50).
143. See Popov and Milshtein (2006, chap. 6).
144. Brzezinski (1998: 138); Popov and Milshtein (2006: 122).
145. Popov and Milshtein (2006: 171, 183).
146. Popov and Milshtein (2006: 178).
147. Hromada won 24 seats; NDP, 28. The largest parties in this legislature were the Communists (121 seats); Rukh (46); and the Socialists (34). Together with independents, who tended to support whoever was in power, pro-presidential forces accounted for about 53 percent of seats.

148. Overall, "centrist" and non-aligned deputies voted with the president about 80 percent of the time in 1998–2002 as calculated with data from Protsyk and Wilson (2003).

149. Whitmore (2004: 99); Kulchytsky (2005: 32).

150. Popov and Milshtein (2006: 186–87).

151. Popov and Milshtein (2006: 190).

152. Birch (2002); Wilson (2005b: 42–43).

153. Birch (2002: 340).

154. ODIHR (2000: 18, 21).

155. Bondarenko (2007: 307).

156. Kulchytsky (2005: 33).

157. See "Va-Bank ili nogodnyi zaets," *Zerkalo nedeli* No. 50 (271), 18–19 December 1999.

158. Bondarenko (2007: 379–81).

159. Kulchytsky (2005: 39).

160. Whitmore (2004: 102, 116).

161. Kulchytsky (2005: 38).

162. Whitmore (2004: 102).

163. Kudelia (2008: 90).

164. See Karatnycky (2001); and Kuzio (2005).

165. Bondarenko (2007: 74).

166. Thus, the protests were led by the Russophile Moroz and by Tymoshenko, who had not yet made the shift to Ukrainian identity against a president who became increasingly identified with Russia.

167. Puglisi (2003: 840).

168. Krushelnycky (2002).

169. Bondarenko (2007: 460–62, 473).

170. Kulchytsky (2005: 52).

171. Magaloni (2008: 716).

172. "Ukraina Partiynaya. Chast' ÍÍ. 'Nasha Ukraïna,'" *Zerkalo nedeli*, 16 February 2002.

173. Kokotyukha (2008: 137).

174. Yushchenko thus referred to Kuchma as a "father" figure (Way 2005b: 139).

175. See Karatnycky (2005); Kuzio (2005); Stepanenko (2005); Diuk (2006); Onuch (2014).

176. World Bank World Development Indicators.

177. For example, late in the campaign Yanukovych allies began to simply send cash in the mail to whole categories of individuals.

178. The author is indebted to Serhiy Kudelia and Taras Kuzio for extensive discussions on this question.

179. Kulchytsky (2005: 55).

180. Bondarenko (2007: 494). On the structure of power within Donetsk, see US Embassy Cable, 9 July 2007.

181. Kulchytsky (2005: 53).

182. Rudenko (2007: 103, 108–9).

183. Popov and Milshtein (2006: 270–71).

184. Yushchenko quoted in Kulchytsky (2005: 57).

185. Kuzio (2015). A polling precinct head in Zaporizhzhia reported that polling station workers were paid up to $5,000 depending on the vote for Yanukovych. "Eto pis'mo prishlo mne segodnya po el. Pochte," *Pochta Zaporizhzhia*, 14 December 2004.

186. Petrov and Ryabov (2006: 157).

187. "Zakoni Zhenra," *Grani plus*, 3 November 2004.

188. Myagkov, Ordeshook, and Shakin (2009).

189. "Yak Yanukovych fal'syfikuvav vybory. Chastyna 2," *Ukrainska Pravda*, 25 November 2004, 17:36.

190. Yanukovych garnered about 25 percent more votes in the second than in the third round in Donetsk, Zakarpatiia, and Kirovohrad (where fraud was widely documented) but only 2 and 7 percent more in Zaporizhzhia and Kharkiv (calculated on the basis of data from cvk.gov.ua).

191. Specifically, I observed that some local officials refused to exclude pro-Yushchenko voters from voter lists as dictated by the government.

192. "Eto pis'mo prishlo mne segodnya po el. Pochte," *Pochta Zaporizhzhia*, 14 December 2004.

193. Based on a Kyiv Institute of Sociology survey of 2,044 respondents conducted December 10–17, 2004. I am extremely grateful to Volodymyr Paniotto for giving me access to this data.

194. Karatnycky (2005); also Kuzio (2005, 2010).

195. Beissinger (2013: 575, 582).

196. See Karatnycky (2005); Kuzio (2005: 117); Diuk (2006); Onuch (2014).

197. Estimates range as high as $100 million (interview with Volodymyr Skachko, editor, *Kyivskii Telegraf*, 17 November 2004). On the role of oligarchic businessmen in Yushchenko's campaign, see "Vlast' Yushchenko: kto kogo kuda lobbiroval," *Ukrainska Pravda*, 8 February 2005.

198. Way (2005b).

199. "Anatomiya dushi maidana," *Zerkalo Nedeli*, 11–17 December 2004.

200. Beissinger (2013: 581–82).

201. In her study of Pora, Olga Onuch (2014) identifies these five regions as the areas where Pora was most active during the Orange Revolution.

202. Stepanenko (2005: 600).

203. Haran (2011: 94).

204. Petrov and Ryabov (2006: 148–57).

205. Kuzio (2010: 292).

206. Way (2011).

207. Beissinger (2013: 586).

208. See also Stepanenko (2005: 613); Beissinger (2013).

209. Way (2011: 147).

210. "Anatomiya dushi maidana," *Zerkalo Nedeli*, 11–17 December 2004.

211. Popov and Milshtein (2006: 348).

212. Kulchytsky (2005: 62).

213. Kulchytsky (2005: 62, 63).

214. "Ukraine President Spurned Yanukovich Pressure to Use Troops to Quell Protesters," *Financial Times*, 14 December 2004.

215. See Taras Kuzio, "Security Forces Begin to Defect to Yushchenko," *Eurasia Daily Monitor*, 1 December 2004.

216. Kuzio (2015: 73).

217. "Anatomiya dushi maidana," *Zerkalo Nedeli*, 11–17 December 2004.

218. Ibid.

219. Stepanenko (2005); Diuk (2006).

220. See http://www.razumkov.org.ua/eng/socpolls.php.

221. Hale (2011: 604).
222. Kuzio (2015, chap. 3).
223. "MP Shkil Predicts Blocking of Party of Regions," *Ukrainian News*, 19 December 2004.
224. "Membership of Party of Regions Increases to 1 Million," *Ukrainian News*, 21 March 2006.
225. "Gennadiy Moskal': "Na Akhmetova v 2005-m nichego ne bylo," *Profil*, 11 June 2011; "Yushchenko pogrozhue 'tak zvaniy opozytsii' v'yaznytseyu,'" *Ukrains'ka Pravda*, 10 February 2005.
226. Kudelia and Kuzio (2015).
227. Kuzio (2015, chap. 3).
228. Kuzio (2015, chap. 3).
229. *Nations in Transit 2010: Ukraine* (www.freedomhouse.org).
230. For example, TV journalists were fired for criticizing Our Ukraine and Tymoshenko. See *Nations in Transit 2010: Ukraine*; see also Hale (2011: 602).
231. See Trochev (2010). For example, in early 2009, Yushchenko ordered the SBU to open an investigation into Tymoshenko's gas deals with Russia—an issue later used by Yanukovuch to justify her arrest.
232. US Embassy Cable, 29 December 2006.
233. Hale (2011).
234. Fisun (2010).
235. Popov and Milshtein (2006: 282).
236. "Yushchenko Pochav Stvorennya Yedynoyi Partiyi. Za tse vidpovidatyme ridnyy brat," *Ukrainska Pravda*, 21 January 2005.
237. "Prevratit' porazheniye v pobedu," *Zerkalo nedeli* No. 33, 2 September 2006.
238. Trochev (2011a: 6).
239. Trochev (2010: 136).
240. "Golubaia kontrrevoliutsiia: Viktor Ianukovich likvidiruet posledstviia 'oranzhevoi revoliutsii,'" *Gazeta.ru*, 30 September 2010.
241. Trochev (2010: 136).
242. Trochev (2011a).
243. "Memorandum porozuminnya mizh vladoyu i opozytsieyu," *Ukrainska Pravda*, 22 September 2005, quoted in Kudelia and Kuzio (2015).
244. Eberhardt (2009: 65).
245. "Ukrainskiye media segodnya: iz garema v bordel,'" *Zerkalo nedeli*, 24 May 2008.
246. "Nation's News Media: Free or Still Captive to Their Owners?" *Kyiv Post*, 15 October 2008.
247. US Embassy Cable, 7 September 2007. Lutsenko complained in 2007 that "some of the presidentially-appointed governors in the South and East were now working for all sides, which was hurting" Our Ukraine (US Embassy Cable, 13 September 2007).
248. Yanukovych captured 77 percent of the presidential vote in the east/south in December 2004 and about 60 percent of the regional vote in parliamentary elections in 2006 and 2007. By contrast, before the Orange Revolution, the Party of Regions (together with other pro-Kuchma parties) reaped just 17 percent of the eastern/southern vote in parliamentary elections in 2002, (calculated from cvk.gov.ua.).
249. See, for example, Eberhardt (2009: 56); "Partiya Regionov Ne Namerena Menyat' Lidera, Poskol'ku Reyting Yanukovicha Vdvoye Prevyshayet Reyting Samoy Partii," *Unian*, 4 July 2005.
250. US Embassy Cable, 5 October 2006. Later, Yanukovych allies complained that

Our Ukraine's coalitional character undermined negotiations; "What are we supposed to do? Agree with each party separately [in the coalition]?" "Radi koalitsii Partiya regionov gotova narushit' zakon," *Rosbalt*, 4 March 2010.

251. US Embassy Cable, 30 October 2006.

252. The Orange coalition (including Moroz's Socialist Party) garnered just over 40 percent of the vote and slightly more than half of the legislature. However, Moroz defected to Yanukovych.

253. "Yushchenko likvidiroval sud, kotoryy otmenil vybory," *Ukrainska Pravda*, 13 October 2008.

254. Trochev (2010: 135–36).

255. "BYuT i Partiya regionov pereshli v rezhim ozhidaniya," *Kommersant-Ukraina*, 5 June 2009; Eberhardt (2009: 48).

256. Andriy Kliuev, quoted in US Embassy Cable, 17 October 2008.

257. US Embassy Cable, 17 October 2008.

258. US Embassy Cable, 10 October 2008.

259. "Partiya regionov raskoletsya iz-za Timoshenko," *Ukrainskaia pravda*, 2 June 2009.

260. US Embassy Cable, 24 April 2008; "Partiya Regionov ne verit v soyuz s BYuT," *Rosbalt*, 7 October 2008.

261. "Baba Porazka Viktora Yushchenka," *Ukrainska Pravda*, 26 January 2010.

262. US Embassy Cable, 25 November 2009.

263. Vanderhill (2011: 13).

264. Hale (2011).

265. See "Freedom of the Press 2011: Ukraine," Freedom House (www.freedomhouse. org); ODIHR (2012); "Ukraine: A nation on guard," *Financial Times*, 21 October 2010. Because parliament periodically and successfully challenged Yanukovych, I nonetheless score parliamentary subordination as medium.

266. Popova (2012b: 13). At the same time, opposition parties such as BYuT *were* allowed to campaign for power (ODIHR 2012).

267. "Mnogostradal'naia Konstitutsiia," *Chaspik*, no. 38 (491), 26 September 2010.

268. "Partiya regionov vpervyye v istorii Ukrainy stala partiyey vlasti—politolog," *Unian*, 26 April 2010.

269. "Skoreye Vsego, Partiya Regionov Poydet Na Parlamentskiye Vybory-2006 Samostoyatel'no," *Unian*, 8 February 2005.

270. "Partiya regionov reshila samostoyatel'no uchastvovat' v vyborakh Rady-2006," *Ukrainskiye novosti*, 5 November 2005.

271. Ibid.; "'Partiya Regionov' Viktora Yanukovicha Poydet Na Vybory v Verkhovnuyu Radu Ukrainy Samostoyatel'no," *Telekanal "Rossiya" VESTI*, 5 November 2005.

272. Kushnarev (2007: 106–8).

273. US Embassy Cable, 7 September 2007; Kushnarev (2007).

274. US Embassy Cable, 28 September 2007; "Partiya regionov i 'Yedinyy tsentr' imeyut samyye bol'shiye seti pervichnykh organizatsiy v strane—Minyust," *Unian*, 24 March 2010; US Embassy Cable, 15 April 2008.

275. The party won a plurality (39.4%) of seats in provincial and rayon councils across the country (Haran 2011: 102) and captured as many as 118 of 177 elections for mayor in 2010. "Partiya regionov," *RBK-Ukraina*, 8 November 2010.

276. Bondarenko (2007: 494).

277. Kudelia (2014).

278. Kuzio (2015, chap. 3).

279. "Partiya regionov ne stremitsya k sozdaniyu konstitutsionnogo bol'shinstva—A. Yefremov," *Unian*, 21 September 2010.

280. "Kravchuk schitayet, chto Partiya regionov ne smozhet sformirovat' novuyu deyesposobnuyu koalitsiyu v VR nyneshnego sozyva," *Unian*, 23 February 2010; "Partiya regionov obezoruzhit Timoshenko pri pomoshchi perebezhchika iz BYuT," *Rosbalt*, 15 February 2010.

281. "Partiya regionov gotova stat' partiyey pravitel'stva," *Kommersant*, 11 March 2010.

282. "Partiya regionov v"yekhala v Kabmin," *Delo*, 12 March 2010.

283. Remark in parliament by Leonid Kravchuk, July 17, 2010. See http://www.youtube.com/watch?v=MDbyjsyosik.

284. "Ukraine: A Nation on Guard," *Financial Times*, 21 October 2010.

285. "Partiya regionov polnost'yu zadavila Kiyev'—Sobolev,'" *Ukrainskaia pravda*, 10 September 2010; "Partiya regionov likvidirovala nenadezhnykh," *Ekonomicheskiye izvestiya*, 12 September 2010.

286. "Konservatsiya vlasti Yanukovicha," *Ukrainska pravda*, 3 June 2011.

287. Popova (2012b: 12).

288. "Ukraine: A Nation on Guard," *Financial Times*, 21 October 2010; "Tak prosto . . ." *Zerkalo nedeli*, 25 September 2010.

289. Popova (2012a).

290. Trochev (2010: 136).

291. "Supreme Court Judges Could Oust Onopenko via Vote," *Kyiv Post*, 11 March 2011.

292. Popova (2012b) argues that Yanukovych's success in this case can be attributed to his decision to assign the "landmark case" to a more malleable, inexperienced judge. Yet such a strategy would likely have been resisted by competing political actors absent Yanukovych's domination of the major branches of government.

293. While the courts had the legal authority to revoke the 2004 constitutional changes—they could not put into effect other alterations in law required to immediately re-establish the old 1996 constitutional system. The courts ignored these problems and did so anyway. See Trochev (2011b).

294. Trochev (2011b: 5).

295. "Inna Bogoslovskaya: Yanukovich ugrobil sebya kak prezidenta v 2015-m," *Ukrainska Pravda*, 2 December 2013.

296. Na Maydan prishlo uzhe okolo 1500 vozmushchennykh ostanovkoy yevrointegratsii," *Ukrainska Pravda*, 22 November 2013; "V tsentre Kiyeva uzhe sobralis' boleye 100 tysyach chelovek, kotoryye khotyat v Yevropu," *Ukrainska Pravda*, 24 November 2013.

297. Lichbach (1987); Wilson (2014: 88).

298. "Razgon Maydana. Kak Eto Bylo. Slozhnyy Diagnoz—Yolka," *Ukrainska Pravda*, 30 November 2013.

299. "Yanukovich snyal s sebya otvetstvennost' za razgon mitinga," *Ukrainska Pravda*, 30 November 2013; "Ukraine Protests Persists as Bid to Oust Government Fails," *New York Times*, 2 December 2013.

300. "Amid Unrest, Ukrainian President Defends Choice on Accords," *New York Times*, 2 December 2013.

301. *Ukrainska Pravda* estimated about 300 on the square on November 28 ("'Yevro-Maydan' prodolzhayet stoyat,'" *Ukrainska Pravda*, 28 November 2013).

302. "Mitinguyushchiye zakhvatili Maydan," *Ukrainska Pravda*, 1 December 2013, 13:13; "Video of Police Brutality in Kiev Fuels Rage," *New York Times*, 2 December 2013.

303. See "Vid Maydanu-taboru do Maydanu-sichi: shcho zminylosya?" Fond Demokratichni Initsiatyvy.

304. V. Ishchenko (2014).

305. "Ukraine's Forces Move against Protesters, Dimming Hopes for Talks," *New York Times*, 9 December 2013.

306. According to the series of surveys conducted by Democratic Initiatives, Kyivites represented about half of the protesters in December and about 20 percent by late January. See "Vid Maydanu-taboru do Maydanu-sichi: shcho zminylosya?" Fond Demokratichni Initsiatyvy (http://dif.org.ua/ua/events/vid-ma-zminilosj.htm).

307. "Statystyka protestnykh podiÿ Maÿdanu: uchasnyky, heohrafiya, nasyl'stvo," (http://www.cedos.org.ua).

308. "Richnytsya Maydanu—opytuvannya hromads'koyi ta ekspertnoyi dumky," (http://www.dif.org.ua).

309. Lucan Way, "Six Reasons to Be Cautious about the Chances of Opposition Success," *Kyiv Post*, 18 December 2013.

310. During the demonstrations, the opposition was divided between three parties (Svoboda, Fatherland, and Vitali Klichko's UDAR) and had no consensus presidential candidate. Unity within the regime may also have been encouraged by the regime's threats of violence against potential defectors.

311. "Profile: Ukraine's 'Right Sector' movement," *BBC*, 21 January 2014; "Lider Pravoho sektoru Dmytro Yarosh: Koly 80% krayiny ne pidtrymuye vladu, hromadyans'koyi viyny buty ne mozhe," *Ukrainska Pravda*, 4 February 2014.

312. Lviv, Ternopil, Rivne, Khmelnytskyi, Ivano-Frankivsk, Chernivtsi, and Volyn.

313. Chernihiv, Sumy, Poltava, and Vinnytsia. See "Euromaidan Rallies in Ukraine," *Kyiv Post*, 23 January 2014; "Khronika i karta protestov v Ukraine," Gordon.com, 27 January 2014.

314. "Background Briefing on the Situation in Ukraine," 19 February 2014 (www.state.gov.ua).

315. "Kiev Protesters Set Square Ablaze to Thwart Police," *New York Times*, 18 February 2014. At the same time, Yanukovych seems to have anticipated the crisis. Thus, he began shipping out valuables from his mansion on the night of February 19 (Bartkowski and Stephan 2014).

316. While there is no direct evidence that Yanukovych gave the order, there is evidence of government involvement. See "Ubiystva na Maydane: obnarodovany plany, ikh organizatory i prichastnyye (dokument)," *Zerkalo nedeli*, 24 February 2014; "Photographs Expose Russian-Trained Killers in Kiev," *Daily Beast*, 30 March 2014.

317. "12 'regionalov' ob"yavili o podderzhke naroda i sozyvayut Radu," *Ukrainska Pravda*, 20 February 2014, 13:31.

318. "Makeyenko—Yanukovychu: Zhodna vlada ne varta lyuds'kykh zhertv," *Ukrainska Pravda*, 20 February 2014.

319. "Background Briefing on the Situation in Ukraine," 19 February 2014 (www.state.gov.ua); Bartkowski and Stephan (2014).

320. See "Lutsenko zbyraye u L'vovi pravookhorontsiv dlya zakhystu Maydanu," *Ukrainska pravda*, 20 February 2014; "V frankovskom SBU poobeshchali zashchishchat' Maydan," *Ukrainska pravda*, 21 February 2014, 15:02; "Militsionery iz Zapadnoy Ukrainy priyekhali okhranyat' Maydan," *Ukrainska pravda*, 21 February 2014.

321. "Ukraine Leader's Allies Deserted Him as His Power Melted Away," *New York Times*, 4 January 2015.

322. "Vidnovleno rukh potyahiv iz Zakhodu," *Ukrainska Pravda*, 20 February 2014; "Mosty v Kiyeve rabotayut," *Ukrainska Pravda*, 20 February 2014.

323. For an analysis of the votes, see "Khto ne holosuvav za Postanovu VR pro prypynennya nasyl'stva: analiz Lesi Orobets'," 21 February 2014 (Chesno.org). I thank Serhiy Kudelia for pointing this out.

324. "Spiker Rybak otpravil svoyu sem'yu iz Kiyeva v Budapesht," *Zerkalo nedeli*, 20 February.

325. "Ukraine peace deal negotiator & foreign minister of Poland Radek Sikorski on Fareed Zakaria GPS," cnnpressroom.blogs.cnn.com.

326. "Gritsenko: Kiyev pokidayut svyshe 1000 silovikov," *Ukrainska pravda*, 21 February 2014.

327. "Pravyy sektor nazval zayavleniya Yanukovicha ochkvtiratel'stvom," *Ukrainska pravda*, 21 February 2014.

328. 310 of 450 deputies voted to end the law under which Tymoshenko had been jailed; 332 voted to fire Zakharchenko. "Rada prinyala zakon, kotoryy pozvolit osvobodit' Timoshenko," *Ukrainska pravda*, 21 February 2014; "Rada ot-stranyla Zakharchenko," *Ukrainska pravda*, 21 February 2014. At least, 60 and 80 respectively Party of Regions deputies voted for these measures.

329. "Za dva dnya fraktsiyu Partii regionov pokinuli 40 deputatov," *Zerkalo nedeli*, 21 February.

330. "SBU prekratila podgotovku k antiterroristicheskoy operatsii," *Ukrainska pravda*, 21 February 2014.

331. "Yanukovich vyletel v Khar'kov," *Ukrainska pravda*, 21 February 2014.

332. Puglisi (2014).

333. See, for example, "'Nastroyi Ukrayiny'—Rezul'taty Spil'noho Doslidzhennya Kmis Ta Sotsys," (www.kiis.com.ua).

334. See "Dumky Ta Pohlyady Zhyteliv Pivdenno-Skhidnykh Oblastey Ukrayiny: Kviten' 2014," (www.kiis.com.ua).

335. For the regional origins of those who died in the protests, see Oleh Rozvadovskyy twitter (ole_g), 25 March 2014: "Zvidky lyudy, yaki zahynuly pid chas Maydanu."

336. Haran (1993: 62).

337. "Partiya regionov vpervyye v istorii Ukrainy stala partiyey vlasti—politolog," *Unian*, 26 April 2010.

338. See Netiaga (2009).

339. "Poroshenko i porozhnecha," *Ukrainska Pravda*, 16 May 2014.

340. Thus, Poroshenko won every single province in Ukraine—although he received a somewhat lower share of the vote in the east.

341. "Poroshenko will impose martial law if cease-fire fails," *Kyiv Post*, 14 February 2015.

CHAPTER FOUR: Pluralism by Default in Moldova

Epigraph: "INFOTAG Reports Further on Lucinschi News Conference," *Infotag*, 12 September 1996 (wnc.fedworld.gov).

1. Alexeyeva and Chalidze (1985: 130–31); Crowther (1991: 183); Badescu, Sum, and Uslaner (2004: 340); Quinlan (2005: 487).

2. March and Herd (2006: 351).

3. The AEI shut down the pro-Communist NIT TV station in 2012. In 1991, Snegur maneuvered to exclude any other candidate from the presidential election.

4. March (2007: 601).

5. Katchanovski (2006).

6. Vitu (2004: 156).

7. March (2007: 601).

8. Under Romanian tutelage, literacy increased to 46% from 15.6% at the end of the 19th century (Livezeanu 1995: 94). For a discussion of Romanian nation-building efforts in Bessarabia, see Livezeanu (1995: 101–16; 299); also Darden and Grzymala-Busse (2006: 113).

9. King (2000).

10. Crowther (1991: 189); Chinn (1994: 312); Eyal and Smith (1996: 128); Skvortsova (2002: 171–72).

11. Crowther (1991: 189).

12. Crowther (1991: 189, 201); King (2000).

13. March (2007: 603); see also Socor (1992b). After 1992, Moldova essentially lacked the salient regional differences found in Ukraine.

14. Roper (2006: 88).

15. These figures are from a 1998 survey by Jerry Hough and David Laitin cited in Katchanovski (2006: 181).

16. Roper (2006: 88).

17. On the concept of non-Western or "black knight" support for authoritarianism, see Levitsky and Way (2010).

18. *Vecherniy Kishinev*, 29 January 1990, 1; 18 May 1990, 2, 3; 1 September 1990, 1.

19. *Vecherniy Kishinev*, 18 May 1990, 2, 6; 24 October 1990, 3.

20. King (2000: 191).

21. Socor (1992b: 8).

22. Interview with Iurie Rosca, head of PPCD, Chişinău, Moldova, 8 February 2002; Crowther (1991); Skvortsova (2002: 182).

23. King (1994a: 295–6); IFES (1994: 25).

24. Socor (1992c).

25. Interview with Alexandru Muravschi, parliamentary deputy (1994–2001), Chişinău, 31 January 2002. According to the rules laid out in appendix 1, it was low strength since it had not run in two elections.

26. Interview with Anatol Golea, journalist, Chişinău, 1 February 2002; Interview with Dumutri Diacov, head of parliament (1998–2000), Chişinău, 1 February 2002.

27. Interview with Alexandru Muravschi, Chişinău, 31 January 2002.

28. March (2005); Quinlan (2005: 487).

29. Helsinki Watch (1993: 18–19); Waters (1996: 398); Interviews with Viorel Ciba-toru, former military advisor, Chişinău, Moldova, 7 February 2002, and Nicolai Chirto-aca, former National Security advisor, 5 February 2002.

30. Interview with Nicolae Andronic, legal advisor to Snegur, Chişinău, 23 July 2004; Chirtoaca interview.

31. See King (2000: 192–93); March and Herd (2006: 365).

32. Waters (1996).

33. March and Herd (2006: 365).

34. Military Balance (2006: 398–99).

35. Crowther (2007); EBRD (ND).

36. See *Foreign Broadcast Information Service—SOV*, 4 November 1991, 71.

37. After 1992, no candidates were barred, and according to ODIHR reports, there was relatively little evidence of serious ballot stuffing or other similar fraud in the 1994, 1996, 1998, 2001, and 2005 parliamentary and presidential elections.

38. OSCE report cited in Parmelee (2009: 3).

39. ODIHR (1997: 7). For other examples of state media bias against incumbents in Moldova, see ODIHR (1998: 12, 7); ODIHR (2001a: 7, 8).

40. "Moldovan Political Parties against Early Parliamentary Elections" *Infotag*, 7 July 1997 (wnc.fedworld.gov). See also Roper (2001: 6); Fish (2006: 11).

41. See "Events around Defence Ministry Have Completely Exposed Differences between Power Structures in Moldova," *Infotag*, 23 April 1996 (wnc.fedworld.gov).

42. Crowther (1991: 201).

43. Crowther (1991: 201, 192); King (2000: 123–26, 136).

44. Crowther (1991: 189–190; 1997: 300); King (1994a: 294).

45. Crowther (1991: 192); Man (1994: 122).

46. Chinn (1994: 309–10); King (1994b: 349, 2000: 129–30).

47. King (1994b: 350).

48. "Violence in Moldavia: Emergency Measures Introduced," *BBC Summary of World Broadcasts*, 13 November 1989.

49. "Kremlin Ousts Moldavia Leader," *The Independent*, 17 November 1989.

50. *Vecherniy Kishinev*, 18 May 1990, 2, 3; and *Vecherniy Kishinev*, 1 September 1990, 1; Crowther (1991: 199).

51. Crowther (1994: 343). See also Roper (2006: 83).

52. Socor (1991b); Skvortsova (2002: 185); see also King (1994a: 295).

53. Socor (1992a: 44).

54. Kolsto, Edemsky, and Kalashnikova (1993: 981–89); King (2000: 151).

55. Crowther (1996: 36).

56. *Vecherniy Kishinev*, 18 May 1990, 1; "Moldavia Delays Language Vote," *The Guardian* (London), 31 August 1989; Crowther (1991: 195–96); Kolsto, Edemsky, and Kalashnikova (1993: 981); Chinn (1994: 311).

57. Kolsto, Edemsky, and Kalashnikova (1993: 984).

58. Socor (1992a: 43); Kolsto Edemsky and Kalashnikova (1993: 987); Hill and Jewett (1994: 61).

59. Socor (1993a: 14).

60. Interview with Nicolae Andronic, Chișinău, Moldova, 23 July 2004; Interview with Nicolai Chirtoaca, former KGB official, 5 February 2002.

61. Neukrich (2004: 134).

62. Helsinki Watch (1993); Crowther (1996: 37); Roper (2006: 84).

63. King (1994b: 353).

64. Roper (2002: 156–58).

65. Crowther (2007: 275–76).

66. Thus, in mid-1993, observers were "bewildered" when Snegur's own supporters voted against the presidential efforts to ratify the CIS agreement. See "Parliament 'Split' over Ratification of Moldova's Membership of the CIS," *ITAR-TASS*, 12 August 1993.

67. Andronic interview; *Nezavisimaya Moldova*, 12 July 1994, 1. Nationalists focused exclusively on divisive ethnic issues and largely refused to engage with the constitutional debate. See "Events around Defence Ministry Have Completely Exposed Differences between Power Structures in Moldova," *Infotag*, 23 April 1996 (wnc.fedworld.gov).

68. Andronic interview.

69. Fish (2006).

70. Interview with Mircea Snegur, Chișinău, Moldova, 8 February 2002.

71. "Parliament Rejects Snegur's Language Bid," *Infotag*, 9 February 1996.

72. *Itar-Tass*, 20 November 1996.

73. "Presidential Campaign in Moldova Is Likely to Have Its Own 'Lebed,'" *Infotag*, 13 July 1996.

74. "Events around Defense Ministry Have Completely Exposed Differences between Power Structures in Moldova," *Infotag*, 23 April 1996.

75. "High-Ranking Officers Demand General Creanga's Dismissal," *Basapress*, 26 June 1996.

76. Chirtoaca interview, 2002.

77. "Snegur Accuses Defense Minister of Inciting 'Mutiny,'" *Basapress*, 28 June 1996.

78. *Basapress*, 21 September 1993; 28 September 1993.

79. A law passed in 1992 forbade denigration of heads of state. See *TASS*, 9 January 1992.

80. Socor (1992b: 77, 78); Parmelee (2009: 9, 14–15).

81. Caraus (2004: 331). Parmelee estimates that print media were "divided almost equally between Moldovan and Russian-language papers" (Parmelee 2009: 7).

82. *ITAR-Tass*, 2 September 1992; *Krasnaya zvezda*, 9 September 1992.

83. "Which Candidate Is Supported by Moscow?" *Infotag*, 4 November 1996.

84. Interview with Adrian Usatii, Chişinău, 30 July 2004.

85. ODIHR (1997: 7).

86. "Sangheli Has 'More Chances to Win,'" *Infotag*, 8 November 1996.

87. An official who worked on Sangheli's 1996 campaign reported that local officials almost always promised 100 percent support, "But it was very difficult to follow up on such promises and to know if they would keep their word" (interview with Alexandru Muravschi).

88. *Infotag*, 10 April 1998; Interview with Alexandru Mosanu, leader of the Front, Chişinău, 4 February 2002.

89. "Moldova: Parliament Speaker Calls for Radio, TV Chiefs' Ouster," *Infotag*, 8 July 1997.

90. In the elections, the Communists gained 40 seats; the Democratic Convention of Moldova, 26; the BDPM, 24; and the Party of Democratic Forces, 11.

91. Diacov interview, 2002.

92. Roper (2001: 6).

93. Mosanu interview, 2002; Diacov interview, 2002; Golea interview, 2002.

94. Diacov interview, 2002.

95. Quote from "Political Commentary Examines Ousted TV Chief's Case," *Basapress*, 30 July 1997; also Diacov interview; Golea interview; Muravschi interview.

96. "Moldova: Parliament Approves New Teleradio Management," *Infotag*, 30 November 1997.

97. Interview with Angela Sarbu, Independent Journalism Center, Chişinău, 6 February 2002.

98. For details of these proposed amendments, see Roper (2001: 12).

99. Crowther (2007: 276).

100. *RFE/RL Newsline*, 16 December 1999.

101. *Infotag*, 20 July 2000.

102. Diacov interview, 2002.

103. Nedelciuc (ND).

104. Hill (2001: 132).

105. Hill (2001: 134).

106. Thus, according to a survey commissioned by Grigore Pop-Eleches (Princeton) and the author in 2005, 93 percent of Russian nationals recalled voting for the Communist

Party in 2001. Of those who recalled voting for the Communist Party, 66 percent felt that Moldova should be closer to Russia than to Romania—as compared to 27 percent of those who voted for a non-Communist party. Results are based on a nationally representative sample of 509 adults conducted in March 2005.

107. Close to a third of the vote went to parties unable to pass the 6-percent threshold. In addition, the Communists benefitted from the d'Hondt formula for the distribution of unrepresented votes.

108. *Infotag*, 27 April 2001. According to the National Committee for the Freedom of the Press, approximately a third of journalists working for National Radio and Television were fired after the Communist victory.

109. Way (2002a: 131), ODIHR (2005: 1).

110. Dura (2008).

111. Roper (2006); "Marian Lupu: 'Ya svoboden i bolee nikomu nichego ne dolzhen,'" *Moldavskie vedomosti*, 26 June 2009.

112. ODIHR (2005: 1, 9, 10); ODIHR (2009a; 2009b).

113. Thus, the government carried out tax audits of those with links to the opposition—a fact that likely discouraged contributions (ODIHR 2009a: 11). For this reason, opposition subordination is scored medium.

114. March and Herd (2006: 366); Popescu (2012: 38).

115. ODIHR (2005: 21, 20); see also ODIHR (2009b: 16–18).

116. ODHIR (2009a: 20); also ODIHR (2009a: 2–3); Hale (2013: 497).

117. "Marian Lupu: 'Ya svobden I bole nikomu nichego ne dolzhen," *Moldavskie vedomosti*, 26 June 2009.

118. Dura (2008).

119. Dura (2008); see also Crowther (2007: 289–90).

120. "Moldaviya: ot 'epokha Voronina' k 'epokhu Lupu'?" *Regnum*, 3 August 2009.

121. Way (2002a: 131).

122. Interview with Vladislav Gribincea, lawyer, Chişinău, Moldova, 29 July 2004.

123. "Moldaviya: ot 'epokha Voronina' k 'epokhu Lupu'?" *Regnum*, 3 August 2009.

124. On the concept of non-Western or "black knight" support for authoritarianism, see Levitsky and Way (2010).

125. *RFE/RL Newsline*, 18 May 2001; March (2007: 605, 609, 617).

126. Crow (1992: 12); Socor (1993b: 31); Roper (2006: 84).

127. Popescu (2012: 49).

128. Quinlan (2005: 495).

129. Quinlan (2005: 496).

130. Neukrich (2004: 133).

131. Quinlan (2005: 495); also Crowther (2007: 282).

132. Stavila (2004: 129); McDonagh (2008: 149); "Spiker parlamenta Moldavii oposaetsya post-vybornogo politicheskogo krizisa v strane" *Regnum* 16 March 2009.

133. See *RFE/RL Newsline*, 10 and 11 January, 14 and 15 February 2002.

134. Rosca interview; Crowther (2007: 280)

135. *RFE/RL Newsline*, 5 February 2002; Crowther (2007: 282); McDonagh (2008: 154).

136. McDonagh (2008: 154, 157).

137. McDonagh (2008: 154). The Justice Minister publicly admitted that the lifting of the suspension had been a "response" to the concerns expressed by the Council of Europe (*RFE/RL Newsline* 11 February 2002).

138. Crowther (2007: 273).

139. Interview with Dmitri Chubashenko, chief editor of *Moldavskie Vedomosti*, 22 July 2004.

140. Crowther (2007: 286).

141. March and Herd (2006: 367, 7); Crowther (2007: 284).

142. *RFE/RL Newsline* 30 November 2004; Igor Botan, "Why were new elections necessary?" e-democracy.md June 27, 2005.

143. This story was related to the author by a Western diplomat who served in Moldova at this time.

144. ODIHR (2005: 1, 9, 10).

145. The opposition Democratic Moldova Bloc won 22 seats, and the PPCD won 11 seats.

146. In exchange, Rosca, the head of the PPCD, was elected deputy speaker of parliament.

147. ODHIR (2009b: 10). "Media NGOs Concerned about Fate of Pro TV channel," *Moldova Azi*, 16 December 2008. At the same time, the government did stop transmission of the Romanian TVR1 (Hale 2013: 492).

148. Hale (2013: 490).

149. Hale (2013: 490). Hale argues that the willingness of such businesses to openly support opposition is explained by uncertainty surrounding the election results and term limits on Voronin's power. For a critique of this argument in the CIS, see chapter 7.

150. Ghimpu's Liberal Party and Filat's LDPM each had 15 seats, while Serafim Urechean's Alliance Our Moldova (AMN) secured 11 seats.

151. "Moldova's Dead Souls," *RFE/RL Reports*, 17 April 2009.

152. "Oppozitsiya i vlasti Moldavii dogovorilis' pereschitat' byulleteni," 7 April 2009.

153. "Spiker parlamenta Moldavii obvinil v organizatsii besporiadkov v Kishineve 'vneshnie sili,'" Regnum, 7 April 2009.

154. Ibid.

155. The government was widely believed responsible for the highly inflammatory Romanian flag. See "Vybory bez vyborov," *Kommersant Plus*, 28 May 2009.

156. "Moldovan President Accuses Romania As Protests Continue," *RFE/RL Report*, 8 April 2009; "IFJ Condemns Ban on Romanians Journalists in Moldova," *News Press*, 14 April 2009.

157. Cited in *Romania Libera* 8 April 2009.

158. "Restive Diplomatic, Security Situation Belie Moldovan Calm," *RFE/RL Reports*, 9 April 2009; "Amnesty International Protests Detentions," *Associated Press*, 11 April 2009; "Spiski zaderzhanykh vo vremya massovykh besporyadkov," *Moldavskie Vedemosti*, 15 April 2009.

159. "For One Moldovan Activist, 'We Are Freer, Because We Have Nothing To Lose,'" *RFE/RL Reports*, 15 May 2009.

160. "Nearly 100 Protesters Released from Prison in Chişinău—Moldovan Prosecutors," *Ukraine General Newswire*, 24 April 2009.

161. ODIHR (2009b: 10).

162. "Communist Leadership Splits Ahead of Moldova's Presidential Showdown," *RFE/RL Reports*, 2 June 2009. See also "Vybory bez vyborov," *Kommersant-Plus*, 28 May 2009.

163. "Bor'ba za 'zolotoy golos,'" *Polit.ru*, 5 May 2009.

164. "Communist Leadership Splits Ahead of Moldova's Presidential Showdown," *RFE/RL Reports*, 2 June 2009.

165. "US State Secretary Urges Moldova to Address Election-related Concerns," *Infotag*, 1 June 2009.

166. "EU Foreign Ministers Discussing Growing Eastern Instability," *RFE/RL Reports*, 27 April 2009; "EU's Solana Congratulates Moldova's Outgoing President on Election as Speaker," *BBC Monitoring Kiev Unit*, 13 May 2009.

167. Hale (2013: 499).

168. LeBas (2011).

169. See Pop-Eleches and Way (2010); also "Eks-spiker parlamenta Moldavii Lupu otnositsya k rasryadu 'sistemnoy-sosushchikh'" *Regnum*, 18 June 2009.

170. Pop-Eleches and Way (2010).

171. "Eks-spiker parlamenta Moldavii Lupu otnositsya k rasryadu 'sistemnoy-sosushchikh,'" *Regnum*, 18 June 2009. Serefim Urechean, the leader of the AMN, claimed that Communist victory threatened "the destruction of a nation" and worried that the government wanted to "change the status of the Romanian language, eliminate the tricolor flag, state crest, and hymn that is the face of the sovereign government." See "Vybory bez vyborov," *Kommersant-Plus*, 28 May 2009.

172. "Moldavskie liberal-demokraty obespokoeny poezdkoy glavy MID Moldavii v Moskvu," *Regnum*, 6 May 2009.

173. "Posle sobytii 7 aprelya PKRM trudno poluchit' 'zolotoy golos' oppozitsii," *Moldova Azi*, 1 June 2009. Another commentator noted, "Any opposition deputy who now gives his "golden vote" to the Communists seriously discredits himself [and his party]" ("Bor'ba za 'zolotoiygolos,'" *Polit.ru*, 5 May 2009).

174. "Bor'ba za 'zolotoy golos,'" *Polit.ru*, 5 May 2009; "Vybory bez vyborov," *Kommersant-Plus*, 28 May 2009.

175. "Vybory bez vyborov," *Kommersant-Plus*, 28 May 2009; "Bor'ba za 'zolotoy golos,'" *Polit.ru*, 5 May 2009.

176. "Posle sobytii 7 aprelya PKRM trudno poluchit' 'zolotoy golos' oppozitsii," *Moldova Azi*, 1 June 2009.

177. "Communist Leadership Splits Ahead of Moldova's Presidential Showdown," *RFE/RL Reports*, 2 June 2009. See also "Filat: Nikto i nichto ne smozhet zastavit' moldavskuyu oppozitsiyu progolosovat' za prezidenta-kommunista," *Regnum*, 5 May 2009; "Moldovan Opposition Party Not to Hold Talks with Ruling Communists," *Infotag*, 28 May 2010; "Parliament Moldavii ne isbral prezidenta I budet raspushchen," *PRIME-TASS News* Agency, 3 June 2009.

178. Popescu (2012: 41).

179. Hale (2013: 498).

180. ODIHR (2009b).

181. The PCRM took 48 seats; Filat's LDPM, 18; Ghimpu's Liberal Party, 15; Lupu's Democratic Party, 13; AMN, 7.

182. "Chetyre partii, poluchivshie bol'shinstvo v parlamente v Moldavii, sozdali koalitsiyu," *RIA Novosti*, 8 August 2009.

183. As a result, the legislature was unable to elect a president. However, the constitution does not allow more than two elections per year, and Ghimpu functioned as acting president.

184. See ODIHR (2011); "Freedom House Freedom of the Press 2011: Moldova" (www.freedomhouse.org).

185. ODIHR (2011: 1).

186. See Hale (2015: 415–16).

187. Popescu (2012: 43).
188. Socor (2013).
189. Popescu (2012: 43).
190. Wilson (2013: 2).
191. Crowther (2007: 274).
192. For example, in 1991, Snegur manipulated electoral rules to become the sole candidate in Moldova's first presidential election. In 2012, the AEI shut down a major opposition TV station (NIT)—a step that even the relatively autocratic Communists had refrained from.
193. Crowther (2007: 286).
194. Fish (2006); March and Herd (2006).
195. March and Herd (2006).

CHAPTER FIVE: Authoritarian Consolidation in Belarus

1. See Bekus (2010: 88); Karbalevich (2010: 438).
2. *Narodnaia hazeta*, 9–11 July 1994, 1; Silitski (2004: 76); Interview with Valerii Fadeev, former staff member of the Council of Ministers, Minsk, 28 June 2004.
3. Silitski (2004: 94); see also Feduta (2005: 283).
4. Burger and Minchuk (2006: 33).
5. Guthier (1977a: 38); Wilson (2011: 79).
6. Guthier (1977a: 47).
7. Wilson (2011: 114).
8. Mihalisko (1997: 235).
9. Guthier (1977b: 275).
10. Drakokhurst and Furman (2002: 232); Wilson (2011: 123).
11. According to official results, 83.3 percent voted for giving Russian language the same official status as Belarusian language; 75 percent voted for a return of Soviet-era Belarusian national symbols.
12. Rontoyanni (2005: 133).
13. Wilson (2011: 125).
14. Wilson (2011: 147). In the 1994 presidential elections, Pazniak's support was a bit higher in Grodno on the Polish border but did not come close to reaching 50 percent.
15. In 2006 and 2010, the main opposition—to the extent that it existed—supported closer ties to Europe. However, these candidates were never able to gain a serious following.
16. Sannikov (2002: 222).
17. Wilson (2011: 139).
18. BPF figure from *Narodnaia hazeta*, 26 January 1991, 2. By contrast, the anti-Russian Rukh in Ukraine garnered about a quarter of the seats in 1990; while the Moldovan Popular Front gained about a third of seats in 1990 and took control over the government.
19. Wilson (2011: 151).
20. Rontoyanni (2005: 135).
21. See especially, "'My ne russkiye, my belorusskiye!': kak slomalsya russkiy natsionalist Lukashenko," *Zapadnaya Rus*,' 4 May 2014; see also Wilson (2011: 203–6).
22. Drakokhrust (2012).
23. Under Kebich, a loose parliamentary faction, "Belarus," supported the prime minister but did not exist outside of the legislature, and never nominated candidates for elections.
24. Lukashuk (1998).

25. *Foreign Broadcast Information Service-SOV,* 4 December 1992, 35; interview with Stanislau Shushkevich, Minsk, 23 June 2004.

26. Interview with Vladimir Reznikov, BKGB official, Minsk, 13 July 2004.

27. *Narodnaia hazeta,* 14 September 1991, 4.

28. Kebich (2008: 272). By 1994, the private sector share of GDP had risen to just 15 percent—a figure matched only by Tajikistan and Turkmenistan in the former Soviet Union and much lower than the 40 percent in Moldova and Ukraine, 50 percent in Russia, and 55 percent in Estonia in that same year (EBRD).

29. Kebich (2008: 139).

30. Interview with Nikolai Voitenkov, member of parliament, 12th convocation, Gomel, 9 July 2004; Interview with Alexander Sosnov, member of Presidium of Supreme Soviet 1990–1995, Minsk, 24 June 2004.

31. For example, when the executive of Gomel refused to resign as requested by Kebich in late 1993, she faced few consequences (Interview with Svetlana Gol'dade, head of Executive Committee of the City of Gomel 1990–1994, Gomel, 9 July 2004).

32. Kebich (2008: 338); Voitenkov interview.

33. Kebich (2008: 143, 261–2); Interview with Pavel Kazlauskii, Minister of Defense under Kebich, Minsk, 23 June 2004.

34. Egorov (2003); *Narodnaia hazeta,* 18 May 1991, 1; 19 December 1991, 1.

35. Egorov (2003: 33–34).

36. Reznikov interview; Interview with Sergei Anisko, KGB official in Kontrrazvedki, 1994–1995, Minsk,14 July 2004.

37. Karbalevich (2010: 197, 652).

38. See *Narodnaia hazeta,* 29 November 1994, 1; 30 November 1994, 1; 2 December 1994, 1; 10–12 December 1994, 1; 14 December 1994, 1.

39. "Sobytiya i kommentarii. V voyennom vedomstve Belorussii polnost'yu smeneno rukovodstvo," *Krasnaya zvezda,* 17 August 1994.

40. "Okhranniki Prezidenta Lukashenko Osvaivayut Opyt Rossiyskikh Spetssluzhb," *Izvestiia,* 15 February 1995.

41. "U Sluzhby Bezopasnosti Prezidenta Belarusi Yubiley," *Interfax,* 25 October 2001.

42. "Narodnyy rezhim," *Izvestiia,* 24 January 1997; "V proyekte byudzheta-2001 po-prezhnemu odnoy iz lidiruyushchikh raskhodnykh statey ostayetsya finansirovaniye pravookhranitel'nykh organov," *Belorusskaya delovaya gazeta,* 4 October 2000; Karbalevich (2010: 393).

43. "Belarus'—odna iz samykh militarizovannykh stran mira," *Belorusskaya delovaya gazeta,* 8 November 2000; Karbalevich (2010: 393). According to a study cited by Karbalevich (2010: 393), in Minsk alone there were 1,442 officers per one hundred thousand population in the 2000s—more than twice the average among 15 countries examined.

44. "Okhranniki Prezidenta Lukashenko Osvaivayut Opyt Rossiyskikh Spetssluzhb," *Izvestiia,* 15 February 1995.

45. *Narodnaia hazeta,* 21 October 1994, 1; Karbalevich (2010: 121).

46. Kebich (2008: 338, 339); also Feduta (2005: 258).

47. See appendix I for coding rules.

48. In particular, the BKGB's loyalty remained uncertain. For example, in the fall of 2004, BKGB head Leonid Erin met with protestors in an apparent show of sympathy following fraudulent parliamentary elections (an action that resulted in Erin's dismissal).

49. Karbalevich (2010: 461–62). "Bylo vashe—stanet nashe," *Belorusskaya delovaya gazeta,* 1 April 2005.

50. EBRD. In 2004, the government owned each of the country's 14 most profitable companies. US Embassy Cable, 5 May 2006.

51. "Prezident Belarusi vyrazil nedovol'stvo rabotoy Komiteta goskontrolya," *Belorusskaya delovaya gazeta*, 6 October 2006; also "Komitet Tozika "kopayet" pod pravitel'stvo," *Belorusskaya delovaya gazeta*, 10 November 2000; "Mest' Lukashenko," *Belorusskaya delovaya gazeta*, 20 July 2001.

52. "Lukashenko ubirayet s politicheskoy doski sil'nyye figury," *Belorusskaya delovaya gazeta*, 14 April 2006.

53. Matsuzato (2004: 254); "Komitet goskontrolya v khode respublikanskoy proverki vyyavil pervyye narusheniya zakonodatel'stva pri vyplate zarplat," *Belorusskaya delovaya gazeta*, 7 July 2005; "Prezident poruchil KGK proveryat' usloviya prodazhi belorusskikh tovarov," *Belorusskaya delovaya gazeta*, 3 August 2009.

54. "Prezident Belarusi otmenil 'zolotuyu aktsiyu,'" *Belorusskaya delovaya gazeta*, 4 March 2008; Karbalevich (2010: 475).

55. "Belarus—Extensive Right to Draft Fixed-term Contracts," *Survey of Violations of Trade Union Rights* (survey.ituc-csi.org) (1999).

56. Karbalevich (2010: 301, 299); see also "Prezident Belarusi potreboval ot Upravdelami 'absolyutnoy chistoty,'" *Belorusskaya delovaya gazeta*, 23 January 2010; Feduta (2005: 401).

57. "Nesovmestimost,'" *Izvestiia*, 27 February 1996; see also "PROTSESS. Prezidentskiy vzyatochnik," *Belorusskaya delovaya gazeta*, 19 August 2003. In the late 1990s, UDP had 13,000 employees. "V okruzhenii Lukashenko zreyut peremeny," *Russkyi Telegraf*, 5 February 1998.

58. "V Belorussii arestovano imushchestvo eks-upravlyayushchey delami prezidenta," *Belorusskaya delovaya gazeta*, 13 December 2004; Feduta (2005: 401–2).

59. "V Belorussii arestovano imushchestvo eks-upravlyayushchey delami prezidenta," *Belorusskaya delovaya gazeta*, 13 December 2004; Karbalevich (2010: 299).

60. Martinsen (2002); Feduta (2005: 403–14); Karbalevich (2010: 302).

61. Clem (1996: 219).

62. Hardline factions (Communists and *Soiuz*) accounted for 58 percent (200) of deputies in the legislature, while "industrialists" and "agrarians" accounted for another 22 percent (65). BPF had just 27 deputies (8 percent). *Narodnaia hazeta*, 26 January 1991, 2.

63. *Narodnaia hazeta*, 19 January 1991, 1; 10 April 1991, 1.

64. For example, an effort by Communist leader Anatolii Malofeev to introduce martial law in the early summer of 1991 went nowhere. *Narodnaia hazeta*, 8 June 1991, 1.

65. Kebich (2008: 364).

66. Gerasyuk (1991: 53); Kebich (2008: 65–66, 93).

67. Quote from party activist at a Minsk party meeting in January 1991. "Kriticheskiie zamechanie i predlozhenii vyskazanikh kommunista v khode otchete vyborov v Minskoi gorodskoi partiinoi organizatsii," 9 January 1991, #00076 (Central Committee archives of Belarusian Communist Party).

68. *Narodnaia hazeta*, 28 August 1991, 1; Feduta (2005: 32).

69. Interview with Leonid Kozik, parliamentary deputy 12th and 13th convocations, Minsk, 8 July 2004; Kazlauski interview; Kebich (2008: 103).

70. *Narodnaia hazeta*, 19 September 1991, 1.

71. Interview with Levon Bashevskii, parliamentary deputy in 12th convocation, Minsk, 30 June 2004.

72. *Foreign Broadcast Information Service-SOV*, 4 December 1992, 35. Shushkevich interview. Kebich (2008: 188, 228).

73. Egorov (2003); Kebich (2008: 364–69).

74. Interview with Pastukhov, Minsk, 6 July 2004.

75. Pastukhov interview; also interview with Hary Pahaniaila, Belarusian Helsinki Committee, Minsk, 8 July 2004.

76. For example, in the winter of 1994, ministers in the Kebich government were able to thwart pressures by Kebich to force the firing of the editor of the opposition newspaper *Svaboda* (*Narodnaia hazeta*, 24–26 September 1994, 2).

77. Way (2012a).

78. Feduta (2005: 128).

79. Way (2012a).

80. Feduta (2005: 71).

81. *Narodnaia hazeta*, 23 March 1994, 1; Feduta (2005: 64).

82. Interview with Sergei Antonchik, member of parliament 12th convocation, Minsk, 3 July 2004; Interview with Mechaslav Grib, former head of parliament, Minsk, 24 June 2004.

83. Kebich (2008: 42).

84. Way (2012a).

85. Interview with Anatolii Lebedko, member of parliament 12th convocation, Minsk, 12 July 2004.

86. Reznikov interview; Anisko interview.

87. Feduta (2005: 15–17).

88. Feduta (2005: 121–22).

89. Karbalevich (2010: 76).

90. *Narodnaia hazeta* 7–9 May 1994, p. 2; 12 May 1994, p. 1.

91. Kebich (2008: 10).

92. Interview with Alyaksandr Kornienko, former deputy mayor of Gomel city, Minsk, 30 June 2004.

93. Interview with Vladimir Novosiad, parliamentary deputy, 13th convocation, Minsk, 8 July 2004; Kebich (2008: 18, 14).

94. Kebich (2008: 428).

95. *Narodnaia hazeta*, 30 June 1994, 1.

96. *Narodnaia hazeta*, 7 October 1994, 1.

97. Leonov (2003: 18); Karbalevich (2010: 196).

98. Haerpfer (2003: 97).

99. Haerpfer (2005: 177).

100. Halman (2001).

101. Poll cited in US Embassy Cable, 14 June 2007.

102. Karbalevich (2010: 165, 170).

103. Karbalevich (2010: 272).

104. Feduta (2005: 256).

105. For example, Lukashenka initially appointed Nikolai Egorov to run the KGB despite Egorov's ties to Shushkevich (*Narodnaia hazeta*, 9 August 1994, 1).

106. Bashevskii interview.

107. "Okhranniki Prezidenta Lukashenko Osvaivayut Opyt Rossiyskikh Spetssluzhb," *Izvestiia*, 15 February 1995.

108. Feduta (2005: 232, 234).

109. Feduta (2005: 230).

110. Feduta (2005: 245).

111. Karbalevich (2010: 141).

112. Markus (1996); Feduta (2005: 250).

113. Sahm (1999: 655); Karbalevich (2010: 147).

114. Karbalevich (2010: 164, 171, 165).

115. Markus (1996); Karbalevich (2010: 171).

116. Silitski (2004: 94). See also Feduta (2005: 283).

117. Feduta (2005: 286–88).

118. Leonov (2003: 25); Karbalevich (2010: 189).

119. Karbalevich (2010: 189); Lebedko interview; Bashevskii interview; interview with Pavel Bykovskii, journalist, Minsk, 5 July 2004.

120. Feduta (2005: 279–80).

121. Karbalevich (2010: 147).

122. Interview with Pavel Daneiko, member of Belarusian parliament 13th convocation, Minsk, 6 July 2004.

123. Karbalevich (2010: 182).

124. Feduta (2005: 326).

125. Bykovskii interview.

126. Lebedko interview; see also Wilson (2011: 179).

127. Novosiad interview.

128. Interview with Andrei Sannikov, former Ministry of Foreign Affairs official, Minsk, 3 July 2004.

129. Leonov (2003: 26).

130. Interview with Vincuk Viacorka, chairman BPF, Minsk, 29 June 2004.

131. Of course, Yeltsin was able to suppress parliament despite open resistance—but only with enormous difficulty (see McFaul 2001).

132. Karbalevich (2010: 189).

133. Silitski (2004: 95).

134. Silitski (2005: 87–88).

135. Feduta (2005: 351).

136. "Portuguese President Refuses to Meet with Belarusian Counterpart," *RFE-RL Newsline*, 2 December 1996; Bureau of European and Eurasian Affairs (2009).

137. Kopstein and Reilly (2000); Brinks and Coppedge (2006).

138. Kopstein and Reilly (2000); Bunce and Wolchik (2011).

139. Feduta (2005: 309).

140. US Embassy Cable, 13 January 2006; "Tekhnologii: 'vertikal' beret golosovaniye v svoi ruki," *Belorusskaya delovaya gazeta*, 22 February 2001.

141. See, for example, ODIHR (2000, 2001b, 2006). Lukashenka even admitted publicly to fraud. See US Embassy Cable, 1 December 2006.

142. "Tsenzura: v 2000 godu Goskompechati vynes preduprezhdeniya 20 gazetam," *Belorusskaya delovaya gazeta*, 6 February 2001; US Embassy Cable, 5 October 2006b.

143. "Belarusian Prison Official Confirms Death Squad Allegations," *RFE/RL Reports*, August 29, 2001.

144. Sannikov (2005: 85).

145. Karbalevich (2010: 121).

146. Aslund (2002); Karol (2006).

147. "Gazprom's Grip" *RFE/RL* July 15, 2014 (rferl.org). Averages on the basis of reported prices 1998–2011. As of July 2014, Belarus paid $166—less than half of what was paid in Moldova ($388) or Ukraine ($485). "Minskoe 'Dinamo,'" *Kommersant*, 13 July 1999; "Sochins"kyj hazavat," *Ukrainska Pravda*, 16 October 2000; Silitski (2003); Balmaceda (2013: 51, 172, 2014: 51). Prices paid by Belarus were also about 30 percent lower than

those paid by Georgia (2003–2008 and 2011); 40 percent lower than those paid by Azerbaijan (2000–2007), and less than half of what the Baltics paid (2003–2009). Armenia, which paid 7 percent higher gas prices than Belarus (2003–2010), has been the only country where gas price subsidies have been similar. (Cites available from author on request.)

148. See Suzdaltsev (2007); *The Economist*, 3 January 2007: 44–45.

149. Silitski (2004: 159); Feduta (2005: 407–11).

150. Balmaceda (2014: 39, 65).

151. Aslund (2002); Karol (2006).

152. Aslund (2002: 182); Karol (2006); US Embassy Cable, 31 March 2006.

153. Feduta (2005: 403–15; 418–19).

154. See US Embassy Cable, 22 December 2008; 30 May 2008.

155. Balmaceda (2014: 156, 171, 86, 89).

156. Balmaceda (2014: 125).

157. Balmaceda (2013; 2014). In addition, such subsidies gave middlemen in both countries vast rent-seeking opportunities (Balmaceda 2014: 80, 83). But such opportunities, available to oligarchs throughout the former Soviet Union, cannot explain why Belarus was the recipient of uniquely vast assistance.

158. Lytvyn (1994); Bondarenko (2007).

159. Just before the elections, Russia provided two million tons of oil at substantially subsidized prices (*Narodnaia hazeta*, 17 June 1994, 2).

160. "Belarusian Opposition in 'Status Quo' Survival Mode," *BelarusDigest*, 12 February 2012.

161. Karbalevich (2010: 664).

162. Thus, at least 41 of the top 50 "oligarchs" were state officials or worked for state companies. See US Embassy Cable, 16 June 2006.

163. "Delo direktorov," *Belorusskaya delovaya gazeta*, 10 June 2003.

164. "Arestovan predsedatel' kontserna 'Belneftekhim,'" " *Belorusskaya delovaya gazeta*, 30 May 2007; Feduta (2005: 422); Karbalevich (2010: 413).

165. "Samyi bol'shoi strakh belorusov—tiur'ma," www.charter97.org/rus/news/2006/10/24/turma.

166. "Khans-Georg Vik vyrazhayet trevogu po povodu nomenklaturnykh 'chistok' v Belarusi," *Belorusskaya delovaya gazeta*, 4 December 2001.

167. "1000 organizatsiy na grani zakrytiya," *Belorusskaya delovaya gazeta*, 24 April 2008.

168. US Embassy Cable, 8 February 2008.

169. "1000 organizatsiy na grani zakrytiya," *Belorusskaya delovaya gazeta*, 24 April 2008.

170. US Embassy Cable, 30 November 2006.

171. US Embassy Cable, 23 October 2009.

172. "Tysiača zvolnienych inšadumcaŭ," *sbaboda.org*, 30 April 2008; see also, for example, "Polotsk: uvol'nyayut oppozitsionerov," *Belorusskaya delovaya gazeta*, 29 June 2001.

173. "Belarusian Opposition in 'Status Quo' Survival Mode," *BelarusDigest*, 12 February 2012.

174. Silitski (2006).

175. Drakokhrust (2012).

176. Drakokhrust (2012); Marin (2012: 21).

177. US Embassy Cable, 2 March 2007; 30 April 2007.

178. Ioffe (2008: 68).

179. Bekus (2010: 143).

180. Marin (2012: 5).

181. Reduced support for Lukashenka during economic downturn (despite continued repression) suggests that polls at least partly reflected actual levels of support for the president.

182. US Embassy Cable, 17 March 2006; US Embassy Cable, 4 October 2007; Ioffe (2008: 215).

183. Karbalevich (2010: 541).

184. US Embassy Cable, 2 November 2005.

185. US Embassy Cable, 4 September 2007.

186. US Embassy Cable, 15 March 2007.

187. US Embassy Cable, 5 March 2007.

188. "Has Moscow Had Enough of Belarus's Lukashenka?" *RFE/RL Reports*, July 19, 2010.

189. US Embassy Cable, 21 March 2008.

190. Drakokhrust (2012).

191. By 2014, the Belarusian price for Russian gas was three times lower than the price paid by Ukraine. "Gazprom's Grip," *RFE/RL*, 15 July 2014.

192. US Embassy Cable, 30 January 2007.

193. See US Embassy Cable, 16 May 2008; "Aktsii protiv otmeny l'got proshli v 30 gorodakh Belarusi," *Belorusskaya delovaya gazeta*, 17 December 2007.

194. Marin (2012: 20, 22).

195. "Belarusian Opposition in 'Status Quo' Survival Mode," *BelarusDigest*, 12 February 2012.

196. Marin (2012: 27).

197. "Belarusian Opposition in 'Status Quo' Survival Mode," *BelarusDigest*, 12 February 2012.

198. Balmaceda (2013: 160).

199. See, for example, Silitski (2005); Bekus (2010); Karbalevich (2010); Balmaceda (2014).

200. Przeworski (1986).

201. Silitski (2005).

202. Mihalisko (1997); Marples (1999).

203. Bekus (2010: 153); Moser (2013: 51).

204. Nodia (1994); Sannikov (2005).

CHAPTER SIX: Consolidated and Unconsolidated Authoritarianism in the Former Soviet Union

1. Lindberg (2006).

2. The average Freedom House score among post-Soviet countries increased from 4.58 in 1991 to 5.2 twenty years later (on a scale of 1 to 7, with 7 being the most authoritarian). During that period, 9 of 12 post-Soviet regimes had become more authoritarian.

3. See, for example, Furman (2004: 16).

4. I define turnover as cases in which leaders lose power to someone from outside of the regime. Cases experiencing turnover through mid-2014 were Azerbaijan, Belarus, Georgia, Kyrgyzstan, Moldova, Tajikistan, and Ukraine.

5. Party substitutes refer to well-established regional and other patronage networks. See Hale (2006).

6. On the breakdown of the Russian state in the 1990s, see Kahn (2002); Stoner-Weiss (2006).

7. McFaul (2001: 154–56); also Baturin et al. (2001: 255); Hale (2006). For example, Yeltsin chose a drinking buddy (Viktor Barannikov) to run the security services and expected officials such as Ruslan Khasbulatov, the head of parliament, to remain loyal out of gratitude for Yeltsin's role in advancing them to their positions (Sukhanov 1992: 313; Mlechin 2002: 742, 746).

8. Yeltsin (2000: 254).

9. Petrov and Slider (2005); Gelman (2006); Stoner-Weiss (2006: 62).

10. Hale (2006).

11. Ivanov (2008: 187); Reuter and Remington (2009: 502).

12. Baturin et al. (2001: 504).

13. Filatov (2001: 70, 171).

14. See Yeltsin (1994: 12, 172–78), and Kulikov (2002: 160–70).

15. Huskey (1999: 41).

16. Kostikov (1997: 290–92).

17. Kostikov (1997: 115–16).

18. Yeltsin (2000: 23–25); Kulikov (2002: 394–402).

19. Fish (2001).

20. Colton (2008: 433–34).

21. Gelman (2006: 240).

22. Colton and McFaul (2003: 180–82).

23. See Remington (2003: 233); Ivanov (2008: 183–84).

24. Myagkov, Ordeshook and Shakin (2009: 178).

25. Goldenberg (1994: 154, 162).

26. Wheatley (2005: 27–28); Bolukbasi (2011).

27. Goldenberg (1994: 154, 162).

28. Aves (1996).

29. De Waal (2003: 257).

30. Bremmer and Welt (1997: 88).

31. See Danielian (1996–1997: 128).

32. Liz Fuller, "Armenia: Political Power Grows out of the Barrel of a Gun," *RFE/RL Caucasus Report*, 12 May 1998, Vol. 1, No. 11.

33. See Danielian (1996–1997: 129); Bremmer and Welt (1997: 88).

34. I do not score this as a turnover because Kocharian was a top regime official at the time of power transfer rather than outside the regime.

35. Liz Fuller, "Thousands Protest Armenian Election Falsification," *RFE/RL Caucasus Report*, 24 February 2003, Vol. 7, No. 35.

36. Emil Danielyan, "Armenia: A Dictator in the Making," *Transitions Online*, 24 June 2004.

37. Anna Hakobyan, "Armenia: Authorities Hit Back as Opposition Campaign Mounts," *Transitions Online*, 13 April 2004.

38. Bolukbasi (2011: 188, 199).

39. Aves (1996).

40. Bolukbasi (2011: 193).

41. Bolukbasi (2011: 191).

42. Bolukbasi (2011: 199).

43. Aves (1996).

44. Aves (1996).

45. Aves (1996); Kendall-Taylor (2012).

46. Aves (1996).

47. Kemrova (2001: 230).

48. Suny (1994: 324); Wheatley (2005: 27–28).

49. Wheatley (2003: 135); Zürcher (2007: 137–39); see also Jones (1996: 36).

50. Zürcher (2007: 127).

51. "Stunned, Georgians Reckon the Cost of Independence," *New York Times*, 10 January 1992.

52. See Wheatley (2005: 86–87).

53. See, for example, "People Power Sends a Message to Oppressive Regimes," *Wall Street Journal*, 21 April 2005.

54. Mitchell (2004: 345); Welt (2006: 14).

55. Welt (2006).

56. Karumidze and Wertsch (2005: 39, 15).

57. Fairbanks and Gugushvili (2013: 117).

58. Fairbanks and Gugushvili (2013: 117).

59. Aprasidze (2013: 223); Fairbanks and Gugushvili (2013: 119)

60. Fairbanks and Gugushvili (2013: 120, 121).

61. Fairbanks and Gugushvili (2013: 121).

62. On leverage, see Levitsky and Way (2010).

63. Kopstein and Reilly (2000); McGlinchey (2011: 34).

64. Olcott (1997: 201); Schatz (2004); Collins (2006: 39); Radnitz (2010a).

65. Between 1992 and 2011, natural resource rents as a share of GDP averaged 34 percent in Kazakhstan; 47 percent in Uzbekistan; and 61 percent in Turkmenistan—as compared to 0.2 percent in Kyrgyzstan and 1 percent in Tajikistan (World Bank World Development Indicators). In 2008, Kazakhstan and Turkmenistan each had 4.9 and 4.3 military and paramilitary personnel per million population as compared to 3.9 and 2.15 in Kyrgyzstan and Tajikistan. Uzbekistan, with 3.04, also had lower numbers of personnel. Similarly, Kazakhstan and Turkmenistan each spent $105 and $17 per capita on defense as compared $9 and $11 in Kyrgyzstan and Tajikistan (data is unavailable for Uzbekistan) (calculated from Military Balance 2010).

66. While Kyrgyzstan and Tajikistan were riven by relatively stable regional divisions as in Moldova and Ukraine, the divisions almost entirely reflected demands for resources rather than any broader, deep-seated ideological or cultural divide. As a result, such cleavages were less likely to generate crisis in the absence of weak organizational capacity. In contrast to these cases, division in Kazakhstan manifested itself less as a split within the titular Kazakh identity and more as demands for Russian minority rights. See appendix I for coding rules.

67. Ochs (1997: 341, 325, 328–29), Dagiev (2014: 3).

68. Ochs (1997); Dagiev (2014).

69. Gleason (1997: 116).

70. Ochs (1997: 324, 329).

71. Ochs (1997: 341); Jones Luong and Weinthal (2010: 83–84).

72. Ochs (1997: 314, 349).

73. McGlinchey (2011: 57); see also Jones Luong and Weinthal (2010: 81). According to EBRD (ND) estimates, the state sector accounted for an average 60 percent of GDP between 1992 and 2010—a figure that likely underestimates de facto state control (McGlinchey 2011: 59).

74. McGlinchey (2011: 75).

75. Melvin (2004: 129); McGlinchey (2011: 11). There was approximately one policeman per 10 citizens in the early 2000s (Markowitz 2013: 76).

76. Fierman (1997: 380, 389); McGinchey (2011: 70).
77. Carlisle (1995: 192).
78. Murtazashvili (2012: 79).
79. Markowitz (2013).
80. Olcott (1994: 126); Melvin (2004: 132); Jones Luong and Weinthal (2010).
81. Jones Luong (2002).
82. Olcott (1997: 207, 210). At the same time, in contrast to other examples of divided identity in the former Soviet Union, this division mostly manifested itself not as a split within the titular Kazakh identity but instead as demands for Russian minority rights.
83. World Bank World Development indicators.
84. Jones Luong and Weinthal (2010: 260, 278)
85. Olcott (1997: 218).
86. Based on calculations from data in *Military Balance* (1995–2012).
87. Kolsto (2004: 171); Olcott (2010: 93, 102–4).
88. Olcott (2010: 105).
89. Jones Luong and Weinthal (2010: 280); Olcott (2010: 92).
90. McGlinchey (2011: 40); see also Kolsto (2004: 170).
91. "Nations in Transit 2005: Kazakhstan," (www.freedomhouse.org).
92. Collins (2006: 189); Radnitz (2010a; 2010b). According to Military Balance (1995–2012), per capita defense spending by the Kyrgyz government was between two and four times lower than in Kazakhstan and 40 to 200 percent lower than in Uzbekistan and Turkmenistan during most of the 1990s and 2000s.
93. Collins (2006); Radnitz (2010b).
94. Anderson (1999).
95. Anderson (1999: 29).
96. Collins (2006: 184).
97. Anderson (1999: 24); see also Collins (2006: 192, 176–77, 237–40).
98. Anderson (1999: 60); Collins (2006: 173 n. 6).
99. Spector (2004: 8).
100. McGlinchey (2011: 83).
101. Huskey (1997: 271, 266).
102. Huskey (1997: 271, 266, 259); Anderson (1999: 41); Collins (2006: 244).
103. Huskey (1997: 266).
104. Markowitz (2013: 138, 137); also McGlinchey (2011: 12).
105. See Collins (2006: 248); Radnitz (2010b, chap. 5); Hale (2011: 590).
106. Thus, demonstrations in Bishkek reached 10,000 at their height (about 1 person per thousand in the capital) as compared to 1 million in Kyiv (about 35 protesters per thousand population in the capital).
107. See *The Economist*, 10 April 2010, 43.
108. Radnitz (2010b: 207).
109. Collins (2006); Markowitz (2013). Thus, I score both cases as "medium" national divide.
110. Buisson (2007: 140).
111. Babak (2004: 158).
112. Collins (2006: 201).
113. Collins (2006: 203); Rubin (1998: 153).
114. Buisson (2007: 117).
115. Nourzhanov (2005: 119).
116. Nourzhanov (2005: 120); Buisson (2007: 128–29).

117. Buisson (2007).

118. Rubin (1998: 153).

119. For a similar argument, see Brudny and Finkel (2011). My variable of national divisions focuses on splits within national identity, not the salience of national identity per se. In most of the rest of the former Soviet Union, where national identity has been relatively unified but less salient (e.g., Belarus), the weakness of cleavages has likely hampered the rise of serious challenges, but nationalism has been less effective at unifying the population around a common threat.

120. Relatively high organizational capacity is indicated by a score of medium or above; weak organizational capacity by a low or medium-low score. National unity is indicated by a medium or low national divide score; low unity is indicated by a high national divide coding. See appendix I for coding rules. I exclude from these numbers incumbents—Sarkisian in Armenia, Margvelashvili in Georgia, Atambayev in Kyrgyzstan, the AEI in Moldova, Berdimuhamedov in Turkmenistan, and Poroshenko in Ukraine—who had not fallen from power by early 2015 but who had not been in power for at least two full terms (or 8 years in the case of parliamentary regimes).

121. The average was 5.4 for strong/unified incumbents as compared to 4.3 for weak/divided incumbents.

122. Appendix B shows organizational capacity scores for all incumbents through 2014.

123. Moldova under Snegur until 1996 is the exception here. Freedom House's negative assessment of this period does not accord with my findings presented in chapter 4. It appears that Freedom House included the independent (and quite authoritarian) Transnistria in its codings in the early 1990s—which would explain Moldova's poor score in the early 1990s.

124. Levitsky and Way (2010, 2012).

125. See Hale (2015).

126. See, in particular, Hale (2015).

127. Levitsky and Way (2010).

128. Kopstein and Reilly (2000); Brinks and Coppedge (2006); Levitsky and Way (2010).

CHAPTER SEVEN: Conclusion

1. The share of democracies among low- and lower-middle-income countries nearly doubled from the mid-1980s to the 2000s, while the share of partially free countries increased by almost half, as measured by data from Freedom House (www.freedomhouse.org). Levels of development according to World Bank in 1995 (http://data.worldbank.org/data-catalog/world-development-indicators). On the increased number of competitive authoritarian regimes during this period, see Levitsky and Way (2010); Svolik (2012).

2. All countries were middle income in the early 1990s. On average in 1998–2013, all three countries were in the top third most corrupt countries in the world according to Transparency International (www.transparency.org).

3. Lipset (1959); Dahl (1971); Rueschemeyer, Stephens, and Stephens (1992). Boix (2003) and Acemoglu and Robinson (2005) suggest that development makes democracy less threatening to economic elites.

4. See, for example, Linz (1990); Fish (1998, 2006); McFaul (2002); Howard (2003); Hale (2006, 2015).

5. The wealthiest upper-middle-income cases (Belarus, Russia, and Kazakhstan) all had consolidated highly closed authoritarian regimes in the 2000s, while lower-middle

and lower-income ones included a mix of more and less democratic regimes (www.econ. worldbank.org).

6. Vachudova (2005). All countries were low linkage (Levitsky and Way 2010). While Belarus, Moldova, and Ukraine were closer to democratic Western Europe than the rest of the former Soviet Union, they experienced divergent regime trajectories.

7. See, for example, Howard (2003); Diuk (2006); Bunce and Wolchik (2011).

8. Beissinger (2013: 581–82).

9. Fond Demokratichni Initsiatyvy (2014).

10. See especially Hale (2015).

11. Przeworski (1986: 52).

12. Karbalevich (2010: 196).

13. Haerpfer (2005: 177).

14. Halman (2001).

15. Beissinger (2013); Norris (2014).

16. See, for example, Anderson (1999); Aron (2000).

17. See, for example, Colton and Skach (2005); Fish (2005, 2006); Hale (2011, 2015).

18. Fish (2006); Hale (2011).

19. Easter (1997).

20. Hale (2006, 2015).

21. As defined here, a turnover occurs when an incumbent loses power to an official who is not a top government official at the time of power transfer.

22. By "relatively weak," I mean incumbents with lower than medium organizational capacity. See appendix B. Just 3 of 12 incumbents who were never ousted by someone from outside the regime possessed weak organizational capacity or were in a highly divided country.

23. Those presidents that avoided term limits (either by changing the constitution, ignoring it, or handing the presidency over to a crony) were Ilham Aliev (Azerbaijan), Islam Karimov (Uzbekistan), Lukashenka (Belarus), Nursultan Nazarbayev (Kazakhstan), Vladimir Putin (Russia), Emomalii Rahmon (Tajikistan); and Askar Akaev in 2000 (Kyrgyzstan). Those that lost power in the run-up to the end of their final constitutional term were Eduard Shevardnadze (Georgia); Kurmanbek Bakiev (Kyrgyzstan); Mikheil Saakashvili (Georgia); Vladimir Voronin (Moldova); and Akaev in 2005 in the run-up to his third term. Kuchma in Ukraine left power after his second term but had obtained a court ruling allowing him to run anyway. I do not code the passing of Ter Petrosian in Armenia as a turnover because he was replaced by the top official from within his regime (Kocharian, who was prime minister when he became president).

24. Hale (2015: 305) attributes the failure to abolish term limits to the popularity of the president.

25. See appendix B. These numbers exclude incumbents—Sarkisian in Armenia, Margvelashvil in Georgia, Atambayev in Kyrgyzstan, AEI in Moldova; Berdimukhamedov in Turkmenistan, and Poroshenko in Ukraine) who had not fallen from power by the end of 2014 but who had not been in power for at least two full terms. I also exclude all leaders who came to power explicitly as interim leaders.

26. Appendix B shows organizational capacity scores for all incumbents through 2014.

27. Moldova's Freedom House score until 1996 is the exception here. Freedom House's negative assessment of this period does not accord with strong evidence of democratic pluralism in the early 1990s (see chapter 4).

28. See, for example, Przeworski et al. (2000).

29. See also Levitsky and Way (2010).

30. Thus, autocrats in Ukraine in 2004, Georgia in 2003, and Moldova in 2001 lost power despite economic growth when incumbent weakness and/or identity splits contributed to incumbent failure.

31. See, for example, Geddes (1999); Brownlee (2007); Magaloni (2008); Levitsky and Way (2010, 2012); Svolik (2012).

32. See especially Ross (2001, 2012); Bellin (2004); Smith (2006); see also Mahdavy (1970); Fish (2005, chap. 5).

33. Ross (2001). Other posited mechanisms include increased corruption, lower taxation, and impediments to modernization. For an insightful discussion of these issues as they relate to Russia, see Fish (2005, chap. 5).

34. Fish (2005: 134–37) makes a similar argument.

35. On the durability of oil-based regimes in the face of crisis, see Smith (2006).

36. See Smith (2015).

37. Hofstadter (1969: 109–10).

38. Moore (1966: 14, 22, 32); see also Dahl (1971: 49).

39. Moore (1966: 14).

40. Botswana and Mauritius possessed underdeveloped agencies of authoritarian repression (armies, special security forces) but well-funded and highly developed infrastructural capacity (e.g., tax collection, etc.). By contrast, Benin, Madagascar, Malawi, Mali, and Zambia were weak overall—suffering from severe underfunding and institutional development across the board.

41. Holm (1987: 24); Miles (1999: 99).

42. Mwanakatwe (1994: 151, 175); Decalo (1997: 47); Marcus (2001: 226); Villalón and Idrissa (2005: 56).

43. Derrick (1992: 175); Raftopoulos (2002: 424); Levitsky and Way (2012).

44. Of the 13 most open cases (average total Freedom House score of 2–7, 1991–2010), 10 had weakly developed and/or highly fractious security forces. By contrast, of the nine most closed, non-competitive cases (total Freedom House of 10 or above with no turnovers for twenty years after 1989), eight entered the 1990s with extraordinarily loyal and robust coercive apparatuses (7) and/or heavy reliance on oil (2). (The open/competitive cases are Benin, Botswana, Ghana, Lesotho, Madagascar, Malawi, Mali, Mauritius, Mozambique, Namibia, Senegal, South Africa, and Zambia. The closed, non-competitive cases are Angola, Cameroon, Chad, Eritrea, Ethiopia, Guinea, Rwanda, Swaziland, Togo, and Zimbabwe). I exclude both microstates (population under 500,000) and countries in civil war.

45. See appendix I for definitions of democratic and authoritarian stability/consolidation.

46. "Mali Profile," *BBC News*, 22 May 2014.

47. Huntington (1991); Lindberg (2006).

Bibliography

Acemoglu, Darin, and James A. Robinson. 2005. *Economic Origins of Democracy and Dictatorship*. New York: Cambridge University Press.

Ahmed, Syed Imtiaz. 2006. "Civilian Supremacy in Democracies with 'Fault Lines': The Role of the Parliamentary Standing Committee on Defence in Bangladesh." *Democratization* 13, No. 2: 283–302.

Albats, Evgeniia. 1994. *The State within a State: The KGB and Its Hold on Russia*. New York: Farrar, Straus and Giroux.

Alexeyeva, Liudmilla, and Valery Chalidze. 1985. "Mass Unrest in the USSR." Report No. 19, Office of Net Assessment of the Department of Defense (August).

Aminzade, Ron, and Doug McAdam. 2001. "Emotions and Contentious Politics." In Ronald Aminzade et al. *Silence and Voice in the Study of Contentious Politics*. New York: Cambridge University Press.

Anderson, John. 1999. *Kyrgyzstan: Central Asia's Island of Democracy?* Amsterdam: Harwood Academic Publishers.

Anderson, Julie, and Joseph Albini. 1999. "Ukraine's SBU and the New Oligarchy." *International Journal of Intelligence and CounterIntelligence* 12, No. 3: 282–324.

Andrews, Josephine T. 2002. *When Majorities Fail: The Russian Parliament, 1990–1993*. Cambridge: Cambridge University Press.

Aprasidze, David. 2013. *Nations in Transit 2012: Georgia*. New York: Freedom House.

Arel, Dominique. 1995. "Language Politics in Independent Ukraine: Towards One or Two State Languages?" *Nationalities Papers* 23, No. 3: 597–622.

———. 1998. "Ukraine: The Muddle Way." *Current History* 97, No. 621 (October): 342–46.

Arel, Dominique, and Valeri Khmelko. 1996. "The Russian Factor and Territorial Polarization in Ukraine." *Harriman Review* 9, Nos. 1–2: 81–91.

Aron, Leon. 2000. *Yeltsin: A Revolutionary Life*. New York: St. Martin's Press.

Aslund, Anders. 2002. "Is the Belarusian Economic Model Viable?" In Ann Lewis, ed. *The EU and Belarus: Between Moscow and Brussels*. London: Federal Trust.

Aves, Jonathan. 1996. "Politics, Parties and Presidents in Transcaucasia." *Caucasian Regional Studies* 1: 5–23. Available at www.poli.vub.ac.be/publi/crs/eng/0101-02.htm.

Babak, Vladimir. 2004. "The Formation of Political Parties and Movements in Central Asia." In Yaacov Roi, ed. *Democracy and Pluralism in Muslim Eurasia*. London: Frank Cass.

Badescu, Gabriel, Paul Sum, and Eric M. Uslaner. 2004. "Civil Society Development and Democratic Values in Romania and Moldova." *East European Politics and Societies* 18, No. 2: 316–41.

Balmaceda, Margarita. 2013. *The Politics of Energy Dependency: Ukraine, Belarus, and Lithuania*. Toronto: University of Toronto Press.

———. 2014. *Living the High Life in Minsk: Energy Rents, Domestic Populism, and Belarus' Impending Crisis.* Budapest: Central European University Press.

Barany, Zoltan. 2002. "Ethnic Mobilization without Prerequisites: The East European Gypsies." *World Politics* 54, No. 3: 277–307.

Barrington, Lowell, and Erik Herron. 2004. "One Ukraine or Many? Regionalism in Ukraine and Its Political Consequences." *Nationalities Papers* 32, No. 1 (March): 53–86.

Bartkowski, Maciej, and Maria J. Stephan. 2014. "How Ukraine Ousted an Autocrat: The Logic of Civil Resistance." 1 June. Atlanticcouncil.org.

Batt, Judy. 1998. "Introduction: National Identity and Regionalism." In Taras Kuzio, ed. *Contemporary Ukraine.* Armonk, NY: M. E. Sharpe.

Baturin, Yu, A. Il'in, V. Kalatskiy, V. Kostikov, M. Krasnov, A. Livshchits, K. Nikiforov, L. Pikhoya, and G. Satarov. 2001. *Epokha El'tsina: Ocherki politicheskoy istorii.* Moscow: Vagrius.

Baylies, C., and M. Szeftel. 1992. "The Fall and Rise of Multi-Party Politics in Zambia." *Review of African Political Economy* 19, No. 54: 75–91.

Beissinger, Mark R. 2002. *Nationalist Mobilization and the Collapse of the Soviet State.* New York: Cambridge University Press.

———. 2007. "Structure and Example in Modular Political Phenomena: The Diffusion of Bulldozer/Rose/Orange/Tulip Revolutions." *Perspectives on Politics* 5 (June): 259–76.

———. 2013. "The Semblance of Democratic Revolution: Coalitions in Ukraine's Orange Revolution." *American Political Science Review* 107 (August): 581–82.

Bekus, Nelly. 2010. *Struggle over Identity: The Official and the Alternative 'Belarusianness.'* Budapest: Central European University Press.

Belik, Yurii. 1998. "Changes in the Central Committee Apparatus." In Michael Ellman and Vladimir Kontorovich, eds. *The Destruction of the Soviet Economic System: An Insiders' History.* New York: M. E. Sharpe.

Bellin, Eva. 2004. "The Robustness of Authoritarianism in the Middle East: Exceptionalism in Comparative Perspective." *Comparative Politics* 36, No. 2: 139–57.

Berezin, Mabel. 2001. "Emotions and Political Identity: Mobilizing Affection for the Polity." In J. Goodwin, J. Jasper, and F. Polletta, eds. *Passionate Politics: Emotions and Social Movements.* Chicago and London: University of Chicago Press.

Bienen, Henry and Nicolas van de Walle. 1991. *Of Time and Political Power: Leadership Duration in the Modern World.* Stanford, CA: Stanford University Press.

Birch, Sarah. 2002. "The Presidential Election in Ukraine, October 1999." *Electoral Studies* 21, No. 2: 339–63.

Blackwell, Robert. 1979. "Cadres Policy in the Brezhnev Era." *Problems of Communism* 28, No. 2: 29–42.

Boichenko, O. V. 2004. "Incidence of Wage Arrears in Ukraine." *Magisterium* (National University of Kyiv Mohyla Academy) 14: 22–5.

Boix, Carles. 2003. *Democracy and Redistribution.* New York: Cambridge University Press.

Bojcun, Marko. 1995. "The Ukrainian Parliamentary Elections in March–April 1994." *Europe-Asia Studies* 47, No. 2: 229–49.

Boldin, Valery. 1994. *Ten Years That Shook the World: The Gorbachev Era As Witnessed by His Chief of Staff.* New York: Basic Books.

Bolukbasi, Suha. 2011. *Azerbaijan: A Political History.* London: I. B. Taurus.

Bondarenko, Kost'. 2003. "Evgenii Marchuk: zhizneopisanie kandidata v ukrainskie De Golli. Chast' vtoraia." *ForUM,* 9 September 2004.

———. 2007. *Leonid Kuchma: Portret na fone epokhi.* Kharkiv: Folio.

Bremmer, Ian, and Cory Welt. 1997. "Armenia's New Autocrats." *Journal of Democracy* 8, No. 3: 77–91.

Brinks, Daniel, and Michael Coppedge. 2006. "Diffusion Is No Illusion: Neighbor Emulation in the Third Wave of Democracy." *Comparative Political Studies* 39, No. 4: 463–89.

Brooker, David C. 2004. "How They Leave: A Comparison of How First Presidents of the Soviet Successor States Left Office." *Journal of Communist Studies and Transition Politics* 20, No. 4: 61–78.

———. 2008. "Kravchuk and Yeltsin at Reelection." *Demokratizatsiya* 16, No. 3 (summer): 294–304.

Brown, Archie. 1996. *The Gorbachev Factor.* Oxford: Oxford University Press.

Brownlee, Jason. 2007. *Durable Authoritarianism in an Age of Democratization.* New York: Cambridge University Press.

Brudny, Yitzhak, and Evgeny Finkel. 2011. "Why Ukraine Is Not Russia: Hegemonic National Identity and Democracy in Russia and Ukraine." *East European Politics and Societies.* 25 No. 4: 813–33.

Brzezinski, Matthew. 1998. *Casino Moscow: A Tale of Greed and Adventure on Capitalism's Wildest Frontier.* New York: Free Press.

Buisson, Antoine. 2007. "State Building and Political Legitimacy: The Case of Post-Conflict Tajikistan." *China and Eurasia Forum Quarterly* 5, No. 4: 115–46.

Bulgakov, V. 2006. *Istoriia belorusskogo natsionalizma.* Vilnius, Institut Belorusistiki.

Bunce, Valerie, and Sharon Wolchik. 2011. *Defeating Authoritarian Leaders in Postcommunist Countries.* New York: Cambridge University Press.

Burant, Stephen R. 1995. "Foreign Policy and National Identity: A Comparison of Ukraine and Belarus." *Europe-Asia Studies* 47, No. 7: 1125–44.

Bureau of European and Eurasian Affairs. 2009. "Foreign Operations Appropriated Assistance: Belarus." Washington, DC: U.S. Department of State.

Burger, Ethan S., and Viktar Minchuk. 2006. "Alyaksandr Lukashenka's Consolidation of Power." In Joerg Forbrig, David R. Marples, and Pavol Demes, eds. *Prospects for Democracy in Belarus.* Washington, DC: German Marshall Fund of the United States.

Calhoun, Craig. 1993. "Nationalism and Ethnicity." *Annual Review of Sociology* 19: 211–39.

Caraus, Tamara. 2004. "Moldova." In *Media Ownership and Its Impact on Media Independence and Pluralism.* Lubljana: South East European Network for Professionalisation of the Media (SEENPM).

Carlisle, Donald S. 1995. "Islam Karimov and Uzbekistan: Back to the Future?" In Timothy Colton and Robert Tucker eds. *Patterns in Post-Soviet Leadership.* Boulder, CO: Westview Press.

Chernyaev, Anatoly. 2000. *My Six Years with Gorbachev.* University Park, PA: Penn State University Press.

Chinn, Jeffrey. 1994. "The Politics of Language in Moldova." *Demokratizatsiya* 2, No. 2: 309–15.

Clem, Ralph. 1996. "Belarus and the Belarusians." In G. Smith, ed. *The Nationalities Question in the Post-Soviet States.* New York: Longman.

Collier, Stephen, and Lucan Way. 2004. Beyond the Deficit Model: Social Welfare in Post-Soviet Georgia." *Post-Soviet Affairs* 20, No. 3: 258–84.

Collins, Kathleen. 2006. *Clan Politics and Regime Transition in Central Asia.* New York: Cambridge University Press.

Colton, Timothy. 2006. "Introduction: Governance and Postcommunist Politics." In

T. Colton and S. Holmes, eds. *The State after Communism: Governance in the New Russia*. New York: Rowman & Littlefield.

———. 2008. *Yeltsin: A Life*. New York: Basic Books.

Colton, Timothy J., and Michael McFaul. 2003. *Popular Choice and Managed Democracy: The Russian Elections of 1999 and 2000*. Washington, DC: Brookings Institution Press.

Colton, Timothy, and Cindy Skach. 2005. "The Russian Predicament." *Journal of Democracy* 16, No. 3: 113–26.

Crow, Suzanne. 1992. "Russian Moderates Walk a Tightrope on Moldova." *RFE/RL Research Report* 1, No. 20: 9–12.

Crowley, Steve. 1997. *Hot Coal, Cold Steel: Russian and Ukrainian Workers from the End of the Soviet Union to the Post-Communist Transformations*. Ann Arbor: University of Michigan Press.

Crowther, William. 1991. "The Politics of Ethno-National Mobilization: Nationalism and Reform in Soviet Moldavia." *Russian Review* 50, No. 2: 183–202.

———. 1996. "The Moldovan Ethno-National Movement." In D. Dyer, ed. *Studies in Moldovan: The History, Culture, Language, and Contemporary Politics of the People of Moldova*. Boulder, CO: East European Monographs.

———. 1997. "The Politics of Democratization in Postcommunist Moldova." In K. Dawisha and B. Parrott, eds. *Democratic Changes and Authoritarian Reactions in Russia, Ukraine, Belarus, and Moldova*. New York: Cambridge University Press.

———. 2007. "Moldova, Transnistria, and the PCRM's Turn to the West." *East European Quarterly* 61, No. 3: 273–304.

D'Anieri, Paul. 1999. *Economic Interdependence in Ukrainian-Russian Relations*. Albany: SUNY Press.

———. 2006. *Understanding Ukrainian Politics: Power, Politics, and Institutional Design*. Armonk, NY: M. E. Sharpe.

Dagiev, Dagukhudo. 2014. *Regime Transition in Central Asia*. London: Routledge.

Dahl, Robert. 1971. *Polyarchy: Participation and Opposition*. New Haven, CT: Yale University Press.

Danielian, Mikael. 1996–97. "Elections in Armenia: A Funeral for Democracy." *Uncaptive Minds* 9, No. 1–2: 125–31.

Darden, Keith. 2008. "The Integrity of Corrupt States: Graft as an Informal State Institution." *Politics and Society* 36, No. 1: 35–59.

———. Forthcoming. *Resisting Occupation in Eurasia*. New York: Cambridge University Press.

Darden, Keith, and Grzymala-Busse, Anna. 2006. "The Great Divide: Literacy, Nationalism, and the Communist Collapse." *World Politics* 59, No. 1: 83–115.

de Waal, Thomas. 2003. *Black Garden: Armenia and Azerbaijan through Peace and War*. New York: NYU Press.

Decalo, Samuel. 1997. "Benin: The First of the New Democracies." In John F. Clark and David E. Gardinier, eds. *Political Reform in Francophone Africa*. Boulder, CO: Westview Press.

Democratic Elections in Ukraine. 1994. *Report on the 1994 Presidential Elections*. Kyiv, Ukraine.

Depoy, Erik. 1996. "Boris Yeltsin and the 1996 Russian Presidential Election." *Presidential Studies Quarterly* 26, No. 4 (Fall): 1140–64.

Derrick, Jonathan. 1992. "Cameroon: One Party, Many Parties and the State." *Africa Insight* 22, No. 3: 165–78.

Diamond, Larry. 1999. *Developing Democracy: Toward Consolidation*. Baltimore: Johns Hopkins University Press.

———. 2002. "Thinking about Hybrid Regimes." *Journal of Democracy* 13, No. 2: 21–35.

———. 2008. *The Spirit of Democracy: The Struggle to Build Free Societies throughout the World*. New York: Times Books.

———. 2010. "Liberation Technology." *Journal of Democracy* 21, No. 3 (July): 69–83.

Diuk, Nadia. 2006. "The Triumph of Civil Society." In Anders Åslund and Michael Mc-Faul, eds. *Revolution in Orange: The Origins of Ukraine's Democratic Breakthrough*. Washington, DC: Carnegie.

Dowley, Kathleen M., and Brian D. Silver. 2002. "Social Capital, Ethnicity, and Support for Democracy in Post-Communist States." *Europe-Asia Studies* 54, No. 4: 516–17.

Drakokhrust, Yuri. 2012. "Spiral' Nezavisimosti." *Globalaffairs.ru*, February 19.

Drakokhrust, Yuri, and Dmitri Furman. 2002. "Belarus and Russia: The Game of Virtual Integration." In Margarita M. Balmaceda, James I. Clem, and Lisbeth L. Tarlow, eds. *Independent Belarus: Domestic Determinants, Regional Dynamic, and Implications for the West*. Cambridge, MA: Harvard University Press.

Dunlop, John. 1995. *The Rise of Russia and the Fall of the Soviet Empire*. Princeton, NJ: Princeton University Press.

Dura, George. 2008. *Nations in Transit 2007: Moldova*. New York: Freedom House.

Easter, Gerald. 1997. "Preference for Presidentialism: Postcommunist Regime Change in Russia and the NIS." *World Politics* 49, No. 2: 184–211.

EBRD. No Date. "Structural and Institutional Change Indicators, Private Sector Share in GDP (in percent)," at www.ebrd.com.

Eberhardt, Adam. 2009. *Revolution That Never Was: Five Years of 'Orange' Ukraine*. Warsaw: Punkt Widzenia.

Egorov, Vladimir. 2003. *Zvezdy i terni Vladimira Egorova*. Minsk: no publisher indicated.

Ellman, Michael, and Vladimir Kontorovich, eds. 1998. *The Destruction of the Soviet Economic System: An Insiders' History*. New York: M. E. Sharpe.

Eyal, Jonathan, and Graham Smith. 1996. "Moldova and the Moldovans." In Graham Smith, ed. *The Nationalities Question in the Post-Soviet States*. London: Longman.

Fairbanks, Charles H. 1996. "Clientelism and the Roots of Post-Soviet Disorder." In R. Suny, ed. *Transcaucasia, Nationalism, and Social Change*. Ann Arbor: University of Michigan Press.

Fairbanks Charles H. Jr., and Alexi Gugushvili. 2013. "A New Chance for Georgian Democracy." *Journal of Democracy* 24, No. 1 (January): 116–27.

Feduta, Aleksandr. 2005. *Lukashenko: Politicheskaya biografiya*. Moscow: Referendum.

Ferdinand, Peter, ed. 2000. *The Internet, Democracy, and Democratization*. London: Frank Cass.

Fierman, William. 1997. "Political Development in Uzbekistan: Democratization?" In Karen Dawisha and Bruce Parrott, eds. *Conflict, Cleavage, and Change in Central Asia and the Caucasus*. Cambridge: Cambridge University Press.

Filatov, Sergei. 2001. *Sovershenno Nesekretno*. Moscow: Vagrius.

Fish, M. Steven. 1998. "Mongolia: Democracy without Prerequisites." *Journal of Democracy* 9, No. 3: 127–41.

———. 2001. "Authoritarianism Despite Elections: Russia in Light of Democratic Theory and Practice." Paper prepared for the 2001 Annual Meeting of the American Political Science Association, San Francisco, CA, 30 August–2 September.

———. 2005. *Democracy Derailed in Russia: The Failure of Open Politics*. New York: Cambridge University Press.

———. 2006. "Stronger Legislatures, Stronger Democracies." *Journal of Democracy* 17, No. 1: 5–20.

Fisun, Oleksandr. 2010. "Ukrainian Teeter-Totter: Vices and Virtues of a Neopatrimonial Democracy." *PONARS Eurasia Policy Memo*, No. 120.

Freeland, Chrystia. 2000. *Sale of the Century: Russia's Wild Ride from Communism to Capitalism*. New York: Crown Business.

Freinkman, Lev. "Politics and Enterprise Behavior." In Michael Ellman and Vladimir Kontorovich, eds. *The Destruction of the Soviet Economic System: An Insiders' History*. New York: M. E. Sharpe.

Frye, Timothy, and Andrei Shleifer. 1997. "The Invisible Hand and the Grabbing Hand." *American Economic Review* 87, No. 2 (May): 354–58.

Fukuyama, Francis. 2004. *State-Building: Governance and World Order in the Twenty-first Century*. Ithaca, NY: Cornell University Press.

Furman, Dmitrii. 2004. *Postsovetskii politicheskii rezhim Kazakhstana*. Moscow: Ogni.

Gandhi, Jennifer. 2008. *Political Institutions under Dictatorship*. New York: Cambridge University Press.

Gandhi, Jennifer, and Adam Przeworski. 2007. "Authoritarian Institutions and the Survival of Autocrats." *Comparative Political Studies* 40, No. 11: 1279–301.

Geddes, Barbara. 1999. "What Do We Know About Democratization after Twenty Years?" *Annual Review of Political Science* 2: 115–44.

Gelman, Vladimir. 2006. "Vozvrashchenie Leviafona? Politika Retsentralizatsii v sovremennoy Rossii." Manuscript. European University at St. Petersburg, Faculty of Political Sciences and Sociology.

Gerasyuk, Ivan. 1991. *Agoniya Nomenklatury*. Minsk: "Belarus."

Glazer, Nathan. 2010. "Democracy and Deep Divides." *Journal of Democracy* 21, No. 2: 5–19.

Gleason, Gregory. 1997. *Central Asian States: Discovering Independence*. Boulder, CO: Westview.

Goldenberg, Suzanne. 1994. *Pride of Small Nations: The Caucasus and Post-Soviet Disorder*. London: Zed Books.

Greene, Kenneth. 2007. *Why Dominant Parties Lose: Mexico's Democratization in Comparative Perspective*. New York: Cambridge University Press.

Grzymala-Busse, Anna, and Pauline Jones Luong. 2002. "Reconceptualizing the State: Lessons from Post-Communism." *Politics & Society* 30, No. 4: 529–54.

Guthier, Steven L. 1977a. "The Belorussians: National Identification and Assimilation, 1897–1970. Part 1: 1897–1930." *Soviet Studies* 29, No. 1 (January): 37–61.

———. 1977b. "The Belorussians: National Identification and Assimilation, 1897–1970. Part 2: 1939–70." *Soviet Studies* 29, No. 2. (April): 270–83.

Haerpfer, Christian. 2003. "Electoral Politics of Belarus Compared." In Elena Korosteleva et al., eds. *Contemporary Belarus*. London and New York: RoutledgeCurzon.

———. 2005. "Belarus and Postcommunist Democratization." In Elena Korosteleva et al., eds. *Postcommunist Belarus*. Boulder, CO: Rowman & Littlefield.

Hale, Henry. 2006. *Why Not Parties in Russia? Democracy, Federalism, and the State*. New York: Cambridge University Press.

———. 2011. "Formal Constitutions in Informal Politics: Institutions and Democratization in Post-Soviet Eurasia." *World Politics* 63, No. 4: 581–617.

———. 2013. "Did the Internet Break the Political Machine? Moldova's 2009 'Twitter Revolution that Wasn't,'" *Demokratizatsiya* 21, No. 3: 481–505.

———. 2015. *Patronal Politics: Eurasian Regime Dynamics in Comparative Perspective*. New York: Cambridge University Press.

Halman, L. 2001. *The European Values Survey: A Third Wave.* Tilburg, Neth.: Tilburg University.

Haran,' Oleksiy. 1993. *Ubyty Drakona: Z Istorii Rukhu ta novykh partiy Ukrainy.* Kyiv: Lybid.'

———. 2011. "From Viktor to Viktor: Democracy and Authoritarianism in Ukraine." *Demokratizatsiya* 19, No. 2: 93–110.

Harasymiw, Bohdan. 2002. *Post-Communist Ukraine.* Edmonton, AL: CIUS Press.

———. 2003. "Policing, Democratization, and Political Leadership in Postcommunist Ukraine." *Canadian Journal of Political Science* 36, No. 2 (June): 319–40.

Helsinki Watch. 1993. *Human Rights in Moldova: The Turbulent Dniestr.* New York: Human Rights Watch.

Hesli, Vicki. 1995. "Public Support for the Devolution of Power in Ukraine: Regional Patterns." *Europe-Asia Studies* 47, No. 1: 91–121.

Hill, Fiona, and Pamela Jewett. 1994. *Back in the USSR: Russia's Intervention in the Internal Affairs of the Former Soviet Republics.* Cambridge, MA: Strengthening Democratic Institutions Project, Harvard University.

Hill, Ronald J. 2001. "Moldova Votes Backwards: The 2001 Parliamentary Election." *Journal of Communist Studies and Transition Politics* 17, No. 4: 130–39.

Hofstadter, Richard. 1969. *The Idea of a Party System: The Rise of a Legitimate Opposition in the United States, 1780–1840.* Oakland: University of California Press.

Holm, John D. 1987. "Botswana: A Paternalistic Democracy." *World Affairs* 150, No. 1: 21–30.

Holmes, Stephen. 1997. "What Russia Teaches Us Now: How Weak States Threaten Freedom." *American Prospect* 8 (July 1–August 1): 30–39.

———. 2002. "Simulations of Power in Putin's Russia." In A. Kuchins, ed. *Russia after the Fall.* Washington, DC: Carnegie Endowment for International Peace.

Holovaty, Serhiy. 1993. "Ukraine: A View from Within." *Journal of Democracy* 4, No. 3: 110–13.

Hough, Jerry. 1997. *Democratization and Revolution in the USSR, 1985–1991.* Washington, DC. Brookings.

Howard, Marc. 2003. *The Weakness of Civil Society in Post-Communist Europe.* New York: Cambridge University Press.

Hritsenko, O. 1995. *Khto e khto v ukrains'kiy polititsi.* Kyiv: TOV. K.I.S.

Huntington, Samuel P. 1968. *Political Order in Changing Societies.* New Haven, CT: Yale University Press.

———. 1991. *The Third Wave.* Norman: University of Oklahoma Press.

Huskey, Eugene. 1995. "The Rise of Contested Politics in Central Asia: Elections in Kyrgyzstan, 1989–90." *Europe-Asia Studies* 47, No. 5: 813–45.

———. 1997. "The Fate of Political Liberalization in Kyrgyzstan." In Karen Dawisha and Bruce Parrott, eds. *Conflict, Cleavage, and Change in Central Asia and the Caucasus.* Cambridge: Cambridge University Press.

———. 1999. *Presidential Power in Russia.* Armonk, NY: M. E. Sharpe.

International Foundation for Electoral Systems (IFES). 1994. *Republic of Moldova Parliamentary Elections, February 27, 1994.* Washington, DC: IFES.

Ioffe, Grigorii. 2008. *Understanding Belarus and How Western Foreign Policy Misses the Mark.* Lanham, MD: Rowman & Littlefield.

Ishchenko, Nataliya. 1996. "Aleksandr Emets: 'Vse dolzhny byt' prichastnyy k sozdaniyu konstitutsii sobstvennoy strany'" *Zerkalo Nedeli,* No.15 (80), 13–19 April.

Ishchenko, Vladimir. 2014. "Maidan, the Right-Wing and Violence in Protest Events." Presentation at the 10th Annual Danyliw Seminar on Ukraine, University of Ottawa.

Ivanov, Vitali. 2008. *Partiya Putina. Istoriya 'Edinoy Rossii.'* Moscow: Olma.

Jones, Stephen F. 1996. "Adventurers or Commanders? Civil Military Relations in Georgia since Independence." In Constantine Danopolous and Daniel Zirker, eds. *Civil–Military Relations in the Soviet and Yugoslav Successor States*. Boulder, CO: Westview Press.

Jones Luong, Pauline. 2002. *Institutional Change and Political Continuity in Post-Soviet Central Asia: Power, Perceptions, and Pacts*. New York: Cambridge University Press.

Jones Luong, Pauline, and Erika Withal. 2010. *Oil Is Not a Curse: Ownership Structure and Institutions in Soviet Successor States*. New York: Cambridge University Press.

Jowitt, Ken. 1992. *New World Disorder: The Leninist Extinction*. Berkeley: University of California Press.

Kahn, Jeffrey. 2002. *Federalism, Democratization, and the Rule of Law in Russia*. New York: Cambridge University Press.

Kalugin, Olg. 1994. *The First Directorate: My 32 Years in Intelligence and Espionage against the West*. New York: St. Martins Press.

Kapto, Aleksandr. 1996. *Na perekrestkakh zhizni: Politicheskie memuary*. Moscow: "Poligraf."

Karatnycky, Adrian. 2001. "Meltdown in Ukraine." *Foreign Affairs* 80, No. 3 (May–June): 73–86.

———. 2005. "Ukraine's Orange Revolution." *Foreign Affairs* 84, No. 2 (March–April): 35–52.

Karbalevich, Valery. 2010. *Aleksandr Lukashenko: Politicheskii Portret*. Moscow: Partizan.

Karol, Siarhej. 2006. "The Belarusian Economic Model: A 21st Century Socialism?" *RFE/RL Reports*. 13 March.

Karumidze, Zurab, and James V. Wertsch, eds. 2005. *Enough! The Rose Revolution in the Republic of Georgia 2003*. New York: Nova Science Publishers.

Katchanovski, Ivan. 2006. *Cleft Countries: Regional Political Divisions and Cultures in Post-Soviet Ukraine and Moldova*. Stuttgart: Ibidem-Verlag.

Kebich, Viacheslav. 2008. *Iskushenie vlastyu: Iz zhizni premier-ministra*. Minsk: Paradoks.

Keck, Margaret E., and Kathryn Sikkink. 1998. *Activists beyond Borders: Advocacy Networks in International Politics*. Ithaca, NY: Cornell University Press.

Kelley, Judith. 2012. *Monitoring Democracy*. Princeton, NJ: Princeton University Press.

Kemrova, Mehran. 2001. "State Building in Azerbaijan: The Search for Consolidation." *Middle East Journal* 55, No. 2: 216–36.

Kendall-Taylor, Andrea. 2012. "Purchasing Power: Oil, Elections and Regime Durability in Azerbaijan and Kazakhstan." *Europe-Asia Studies* 64, No. 4 (June): 737–60.

Khmelko, Valeri, and Andrew Wilson. 1998. "Regionalism and Ethnic and Regional Cleavages in Ukraine." In Taras Kuzio, ed. *Contemporary Ukraine*. Armonk, NY: M. E. Sharpe.

King, Charles. 1994a. "Moldova." In Bogdan Szajkowski, ed. *Political Parties of Eastern Europe, Russia, and the Successor States*. London: Longman.

———. 1994b. "Moldovan Identity and the Politics of Pan-Romanianism." *Slavic Review* 53, No. 2: 345–68.

———. 2000. *The Moldovans: Romania, Russia, and the Politics of Culture*. Palo Alto, CA: Hoover Institution Press.

Knight, Amy. 1990. *The KGB: Police and Politics in the Soviet Union*. Crows Nest, UK: Unwin Hyman.

———. 1996. *Spies without Cloaks: The KGB's Successors*. Princeton, NJ: Princeton University Press.

Kohli, Atul. 1990. *Democracy and Discontent: India's Growing Crisis of Governability.* New York: Cambridge University Press.

Kokotyukha, Andriy. 2008. *Yulia: vtoroe dykhanie.* Kharkov: Folio.

Kolsto, Pal. 2004. "The Price of Stability: Kazakhstani Control Mechanisms under Conditions of Cultural and Demographic Bipolarity." In Yaacov Roi, ed. *Democracy and Pluralism in Muslim Eurasia.* London: Frank Cass.

Kolsto, Pal, and Andrei Edemsky, with Natalya Kalashnikova. 1993. "The Dniester Conflict: Between Irredentism and Separatism." *Europe-Asia Studies* 45, No. 6: 973–1000.

Kopstein, Jeffrey S., and David A. Reilly. 2000. "Geographic Diffusion and the Transformation of the Postcommunist World." *World Politics* 53, No. 1: 1–37.

Korzh, Gennadiy. 2004. *Leonid Kuchma: Nastoyashchaya biografiya vtorogo Prezidenta Ukrainy.* Kharkov: Folio.

Koshiw, Jaroslaw. 2010. "Politics and Crimes in Ukraine: Study Based on Conversations in the Office of President Kuchma from August 1999–September 2000." Unpublished manuscript. Woodrow Wilson Center.

Kostikov, Vyacheslav. 1997. *Roman s prezidentom.* Moscow: Vagrius.

Kramer, Mark. 1992. "The Armies of the Post-Soviet States." *Current History* 91, No. 567 (October): 327–33.

Kravchuk, Leonid. 2002. *Maemo te, shcho maemo: Spohady i rozdumy.* Kyiv, Ukraine: Stolittia.

Kryuchkov, Vladimir. 1996. *Lichnoe delo: chast' vtoraya.* AST. Moscow.

———. 2001. *Lichnoe delo: Tri dnia I vsia zhizn'.* AST. Moscow.

Krushelnycky, Askold. 2002. "Ukraine: Exploring Kuchma's Motives for Moving toward Parliamentary Democracy." *RFE/RL*, 29 August.

———. 2006. *An Orange Revolution.* London: Harvill Secker.

Kryshtanovskaya, Olga. 2005. *Anatomiya rossiiskoy elity.* Moscow: Zakharov.

Kubicek, Paul. 2000. *Unbroken Ties: The State, Interest Associations, and Corporatism in Post-Soviet Ukraine.* Ann Arbor: University of Michigan Press.

———. 2002. "Civil Society, Trade Unions and Post-Soviet Democratisation: Evidence from Russia and Ukraine." *Europe-Asia Studies*, 54, No. 4: 603–24.

Kudelia, Serhiy. 2008. "Intangible Asset: Society, Elites and the Politics of Constitutional Reform in Ukraine." Ph.D. diss., Johns Hopkins University, the Paul H. Nitze School of Advanced International Studies (SAIS).

———. 2014. "Ukraine in Context: What Happens When Authoritarians Fall." *Foreign Affairs* (February 27).

Kudelia, Serhiy, and Taras Kuzio. 2015. "Nothing Personal: Explaining the Rise and Decline of Political Machines in Ukraine." *Post-Soviet Affairs* 31, No. 3.

Kulchytsky, Stanislav. 2005. *Ukrayins'ka Revolutsiia 2004.* Kyiv: Heneza.

Kulikov, Anatoliy. 2002. *Tyazhelie Zvezdy.* Moscow: Voyna i Mir.

Kushnarev, Evgeniy. 2007. *Vybory i vily.* Kyiv: ADEF-Ukraina.

Kuzio, Taras. 1989. "Unofficial Groups and Semi-Official Groups and Samizdat Publications in Ukraine." In Romana M. Bahry, ed. *Echoes of Glasnost in Soviet Ukraine.* North York: Captus Press.

———. 1994. "Paramilitary Groups in Ukraine." *Jane's Intelligence Review* 6, No. 3 (March): 540–41.

———. 1996. "Kravchuk to Kuchma: The Ukrainian Presidential Elections of 1994." *Journal of Communist Studies and Transition Politics* 12 (June): 117–44.

———. 2000a. *Ukraine: Perestroika to Independence.* New York: St. Martin's Press.

———. 2000b. "The Non-Military Security Forces of Ukraine." *Journal of Slavic Military Studies* 13, No. 4: 29–56.

———. 2005. "Opposition's Road to Success." *Journal of Democracy* 16, No. 2: 117–30.

———. 2010. "Nationalism, Identity and Civil Society in Ukraine: Understanding the Orange Revolution." *Communist and Post-Communist Studies* 43, No. 3 (September): 285–296.

———. 2015. *Ukraine: Democratization, Corruption, and the New Russian Imperialism.* Santa Barbara, CA: Praeger International.

Lachapelle, Jean, Lucan Way, and Steven Levitsky. 2012. "Crisis, Coercion, and Authoritarian Durability: Explaining Diverging Responses to Anti-Regime Protest in Egypt and Iran." Unpublished manuscript. University of Toronto.

LeBas, Adrienne. 2011. *From Protest to Parties: Party-Building and Democratization in Africa.* New York: Oxford University Press.

Lebed, Aleksandr. 1995. *Za derzhavu obidno . . .* Moskovskaya Pravda. Moscow.

Leonov, Vasiliy. 2003. *Rabota nad oshibkami.* Smolensk.

Levitsky, Steven, and María Victoria Murillo. 2009. "Variation in Institutional Strength." *Annual Review of Political Science* 12: 115–33.

Levitsky, Steven, and Lucan A. Way. 2002. "The Rise of Competitive Authoritarianism." *Journal of Democracy* 13, No. 2 (April): 51–65.

———. 2010. *Competitive Authoritarianism: Hybrid Regimes after the Cold War.* New York: Cambridge University Press.

———. 2012. "Beyond Patronage: Violent Struggle, Ruling Party Cohesion and Authoritarian Durability." *Perspectives on Politics* 10, No. 4: 869–89.

———. 2013. "The Durability of Revolutionary Regimes." *Journal of Democracy* 24, No. 3: 5–17.

Levitz, Philip, and Grigore Pop-Eleches. 2010. "Why No Backsliding? The EU's Impact on Democracy and Governance Before and After Accession." *Comparative Political Studies* 43, No.4: 457–85.

Lichbach, Mark. 1987. "Deterrence or Escalation? The Puzzle of Aggregate Studies of Repression and Dissent." *Journal of Conflict Resolution* 31, No. 2: 266–97.

Lieven, Anatol. 1993. *The Baltic Revolution: Estonia, Latvia, Lithuania and the Path to Independence.* New Haven, CT: Yale University Press.

Ligachev, Yegor. 1996. *Inside Gorbachev's Kremlin.* Boulder, CO: Westview.

Lijphart, Arend. 1977. *Democracy in Plural Societies.* New Haven, CT: Yale University Press.

Lindberg, Staffan I. 2006. *Democracy and Elections in Africa.* Baltimore: Johns Hopkins University Press.

Linz, Juan J. 1990. "The Perils of Presidentialism." *Journal of Democracy* 1, No. 1: 51–69.

Linz, Juan J., and Alfred Stepan. 1996. *Problems of Democratic Transition and Consolidation: Southern Europe, South America, and Post-Communist Europe.* Baltimore: Johns Hopkins University Press.

Lipset, Seymour Martin. 1959. "Some Social Requisites of Democracy: Economic Development and Political Legitimacy." *American Political Science Review* 53. No.1: 69–105.

Lipset, Seymour Martin, and Stein Rokkan. 1990 [1967]. "Cleavage Structures, Party Systems, and Voter Alignments." In Peter Mair, ed. *The West European Party System.* New York: Oxford University Press.

Livezeanu, Irina. 1995. *Cultural Politics in Greater Romania: Regionalism, Nation Building, and Ethnic Struggle, 1918–1930.* Ithaca, NY: Cornell University Press.

Lukanov, Yuryi. 1996. *Tretyi Prezident: Polytichnii portret Leonida Kuchmi.* Kyiv: Tak Spravi.

Lukashuk, Alexander. 1998. "Yesterday as Tomorrow: Why It Works in Belarus." *East European Constitutional Review* 7, No. 3.

Lytvyn [Litvin], Vladimir. 1997. *Ukraina: politika, politiki, vlast' na fone politicheskogo portreta L. Kravchuka.* Kyiv: Izdatel'skiy dom "Al'ternativy."

Magaloni, Beatriz. 2006. *Voting for Autocracy: Hegemonic Party Survival and Its Demise in Mexico.* New York: Cambridge University Press.

———. 2008. "Credible Power Sharing and the Longevity of Authoritarian Rule." *Comparative Political Studies* 41: 4/5: 715–41.

Mahdavy, H. 1970. "The Patterns and Problems of Economic Development in Rentier States: The Case of Iran." In *Studies in the Economic History of the Middle East*, ed. M. A. Cook, 428–67. London: Oxford University Press.

Mainwaring, Scott, and Timothy R. Scully, eds. 2003. *Christian Democracy in Latin America: Electoral Competition and Regime Conflicts.* Stanford, CA: Stanford University Press.

Man, Liviu. 1994. "Moldavia, Past and Present: Why the Communists Won the Election." *Uncaptive Minds* 7, No. 1 (25): 119–27.

Mandler, Peter. 2006. "What Is 'National Identity'? Definitions and Applications in Modern British Historiography." *Modern Intellectual History* 3, No. 2: 271–97.

Mann, Michael. 1984. "The Autonomous Power of the State: Its Origins, Mechanisms, and Results." *Archives européenes de sociologie* 25: 185–213.

March, Luke. 2005. "The Moldovan Communists: From Leninism to Democracy?" *Journal of Foreign Policy of Moldova* 9: 1–25.

———. 2007. "From Moldovanism to Europeanization? Moldova's Communists and Nation-Building." *Nationalities Papers* 35, No. 4: 601–26.

March, Luke, and Graeme P. Herd. 2006. "Moldova between Europe and Russia: Inoculating against the Colored Contagion?" *Post-Soviet Affairs* 22, No. 4: 349–79.

Marcus, Richard R. 2001. "Madagascar: Legitimizing Autocracy." *Current History* 100, No. 646 (May): 226–31.

Marin, Anaïs. 2012. *Sociological Study on the Composition of the Belarusian Society.* Brussels: Directorate-General for External Policies of the Union.

Marinov, Nikolay, and Hein Goemans. 2013. "Coups and Democracy." *British Journal of Political Science* (July): 1–27.

Markov, Ihor. 1993. "The Role of the President in the Ukrainian Political System." *RFE/RL Research Report* (3 December): 31–5.

Markowitz, Lawrence P. 2013. *State Erosion: Unlootable Resources and Unruly Elites in Central Asia.* Ithaca, NY: Cornell University Press.

Markus, Ustina. 1996. "Belarus: A New Parliament, Despite the President." *Transitions Online* (12 January). (Online: www.tol.org).

———. 1998. "Belarus: From Bad to Worse." *Transitions Online* (18 January).

Marples, David. 1990a. "The Communist Party of Ukraine: A Fading Force?" *Report on the USSR* 2, No. 23 (June 8): 21–22.

———. 1990b. "The First Session of the Ukrainian Parliament." *Report on the USSR* 2, No. 39 (September 28): 15–7.

———. 1990c. "Ukrainian Premier on the Way Out?" *Report on the USSR* 2, No. 43 (October 26): 16–7.

———. 1999. *Belarus: A Denationalized Nation.* New York: Harwood.

Martinsen, Kaare Dahl. 2002. "The Russian Takeover of Belarus." *Comparative Strategy* 21: 401–416.

Matsuzato. Kimitaka. 2004. "A Populist Island in an Ocean of Clan Politics: The

Lukashenka Regime as an Exception among CIS Countries." *Europe Asia Studies* 56, No. 2: 235–61.

Matviiuk, Maria. 1994. "Evgenii Marchuk—Povyshenie ili Zapadnia." *Zerkalo nedeli* 5, No. 11 (November).

McAdam, Doug. 1996. "Political Opportunities: Conceptual Origins, Problems, Future Directions." In Doug McAdam, John McCarthy, and Mayer Zald, eds. *Comparative Perspectives on Social Movements: Political Opportunities, Mobilizing Structures and Cultural Framings.* New York: Cambridge University Press.

McCauley, Martin. 1997. *Who's Who in Russia since 1900.* London: Routledge.

McDonagh, Ecaterina. 2008. "Is Democracy Promotion Effective in Moldova?" *Democratization* 15, No. 1: 142–61.

McFaul, Michael. 2001. *Russia's Unfinished Revolution: Political Change from Gorbachev to Putin.* Ithaca, NY: Cornell University Press.

———. 2002. "The Fourth Wave of Democracy and Dictatorship: Noncooperative Transitions in the Postcommunist World." *World Politics* 54, No. 2: 212–44.

McGlinchey, Eric. 2011. *Chaos, Violence, Dynasty: Politics and Islam in Central Asia.* Pittsburgh, PA: University of Pittsburgh Press.

McMann, Kelly. 2006. *Economic Autonomy and Democracy: Hybrid Regimes in Russia and Kyrgyzstan.* New York: Cambridge University Press.

Melnychenko, N. 2002. *Kto est' Kto na divane Prezidenta Kuchmy.* Kyiv.

Melvin, Neil J. 2004. "Authoritarian Pathways in Central Asia: A Comparison of Kazakhstan, the Kyrgyz Republic and Uzbekistan." In Yaacov Roi, ed. *Democracy and Pluralism in Muslim Eurasia.* London: Frank Cass.

Mihalisko, Kathleen. 1997. "Belarus: Retreat to Authoritarianism." In Karen Dawisha and Bruce Parrott, eds., *Democratic Changes and Authoritarian Reactions in Russia, Ukraine, Belarus, and Moldova.* New York: Cambridge University Press.

Miles, William. 1999. "The Mauritius Enigma." *Journal of Democracy* 10, No. 2: 91–104.

Military Balance. 2006. London: International Institute for Strategic Studies.

Miller, Arthur H, Thomas F. Klocubar, and William M. Reisinger. 2000. "Establishing Representation: Mass and Elite Political Attitudes in Ukraine." In Sharon L. Wolchik and Volodymyr Zviglyanich, eds. *Ukraine: The Search for a National Identity.* Lanham, MD: Rowman & Littlefield.

Miller, William L., Stephen White, and Paul Heywood. 1998. *Values and Political Change in Postcommunist Europe.* Houndmills: Macmillan Press.

Mitchell, Lincoln. 2004. "Georgia's Rose Revolution." *Current History* 103, No. 675: 342–53.

Mlechin, Leonid. 2002. *KGB: Predsedateli organov gosbezopasnosti rassekrechenye sud'by.* Moscow: Tsentrpoligraf.

Moore, Barrington. 1954. *Terror and Progress: USSR.* Cambridge, MA: Harvard University Press.

———. 1966. *Social Origins of Dictatorship and Democracy: Lord and Peasant in the Making of the Modern World.* Boston: Beacon Press.

Moran, John P. 2002. *From Garrison State to Nation State: Political Power and the Russian Military under Gorbachev and Yeltsin.* Praeger.

Moser, Michael. 2013. *Language Policy and the Discourse on Languages in Ukraine under President Yanukovych.* Stuttgart: ibidem Press.

Mozhin, Vladimir. 1998. "The Party and the Economic Reform." In Michael Ellman and Vladimir Kontorovich, eds. *The Destruction of the Soviet Economic System: An Insiders' History.* New York: M. E. Sharpe.

Murawiec, Laurent, and Clifford Gaddy. 2002. "The Higher Police: Vladimir Putin and His Predecessors." *National Interest* (Spring): 29–36.

Murtazashvili, Jennifer. 2012. "Coloured by Revolution: The Political Economy of Autocratic Stability in Uzbekistan." *Democratization* 19, No. 1: 78–97.

Mwanakatwe, John M. 1994. *End of the Kaunda Era.* Lusaka, Zambia: A Multimedia Publication.

Myagkov, Mikhai, Peter C. Ordeshook, and Dimitri Shakin. 2009. *The Forensics of Election Fraud: Russia and Ukraine.* New York: Cambridge University Press.

Nedelciuc, Vasile. No Date. *The Republic of Moldova: An Historical Background.* Kishinev, Moldova: Compudava Foundation.

Neidhart, Christoph. 2003. *Russia's Carnival: The Smells, Sights, and Sounds of Transition.* Boulder, CO: Rowman & Littlefield.

Nesvetailova, Anastasia. 2002. "Russia and Belarus: The Quest for Union." In Elena Korosteleva, Colin Lawson, and Rosalind Marsh, eds. *Contemporary Belarus: Between Democracy and Dictatorship.* New York: Routledge.

Netiaga, Mykola. 2009. "Ways of Political Corruption Alleviation in Ukraine." Master's thesis, MTEC Master in Public Administration, University of Twente.

Neukrich, Claus. 2004. "Moldova's Eastern Dimension." In Ann Lewis, ed. *The EU and Moldova: On a Fault-line of Europe.* London: The Federal Trust.

Nodia, Ghia. 1994. "Nationalism and Democracy." In Larry Diamond and Marc Plattner, eds. *Nationalism, Ethnic Conflict, and Democracy.* Baltimore: Johns Hopkins University Press.

———. 2002. "The Democratic Path." *Journal of Democracy* 13, No. 3: 13–19.

Norris, Pippa. 2014. "Ukrainians Are Not That Divided in Their Views of Democracy." Washingtonpost.com. 3 March.

Nourzhanov, Kirill. 2005. "Saviours of the Nation or Robber Barons? Warlord Politics in Tajikistan." *Central Asian Survey* 24, No. 2 (June): 109–30.

O'Donnell, Guillermo. 1993. "On the State, Democratization, and Some Conceptual Problems: A Latin American View with Some Post-Communist Countries." *World Development* 21, No. 8: 1355–69.

O'Donnell, Guillermo, and Philippe C. Schmitter. 1986. *Transitions from Authoritarian Rule: Tentative Conclusions about Uncertain Democracies.* Baltimore: Johns Hopkins University Press.

O'Loughlin, Gerard Toal, and Rebecca Chamberlain-Creangă. 2013. "Divided Space, Divided Attitudes? Comparing the Republics of Moldova and Pridnestrovie (Transnistria) Using Simultaneous Surveys." *Eurasian Geography and Economics* 54, No. 2: 227–58.

Ochs, Michelle. 1997. "Turkmenistan: the Quest for Stability and Control." In Karen Dawisha and Bruce Parrott, eds. *Conflict, Cleavage, and Change in Central Asia and the Caucasus.* Cambridge: Cambridge University Press.

ODIHR. 1997. *Final Report on the Presidential Election in Moldova, 17 November and 1 December 1996.* Warsaw: OSCE.

———. 1998. *Moldovan Parliamentary Elections.* Warsaw: OSCE.

———. 2000. *Ukraine Presidential Elections, 31 October and 14 November 1999, Final Report.* Warsaw: OSCE.

———. 2001a. *Final Report on the Parliamentary Elections in Moldova, 25 February 2001.* Warsaw: OSCE.

———. 2001b. *Final Report on the Presidential Election in Belarus, 9 September 2001.* Warsaw: OSCE.

———. 2005. *Moldova: Parliamentary Elections, 6 March 2005, Election Observation Mission Report.* Warsaw: OSCE.

———. 2006. *Final Report on the 19 March 2006 Presidential Election in Belarus.* Warsaw: OSCE.

———. 2009a. *Moldovan Parliamentary Elections, 5 April 2009.* Warsaw: OSCE.

———. 2009b. *Early Parliamentary Elections, 29 July 2009.* Warsaw: OSCE.

———. 2011. *Republic of Moldova Early Parliamentary Elections 28 November 2010.* Warsaw: OSCE.

———. 2012. *Election Observation Mission, Ukraine, "Post-Election Interim Report."* 29 October– 6 November. Warsaw: OSCE.

Odom, William. 1998. *The Collapse of the Soviet Military.* New Haven, CT: Yale University Press.

Ogushi, Atsushi. 2008. *The Demise of the Soviet Communist Party.* London: Routledge.

Olcott, Marta Brill. 1994. "Kazakhstan." In Mohiaddin Mesbahi, ed. *Central Asia and the Caucasus after the Soviet Union.* Gainesville: University Press of Florida.

———. 1997. "Kazakhstan." In Karen Dawisha and Bruce Parrott, eds. *Conflict, Cleavage, and Change in Central Asia and the Caucasus.* Cambridge: Cambridge University Press.

———. 2010. *Kazakhstan: Unfulfilled Promise?* Washington, DC: Carnegie Endowment.

Olynyk, Stephen D. 1994. "Emerging Post-Soviet Armies: The Case of the Ukraine." *Military Review* 74, No. 3 (March): 5–18.

Onuch, Olga. 2014. *Mapping Mass Mobilization: Understanding Revolutionary Moments in Argentina and Ukraine* Basingstoke: Palgrave.

Parmelee, John. 2009. "Media Pluralism by Default: The Case of Moldova." Paper presented at the annual meeting of the International Communication Association, Chicago, May 21.

Pavlychko, Solomea. 1992. *Letters from Kyiv.* Edmonton: Canadian Institute of Ukrainian Studies Press.

Petrov, Nikolai, and Andrei Ryabov. 2006. "Russia's Role in the Orange Revolution." In Anders Åslund and Michael McFaul, eds. *Revolution in Orange: The Origins of Ukraine's Democratic Breakthrough.* Washington, DC: Carnegie.

Petrov, Nikolai, and Darrell Slider. 2005. "Putin and the Regions." In Dale Herspring, ed. *Putin's Russia: Past Imperfect, Future Uncertain.* Boulder, CO: Rowman & Littlefield.

Plokhy, Serhii. 2011. "The 'New Eastern Europe': What to Do about the Histories of Ukraine, Belarus, and Moldova." *East European Politics and Societies* 25, No. 4: 763–69.

Pop-Eleches, Grigore, and Lucan Way. 2010. "Political Crisis and Opinion Formation: Moldova's Twitter Revolution." Unpublished manuscript. Princeton University.

Popescu, Nicu. 2012. "Moldova's Fragile Pluralism." *Russian Politics and Law* 50, No. 4 (July–August): 37–50.

Popov, Dmitrii, and Ilia Milshtein. 2006. *Oranzhevaia printsessa: zagadka Iulii Tymoshenko.* Kyiv: Izdatelstvo Ol'gy Morozovoi.

Popova, Maria. 2012a. *Politicized Justice in Emerging Democracies: A Study of Courts in Russia and Ukraine.* New York: Cambridge University Press.

———. 2012b. "Authoritarian Learning and the Politicization of Justice: The Tymoshenko Case in Context." Paper prepared for ASEEES 44th Annual Convention, New Orleans, LA, November 15–18.

Protsyk, Oleh, and Andrew Wilson. 2003. "Center Party Politics in Russia and Ukraine: Power, Patronage, and Virtuality." *Party Politics* 9, No. 6: 703–27.

Przeworski, Adam. 1986. "Some Problems in the Study of the Transition to Democracy." In Guillermo O'Donnell, Philippe C. Schmitter, and Laurence Whitehead, eds. *Tran-*

sitions from Authoritarian Rule: Comparative Perspectives. Baltimore: Johns Hopkins University Press.

Przeworski, Adam, Michael E. Alvarez, José Antonio Cheibub, and Fernando Limongi. 2000. *Democracy and Development: Political Institutions and Well-Being in the World, 1950–1990.* New York: Cambridge University Press.

Puglisi, Rosaria. 2003. "Clashing Agendas? Economic Interests, Elite Coalitions and Prospects for Cooperation between Russia and Ukraine." *Europe–Asia Studies* 55, No. 6: 827–45.

———. 2014. "A Regional Perspective on Post-Maidan Domestic Security." Presentation at the 10th Annual Danyliw Seminar on Ukraine, University of Ottawa, 30–31 October.

Pyskir, Bohdan. 1993. "The Silent Coup: The Building of Ukraine's Military." *European Security* 2, No. 1: 140–61.

Quinlan, Paul D. 2005. "Back to the Future: An Overview of Moldova under Voronin." *Demokratizatsiya* 12, No. 4: 485–504.

Radnitz, Scott. 2010a. "The Color of Money: Privatization, Economic Dispersion, and the Post-Soviet 'Revolutions.'" *Comparative Politics* 42, No. 2: 127–46.

———. 2010b. *Weapons of the Wealthy.* Ithaca, NY: Cornell University Press.

Raftopoulos, Brian. 2002. "Briefing: Zimbabwe's 2002 Presidential Election." *African Affairs* 101: 413–26.

Remington, Thomas F. 2003. "Coalition Politics in the New Duma." In Vicky Hesli and William Reisinger, eds. *The 1999–2000 Elections in Russia: Their Impact and Legacy.* New York: Cambridge University Press.

Reuter, Ora John, and Thomas F. Remington. 2009. "Dominant Party Regimes and the Commitment Problem: The Case of United Russia." *Comparative Political Studies* 42, No. 4: 501–26.

Rontoyanni, Clelia. 2005. "Belarus and the East." In Stephen White, Elena Korosteleva, and John Lowenhardt, eds. *Postcommunist Belarus.* Lanham, MD: Rowman & Littlefield.

Roper, Steven D. 2001. "From Semi-Presidentialism to Parliamentarism: Constitutional Change in Post-Soviet Moldova." American Political Science Association meeting, San Francisco.

———. 2002. "The Impact of Moldovan Parliamentary Committees on the Process of Institutionalization." In David Olsen and William Crowther, eds. *Committees in Post-Communist Democratic Parliaments.* Columbus: Ohio State University Press.

———. 2006. "Post-Soviet Moldova's National Identity and Foreign Policy." In Oliver Schmidtke and Serhy Yekelchyk, eds. *Europe's Last Frontier? Belarus, Moldova, and Ukraine between Russia and the European Union.* New York: Palgrave Macmillan.

Ross, Michael. 2001. "Does Oil Hinder Democracy?" *World Politics* 53, No. 3: 325–61.

———. 2012. *The Oil Curse: How Petroleum Wealth Shapes the Development of Nations.* Princeton, NJ: Princeton University Press.

Rothschild, Joseph. 1981. *Ethnopolitics: A Conceptual Framework.* New York: Columbia University Press.

Rubin, Barnett. 1998. "Russian Hegemony and State Breakdown in the Periphery: Causes and Consequences of the Civil War in Tajikistan." In Barnett Rubin and Jack Snyder, eds. *Post-Soviet Political Order: Conflict and State Building.* New York: Routledge.

Rudenko, Sergey. 2007. *Vsya prezidentskaya rat': okruzhenie iktora Yushchenko ot 'A' do 'Ya.'* Kyiv: Sammit-Kniga.

Rueschemeyer, Dietrich, Evelyne Huber Stephens, and John D. Stephens. 1992. *Capitalist Development and Democracy.* Chicago: University of Chicago Press.

Russell, Mathew. 2003. "The Separation of Powers and the Republic of Belarus." *European Commission for Democracy through Law.* Venice Commission CDL-JU (2003) 23.

Rustow, Dankwart. 1970. "Transitions to Democracy: Toward a Dynamic Model." *Comparative Politics* 2, No. 3: 337–63.

Ryabinska, Natalya. 2011. "Media: The Media Market and Media Ownership in Post-Communist Ukraine's Impact on Media Independence and Pluralism." *Problems of Post-Communism* 58, No. 6 (November/December): 3–20.

Sahm, Astrid. 1999. "Political Culture and National Symbols: Their Impact on the Belarusian Nation-Building Process." *Nationalities Papers* 27, No. 4: 549–77.

Sannikov, Andrei. 2002. "Russia's Varied Roles in Belarus." In Margarita Balmaceda, James Clem, and Lisbeth Tarlow, eds. *Independent Belarus: Domestic Determinants, Regional Dynamics, and Implications for the West.* Cambridge, MA: HURI Press.

———. 2005. "The Accidental Dictatorship of Alexander Lukashenko." *School of Advanced International Studies of Johns Hopkins University Review* (Winter–Spring): 75–88.

Sasse, Gwendolyn. 2007. *The Crimea Question: Identity, Transition, and Conflict.* Cambridge, MA: Harvard University Press for the Harvard Ukrainian Research Institute.

Schatz, Edward. 2004. *Modern Clan Politics.* Seattle: University of Washington Press.

Schedler, Andreas. 2002. "The Menu of Manipulation." *Journal of Democracy* 13, No. 2: 36–50.

———, ed. 2006. *Electoral Authoritarianism: The Dynamics of Unfree Competition.* Boulder, CO: Lynne Rienner Publishers.

Schimmelfennig, Frank, and Ulrich Sedelmeier, eds. 2005. *The Europeanization of Central and Eastern Europe.* Ithaca, NY: Cornell University Press.

Schurmann, Franz. 1966. *Ideology and Organization in Communist China.* Berkeley: University of California Press.

Senn, Alfred. 1995. *Gorbachev's Failure in Lithuania.* New York: St. Martin's Press.

Shelley, Louise. 1996. *Policing Soviet Society: The Evolution of State Control.* London: Routledge 1996.

Sheremet, Pavel, and Svetlana Kalinkina. 2004. *Sluchainiy president.* St. Petersburg: Limbus Press.

Shlapentokh, Vladimir. 2001. *A Normal Totalitarian Society: How the Soviet Union Functioned and How It Collapsed.* New York: M. E. Sharpe.

Shulman, Stephen. 2005. "National Identity and Public Support for Political and Economic Reform in Ukraine." *Slavic Review* 64, No. 1 (Spring): 59–87.

Silitski, Vitali. 2003. "What Are the Consequences of the Russian 'Gas Attack'?" *RFE/RL Belarus Ukraine Report,* 23 September.

———. 2004. *Post-Communist Authoritarianism in Eastern Europe: Serbia and Belarus Compared.* Unpublished manuscript. Belarusian Institute for Strategic Studies.

———. 2005. "Preempting Democracy: The Case of Belarus." *Journal of Democracy* 16, No. 4: 83–97.

———. 2006. "Belarus: Learning from Defeat." *Journal of Democracy* 17, No. 4: 139–51.

Skocpol, Theda. 1979. *States and Social Revolutions.* New York: Cambridge University Press.

Skvortsova, Alla. 2002. "The Cultural and Social Makeup of Moldova." In Pal Kolsto, ed. *National Integration and Violent Conflict in Post-Soviet Societies: The Cases of Estonia and Moldova.* Boulder, CO: Rowman & Littlefield.

Slater, Dan. 2010. *Ordering Power: Contentious Politics, State-Building, and Authoritarian Durability in Southeast Asia.* New York: Cambridge University Press.

Smith, Benjamin. 2006. "The Wrong Kind of Crisis: Why Oil Booms and Busts Rarely

Lead to Authoritarian Breakdown." *Studies in Comparative International Development* 40, No. 4: 55–76.

———. 2015. "Oil Wealth, Order and Conflict: Evidence from New Data." Unpublished manuscript. University of Florida.

Snyder, Jack. 2000. *From Voting to Violence: Democratization and Nationalist Conflict*. New York: Norton.

Socor, Vladimir. 1991. "The Moldavian Communists: From Ruling to Opposition Party." *Report on the USSR* 3, No. 14 (April 5): 15–21.

———. 1991b. "The Moldavian Communists: From Ruling to Opposition Party." *Report on the USSR* 3, No. 14 (April 5): 15–21.

———. 1992a. "Moldavia Builds a New State." *RFE/RL Research Report* 1, No. 1: 42–5.

———. 1992b. "The Media in Regions of Conflict: Moldova." *RFE/RL Research Report* 1, No. 39: 77–81.

———. 1992c. "Moldova's New 'Government of National Consensus.'" *RFE/RL Research Report* 1, No. 47: 5–10.

———. 1993a. "Moldova's 'Dniester' Ulcer." *RFE/RL Research Report* 2, No. 1: 12–16.

———. 1993b. "Dniester Involvement in the Moscow Rebellion." *RFE/RL Research Report* 2, No. 46: 25–32.

———. 2013. "Demise of Moldova's Alliance for European Integration Surprises European Union's Leaders." *Eurasia Daily Monitor* 10, Issue 90.

Solchanyk, Roman. 1989. "Shcherbitsky Leaves the Political Arena: The End of an Era?" *Report on the USSR* 1, No. 40 (October 6): 1–3.

———. 1990a. "Ferment in Western Ukraine: An Interview with Rostyslav Bratun.'" *Report on the USSR* 2, No. 18 (May 4): 12–16.

———. 1990b. "The Communist Party and the Political Situation in Ukraine: An Interview with Stanislav Hurenko." *Report on the USSR* 2, No. 50 (December 14): 12–5.

———. 1994. "The Politics of State-Building: Centre-Periphery Relations in Post-Soviet Ukraine." *Europe-Asia Studies* 46, No. 1: 47–68.

———. 2001. *Ukraine and Russia: The Post-Soviet Transition*. Oxford, UK: Rowman & Littlefield.

Solomon, Peter. 2010. "Authoritarian Legality and Informal Practices: Judges, Lawyers and the State in Russia and China." *Communist and Post-Communist Studies* 43, No. 4: 351–62.

Solomon, Susan. 1983. "'Pluralism' in Political Science: The Odyssey of a Concept." In Susan Solomon, ed. *Pluralism in the Soviet Union: Essays in Honour of H. Gordon Skilling*. New York: Palgrave.

Spector, Regine. 2004. "The Transformation of Askar Akaev, President of Kyrgyzstan." *Berkeley Program in Soviet and Post-Soviet Studies Working Papers Series* (Spring).

Sperling, Valerie, ed. 2000. *Building the Russian State: Institutional Crisis and the Quest for Democratic Governance*. Boulder, CO: Westview Press.

Stavila, Ion. 2004. "Moldova between East and West: A Paradigm of Foreign Affairs." In Ann Lewis, *The EU and Moldova: On a Fault-line of Europe*. London: The Federal Trust.

Stepan, Alfred. 2005. "Ukraine: Improbable Democratic 'Nation-State' but Possible Democratic 'State-Nation'?" *Post-Soviet Affairs* 21, No. 4: 279–308.

Stepanenko, Viktor. 2005. "How Ukrainians View the Orange Revolution." *Demokratizatsiya* 13, No. 4: 595–616.

Stoner-Weiss, Kathryn. 2006. *Resisting the State: Reform and Retrenchment in Post-Soviet Russia*. New York: Cambridge University Press.

Sukhanov, Lev. 1992. *Tri goda s El'tsinom: zapiski pervogo pomoshchnika*. Riga, Latvia: Vaga.

Suny, Ronald. 1994. *The Making of the Georgian Nation*. Bloomington: Indiana University Press.

———. 1999/2000. "Provisional Stabilities: The Politics of Identities in Post-Soviet Eurasia." *International Security* 24, No. 3: 139–78.

Suzdaltsev, Andrei. 2007. "Lukashenko: Russia's Ally or Sponge?" *RIA Novosti*, 11 January.

Svolik, Milan W. 2012. *The Politics of Authoritarian Rule*. Cambridge: Cambridge University Press.

Szporluk, Roman. 1979. "West Ukraine and West Belorussia." *Soviet Studies* 31, No. 1: 76–98.

———. 1991. "The Soviet West—or Far Eastern Europe?" *East European Politics and Societies* 5, No. 3: 466–82.

Tarrow, Sidney. 1996. "States and Opportunities: The Political Structuring of Social Movements." In Doug McAdam, John McCarthy, and Mayer Zald, eds. *Comparative Perspectives on Social Movements*. New York: Cambridge University Press.

———. 1998. *Power in Movement: Social Movements and Contentious Politics*. Cambridge: Cambridge University Press.

Taylor, Brian. 2011. *State Building in Putin's Russia: Policing and Coercion after Communism*. New York: Cambridge University Press.

Taylor, Ian. 2003. "As Good as It Gets? Botswana's 'Democratic Development.'" *Journal of Contemporary African Studies* 21, No. 2: 215–31.

Tilly, Charles, ed. 1975. *The Formation of National States in Western Europe*. Princeton, NJ: Princeton University Press.

———. 1985. "War Making and State Making as Organized Crime." In Peter Evans, Dietrich Rueschemeyer, and Theda Skocpol, eds. *Bringing the State Back In*. Cambridge: Cambridge University Press.

Trochev, Alexei. 2010. "Meddling with Justice: Competitive Politics, Impunity and Distrusted Courts in post-Orange Ukraine." *Demokratizatsiya* 18, No. 2 (Spring): 122–47.

———. 2011a. "Editor's Introduction." *Statutes and Decisions* 46, No. 2 (March–April): 4–7.

———. 2011b. "Editor's Introduction." *Statutes and Decisions* 46, No. 3 (May–June): 4–6.

US Embassy Cable, "Belarus and Russia to Unite? Not this Year." 2 November 2005.

———, "Ukraine Election 2006: Winners, Losers, Trends." 30 March 2006.

———, "USD 2.5 Billion in Russian Subsidies in 2005." 31 March 2006.

———, "Minsk Regime Nationalizing and Milking Economy." 5 May 2006.

———, "The Political Chess Game: Views from the Second Bench." 21 July 2006.

———, "Ukraine: Engaging the New Ukrainian Reality after 50 Days of PM Yanukovych." 28 September 2006.

———, "New EU Interest in Visa Bans on State Media." 5 October 2006.

———, "PM Yanukovych—Defender of the Constitution?" 5 October 2006.

———, "Our Ukraine Hampered by Disorganization and Infighting." 30 October 2006.

———, "Our Ukraine Regrouping." 6 December 2006.

———, "Ukraine: Confrontation and Compromise—A Tale of Two Viktors." 29 December 2006.

———, "Independent Surveys Having Effect on Voters." 2 March 2007.

———, "Polling Results: Lukashenko Support Remains High in Wake of Energy Crisis." 30 April 2007.

———, "Ukraine: IUD's Taruta on Regions, Elections, and Gas Deals." 9 July 2007.

———, "Replacing PM Sidorskiy Easier Said Than Done." 17 August 2007.

——, "Even Small Election Abuses Could Influence Outcome of September Vote." 7 September 2007.

——, "Our Ukraine Discouraged from the Top Down." 13 September 2007.

——, "Ukraine: Region Focuses on Campaign; Puts Aside Internal Differences." 23 September 2007.

——, "No Split in Party of Regions Expected." 15 April 2008.

——, "Tymoshenko Enters Constitutional Game." 24 April 2008.

——, "Akhmetov Holds Forth on Ukrainian Politics and Economics." 10 October 2008.

——, "Regions-Byut Coalition Deal: Why It Fell Apart." 17 October 2008.

——, "Party of Regions' Internal Divisions." 13 February 2009.

——, "Belarus: Regime Crying Over Spilt Milk as Spat with Moscow Widens." 8 June 2009.

——, "Yushchenko and Yanukovych Find Common Ground—Tymoshenko Defeat." 25 November 2009.

Vachudova, Milada. 2005. *Europe Undivided: Democracy, Leverage and Integration after Communism.* London: Oxford University Press.

Vanderhill, Rachel. 2011. "The Ukrainian 2010 Presidential Elections: What Was the Role of Russia? What Do They Mean for the Future of Democracy in Ukraine?" International Studies Association Annual Meeting, Montreal, Canada, March 16.

Villalón, Leonardo A., and Abdourahmane Idrissa. 2005. "The Tribulations of a Successful Transition: Institutional Dynamics and Elite Rivalry in Mali." In Leonardo A. Villalón and Peter VonDoepp, eds. *The Fate of Africa's Democratic Experiments: Elites and Institutions.* Bloomington: Indiana University Press.

Vitu, Liliana. 2004. "Moldova and the Baltic States: Lessons of Success and Failure." In Ann Lewis, ed. *The EU and Moldova: On a Fault-line of Europe.* London: The Federal Trust.

Walder, Andrew. 1986. *Communist Neotraditionalism.* Berkeley: University of California Press.

Walker, Edward. 2003. *Dissolution: Sovereignty and the Breakup of the Soviet Union.* Lanham, MD: Rowman & Littlefield.

Waller, J. Michael. 2004. "Russia: Death and Resurrection of the KGB." *Demokratizatsiya* 12, No. 3 (Summer): 333–55.

Waters, Trevor. 1996. "Moldova: Continuing Recipe for Instability." *Jane's Intelligence Review* 8, No. 9 (18 September): 398–401.

Way, Lucan. 2002a. "Pluralism by Default in Moldova." *Journal of Democracy* 13, No. 4: 127–41.

——. 2002b. "The Dilemmas of Reform in Weak States: The Case of Post-Soviet Fiscal Reform." *Politics & Society* 30, No. 4: 579–98.

——. 2003. "Weak States and Pluralism: The Case of Moldova." *East European Politics and Societies* 17, No. 3: 454–82.

——. 2005a. "Authoritarian State-Building and the Sources of Regime Competitiveness in the Fourth Wave." *World Politics* 57, No. 2: 231–61.

——. 2005b. "Kuchma's Failed Authoritarianism." *Journal of Democracy* 16, No. 2: 131–45.

——. 2008. "The Real Causes of the Color Revolutions." *Journal of Democracy* 19, No. 3: 55–69.

——. 2011. "National Identity and Authoritarianism: Belarus and Ukraine Compared." In Paul D'Anieri, ed. *Social Mobilization in Ukraine.* Washington, DC: Woodrow Wilson Center Press.

———. 2012a. "Deer in Headlights: Incompetence and Weak Authoritarianism after the Cold War." *Slavic Review* 71, No. 3: 619–46.

———. 2012b. "The Sources of Authoritarian Control after the Cold War: East Africa and the Former Soviet Union." *Post-Soviet Affairs* 28, No. 4: 424–48.

———. 2014. "The Maidan and Beyond: Civil Society and Democratization." *Journal of Democracy* 25, No.3: 35–43.

Welt, Cory. 2006. "Georgia's Rose Revolution: From Regime Weakness to Regime Collapse." Working Paper. Stanford, CA: Center of Democracy, Development, and the Rule of Law.

Wheatley, Jonathan. 2003. "The Problems of Post-Soviet Regime Change: Dynamic and Static Elements of the Georgian Regime 1989–2001." Ph.D. diss. Florence: European University Institute.

———. 2005. *Georgia from National Awakening to Rose Revolution: Delayed Transition in the Former Soviet Union.* Aldershot, UK: Ashgate Publishing.

White, Stephen. 1993. "Russia: Yeltsin's Kingdom or Parliament's Playground?" *Current History* 92, No. 576: 309–13.

Whitmore, Sarah. 2004. *State Building in Ukraine: The Ukrainian Parliament, 1990–2003.* London: RoutledgeCurzon.

Wilson, Andrew. 1993. "The Growing Challenge to Kiev from the Donbas." *RFE/RL Research Report* (20 August).

———. 1997. "The Ukrainian Left: In Transition to Social Democracy or Still in Thrall to the USSR?" *Europe-Asia Studies* 49, No. 7: 1293–316.

———. 2000. *The Ukrainians: Unexpected Nation.* New Haven, CT: Yale University Press.

———. 2005a. *Virtual Politics: Faking Democracy in the Post-Soviet World.* New Haven, CT: Yale University Press.

———. 2005b. *Ukraine's Orange Revolution.* New Haven, CT: Yale University Press.

———. 2011. *Belarus: The Last European Dictatorship.* New Haven, CT: Yale University Press.

———. 2013. "Filat's Gamble." *OpenDemocracy*, 23 May. Available at www.opendemocracy .net.

———. 2014. *Ukraine Crisis: What It Means for the West.* New Haven, CT: Yale University Press.

Wolczuk, Kataryna. 1998. *The Moulding of Ukraine: The Constitutional Politics of State Formation.* CEU Press: Budapest.

World Bank. 1995. *World Development Report: Workers in an Integrating World.* Washington, DC: World Bank.

Yasin, Yevgenii. 1998. "How the Chinese Path of Reform Failed in the USSR." In Michael Ellman and Vladimir Kontorovich, eds. *The Destruction of the Soviet Economic System: An Insiders' History.* New York: M. E. Sharpe.

Yeltsin, Boris. 1994. *The Struggle for Russia.* New York: Random House.

———. 2000. *Prezidentskiy marafon.* Moscow: AST.

Zürcher, Christoph. 2007. *The Post-Soviet Wars: Rebellion, Ethnic Conflict, and Nationhood in the Caucasus.* New York: New York University Press.

Index

Abdullajanov, Abdumalik, 161
Abkhazia, 139, 153
Agrarian Democratic Party (ADP, Moldova), 96, 99–100, 102
Akaev, Askar, 5, 158–59, 160, 168, 190, 229n23
Akhmetov, Rinat, 73, 77
Alexeyeva, Liudmilla, 199n7
Aliev, Ilham, 229n23
Aliev, Heidar, 152–53
Alliance for Democracy and Reform (ADR, Moldova), 102, 103, 104
Alliance for European Integration (AEI, Moldova), 92, 96, 110, 111, 113, 211n3
Alliance Our Moldova (AMN), 109, 216n150, 217n171
Amnesty International, 6, 109
Armenia, 41, 150–52, 163, 190–91
Armenian National Movement (ANM), 41, 150
authoritarianism: in Belarus, 3, 27, 115, 127–39, 140–41; in Caucasus, 149–55; and centralized economic control, 16, 141, 169; competitive, 2, 8, 97, 166; defined, 5, 184; and economics, 175–76; Freedom House scores on, 162–63, 174–75; and national identity, 18, 22, 26, 47, 140–41, 162–63, 228n119; and natural resources, 176–77; obstacles to, 6–7, 23, 132, 158; and organizational capacity, 163, 174–75; and polarized divisions, 18, 31, 114; political parties and, 10–12, 163, 176; in Russia, 146; scholarship on, 4–5, 176; state power relationship to, 12–13, 40–41, 163; in Ukraine, 1, 74, 78–81
Azarov, Mykola, 49, 59, 60, 80, 82, 84
Azerbaijan, 41, 151–53, 163, 190–91

Bakiyev, Kurmanbek, 160, 229n23
Balmaceda, Margarita, 134–35
Baltic countries, 41
Bandera, Stepan, 83, 86
Bangladesh, 20
Barannikov, Viktor, 225n7
Beissinger, Mark, 19, 37, 68, 69, 70, 167, 168
Belarus, 113, 115–42, 190–91; authoritarian state building in, 120–23; civil society in, 167–68; closed authoritarianism in, 3, 26, 127–39; constitution in, 117, 122, 130–31; economic controls in, 13, 17, 120, 122–23, 134, 136–37, 141, 172, 177, 220n50; elections in, 116, 117, 118–19, 127, 132, 133, 135, 218n14; under Kebich, 119–20; media in, 117, 125, 129, 133, 221n76; national identity in, 26, 41, 116, 117–19, 128–30, 135, 137–38, 140–41, 173; organizational capacity in, 119–23; oligarchs in, 136, 223n162; parliament in, 117, 125, 130–32; political culture in, 28, 128, 139, 169; and political parties, 120–21, 141–42; private sector in, 122, 219n28; protests and demonstrations in, 130, 137; repression in, 133–34; and Russia, 21, 118, 119, 129, 132, 134–36, 138–39, 173, 222–23n147, 223n157; security services in, 119–20, 121–22, 133, 197n77, 219n43; support for Russian language in, 118, 218n11; Western condemnation of, 132
Belarusian Popular Front (BPF), 118, 130, 131, 137
Belovezhskaia Accord, 124
Benin, 178, 179, 230n40
Bessarabia, 93
Bessmertnyi, Roman, 65, 69

Birlik, 157
Bloc for a Democratic and Prosperous
    Moldova (BDPM), 96, 102, 103
Bohoslovska, Inna, 82
Botswana, 178, 230n40
Brezhnev, Leonid, 33, 34

Cameroon, 179
Caucasus, 149–55
Chalidze, Valery, 199n7
chaos, 81, 86, 93, 152, 179; democracy and, 23
Chechnya, 148
Chernomyrdin, Viktor, 132, 148, 197n70
Chigir, Mikhail, 131
Chornovil, Viacheslav, 52
Christian-Democratic People's Party
    (PPCD, Moldova), 106–7, 108
civil society, 10, 11, 39, 143; defined,
    198n114; democratization literature on,
    27, 167–68; in Ukraine, 65–66, 69, 167
coercive capacity, 13–16, 40; in Belarus, 15,
    136; defined, 13, 185–86; in Georgia, 151,
    154; in Moldova, 96–97; in Ukraine, 52,
    89, 121; weakness in, 14–15, 146, 161, 163,
    178. *See also* security forces
Committee for State Control (KGK,
    Belarus), 13, 122, 123, 169
Commonwealth of Independent States (CIS),
    39, 43, 52; pluralism in, 144, 166–67,
    228–29n5
Communist Party (Azerbaijan), 151–52
Communist Party (Belarus), 119, 120,
    123–24, 131, 220n62
Communist Party (Moldova), 92, 94, 95, 96,
    98, 173; authoritarian regime led by,
    104–11; downfall of, 101, 113; electoral
    victory of, 104, 112–13, 214–15nn106–7
Communist Party (Soviet Union), 32–33,
    34; demise of, 26, 39, 172; Gorbachev and,
    35, 36, 39, 89, 124
Communist Party (Tajikistan), 160
Communist Party (Turkmenistan), 156, 157
Communist Party (Ukraine), 47–48, 58, 59;
    fall from power of, 50–52; membership
    and support for, 51, 202n45; strengthened
    identity of, 60, 63, 204n147
Communist Party (Uzbekistan), 157
competitive authoritarianism, 2, 8, 26, 171,
    228n1

constitutions, 27–28; in Belarus, 117, 122,
    130–31; in Moldova, 100, 103–4, 113; in
    Ukraine, 52, 58–59, 72, 73–74, 81, 170,
    209n293
Council of Europe, 107, 215n137
Creanga, Pavel, 100
Crimea, 86, 91, 149

Darden, Keith, 37, 46
democratic consolidation, 2, 8, 23, 179–80,
    184; and political competition, 26–27
Democratic Party (Moldova), 110, 112
democratic values, 28, 47, 65, 68, 143, 168
democratization literature, 4, 7–8, 27, 166
Diacov, Dumitru, 102, 103, 110
Donbas, 54, 79, 88, 91
Donetsk, 66, 68, 79, 86
Druc, Mircea, 98
Dzerzhinsky, Felix, 33, 124

economic control, 16–17, 186; in Belarus, 13,
    17, 120, 122–23, 134, 136–37, 141, 172, 177,
    220n50; in Central Asia, 156–57, 226n73;
    in Moldova, 96–97; Soviet Union and, 33,
    39–40; in Ukraine, 50, 72–73
Elchibey, Abulfaz, 152
electoral fraud, 14, 181; in Armenia, 151; in
    Belarus, 132, 133; in Russia, 16, 148, 149;
    in Ukraine, 56, 62, 66, 67, 68, 72, 78,
    203n105, 205n185
electoral turnover. *See* leadership turnover
elite collusion, 18, 20–21, 22; in Moldova,
    94, 109, 110; in Ukraine, 76, 77, 89
elite defection, 10, 11, 12, 17, 60, 97, 105,
    159
Erin, Leonid, 219n48
Eritrea, 179
Ethiopia, 179
Euromaidan protests, 81–86, 167, 210n306
European Union, 6, 7, 41, 81, 107, 109

Fatherland party (Ukraine), 60, 63, 74,
    210n310
Filat, Vlad, 108, 109–10, 112
Fokin, Vitold, 54

Gamsakhurdia, Zviad, 153, 164
Gaziev, Rahim, 152
Georgia, 5, 139, 150, 153–55, 163, 164–65,

190–91, 200n50; civil war in, 41, 153; Rose Revolution in, 11, 15, 71, 154
Georgian Dream coalition, 154
Ghimpu, Mihai, 108, 110, 112, 217n183
Goemans, Hein, 14
Gongadze, Georgi, 63
Gorbachev, Mikhail, 37, 52, 152; and Communist Party, 35, 36, 39, 89, 124; coup against, 38; Soviet reforms by, 16, 32, 34–35
Great Britain, 178
Grossu, Semyon, 98

Hale, Henry, 27, 170, 171, 216n149
Hamidov, Iskander, 152
Hanchar, Victor, 130–31
Howard, Marc, 7, 34
Hromada Party (Ukraine), 61, 63, 204n147
Huntington, Samuel, 9, 196n45
Hurenko, Stanislav, 51–52
Husseinov, Surat, 152

Iskandarov, Akbarshoh, 161

Jowitt, Ken, 34

Karimov, Islam, 156–67, 229n23
Kazakhstan, 163, 190–91; economic situation of, 116n65, 157; national identity and divisions in, 155, 157, 200n58, 226n66, 227n82; organizational capacity in, 157–58; security apparatus in, 157–58
Kebich, Viacheslau, 13, 116–17, 135, 218n23; state power under, 119–20; weak authoritarianism under, 123–27
KGB, 33–34, 38–39, 40; in Belarus, 120, 133, 219n48; in Moldova, 99, 102
Khasbulatov, Ruslan, 12, 147, 225n7
Khrushchev, Nikita, 33
Khudunozar, Davlat, 160
Kocharian, Robert, 151, 225n34
Kolesnikov, Boris, 73
Kravchuk, Leonid: and breakup of Soviet Union, 39, 52, 124; lack of party organization of, 10, 26, 47–48, 53; lack of regional network of, 53, 89; loss of power by, 1–2, 176; personal skills of, 52, 135; rise to power of, 52, 202n56; undemocratic practices of, 5, 48, 52, 168–69, 202n59

Kuchma, Leonid: constitutional power of, 58–59, 169–70; in elections, 2, 61–62, 89; "multi-party ruling party" of, 50, 59–60, 67; and Orange Revolution, 65–67, 71; regional network of, 48, 57, 90, 203n111; repressive economic instruments of, 13, 59, 61; and Russia, 55–56, 57–58, 64, 66, 135; and tapes scandal, 63–65
Kulikov, Anatolii, 15
Kushnarev, Evheniy, 79
Kyrgyzstan, 5, 158–60, 190–91, 226n65; as "island of democracy," 158; national identity and divisions in, 200n58, 226n66; organizational capacity in, 158–60; party weakness in, 159, 200n56; protests and demonstrations in, 15, 159–60, 227n106; security forces in, 15, 158, 159

Latvia, 41
Lazarenko, Pavlo, 61
leadership tolerance, 5, 149, 160, 164, 168–69
leadership turnover, 144, 145, 184; defined, 224n4, 229n21; in Moldova, 22, 92, 173, 230n30; and national identity and divisions, 20, 22, 173, 175; and organizational capacity, 23, 26, 154, 163, 170–71; in Ukraine, 2, 22, 43, 45, 85, 89, 173, 230n30
LeBas, Adrienne, 20–21, 109
Lebed, Alexander, 37
Lenin, V. I., 33
Liberal Democratic Party (LDPM, Moldova), 108, 112
Liberal Party (Moldova), 108, 109, 112
Lindberg, Staffan, 143–44
Lucinschi, Petru, 13, 26, 28, 92, 95, 96, 97, 98, 100, 102–3, 112, 113, 135
Lukashenka, Alyaksandr: authoritarianism of, 115, 120–23, 127–39, 229n23; economic control by, 13, 17, 136; in elections, 127, 135; popularity of, 138, 139; rise of, 125–26; and Russia, 21, 119, 129, 132, 139, 173; style and personality of, 115–16, 128, 135, 139–40
Lupu, Marian, 110–11, 112
Lutsenko, Yuriy, 63, 71, 78, 207n247
Luzhkov, Yurii, 148
Lyovochkin, Serhiy, 82
Lytvyn, Volodymyr, 64, 66, 70–71, 80

Madagascar, 178, 230n40
Malawi, 178, 230n40
Mali, 178, 179, 230n40
Mamedov, Yaqub, 152
Manukian, Vazgen, 150–51
Marchuk, Evheniy, 48, 53, 55, 56
Margvelashvili, Giorgi, 154
Marinov, Nikolay, 14
Masol, Vitalii, 51–52
Mauritius, 178, 230n40
media, 35, 164, 181–82; in Belarus, 117, 125,
    129, 133, 221n76; in Moldova, 92, 97, 101,
    103, 104, 111, 211n3, 215n108; in Ukraine,
    50, 54, 75, 78, 202n59
Medvedchuk, Viktor, 60, 64
Milinkevich, Aliaksandr, 137
Moldova, 3, 92–114, 192–93; civil war in, 95,
    98–99, 102, 112; Communist authoritari-
    anism in, 104–11; constitution in, 100,
    103–4, 113; demonstrations and protests
    in, 98, 102, 106, 108; elections in, 96, 97,
    99, 101, 104, 108, 110, 114n87, 212n37; and
    external vulnerability, 113–14, 164–65;
    Freedom House scores for, 162–63,
    228n123, 229n27; language issue in, 93,
    97–98; leadership turnovers in, 22, 92,
    173, 230n30; media in, 92, 97, 101, 103,
    104, 111, 211n3, 215n108; national identity
    and divisions in, 22, 24, 41–42, 93–95,
    96–99, 102, 112, 113–14, 173; oligarchs
    in, 107, 108, 112, 216n149; organizational
    capacity in, 26, 95–97; ousting of Com-
    munist rule in, 109–11; parliament in,
    100–101, 103, 112; party strength and
    weakness in, 10, 95–96, 99, 102–3,
    111–12, 170, 173; patronage and cor-
    ruption in, 100, 112; polarization in,
    94, 99, 109, 110, 111, 112, 173; privatiza-
    tion in, 97, 173; repression in, 5, 103, 105,
    107, 108–9, 215n113; under Romanian
    rule, 93, 212n8; and Russia, 21, 99, 105–6,
    107, 113; security forces in, 96, 100,
    200n50
Moldovan Popular Front, 95–96, 98, 99,
    218n18
Moore, Barrington, 16, 178
Moroz, Oleksandr, 60, 62, 63, 65
Mutalibov, Ayaz, 144, 151–52

Nabiev, Rahmon, 160–61, 164
Nagorno-Karabagh, 41, 150, 151
national identity and divisions: appeals to,
    18, 19–20; and authoritarianism, 18, 22,
    140–41, 162, 228n119; in Belarus, 26, 41,
    116, 117–19, 128–30, 135, 137–38, 140–41,
    173; in Caucasus, 41, 150–51; in Central
    Asia, 155, 157, 160, 200n58, 226n66,
    227n82; and chaos, 23; defined, 188–89,
    198n89; and elite collusion, 18, 20–21; and
    external vulnerability, 18–19, 21–22; in
    Moldova, 22, 24, 41–42, 93–95, 96–99,
    102, 112, 113–14, 173; and opposition
    mobilization, 19, 22; and organizational
    capacity, 22, 173; and political competi-
    tion, 4, 18–19, 30, 41, 144; as regime
    evolution factor, 172, 173; in Russia, 146,
    148–49; in Soviet Union, 36–38; in
    Ukraine, 22, 24, 26, 41–42, 45–47, 54,
    56–57, 63, 67, 69–72, 74, 77–78, 88–89,
    90, 173
nationalism: anti-Russian, 21, 22, 37, 41, 42,
    69, 129–30, 138; and authoritarianism,
    22, 162; Belarusian, 117, 118–19, 129,
    137; Moldovan, 97–98, 100, 109–10; as
    oppositional tool, 19–20; Ukrainian, 46,
    50–51, 55, 69, 70, 83, 86, 91
natural resources, 157, 176–77
Nazarbayev, Nursultan, 156, 157, 158,
    229n23
New Azerbaijan Party, 152–53
Niyazov, Saparmurat, 156
Nyerere, Julius, 20

oil wealth: and authoritarian stability,
    176–77; in Azerbaijan, 152; in Central
    Asia 156, 157; in Russia, 134, 138, 139
Okhmakevich, Mykola, 54
oligarchs, 16–17; in Belarus, 136, 223n162; in
    Georgia, 154; in Moldova, 107, 108, 112,
    216n149; in Russia, 149; in Ukraine, 44,
    57–58, 59, 60, 61, 64–65, 69, 73, 79–80,
    82, 90
Omelchenko, Grigoriy, 64, 70
Onuch, Olga, 69, 206n201
Orange coalition (Ukraine), 74–76, 77–78,
    90, 208n252
Orange Revolution (Ukraine), 65–72, 90, 167

organizational capacity, 17, 24, 72, 161–62, 172, 173; and authoritarianism, 163, 174–75; in Belarus, 119–123; in the Caucasus, 149–55; defined, 9, 17, 185–87; in Kyrgyzstan and Tajikistan, 158–61, 200n56; and leadership turnover, 23, 26, 154, 163, 170–71; in Moldova, 26, 96–97; and national identity, 22, 173; and regime competition, 26, 144–45; in Russia, 146, 147–48, 149; in Turkmenistan, Uzbekistan, and Kazakhstan, 155–57; in Ukraine, 47–50

organizations, defined, 196n45

Ossetia, 139, 153

Our Ukraine, 49, 65, 74, 76, 79, 207–8n250

parliament, 37–38, 182; in Belarus, 131; in Moldova, 100–101, 103, 112; party disorganization and, 11–12; in Russia, 12; in Ukraine, 53, 58–59, 62, 73, 80, 204n119, 204n148

Party of Regions (Ukraine), 49, 60, 76, 77, 79–80, 84, 85, 208n275

party strength/weakness, 187–88; in Belarus, 119; in Central Asia, 158, 161, 200n56; and democratic accountability, 3, 23; as factor explaining regime evolution, 8, 9, 10–12, 17, 22, 24, 26, 29, 30, 56, 163–65, 170, 173, 176; in Moldova, 95–97, 99, 102–3, 112, 113, 170, 173; in Russia under Putin, 146; in Russia under Yeltsin, 34, 147; in Soviet Union, 32–34, 89, 164; in Ukraine, 44, 47–50, 56, 63, 74–78, 88–89, 173

Pastukhov, Mikhail, 125

patronage, 10–11; in Moldova, 100; in Ukraine, 58, 62–63, 87

Pazniak, Zenon, 118, 124, 125, 218n14

people power, 15, 29, 154, 162, 180

Perestroika, 35

Pinchuk, Viktor, 73

Plahotniuc, Vladimir, 110, 112

pluralism by default, causal mechanisms of, 9; defined, 2, 8; indicators of, 29–30; organizational capacity and, 9–17; national divisions and, 18–22

Plyushch, Ivan, 52, 53–54

polarization: and elite collusion, 20–21; in Moldova, 94, 99, 109, 110, 111, 112, 173; in Ukraine, 47, 59, 60, 73, 77, 88, 91, 173

political competition/closure, see regime competition/closure political culture, 28, 128, 139, 168, 169

popular support, 10, 27, 61, 118, 128–29, 168, 173

Poroshenko, Petro, 65, 69, 74, 86–87, 91, 211n340

Presidential Business Administration (UDP, Belarus), 122–23, 136

Primakov, Evgenii, 148

privatization, 16, 173; in Kazakhstan, 157, 158; in Kyrgyzstan, 158; in Moldova, 97, 173; in Ukraine, 60, 173

Pro-European Coalition (Moldova), 96, 112

Przeworski, Adam, 140, 168

Pustovoitenko, Valery, 61, 62

Putin, Vladimir, 16, 28, 120147, 229n23; autocratic proclivities of, 147, 164; and Belarus, 119, 135, 138; organizational capacity of, 146, 149; and Russia's national identity, 148–49; and Ukraine, 64, 66, 67, 69, 86, 88

Rahmon, Emomalii, 161, 229n23

Regime competition/closure, 8 defined, 196n44; indicators of, 181–84

regional context, 132, 165, 174

Rizhak, Ivan, 73

Rose Revolution (Georgia), 11, 15, 71, 154

Rukh movement (Ukraine), 51, 53, 218n18

Russia, 146–49, 161, 192–93; and Belarus, 21, 118, 119, 129, 132, 134–36, 138–39, 173, 222–23n147, 223n157; and Chechnya, 148; and Crimea, 86, 149; crisis of 1992 in, 12; electoral fraud in, 16, 148, 149; and Moldova, 21, 99, 105–6, 107, 113; national identity in, 146, 148–49; oil wealth of, 134, 138, 139; oligarchs in, 149; organizational capacity in, 146, 147–48, 149; political parties in, 146, 147; security services in, 5, 13, 15; state controls in, 146, 149; and Ukraine, 21, 45, 56, 64, 66, 67, 80, 83, 91

Rybak, Volodymyr, 85

Saakashvili, Mikheil, 5, 71, 153, 154–55, 229n23

Sakharov, Andrei, 35, 36

Sangheli, Andrei, 99, 100, 101, 214n87

Sarkisian, Serge, 151

Schurmann, Franz, 196n45

security forces, 33, 40, 151, 178–79; in Belarus, 119–20, 121–22, 133, 197n77, 219n43; in Central Asia, 15, 156, 157–58, 159, 200n50, 226n75; in Moldova, 96, 100, 200n50; non-material ties among, 15, 197n75; in Russia, 5, 13, 15; in Ukraine, 15, 49, 55, 66, 71, 84–85. *See also* coercive capacity

Sharetskii, Semion, 130, 131–32

Sheiman, Viktor, 121

Shevardnadze, Eduard, 71, 153, 154, 229n23

Shushkevich, Stanislau, 119, 123–24, 125, 126, 197n77; and formation of CIS, 39, 52, 124

Sikorski, Radoslaw, 85

Silitski, Vitali, 140

Snegur, Mircea, 26, 97, 98, 101–2, 106, 112, 176; lack of party support by, 10, 95–96, 99–100; undemocratic moves by, 92, 113

Social Democratic Party (Ukraine), 60

Soviet Union: and Belarus, 118, 123–24; in Central Asia, 155–56; collapse of, 10, 26, 39, 52, 124, 144; failed coup in, 38–39, 124; and Georgia, 41, 153; Gorbachev reforms in, 16, 32, 34–36; KGB in, 33–34; legacy of, 39–42; and Moldova, 93–94, 97–99; nationalities crisis in, 36–38; repression in, 33, 143–44, 199n7; system of control in, 32–34, 164

Stalin, Joseph, 33

state building, 5, 26, 32, 40; in Belarus, 116, 120–23; in Caucasus, 149–55; and national divisions, 150, 153; reducing space for pluralism in, 12–13, 15–16, 171; in Ukraine, 57–63

Stroev, Egor, 132

Sub-Saharan Africa, 178–79, 230nn40–44

Svaboda (newspaper, Belarus), 117, 129

Svoboda Party (Ukraine), 83, 86, 210n310

Symonenko, Petro, 62

Tajikistan, 174, 192–93, 200n50, 226n65; demonstrations and civil war in, 161;

elections in, 160, 161; low organizational capacity in, 160–61, 200n56; national identity and divisions in, 160, 200n58, 226n66

Tanzania, 20

Tarrow, Sidney, 15

Taylor, Brian, 4

term limits, 170–71, 229n23

Ter-Petrosian, Levon, 150, 151, 229n23

Timofti, Nicolae, 112

Transnistria, 93, 94, 96, 106

Turchynov, Oleksandr, 63, 85

Turkmenistan, 155–56, 163, 192–93, 226n65

Tyhypko, Serhiy, 66, 70, 79, 84

Tymoshenko, Yulia, 60, 61, 63, 64, 65; jailing of, 78, 85; and Orange coalition, 74–75, 76, 90; and Ukrainian national identity, 67; and Yushchenko, 48, 72–73, 76–77

Ukraine, 43–91, 162–63, 192–93; authoritarian state building in, 57–63; civil society in, 65–66, 69, 167; constitution in, 52, 58–59, 72, 73–74, 81, 170, 209n293; and Crimea, 86, 91, 149; demonstrations and protests in, 11, 47, 51, 54, 63, 68–69, 72, 81–86, 167, 201n42, 205n166, 210n306; economic decline in, 55, 203n94; economic resources of, 50, 62, 177; elections in, 1–2, 47, 55–56, 61–62, 65, 66, 75, 76, 77, 203n98, 206n190, 207n248, 208n252; electoral fraud in, 56, 62, 66, 67, 68, 72, 78, 203n105, 205n185; external debt of, 58, 203n116; fall of Soviet rule in, 50–52; Kravchuk regime in, 50–57; leadership turnovers in, 2, 22, 43, 45, 85, 89, 173, 230n30; media in, 50, 54, 75, 78, 202n59; national identity and divisions in, 3, 22, 24, 26, 41–42, 45–47, 50, 54, 56–57, 63, 67, 69–72, 73, 74, 75–78, 82–83, 86–89, 90, 173, 201n19; organizational capacity in, 47–50; oligarchs in, 59, 60, 61, 64–65, 69, 73, 79–80, 82, 90; Orange coalition in, 74–76, 77–78, 90, 208n252; Orange Revolution in, 65–72, 90, 167; parliament in, 53, 58–59, 62, 73, 80, 204n119, 204n148; party strength and weakness in, 8–89, 44, 47–50, 60, 72–79, 91, 173; patronage in, 58, 62–63, 87; privatization in, 60, 173; regime collapse in, 14, 78–81, 84, 90, 176;

repressive moves in, 5, 13, 73, 78, 84, 202n59, 207n207; and Russia, 21, 45, 56, 64, 66, 67, 80, 83, 91; security apparatus in, 15, 49, 55, 66, 71, 84–85; state strength in, 47–50, 57; state weakness in, 88–89; tapes scandal in, 63–65
Ukrainka, Lesia, 67
United National Movement (Georgia), 154
United Russia party, 146
United States, 132, 178
Urechean, Serafim, 107–8, 217n171
Usatii, Adrian, 101, 103
Uzbekistan, 161, 163, 192–93; economy of, 156–57, 226n65, 226n73; high organizational capacity in, 156–57; national identity in, 155; security apparatus in, 156, 226n75

Vasilishin, Andrii, 55
Venice Commission, 103
Voronin, Vladimir, 104, 105–6, 107–9, 110–11, 135, 229n23

Wilson, Andrew, 118

Yanukovych, Viktor, 26, 28, 45, 135, 169–70; control over judiciary by, 80–81, 209n292;

downfall of, 14, 84–88; in elections, 47, 68, 74, 76, 77; Kuchma and, 66, 71; and maidan demonstrations, 81–83; monopolization of power by, 50, 74; party structure of, 49, 60, 78–80, 173; Russian support for, 72, 83
Yavlinskii, Grigorii, 148
Yazov, Dmitry, 38, 39
Yeltsin, Boris, 10, 135; abuses of democratic norms by, 5, 13, 15, 168–69; and Communist Party, 34, 146; and dissolution of Soviet Union, 39, 52, 124, 146; under Gorbachev, 36, 38; and Moldova, 99, 106; personal ties of, 146, 147, 225n7; weak organizational capacity of, 12, 147–48
Yushchenko, Viktor, 26, 62, 64, 72–78; abuses of democratic norms by, 67–68, 73, 168–69, 207n231; coalitional structure of regime of, 48, 50, 74–76, 90; Kuchma appointment of, 58, 134

Zakharchenko, Vitalii, 85
Zambia, 178, 179, 230n41
Zhvania, David, 82
Zimbabwe, 179
Zinchenko, Alexander, 67, 69
Zyuganov, Gennady, 148